Gradient Acceptability and Linguistic Theory

OXFORD SURVEYS IN SYNTAX AND MORPHOLOGY

General Editor

Robert D. Van Valin, Jr., Heinrich-Heine University and the University at Buffalo,
State University of New York

Advisory Editors

Guglielmo Cinque, University of Venice
Daniel Everett, Illinois State University
Adele Goldberg, Princeton University
Kees Hengeveld, University of Amsterdam
Caroline Heycock, University of Edinburgh
David Pesetsky, Massachusetts Institute of Technology
Ian Roberts, University of Cambridge
Masayoshi Shibatani, Rice University
Andrew Spencer, University of Essex
Tom Wasow, Stanford University

RECENTLY PUBLISHED IN THE SERIES

6. Processing Syntax and Morphology
A Neurocognitive Perspective
Ina Bornkessel-Schlesewsky and Matthias Schlesewsky

7. Syntactic Categories
Gisa Rauh

8. The Interplay of Morphology and Phonology
Sharon Inkelas

9. Word Meaning and Syntax
Approaches to the Interface
Stephen Wechsler

10. Unbounded Dependency Constructions
Theoretical and Experimental Perspectives
Rui P. Chaves and Michael T. Putnam

11. Gradient Acceptability and Linguistic Theory
Elaine J. Francis

For a complete list of titles published and in preparation for the series, see p. 272

Gradient Acceptability and Linguistic Theory

ELAINE J. FRANCIS

OXFORD
UNIVERSITY PRESS

OXFORD
UNIVERSITY PRESS

Great Clarendon Street, Oxford, OX2 6DP,
United Kingdom

Oxford University Press is a department of the University of Oxford.
It furthers the University's objective of excellence in research, scholarship,
and education by publishing worldwide. Oxford is a registered trade mark of
Oxford University Press in the UK and in certain other countries

Published in the United States of America by Oxford University Press
198 Madison Avenue, New York, NY 10016, United States of America

British Library Cataloguing in Publication Data
Data available

Library of Congress Control Number: 2021937207

ISBN 978-0-19-289894-4 (hbk.)
ISBN 978-0-19-289895-1 (pbk.)

DOI: 10.1093/oso/9780192898944.001.0001

Printed and bound by
CPI Group (UK) Ltd, Croydon, CR0 4YY

Contents

General Preface	viii
Acknowledgments	ix
List of Figures	xii
List of Abbreviations	xiv

1. The problem of gradient acceptability — 1
   1.1 Knowledge of grammar and linguistic intuitions — 1
   1.2 Gradient acceptability: the case of selectional restrictions — 7
   1.3 Formal syntactic explanations: superficial similarities can mask underlying structural differences — 8
   1.4 Prosodic explanations: ill-formed prosodic structures may be confusable with syntactic rule violations — 10
   1.5 Semantic explanations: semantic anomalies may be confusable with syntactic rule violations — 11
   1.6 Pragmatic explanations: grammatical sentences may appear ill-formed in an inappropriate discourse context — 12
   1.7 Processing explanations: grammatical sentences may appear ill-formed when they are hard to process — 13
   1.8 Processing explanations: ungrammatical sentences may appear well-formed when they are hard to process — 15
   1.9 Overview of the book — 16

2. Theories of grammatical knowledge in relation to formal syntactic and non-syntactic explanations — 18
   2.1 Derivational grammars — 20
      2.1.1 Form–meaning correspondences in derivational grammars — 22
      2.1.2 Processing-based explanations in derivational grammars — 24
   2.2 Constraint-based grammars — 26
      2.2.1 Form–meaning correspondences in level-mapping grammars — 27
      2.2.2 Form–meaning correspondences in sign-based grammars — 29
      2.2.3 Processing-based explanations in constraint-based grammars — 33
   2.3 OT — 35
      2.3.1 Form–meaning correspondences in OT — 37
      2.3.2 Stochastic OT, gradient grammar, and processing-based explanations — 38
   2.4 Gradient grammaticality in derivational theories: a look back — 42
   2.5 Usage-based approaches: grammar as a complex adaptive system — 47
   2.6 Conclusions — 52

3. On distinguishing formal syntactic constraints from other aspects of linguistic knowledge — 55
   3.1 Outbound anaphora in English — 57
   3.2 Factive islands and manner-of-speaking islands in English — 59

3.3 Word order and prosody in Czech 63

3.4 Auxiliary selection and impersonal passives in German 66

3.5 Conclusions 71

4. On distinguishing formal syntactic constraints from processing constraints 74

4.1 Amelioration and isomorphism 75

4.2 Syntactic satiation 80

4.3 Working memory capacity 84

4.4 Overgeneration of ungrammatical sentences 87

4.5 Cross-linguistic differences: superiority effects in Czech, English, German, and Russian 92

4.6 Conclusions 101

5. On the relationship between corpus frequency and acceptability 103

5.1 Evidence from close correlations: acceptability mirrors corpus frequency 107

5.2 Evidence from mismatches: differences in acceptability among low-frequency forms 110

5.3 Evidence from statistical preemption: judgments of unusual verb-construction combinations 115

5.4 Evidence from machine learning: deriving acceptability judgments from corpus patterns 117

5.5 Conclusions 123

6. Relative clause extraposition and PP extraposition in English and German 126

6.1 NPI licensing in RCE as evidence for syntactic structure? 128

6.2 Freezing effects as grammar or processing? 131

6.3 Subclausal locality: hard constraint, soft constraint, or neither? 136

6.4 What are the Predicate Constraint and the Name Constraint? 144

6.5 Conclusions 155

7. Resumptive pronouns in Hebrew, Cantonese, and English relative clauses 157

7.1 Resumption in contexts where gaps are permitted: object relatives in Hebrew and English 160

7.2 Resumption in contexts where gaps are not permitted: coverb stranding in Cantonese 172

7.3 Does resumption rescue islands? Evidence from Hebrew and English 178

7.4 Gradient judgment data and the distinction between grammatical and intrusive resumption 189

8. Gradient acceptability, methodological diversity, and theoretical interpretation 194

8.1 Form–meaning isomorphism and the syntactic status of semantic contrasts 195

8.2 The case for gradient grammars 201

8.3 The place of acceptability judgments in an expanding syntactic toolkit 211

8.3.1 How corpus data, production tasks, and self-paced reading
tasks can inform our syntactic analyses 211
8.3.2 Split intransitivity in Spanish and English: evidence from
acceptability judgments, visual probe recognition, structural
priming, and cross-modal lexical priming 213
8.4 Expanding the toolkit further: some thoughts on big data,
neurolinguistics, and the future of syntactic theory 227
8.5 Conclusions 235

Glossary 237
References 245
Name Index 263
Subject Index 267

Appendix: Common experimental paradigms for syntax research
(supplemental resource available at www.oup.co.uk/companion/Francis)

General Preface

Oxford Surveys in Syntax and Morphology provides overviews of the major approaches to subjects and questions at the center of linguistic research in morphology and syntax. The volumes are accessible, critical, and up to date. Individually and collectively they aim to reveal the field's intellectual history and theoretical diversity. Each book published in the series will characteristically contain: (1) a brief historical overview of relevant research in the subject; (2) a critical presentation of approaches from relevant (but usually seen as competing) theoretical perspectives to the phenomena and issues at hand, including an objective evaluation of the strengths and weaknesses of each approach to the central problems and issues; (3) a balanced account of the current issues, problems, and opportunities relating to the topic, showing the degree of consensus or otherwise in each case. The volumes will thus provide researchers and graduate students concerned with syntax, morphology, and related aspects of semantics with a vital source of information and reference.

Gradient Acceptability and Linguistic Theory explores fundamental methodological questions about the nature of linguistic data and its ramifications for theoretical linguistics. The data that linguists use for argumentation and theory building in syntax, whether obtained from elicitation with native speakers, corpus analysis, or experimentation, are often not clear-cut, and the author exemplifies this with data from a wide range of languages and investigates the implications of this for different theories of syntax. The results of this inquiry are relevant to scholars across the theoretical spectrum, and the volume constitutes a significant contribution to the series.

Van Valin, Robert D. Jr.
General Editor

University at Buffalo,
The State University of New York
Heinrich Heine University,
Düsseldorf

Acknowledgments

This book could never have been completed without the support of many people. I would first like to thank the current and former graduate students in my lab at Purdue, who have inspired me with their insights and their incredible research: John Hitz, Charles Lam, Ethan Myers, Maria Pritchett, Vanessa Sheu, Carol Zheng, and Josh Weirick. I also thank the students in my Experimental Syntax classes at Purdue, especially the class members from Fall 2018 who provided helpful feedback and discussion of early chapter drafts: Brittlea Jernigan-Hardrick, Jian Jiao, Lauren "Nik" Nikolai, Sharry Vahed, Josh Weirick, and René Zúñiga Argüello. In 2019, I had the privilege to co-teach a mini-course on Experimental Syntax at the Linguistic Institute in Davis, California with Savithry Namboodiripad. I thank the students in that class for their incisive questions and comments, and I especially thank Savithry for teaching me all sorts of things I did not know and for encouraging me on this project.

Diane Brentari met with me during a conference in Chicago in 2014 and suggested that I develop this book idea into a submission for a new linguistics series at the University of Chicago Press. I was sorry when the series did not materialize, but I am grateful to Diane and the other series editors at Chicago for believing in me and helping me get started.

Several colleagues have returned feedback on chapter drafts, without whom this book would be much poorer. Of course, they are in no way responsible for the remaining shortcomings. First and foremost, I am grateful to Tom Wasow. Tom gave me feedback on every chapter. He also met with me numerous times at conferences and over video calls to discuss the book. I have never met a kinder or more generous colleague than Tom. I am also grateful to Edith Moravcsik, who provided helpful comments on several chapters and pointed me to important references. I thank John Goldsmith, Tom Juzek, David Kemmerer, Laura Michaelis, and Savithry Namboodiripad for their feedback on specific chapters. I benefitted greatly from four anonymous reviews, two from the University of Chicago Press and two from Oxford University Press. The first two reviews helped me reorganize the book in a more reader-friendly way and to narrow the focus, while the second two were invaluable for improving the coverage of the literature review, correcting some inaccuracies and inconsistencies, and better developing the main arguments. I am grateful to series editor Robert Van Valin for his valuable feedback and for the amazing opportunity to publish this book in Oxford Surveys in Syntax and Morphology. Finally, I want to thank commissioning editors Vicki Sunter and Julia Steer and everyone at Oxford University Press who has helped put this book through production.

I am grateful for financial support for this project from Purdue University. A fellowship from the Center for Social Sciences in the College of Liberal Arts provided a teaching release in Fall 2015, which allowed me to get started writing. I am grateful to Edith Moravcsik, Tom Wasow, and Peter Culicover for writing letters in support of the fellowship. I received an Aspire grant from the College of Liberal Arts in 2018, which allowed me to hire Josh Weirick as a research assistant. I thank Josh for building the Zotero reference database and creating the bibliography for the first submission. I also thank Dave Zwicky, a professor from Libraries and School of Information Studies, for helping us get started with Zotero. I thank Maria Pritchett for additional assistance with the Zotero database and the Department of Linguistics for funding Maria's position. I am grateful to the Department of English and Purdue University for granting me a sabbatical leave in 2018–19, which gave me the time to complete several chapters. I thank my friend and department head, Dorrie Armstrong, for providing departmental funds to hire assistants to format the final typescript, and for her endless confidence in me during the final stages of the project. I am grateful to Josh Weirick and Amy Hutchinson for completing the formatting work quickly, meticulously, and with good cheer.

I am indebted to my dissertation advisor, Salikoko Mufwene, and committee members Amy Dahlstrom, Jerry Sadock, and the late Jim McCawley for providing incredible intellectual inspiration during my grad school days at Chicago and beyond. Chapters 1 and 8 are for Jim, who opened my eyes to subtle variations in acceptability judgments, inspiring me to eventually pursue this book project. Chapter 2 is for Amy, who brought a little of Berkeley to Chicago and introduced me to constraint-based theories. Chapter 3 is for Jerry, who inspired me with Automodular Grammar and showed me that semantics and pragmatics really matter. Chapter 7 is for Sali, who taught me to embrace the complexities of linguistic data and to be suspicious of simple, elegant explanations. Your influences have been felt throughout the writing process.

I am grateful to my collaborators, who helped me develop the ideas for this book: Jana Häussler, John Hitz, Jessica Huber, Tom Juzek, Charles Lam, Stephen Matthews, Laura Michaelis, Etsuyo Yuasa, and Carol Zheng. This work has also benefitted from discussions with many other colleagues, including Lauren Ackerman, Ann Bunger, Dustin Chacón, Bill Croft, Peter Culicover, Alejandro Cuza, Brian Dillon, Alex Francis, Ted Gibson, April Ginther, Nik Gisborne, Adele Goldberg, Jack Hawkins, Ray Jackendoff, David Kemmerer, Jean-Pierre Koenig, Ryan Lepic, Charles Lin, Maryellen MacDonald, Savithry Namboodiripad, Mary Niepokuj, Fritz Newmeyer, Joanna Nykiel, Felicia Roberts, Tom Wasow, Ronnie Wilbur, and others.

For their incredible support throughout the writing process, I thank my good friends and fellow writing accountability group members, Maren Linett and Jen William. I am also thankful to many other friends and colleagues who encouraged and supported me along the way and helped me find joy and humor when everything was just too much.

I am so thankful for the love and support of my family. My parents, Dan and Reta Jones, have been a constant source of encouragement and have somehow kept me out of trouble all of these years. My parents-in-law, George and Bettina Francis, and my siblings-in-law Jennifer Liberto and Theo Francis, have cheered for me in every stage of writing. My children, William and Lyris, have graciously endured my work habits, entertained me with their goofy antics, and cheerfully loaded and unloaded the dishwasher. My husband, Alex Francis, more than anyone, made this work possible with his enduring love, his constant encouragement, and his promise to clean out the basement office as soon as the book goes to press. I dedicate this book to Alex.

List of Figures

2.1. A basic Minimalist analysis of an English passive sentence   21

2.2. A basic Automodular analysis of an English passive sentence   28

2.3. A basic Construction Grammar analysis of the English passive   30

2.4. OT constraint interaction in English (top) and Italian (bottom)   36

3.1. Sample stimuli for reading comprehension of outbound and regular anaphora in topical and non-topical contexts   58

3.2. Correlation between difference in acceptability and negation test scores   61

3.3. Effects of word order, stress, and definiteness on the acceptability of Czech transitive clauses   65

3.4. Acceptability of impersonal passives by verb class   69

3.5. Acceptability of auxiliaries *haben* and *sein* by verb class   69

4.1. Mean acceptability ratings of bare and D-linked *wh*-questions in CNPC island, *wh*-island, and non-island (*that*-clause) conditions   79

4.2. Mean acceptability ratings for island and non-island Complex NP questions   85

4.3. Mean acceptability ratings for multiple *wh*-questions in English and Russian   94

4.4. Mean acceptability ratings for multiple *wh*-questions in English and German   100

5.1. Sample item from the judgment task   109

5.2. Mean rating of prepositional dative option by corpus probability   110

5.3. Acceptability ratings (left) and corpus frequencies (right) for six word order permutations in German clauses   111

5.4. A comparison of corpus frequency, Magnitude Estimation judgments, and binary grammaticality judgments   112

5.5. Acceptability ratings for familiar and novel sentence types, with and without a competing alternative   117

6.1. Acceptability ratings by condition for extraposed (ex situ) and adjacent (in situ) relative clauses in English   129

6.2. Acceptability ratings for English interrogative and non-interrogative clauses, with and without extraposition   133

6.3. Acceptability ratings for extraposed and adjacent (integrated) relative clauses in German, with low vs. high attachment   140

6.4. Rate of extraposition as a function of depth of embedding of the antecedent noun   142

6.5. Acceptability ratings for RCE in English according to definiteness of the subject NP and verb type   145

6.6. Percentage of RCE use for four categories of definiteness and verb type   149

6.7. Percentage of RCE use for increasing ratios of VP to relative clause length   151

7.1. Mean acceptability ratings for simple (left) and embedded (right) object relative clauses in Hebrew with gap (dark bar) or resumptive pronoun (light bar)   162

7.2. Mean acceptability ratings for simple (right) and embedded (left) object relative clauses in English   165

7.3. Relative clause types produced in restrictive and nonrestrictive contexts in Hebrew   167

7.4. Relative clause types produced with animate and inanimate patient arguments in Hebrew   168

7.5. Acceptability ratings of gaps and resumptive pronouns in subject, direct object, and coverb object positions in Cantonese relative clauses   174

7.6. Percent resumptive pronouns produced in subject, direct object, and coverb object positions in Cantonese relative clauses   175

7.7. Acceptability ratings of Cantonese relative clauses by individual verb   176

7.8. Percent of resumptive pronouns produced in direct object and coverb object positions in Cantonese relative clauses, by individual verb   176

7.9. Acceptability of gaps (dark bars) and resumptive pronouns (light bars) in island and non-island contexts in Hebrew relative clauses   180

7.10. Acceptability of gaps (dark bars) and resumptive pronouns (light bars) in wh-island contexts in English   184

7.11. Mean reading time for the spillover region following a gap or a resumptive pronoun in a wh-island or non-island sentence   186

8.1. Acceptability of transitive and intransitive control sentences with *promise* and their finite paraphrases   198

8.2. Acceptability of grammatical and ungrammatical filler sentences and TSC sentences with *promise*   198

8.3. Acceptability of transitive and intransitive control sentences with *vow*, *pledge*, *commit*, and *guarantee*, and their finite paraphrases   199

8.4. Mean acceptability ratings of items marked grammatical and ungrammatical in the original *Linguistic Inquiry* publication. Items in the middle range of 3–5 are highlighted   206

8.5. Mean response times by verb type and semantic subclass for monolingual Spanish speakers in the Spanish visual probe recognition task   218

8.6. Mean response times by verb type and semantic subclass for monolingual English speakers in the English visual probe recognition task   218

List of Abbreviations

ADJ	adjective
AGT	agent
BCG	Berkeley Construction Grammar
BNC	British National Corpus
C	complementizer
CL	clitic
CNPC	complex noun phrase constraint
COCA	Corpus of Contemporary American English
CP	complementizer phrase
DD	differences-in-differences
DEP-IO	Dependence Constraint on Input–Output Correspondence
D-linking	discourse linking
DO	direct object
ECP	Empty Category Principle
EEG	electroencephalography
EPP	Extended Projection Principle
ERP	event-related potential
EVAL	harmony evaluation
F/A	function-argument structure
fMRI	functional magnetic resonance imaging
GB	Government and Binding
GEN	candidate generation
HPSG	Head-Driven Phrase Structure Grammar
ICE-GB	International Corpus of English Great Britain
intP	intermediate phrase
iP	intonation phrase
IP	inflection phrase
ISC	intransitive subject control
LFG	Lexical-Functional Grammar
MDP	Minimal Distance Principle
ME	magnitude estimation
N	noun
NP	noun phrase
NPI	negative polarity item
OGJ	offline grammaticality judgement
ORC	object relative clause
OT	Optimality Theory
OV	object-verb
PP	preposition phrase
PPE	preposition phrase extraposition
PRAG	pragmatics and information structure specifications
PRO	pronominal determiner phrase without phonological content
RC	relative clause
RCE	relative clause extraposition
RNN	recurrent neural network
S	sentence
SCR	Sentential Complement Ratio
SEM	semantic properties
SOSP	self-organized sentence processing

Spec	specifier
SRC	subject relative clause
SSC	Sentential Subject Constraint
SVO	subject-verb-object
SYN	external syntactic and categorial properties
T	tense
TP	tense phrase
TSC	transitive subject control
TüBa-D/Z	Tübingen Treebank of Written German
V	verb
VAL	valence
VO	verb-object
VP	verb phrase

1

The problem of gradient acceptability

This chapter introduces the main problem on which this book is focused: the problem of interpreting speakers' judgments of sentence acceptability in relation to theories of grammatical knowledge. Although this problem is not always acknowledged as an important or difficult one, I will argue that it is both important and difficult. It is important because most of the research about grammatical knowledge within the tradition of generative grammar has been supported with data from speakers' intuitive judgments of researcher-constructed sentences. With the introduction of new technologies such as eye-tracking, functional magnetic resonance imaging (fMRI), and electroencephalography (EEG), and with the availability of large electronically searchable corpora of texts and speech, this heavy reliance on sentence judgments is slowly beginning to change. Given the low cost, convenience, and high success rate of this method, however, sentence judgments are likely to remain as the primary means for testing hypotheses about grammatical knowledge for years to come. As such, it is important to reflect on how we are using these judgments in our theory building, and how our interpretation of judgment patterns is potentially affected by particular theoretical assumptions. The problem of interpreting sentence judgments is difficult because such judgments do not and cannot directly reflect grammatical knowledge. Rather, they are subject to the effects of extraneous factors that can, at times, be difficult to tease apart from the effects of grammatical knowledge. These include semantic and pragmatic factors, constraints on sentence prosody, and general cognitive mechanisms involved in language processing. In this book, I explore this problem in the context of linguistic examples involving *gradient acceptability*, in which sentences that share the same or similar structures differ to varying degrees in acceptability. The current chapter first provides an overview of the relation between grammatical knowledge and sentence judgments as it has been understood in generative grammar, and then illustrates the concept of gradient acceptability using several examples from the literature. The chapter concludes by giving a preview of the chapter contents and the major themes of the book.

1.1 Knowledge of grammar and linguistic intuitions

Language users possesses a vast knowledge of grammatical patterns, some of which appear to be highly general, and others of which appear to be highly specific. For example,

Gradient Acceptability and Linguistic Theory. Elaine J. Francis, Oxford University Press.
© Elaine J. Francis (2022). DOI: 10.1093/oso/9780192898944.003.0001

English speakers know that articles come before nouns (as in *the book*, as opposed to **book the*), transitive verbs come before their objects (as in *read a book*, as opposed to **a book read*), and finite verbs agree with third person singular subjects (as in *Jane is dancing* as opposed to **Jane are dancing*). At the same time, they know that the preposition *with* allows a gerund clause, as in (1a), but not an infinitival clause, as in (1b), as its complement, and that the verb *have* negates like a lexical verb when preceding an infinitive, as in (2a), despite having a modal-like meaning similar to *ought* (2c).

(1)   a. We're content with the cleaners returning the drapes next week.
      b. *We're content with for the cleaners to return the drapes next week.

(McCawley 1998: 121)

(2)   a. Joe doesn't have to wash the dishes.
      b. *Joe hasn't to wash the dishes.
      c. Joe oughtn't to wash the dishes.

Similarly, English speakers know that matrix questions with *why* must occur with an inverted auxiliary (3a–b), while matrix questions with *how come* must not (4a–b).

(3)   a. Why did I agree to this?
      b. *Why I agreed to this?

(4)   a. *How come did I agree to this?
      b. How come I agreed to this?

Chances are that as a reader, you are not at this point questioning my assertion that the contrasts between the 'good' and 'bad' (i.e. well-formed and ill-formed) sentences in (1–4) reflect some kind of grammatical knowledge. Indeed, for today's linguists and students of linguistics, it is completely normal and conventional to talk about speakers' knowledge of grammatical patterns in terms of example sentences such as these. This link between 'good' and 'bad' example sentences and mental knowledge of grammatical patterns is not self-evident, however. It is, rather, based on the assumption that speakers' intuitions about sentences—that is, their ability to hear or read a sentence and recognize whether it is well-formed or not—reflect their underlying grammatical knowledge. This assumption has been necessary because the grammatical status of sentences such as those in (1–4), which is conventionally indicated by the assignment of '*' where a sentence is ill-formed, has depended primarily on speakers' intuitive judgments. This idea that intuitive judgments provide access to grammatical knowledge has been a standard assumption in modern syntactic research within the generative tradition. To understand why this is so, it is necessary to consider why the use of intuitions has been so important to the development of modern generative theories, and how the reliance on such judgments has been justified.

As the founder of modern generative grammar, Noam Chomsky (1965; 1986b) characterized grammar as a mental entity—a form of implicit knowledge in the mind of a speaker. In doing so, Chomsky broke with the American structuralist tradition of the time, according to which grammar was understood as a system of social conventions, and the task of a linguist was, as Leonard Bloomfield put it, to "describe the speech habits of a community" (Bloomfield 1933: 37). According to Bloomfield, a linguist "must record every form he can find and not try to excuse himself from this task by appealing to the reader's common sense or to some other language or to some psychological theory, and above all, he must not select or distort the facts according to his views of what the speakers ought to be saying" (Bloomfield 1933: 38). Besides urging linguists to be meticulous, avoid their own biases, and take a descriptive rather than a prescriptive approach, Bloomfield specifically warned against the dangers of a mentalistic view of language, which "may tempt the observer to appeal to purely spiritual standards instead of reporting the facts" (Bloomfield 1933: 38). He gave the hypothetical example of a linguist reporting that "combinations of words which are 'felt to be' compounds have only a single high stress" and criticized this approach on the grounds that "we have no way of determining what the speakers may feel" (Bloomfield 1933: 38). This is not to say that Bloomfield and other American linguists of the time never relied on their own intuitions or the intuitions of their language consultants. However, Bloomfield upheld an objective approach to linguistic description based on observations of linguistic behavior as the ideal practice.[1] Chomsky, by contrast, conceived of grammar as fundamentally psychological rather than social or behavioral. Accordingly, the task of a linguist was "discovering a mental reality underlying actual behavior" (Chomsky 1965: 4). He referred to this mental reality as *competence*, which he clearly distinguished from actual language use, or *performance*. As Chomsky (1965: 4) acknowledged, this distinction was closely related to the distinction between *langue* 'language system' and *parole* 'speech,' as proposed by the Swiss linguist Ferdinand de Saussure in *Cours de Linguistique Générale* (Saussure 1916). Chomsky's idea of competence differed from Saussure's *langue* in at least two important respects, however. First, for Saussure, *langue* was a collective entity belonging to a speech community, rather than a mental entity belonging to each individual. To the extent that *langue* existed in an individual's mind, it existed only in a partial, imperfect form: "the language is never complete in any single individual, but exists perfectly only in the collectivity" (Saussure 1983: 13). Second, while Saussure's *langue* was an interconnected system of linguistic signs, Chomsky's competence was "a system of generative processes" (Chomsky 1965: 4). As Newmeyer (1996: 25) observes, Chomsky put syntax—the system for generating an infinitively diverse variety of novel sentences by means of productive processes—into the forefront of linguistic inquiry, highlighting the creative aspect of language more so than his predecessors had done.

Chomsky was critical of traditional and structuralist grammars in that they tended to focus on exceptions and irregularities but "provide only examples and hints concerning the regular and productive syntactic processes" (Chomsky 1965: 5).

---

[1] Bloomfield (1933) occasionally used '*' to mark ill-formed structures, and surely made use of his own and others' intuitive judgments. However, he explained in a footnote that '*' is used to mark forms that are "theoretically posited" but unattested (Bloomfield 1933: 516), thus emphasizing the importance of attested forms.

To overcome these limitations, he saw as essential the development of an explicit formal metalanguage through which syntactic rules could be formulated to predict the set of well-formed sentences. Hence, the permissible structures of a language (such as in 1a, 2a, 2c, 3a, and 4b) should be licensed by the appropriate formal rules, while logically possible but non-permissible structures (such as in 1b, 2b, 3b and 4a) should be excluded.[2] How should this distinction between permissible and non-permissible structures be justified? Chomsky (1965: 19–20) acknowledged a variety of potential sources of information, including observations of actual linguistic behavior and experimental procedures, but asserted that the most useful and decisive evidence came from the intuitive judgments of speakers: "The structural descriptions assigned to sentences by the grammar, the distinctions that it makes between well-formed and deviant, and so on, must, for descriptive adequacy, correspond to the linguistic intuition of the native speaker (whether or not he may be immediately aware of this) in a substantial and significant class of crucial cases" (1965: 24).

Now more than fifty years later, the research program of generative grammar encompasses a wide range of distinct formalisms and theoretical perspectives, all of which differ substantially from the proposals put forth in Chomsky's early work. Regardless of their differences, however, practitioners of generative grammar have remained committed to the study of implicit knowledge, or competence, and have continued to emphasize the creative abilities of language users. Furthermore, intuitive judgments have remained as their primary data source. As Schütze (1996: 2) observes, this heavy reliance on intuitive judgments, which are more commonly known today as 'acceptability judgments', has been well justified, given the aims of generative theories. Most importantly, acceptability judgments provide a simple method for showing minimal contrasts between sentences hypothesized to differ in grammatical status due to the presence or absence of a particular structural property (e.g. the syntactic category of the complement of *with* in (1a–b)). Data from spontaneous discourse, by contrast, do not contain direct evidence for structures that fail to occur, making it difficult to distinguish between grammatical but rarely produced sentence types and ungrammatical sentence types. Furthermore, this reliance on acceptability judgments has been fruitful. Practitioners of generative grammar have been able to achieve remarkable success in elucidating the human capacity for language, providing both detailed analyses of the syntactic patterns of individual languages as well as broader generalizations that apply across typologically diverse signed and spoken languages.

The continued reliance on intuitive judgments has not been without controversy, however. From early on, linguists and psychologists have expressed skepticism over the validity of intuitive judgments for discovering facts about the underlying competence grammar. In part, these concerns were due to the informal and uncontrolled

---

[2] This formal metalanguage initially took the form of string rewriting rules which followed the mathematical framework of Emil Post (1943). According to Pullum (2010: 242), Chomsky acknowledged Post's ideas but never cited his technical papers. Pullum notes that Chomsky (1956) cited Post's proposals indirectly through Rosenbloom (1950). Thus, the formal basis for generative grammar followed from Post (1943), while the application to linguistic theory was an innovation.

manner in which judgments were typically collected, either through interviews with a small number of speakers or through the researcher consulting their own intuitions. In cases where speakers disagreed with each other as to the status of a particular sentence type, informal methods provided no systematic method of resolving data disputes. Labov (1972: 106) laments: "It is unfortunate that this proliferation of the intuitive data has not been accompanied by a methodological concern for the reduction of error, or a search for intersubjective agreement." Other concerns were regarding the nature of judgments themselves as a type of metalinguistic performance which may be affected by many other factors besides speakers' underlying competence grammar—a problem which Chomsky himself recognized (1965: 11). For example, pointing to the secondary status of linguistic intuitions as imagined episodes of language use, Levelt (1972: 22) states: "It is not at all obvious that intuitions will reveal the underlying competence." These and other similar criticisms inspired numerous empirical studies testing the validity of intuitive judgments (Greenbaum 1976; Nagata 1988; Snow and Meijer 1977; Spencer 1973; Vetter, Volovecky, and Howell 1979), which in turn inspired the development of more rigorous standards for data collection.

In the most comprehensive and important work on this topic to date, *The Empirical Base of Linguistics*, Schütze (1996) provides a detailed review of these early criticisms and empirical studies of linguistic intuitions. His approach is fair and even-handed, pointing out the flaws and limitations of previous empirical studies on linguistic intuitions, while acknowledging the genuine insights and highlighting the real problems which these studies revealed, and with which linguists who rely on acceptability judgments ought to concern themselves. While agreeing that judgments can be affected by a variety of factors related to the speaker's background, the task, the sentence materials, and the judgment process, Schütze argues convincingly that judgment data, when properly controlled, provide a rich source of information about grammatical knowledge. He points toward some exemplary studies that had already been conducted at the time (Cowart 1994; Snyder 1994), lays out a set of practical suggestions for collecting judgment data by means of well-controlled experimental tasks, and outlines a proposal for a psychological model of sentence judgments. Importantly, he considers how the data can best be interpreted in the face of the common problem that Labov (1972) and many others had noted: variation within and across speakers. Essentially, Schütze argues in favor of using carefully chosen speaker populations and carefully controlled sentence materials to eliminate known confounds (e.g. regional dialect, lexical frequency), and statistical techniques to identify systematic variation and factor out random variation in the results. When the expected systematic variation is confirmed through tests of statistical significance, for example a systematic difference in acceptability between sentences like (2a) and (2b) *as averaged across multiple speakers and across multiple sentence sets with different lexical content*, this can be taken to provide evidence of grammatical knowledge. When unexpected systematic variation is discovered, for example a difference in acceptability between two sentence types hypothesized to be fully grammatical, it can then be studied separately: "[Extraneous factors] might add sufficient noise to obscure actual grammatical phenomena, but they cannot systematically change the pattern of results unless they too are stable. If so, they can be studied directly and then factored out..." (1996: 121). Finally, Schütze (1996: 180) argues in favor of using data from other sources in addition to sentence judgments, such as corpus data from spontaneous speech and data from other types of psycholinguistic experiments, in order to provide converging evidence for a particular grammatical construct.

Over the past 25 years, Schütze's (1996) proposals for rigorous data collection techniques, along with similar proposals elaborated by Cowart (1997) in his foundational textbook *Experimental Syntax*, have failed to cause any sweeping methodological revolution in syntax. The vast majority of studies in recent years have continued to use informally collected judgments. These groundbreaking proposals have, however, influenced a growing minority of linguists to begin to apply such techniques to the study of syntax. These empirical studies have been successful in showing quantitative support for (or in some cases, against) numerous theoretical constructs in syntax (Myers 2009). Consequently, the strong criticisms of intuitive judgments, such as those expressed by Labov (1972) and Levelt (1972) have died down. Although we still lack any established psychological model of the judgment process (Lewis and Phillips 2015: 42), it is now generally accepted, at least among those linguists who see generative grammar as a worthwhile research program, that intuitive judgments *can* be a reliable and valid source of data for building theories of grammatical knowledge. Currently two major controversies concerning acceptability judgments persist. The first concerns the extent to which traditional informal methods of data collection are acceptable for supporting theories of syntax. While the majority of syntax researchers find them to be generally acceptable for most purposes, a vocal minority argue that well-controlled experimental methods are almost always to be preferred (Edelman and Christiansen 2003; Featherston 2007; Gibson and Fedorenko 2013; Wasow and Arnold 2005). The second concerns how to tease apart the different factors *in addition to grammatical knowledge* that may affect speakers' judgments of sentences. It is my purpose in this book to explore the second controversy, with some implications for the first as well. In particular, I will explore how linguists can distinguish grammatical knowledge (specifically, knowledge of syntax, to the exclusion of phonology and semantics) from other factors that affect speakers' intuitions in cases that are less clear than those introduced so far. My focus will be on a few factors that are easily confusable with syntactic knowledge, namely knowledge of semantic, pragmatic, and prosodic constraints, and effects of general cognitive mechanisms such as working memory capacity. I will explore these issues in the context of linguistic examples involving *gradient acceptability*, in which sentences that share the same or very similar structures differ in acceptability to varying degrees. In the following section, I will introduce the concept of gradient acceptability and discuss two possible ways of explaining it, using Chomsky's (1965) example of selectional restrictions.

1.2 Gradient acceptability: the case of selectional restrictions

Chomsky (1965) recognized that speakers' intuitions are not always clear-cut, and that for certain types of grammatical phenomena we must recognize different degrees of acceptability. For example, he identifies three "degrees of deviance" for the following sentences, with (5a) being the strongest deviation from a normal grammatical sentence and (5c) being the weakest deviation. I have included a fully grammatical example in (5d) for the sake of comparison.

(5)   a. Sincerity may virtue the boy.
      b. Sincerity may elapse the boy.
      c. Sincerity may admire the boy.
      d. Sincerity may frighten the boy.

At least superficially, all three sentences in (5a–c), from Chomsky (1965: 152), conform to the typical structure of a transitive clause in English as in (5d), but each deviates in some way from the norm. While (5a) violates the requirement for a verb to act as head of VP (*virtue* is a noun), and (5b) violates the strict subcategorization of the verb *elapse* (which is normally intransitive), (5c) violates only the selectional feature of the transitive verb *admire* (which normally requires a sentient subject). To account for these differences in acceptability, Chomsky considers two possibilities: (1) that all three sentences are ungrammatical and that therefore we must recognize different "degrees of grammaticalness" (1965: 153); and (2) that (5a–b) are ungrammatical, while (5c) is grammatical (i.e. syntactically well-formed) but deviant in its combination of semantic properties. In favor of the second option, he notes that sentences which violate selectional restrictions can often be interpreted figuratively, given an appropriate context (1965: 149). For example, (5c) could involve personification of the abstract concept of sincerity. However, he ultimately settles on the first option—including selectional features within the syntax—citing examples in which selectional features such as animacy appear to cause structural deviance (e.g. *the book who you read*). He proposes a hierarchy of dominance to account for the observed differences in degree of deviance in sentences like (5a–c): "features introduced by strict subcategorization rules dominate features introduced by selection rules, and…all lexical features are dominated by the symbols for lexical categories" (1965: 153). Incidentally, McCawley (1968) rejects Chomsky's proposal and instead argues in favor of the first option, in which sentences such as (5c) are syntactically well-formed, and selectional features are purely semantic in nature.

The sentences in (5a–d) exemplify the key concept of *gradient acceptability*. While example (5a) is clearly ill-formed, and example (5d) is clearly acceptable, examples (5b–c) are intermediate in acceptability, meaning that speakers are likely to judge them as neither fully acceptable nor fully unacceptable. Often such sentences are marked with '?' or '??' instead of '*' in studies of syntax. Significantly, examples (5a–d) appear to share the same grammatical structure, in this case the structure of a simple transitive clause, but differ incrementally in terms of speakers' judgments of their acceptability. Chomsky's (1965) discussion of these examples illustrates two possible types of explanations, which, following Phillips (2013a: 157), I will refer to as *formal syntactic* and *non-syntactic*.[3] A formal syntactic explanation requires reference to some properties of the sentence that are purely structural, such as a syntactic category (e.g. verb), feature (e.g. nominative case), or relation (e.g. subject of). A formal syntactic explanation does not require that structural features be the *only* thing accounting for the deviance of the less acceptable sentence, however. In (5a), for example, it is clear that there are semantic anomalies, in addition to the syntactic category error. But Chomsky's explanation for the deviance of (5a–c) crucially refers to formal syntactic features. A non-syntactic explanation, by contrast, does not require reference to any syntactic property of the sentence. In this case, Chomsky considered (but rejected) an explanation in which selectional features, such as animacy, are stated only at the level of semantics. McCawley (1968) later took up this suggestion and developed a purely semantic account of selectional restrictions. Thus, McCawley (1968) represents a non-syntactic account of selectional restrictions, or more specifically, a semantic account.

Throughout the history of generative grammar, non-syntactic accounts—especially involving semantics and pragmatics—have been proposed as an alternative to formal syntactic accounts of certain phenomena (e.g. Erteschik-Shir and Lappin 1979; Ginzburg and Sag 2000; Jackendoff 1992; Levinson 1987, 1991; Oshima 2006). More recently, non-syntactic accounts involving working memory capacity or other general cognitive mechanisms have become more common, especially with respect to phenomena involving long-distance dependencies (Chaves 2013; Goldberg 2013; Hofmeister and Sag 2010; Hofmeister et al. 2013). In the following sections, I will discuss some additional examples of gradient acceptability with the aim of briefly introducing the major types of explanations for contrasts in acceptability that have appeared in the literature.

1.3 Formal syntactic explanations: superficial similarities can mask underlying structural differences

A formal syntactic explanation for a contrast in acceptability says that the less acceptable sentence differs from the more acceptable sentence according to some crucial syntactic property, with the less acceptable sentence violating a grammatical constraint. The examples I am considering here are distinctive in that the contrasting sentences appear, at least superficially, to share the same grammatical structure.

---

[3] Following the suggestion of an anonymous reviewer, I have replaced Phillips's original term, *reductionist*, with a more neutral term, *non-syntactic*. This avoids the ambiguity and negative connotations associated with the term *reductionist* while maintaining the two-way distinction that Phillips used. This two-way distinction is not intended to detract from the individual importance of semantic, pragmatic, prosodic, or processing-based factors but rather reflects the focus of the current book, which is to explore the implications of gradient judgment data for theories of syntax and notions of syntactic well-formedness.

It is precisely for these types of cases that non-syntactic accounts become plausible, and that formal syntactic accounts become especially tricky. The example given in (6) illustrates this phenomenon with respect to the constraint commonly known as a comp-trace or *that*-trace violation. The status of (6a) is uncontroversial: it is an acceptable sentence in which the relativized element *which* functions as the subject of the complement clause. Assuming a traditional movement-based analysis, *which* moves from its original position and leaves behind a trace, as indicated by '__'. Example (6b) illustrates the same type of relative clause formation, but with an overt complementizer *that* introducing the complement clause. This is an example of a classic comp-trace violation, resulting in ungrammaticality and degraded acceptability as compared with (6a). Example (6c) is the same as (6b), except that an adverbial PP *for the most part* is added following the complementizer *that*, causing the sentence to again become more acceptable. This amelioration effect (i.e. the increase in acceptability associated with the addition of an adverbial phrase) has been confirmed experimentally by Sobin (2002: 543), using an acceptability rating task administered to 23 participants using slightly different sentence materials (involving interrogatives with comp-trace violations rather than relative clauses).

(6)   a. These are all ideas which I think __ should be easy to implement.
       b. *These are all ideas which I think that __ should be easy to implement.
       c. These are all ideas which I think that for the most part __ should be easy to implement.

Various syntactic analyses have been proposed to account for comp-trace violations as in (6b) (Chomsky 1981; Chomsky and Lasnik 1977; Culicover 1993; Pesetsky 1982; Stowell 1981). Many of them depend on some version of the Empty Category Principle (Chomsky 1981; Hornstein and Weinberg 1995), which requires that a trace in subject position be properly governed by a coindexed antecedent in a higher position. Comp-trace effects as in (6b) occur because an overt complementizer, such as *that*, cannot itself act as an antecedent and blocks government by the antecedent of the trace (*which*), leaving the trace in subject position unlicensed. For a grammatical sentence such as (6a), the null complementizer fails to block proper government by the coindexed antecedent. Under this type of account, it is not obvious why a sentence like (6c), which also appears to contain a comp-trace violation, should be judged as more acceptable. A few studies have explicitly addressed this issue, only one of which I will consider here. (For ease of exposition, I am omitting some of the technical details.) Sobin (2002) proposes that null complementizers but not overt complementizers have properties allowing them to license a trace in subject position, resulting in the observed contrast between (6a) and (6b). For a sentence such as (6c), however, the overt complementizer *that* merges with the adverbial PP. The resulting structure contains a null complementizer in head position followed by *that*+PP in an adjunct position. Thus, the subject trace in (6c) is licensed by the null complementizer just as it is in (6a), and only (6b) contains any comp-trace violation. In more general terms, the presence of the adverbial phrase in (6c), which might appear to be irrelevant to the licensing of the subject trace, actually changes the structure in a crucial way, according to Sobin's (2002) analysis.

1.4 Prosodic explanations: ill-formed prosodic structures may be confusable with syntactic rule violations

Phenomena commonly believed to be syntactic in nature have occasionally been analyzed as instead involving constraints on prosodic structure. Again considering the case of comp-trace violations in English and their mitigation by the addition of an adverbial phrase, Kandybowicz (2006) presents an alternative to the Empty Category Principle and other syntactic explanations that have been proposed. Under this analysis, comp-trace sentences do not violate any syntactic rules but instead show an ill-formed prosodic contour: "In English, the sequence <C_0,trace> is illicit when C_0 and trace are adjacent within the same prosodic phrase and C_0 is aligned with a prosodic phrase boundary" (Kandybowicz 2006: 223). Here I repeat the examples from (6a–c), this time showing the relevant prosodic boundaries. Following the original notation, iP indicates Intonation Phrase and intP indicates Intermediate Phrase (Kandybowicz 2006: 223).

(7)   a. These are all [$_\text{iP}$ ideas which I think __ should be easy to implement].
      b. *These are all [$_\text{iP}$ ideas which I think [$_\text{intP}$ that __ should be easy to implement]].
      c. These are all [$_\text{intP}$ ideas which I think that] [$_\text{iP}$ for the most part] __ [$_\text{intP}$ should be easy to implement].
      d. These are all [$_\text{iP}$ ideas that __ should be easy to implement].

According to this analysis, the addition of an overt complementizer, as in (7b), introduces an intermediate prosodic boundary, causing an illicit prosodic structure in which the intermediate boundary is followed by an overt complementizer and a trace. However, the addition of an adverbial PP, as in (7c), repairs the prosody of the sentence by introducing an additional prosodic phrase before the trace, and therefore preventing the type of prosodic structure in (7b) from occurring. As Kandybowicz acknowledges, this solution is of the same flavor as the filter-based approach of Chomsky and Lasnik (1977), who proposed a simple constraint barring an adjacent complementizer and trace. The difference here is that the constraint on adjacency is stated at the level of prosody, leaving unacceptable sentences such as (7b) syntactically well-formed. This solution also accounts for the acceptability of simple relative clauses such as in (7d) in terms of prosody, claiming that even though there is an adjacent complementizer and trace, there is no prosodic boundary before the complementizer.

1.5 Semantic explanations: semantic anomalies may be confusable with syntactic rule violations

We have seen that Chomsky (1965) suggested and then rejected a purely semantic explanation of selectional restrictions. Because of the undeniably close relationship between structure and meaning, the division of labor between the syntactic and semantic components of linguistic knowledge has been one of active controversy throughout the history of generative grammar. As I will argue in Chapter 2, this division depends largely on one's theoretical assumptions regarding the degree of isomorphism between syntax and semantics. For now, I will provide one additional example of a semantic explanation for acceptability contrasts often assumed to reflect a syntactic difference. Starting with Chomsky (1973), the standard analysis of examples such as (8a) has been that the verb *believe* takes an infinitive clause *Chris to be a spy* as its complement. This contrasts with the analysis of similar sentences such as (8b), in which *Chris* is the object of the matrix verb *persuade*, and the infinitive clause *to be a spy* takes a null (PRO) subject which is co-referential with *Chris*. This type of analysis accounts for the contrast in acceptability between sentences like (8c) and (8d) as being due to this difference in structure. For example, Chomsky (1981: 37) attributed this contrast to one component of the Projection Principle, which required that elements in object position should always receive a semantic role (theta role) in that position. Because *there* is an expletive element (i.e. is non-referential) and does not receive any semantic role, it should not occur in an object position. For this reason, (8d) is ungrammatical. Such a problem does not apply to (8c), however, as long as *there* resides in the subject position of the infinitive clause.

(8) a. Pat believes Chris to be a spy.   (Pollard and Sag 1994: 112)
  b. Pat persuaded Chris to be a spy.
  c. Pat believes there to be a problem.
  d. *Pat persuaded there to be a problem.

Pollard and Sag (1994: 112–23) are critical of this type of analysis, on the grounds that it fails to straightforwardly account for the numerous object-like properties of the NP following the verb *believe*, which had under earlier transformational accounts been treated as the effect of a transformation of subject-to-object raising (i.e. moving the subject NP of the infinitive clause up into object position) (Postal 1974; Rosenbaum 1967). Pollard and Sag do not themselves adopt a raising analysis, but instead argue for a purely semantic account of contrasts such as the one in (8c–d). They claim that sentences like (8a) and (8b) share the same syntactic structure (in which *Chris* is the object of the matrix verb), but differ in semantic content (1994: 122). A sentence such as (8d) is semantically ill-formed because existential *there* does not refer to any entity which would be capable of being persuaded, whereas *Chris* does. A sentence such as (8c) is acceptable because the verb *believe*, unlike the verb *persuade*, does not impose any semantic requirements on the NP in object position. While proponents of both types of analysis would agree that there is a semantic anomaly in (8d), Pollard and Sag (1994) recognize *only* the semantic anomaly, whereas Chomsky (1981) posits a syntactic rule violation which correlates with the semantic anomaly. Pollard and Sag's (1994) analysis is therefore non-syntactic in our sense.

1.6 Pragmatic explanations: grammatical sentences may appear ill-formed in an inappropriate discourse context

Similar to semantic explanations for gradient acceptability, pragmatic explanations propose that variations in the acceptability of structurally similar sentences are due to factors in the discourse context rather than syntactic rule violations. Ward et al. (1991) present such a pragmatic account of the phenomenon known as 'outbound anaphora'. Their analysis is presented as an alternative to several previous analyses, starting with Postal (1969), which treat the reduction in acceptability for sentences such as (9b) as being due to a syntactic rule violation. According to Postal (1969), a personal pronoun, such as *its*, cannot take a morpheme in a word-internal position as its antecedent due to a syntactic constraint on anaphora, i.e. pronoun–antecedent relations. Because *coffee* is part of a compound in (9b), it cannot act as an antecedent of *its* and the sentence is unacceptable under such an interpretation. In (9a), this problem does not arise, since *coffee* is an independent word acting as the complement of a preposition.

(9)   a. Drinkers of *coffee* tend to enjoy *its* taste.
      b. **Coffee* drinkers tend to enjoy *its* taste.   (adapted from Postal 1969: 230)
      c. At the same time as *coffee* beans were introduced, the Arabs made changes in *coffee* preparation that greatly improved *its* flavor.   (Ward et al. 1991: 452)
      d. *Changes in *coffee* preparation greatly improved *its* flavor.

In defense of their pragmatic account of this type of anaphora, Ward et al. (1991) demonstrate that the supposed rule against word-internal antecedents is routinely violated in discourse, citing the example in (9c) (from a book about coffee and tea) and a number of similar examples from spontaneous speech and from various written sources. They propose that pronouns refer to discourse entities rather than linguistic antecedents. While a linguistic antecedent can help evoke the relevant discourse entity, there is no necessary syntactic relationship between the pronoun and its linguistic antecedent. In this view, outbound anaphora is pragmatically infelicitous in those cases for which the discourse entity is not sufficiently accessible from the context. In (9a), *coffee* has independent reference, making it immediately accessible to pronominal co-reference, whereas in (9b), *coffee* acts as a word-internal modifier, making it less accessible. In (9c), although *coffee* still acts as word-internal modifier, the context evokes coffee as a discourse topic. While there is no independent noun phrase to act as the antecedent of the pronoun *its*, the discourse entity 'coffee' is, apparently, sufficiently accessible. If we remove part of the facilitating context, as in (9d), we can see that *coffee* becomes less felicitous as a linguistic antecedent and more similar to (9b). As is typical of pragmatic explanations for variable acceptability, Ward et al. (1991) argue that in an appropriate discourse context, outbound anaphora becomes fully acceptable, thereby removing any need for a syntactic rule to account for contrasts such as (9a–b).

1.7 Processing explanations: grammatical sentences may appear ill-formed when they are hard to process

Processing explanations claim that a syntactic rule is not necessary to explain a reduction in acceptability if that reduction can be attributed to general processing difficulty. One type of argument for such an account is similar to what we have already seen with the example of outbound anaphora: if we can manipulate non-structural factors, such as lexical content, to make a sentence both more acceptable and easier to understand, then perhaps the less acceptable version is simply difficult to process. Kluender and Kutas (1993) present this sort of example as a motivation for their experimental study of processing constraints on interrogative sentence formation.

(10) a. *What do the editors really need to locate [the linguist [who reviewed __]]?
      b. What do we really need to find [someone [to review __]]?

They note that (10a) and (10b) should both be ungrammatical, since both sentences violate a syntactic constraint on interrogative formation known as the Complex Noun Phrase Constraint (Ross 1967), or more generally, the Subjacency condition (Chomsky 1981). On a movement-based account of interrogative formation, these sentences are problematic because the interrogative pronoun *what* originates within a relative clause, which is an island to extraction ('island' being Ross's (1967) clever term for a position in the structure from which movement is prohibited). The Subjacency account, for example, says that the interrogative pronoun must cross both a relative clause boundary and a noun phrase boundary before it can land in any clausal specifier position, and that this type of double boundary crossing is illicit (Chomsky 1981). Such an account does not readily explain why speakers judge (10a) to be less acceptable than (10b), however. Kluender and Kutas (1993) suggest that the difference may lie in the type of referential processing needed to understand each sentence. While (10a) contains two full noun phrases (*the editors, the linguist*) and an overt relative pronoun (*who*), (10b) contains two pronouns (*we, someone*) and no overt relative pronoun. The difficulty of processing the interrogative dependency (the relation between the pronoun *what* and its trace, as indicated by '__') then combines with the difficulty of processing the referring expressions in (10a), leading speakers to judge such sentences as unacceptable. Sentences such as (10b) are easier to process because the referring expressions are less complex, leading to increased acceptability. The authors reason that the acceptability of (10b) implies that perhaps it is fully grammatical, which in turn implies that (10a) may also be grammatical, but simply difficult to process.

Kluender and Kutas (1993) test a different type of question formation in their actual experiments, but their proposal for a processing explanation is similar. A subset of their sentence materials is given in (11a–d) (an additional experimental condition is omitted for the purposes of this brief example).

(11)   a. Who isn't he sure [that the TA explained it to __ in lab]?
       b. ?Who isn't he sure [if the TA explained it to __ in lab]?
       c. Isn't he sure [that the TA explained it to them in lab]?
       d. Isn't he sure [if the TA explained it to them in lab]?

While (11a) is, on all accounts, fully grammatical, (11b) again violates a syntactic constraint on interrogative formation. According to the Subjacency account (Chomsky 1981), the interrogative pronoun *who* must cross over a clause boundary in (11b), whereas in (11a) it can stop in the intermediate specifier position of the complementizer *that* before moving to its final sentence-initial position. The long movement required for (11b) is illicit, whereas the shorter movement required for (11a) is permitted. Kluender and Kutas (1993) hypothesize that the lower acceptability of (11b) is not really due to any syntactic constraint, but rather due to the difficulty of processing the interrogative complementizer *if* as compared with the declarative complementizer *that* at the clause boundary, combined with the difficulty of processing the long-distance dependency between *who* and its trace. Their argument in this case is slightly more complicated. They must tease apart the effects of the complementizer choice from the effects of the long-distance dependency. To do so, they included yes–no questions such as those in (11c–d). Since there is no long-distance dependency in yes–no questions, they were able to manipulate the complementizer choice independently of the interrogative dependency. The results of an acceptability rating task showed that as expected under either a formal syntactic or a processing account, participants rated (11b) as less acceptable than (11a). However, they also found that participants uniformly rated *wh*-questions as less acceptable than yes–no questions, even finding a contrast between the fully grammatical sentences in (11a) and (11c). In addition, they rated the sentences with *if* as uniformly less acceptable than the sentences with *that*, finding a contrast between the fully grammatical yes–no questions in (11c) and (11d). They reasoned that the lower acceptability of (11b) must have been the result of non-syntactic factors which equally applied to the grammatical sentences, but which had an additive effect on (11b), since this sentence type contained the complementizer *if* in combination with a long-distance dependency.

The reasoning in this case is slightly different than the reasoning given for (10). For the contrast in (10), they argued that two sentences sharing the same structural properties differ in acceptability due to processing constraints that affect (10a) more than (10b). This is known as an amelioration effect (Phillips 2013a: 164), and is comparable to the pragmatic amelioration effect that Ward et al. (1991) found for outbound anaphora. For the sentences in (11), they showed that sentences which are uncontroversially grammatical appear to be sensitive to the same processing factors hypothesized to affect Subjacency-violating sentences. For both (10) and (11), they argued that Subjacency-violating sentences are generally less acceptable not because they violate any syntactic rule, but rather because they involve the combined effects of different types of difficult-to-process elements. These arguments are typical of processing-based explanations for variation in acceptability and will be considered in more depth in Chapter 4.

1.8 Processing explanations: ungrammatical sentences may appear well-formed when they are hard to process

So far, we have been considering explanations which argue that a particular sentence type is syntactically well-formed, despite the fact that it is often judged as unacceptable. As Phillips (2013a) observes, the reverse type of situation is also possible in which speakers judge certain ungrammatical sentences to be acceptable. One example of this type comes from subject–verb agreement errors. Although a finite verb in English generally agrees in number with the head noun of the subject NP, English speakers sometimes produce and accept sentences in which the finite verb agrees with a non-head noun within the subject NP. For example, in Francis (2011), I investigated subject–verb agreement in sentences containing possessive relative clauses, as in (12a–b).

(12) a. The guy whose dogs got loose is in trouble.
     b. Whoever's dogs got loose is in trouble.
     c. *The guy whose dogs got loose are in trouble.
     d. *Whoever's dogs got loose are in trouble.
     e. Whichever dogs got loose are in trouble.
     f. Whoever is/*are going should let me know.

In (12a), the verb *is* takes a singular form, to agree with the singular head noun *guy*. In (12b), the phrase *whoever's dogs got loose* is a free relative clause, meaning that there is no overt head noun (*whoever's* is analyzed as a possessive relative pronoun). However, the covert head (co-referential with *whoever's*) is apparently singular, again requiring a singular verb form. The analysis of *whoever's* as singular is supported by the general unacceptability of *whoever* with a plural verb form, as in (f). Based on this analysis, the sentences in (12c–d) are ungrammatical due to the plural verb form *are*. Although I did not elicit acceptability judgments for these sentences, the results of a verb selection task showed an interesting effect. Participants were presented with a series of sentences like (12a–b), but with the verb omitted, and their task was to select the correct verb form, *is* or *are*. In cases like these in which the head noun was singular and the embedded noun (*dogs*) was plural, participants responded with the incorrect plural verb form 10% of the time for sentences like (12a), but 41% of the time for sentences like (12b). While a 10% error rate is not unusual for this type of task, a 41% error rate is surprising. My interpretation of this effect was that sentences like (12d) are just as ungrammatical as sentences like (12c), but that participants had more trouble identifying and interpreting the head noun in (12d) as compared with (12c). This was possibly due to the surface similarity of (12d) to more common free relative clauses such as (12e) which contain only one possible head. My explanation in Francis (2011) was non-syntactic in that it appealed to processing factors to account for the observed difference between two ungrammatical sentences types. A formal syntactic account is also possible, however. An alternative interpretation of the observed difference between (12c) and (12d) would be that sentences like (12d) are not really ungrammatical. According to this analysis, *whoever's* is ambiguous in number, causing participants to vary in their verb form choices. This alternative explanation is a formal syntactic explanation in that it appeals to two possible feature specifications (singular and plural) for *whoever's* in (12d), but only one possible feature specification for *who* in (12c), due to the presence of the (unambiguously) singular head noun *guy*.

Francis (2011) claimed that two *ungrammatical* sentence types differ in acceptability due to the *more* acceptable sentence type being more difficult to process, making it more difficult for speakers to detect the syntactic anomaly. This type of processing explanation is in contrast to the type of explanation given by Kluender and Kutas (1993), in which two *grammatical* sentence types were said to differ in acceptability due to the *less* acceptable sentence type being more difficult to process. These different types of explanations underline the fact that acceptability judgments do not bear a straightforward relationship with ease of processing, and that indeed 'processing' is itself a multifaceted phenomenon.

1.9 Overview of the book

This brief chapter has introduced some of the problems that gradient acceptability judgments pose for interpreting the results of judgment tasks in relation to theoretical claims in syntax. We have seen that in addition to formal syntactic explanations, which are the most common type of explanation in the syntax literature, various types of non-syntactic explanations have also been proposed. These include explanations that make reference to semantic, pragmatic, or prosodic factors, as well as explanations that appeal to general cognitive mechanisms involved in language processing. Crucially, while formal syntactic explanations may include reference to other factors in addition to the purported syntactic constraints, non-syntactic approaches avoid invoking any specific syntactic constraints, and instead attribute the relevant patterns of judgments entirely to other factors. Like Phillips (2013a), I take the position in this book that both formal syntactic and non-syntactic solutions may be appropriate, but in different cases. I will show that some patterns of judgments which have traditionally been given a formal syntactic interpretation turn out to be better understood in terms of non-syntactic factors, while others cannot be understood (or at least not fully understood) in this way. In my exploration of several challenging cases, I will argue for two main positions: (1) converging evidence from additional data sources, such as spontaneous language use and elicited production tasks, can help determine the source(s) of deviance for a particular sentence type; and (2) the interpretation of gradient judgment data depends crucially on one's theoretical commitments and assumptions. It is notable that the ongoing controversy surrounding formal syntactic versus non-syntactic explanations for variable acceptability has played out primarily among the minority of linguists who are already using experimental methods (Sprouse and Hornstein 2013). I will argue, however, that *all* linguists who study syntax can benefit from more systematically exploring cases of gradient acceptability, from taking various non-syntactic factors into account, from examining their own theoretical assumptions, and from consulting alternative data sources even when the judgment data show clear patterns. Finally, I will show that some gradient patterns of judgments are neither reducible to non-syntactic factors nor adequately described by formal syntactic constraints that categorically exclude a certain type of structure from the language. For such cases, I will argue that 'soft constraints' (non-categorical grammatical constraints) are needed.

The remainder of the book is organized as follows. Chapter 2 examines the major current theories of syntax and their underlying assumptions as relevant to interpreting judgment data. Two concepts are of particular importance: form–meaning isomorphism (the tightness of the relationship between meaning and syntactic form) and gradient grammaticality (whether the theory allows for soft constraints in the grammar). Chapter 3 discusses the ongoing debate over how to distinguish the effects of strictly syntactic knowledge from other aspects of linguistic knowledge (semantics, pragmatics, prosody) and surveys the major criteria that have been proposed for making this distinction. Similarly, Chapter 4 explores the criteria for distinguishing the effects of syntactic knowledge from the effects of general processing constraints operating in production and comprehension. Chapter 5 explores the relationship between acceptability and corpus frequency, especially for cases where low-frequency constructions differ in acceptability. Chapters 6 and 7 present detailed case studies examining previously published acceptability judgment studies of specific linguistic phenomena: relative clause and PP extraposition in English and German, and resumptive pronouns in Hebrew, Cantonese, and English relative clauses. For each of these case studies, I examine how certain theoretical assumptions, especially regarding degree of form–meaning isomorphism and inclusion or noninclusion of soft constraints in the grammar, can lead to different interpretations of the same data. Each case study also shows how data from other types of experimental tasks and from spontaneous language use can supplement judgment data to inform our theoretical proposals. Chapter 8 elaborates on the theoretical implications of the case studies, arguing in favor of a model of grammar that includes soft constraints. This chapter concludes by considering the future of acceptability judgments in theoretical syntax within an increasingly multimethodological research landscape.

2

Theories of grammatical knowledge in relation to formal syntactic and non-syntactic explanations

Thus far, I have been using the term 'generative grammar' as a cover term for a variety of unspecified formalisms and theoretical approaches, all of which share the goal of elucidating language users' implicit grammatical knowledge, including their creative capacity for generating novel sentences. The examples introduced so far have come from a variety of sources and time periods, and I think it is safe to say that none of the authors cited has the exact same theoretical assumptions as any other author. In this chapter, I will describe some of the key theoretical assumptions that distinguish among the different varieties of generative grammar in use today, and show how those assumptions can influence the interpretation of acceptability judgment data and in particular the likelihood of offering either a formal syntactic or non-syntactic explanation for a given contrast in acceptability.

The program of generative grammar set forth by Chomsky (1957) has inspired the development of a multitude of specific approaches and formalisms, each corresponding to a different set of theoretical assumptions. Chomsky himself has been the leading architect of a series of theoretical proposals which Culicover and Jackendoff (2005) call Mainstream Generative Grammar (due to their prominent status in the field) and which I will refer to as derivational theories (due to a shared aspect of their architecture). These proposals, which have strongly influenced the development of syntactic theory during particular time periods, include Standard Theory (Chomsky 1957), Extended Standard Theory (Chomsky 1965), Government and Binding (Chomsky 1981), Principles and Parameters (Chomsky and Lasnik 1993), and, most recently, the Minimalist Program (Chomsky 1995). All of the derivational approaches share the idea that sentences are generated through a procedural (step-by-step) *derivation*, and that abstract elements of syntactic representation are needed within the phrase structure.[1] In reaction to this, a number of influential alternative frameworks have been

---

[1] As Culicover and Jackendoff (2005: 15) point out, the idea of a procedural derivation is not unique to mainstream Chomskyan approaches to syntax. For example, derivations are also used in Combinatory Categorial Grammar (Steedman 2000) and Tree-Adjoining Grammar (Joshi and Schabes 1997). Since these theories are not discussed in the current work, I will, following Goldberg (2006: 28), use the term derivational more narrowly in reference to Chomskyan approaches.

Gradient Acceptability and Linguistic Theory. Elaine J. Francis, Oxford University Press.
© Elaine J. Francis (2022). DOI: 10.1093/oso/9780192898944.003.0002

developed which lack the technical apparatus of a procedural derivation and which simplify the representation of syntactic phrase structure. These theories instead employ a set of *constraints*, each of which licenses a piece of structure, and some form of *unification*, a process which combines pieces of structure together in no particular order and checks them for compatibility. The phrase structure representation itself is more surface-oriented, with fewer abstract elements, and the various types of grammatically relevant information are distributed across distinct levels of syntactic, semantic, and information structural representations and their interfaces (i.e. the lexicon and linking rules). Among the most influential of these constraint-based theories are Lexical-Functional Grammar (Bresnan 2000; Kaplan and Bresnan 1982), Generalized Phrase Structure Grammar (Gazdar et al. 1985), Head-Driven Phrase Structure Grammar (Pollard and Sag 1994; Sag, Wasow, and Bender 2003), Automodular Grammar (Sadock 1991; 2012; Yuasa 2005), Role and Reference Grammar (Van Valin and LaPolla 1997), Simpler Syntax (Culicover and Jackendoff 2005), Sign-Based Construction Grammar (Kay and Sag 2012; Michaelis 2012; Sag 2012), Berkeley Construction Grammar (Fillmore, Kay, and O'Connor 1988; Kay and Fillmore 1999), Cognitive Construction Grammar (Goldberg 1995; 2006), Fluid Construction Grammar (Steels 2013), and Radical Construction Grammar (Croft 2001). This is necessarily an incomplete list, due to the multitude of alternative generative theories that have been proposed.

An additional outgrowth of generative grammar has been the adaptation of formalisms originally developed for phonology to model constraint interaction in syntax. This general approach, known as Optimality Theory (OT), views as central the idea of competition among ranked or weighted constraints which apply to a set of candidate forms to select the most optimal output. Building on theoretical principles developed either in one of the derivational theories or in one of the constraint-based theories described above, this family of theories includes OT Syntax (Grimshaw 1997), Linear OT (Sorace and Keller 2005), Stochastic OT (Boersma and Hayes 2001; Bresnan, Dingare, and Manning 2001), and the Decathlon Model (Featherston 2008; 2019).

These various approaches which fall under the umbrella of generative grammar have not been developed in isolation, but rather have developed alongside important functionalist approaches to grammar. Most functionalist approaches share with generative approaches the idea that grammar is a form of implicit knowledge, but tend to place more emphasis on the communicative functions of language in use and less emphasis on formal syntactic representations. These include functional-typological approaches (Croft 1991; Givón 1984), cognitive approaches (Lakoff 1987; Langacker 1987; Talmy 1985), and usage-based approaches (Bybee and Hopper 2001; Bybee and McClelland 2005; Tomasello 2003), among others. Although such approaches have had relatively little connection with derivational theories, several of the alternative generative theories mentioned above, especially Role and Reference Grammar (Van Valin and LaPolla 1997), Stochastic OT (Bresnan, Dingare, and Manning 2001), and Cognitive Construction Grammar (Goldberg 2006) share key assumptions with these functionalist

approaches and indeed can most adequately be described as being generative and functionalist at the same time. For example, the idea of 'soft constraints' (i.e. grammatical
constraints that are realized in terms of statistical tendencies) in Stochastic OT is similar to the notion of entrenchment in usage-based theories, and correlated with the
tendency to use data from corpora of spontaneous discourse in testing and formulating
theoretical proposals. Similarly, most construction-based theories treat phrase structure rules as meaningful (symbolic) in the same way that lexical items are, and allow for
(resolvable) semantic conflict between the meaning of a construction and the meaning
of the lexical items that fill the construction (Michaelis 2004). While this distinguishes them from some other constraint-based theories (e.g. Automodular Grammar,
Lexical-Functional Grammar), it is a feature shared with cognitive approaches such as
Cognitive Grammar (Langacker 1987). These two ideas—probabilistic constraint application and symbolic representation of syntax—not only show cross-fertilization of
ideas between generative, cognitive, and usage-based theories, but also turn out to be
important for the interpretation of acceptability judgment data.

The current chapter cannot attempt to do justice to all of the various theories of
grammatical knowledge. For the purposes of exploring the implications of certain theoretical assumptions for the interpretation of acceptability judgments, I focus on just a
few key features of a subset of current generative theories and make no attempt to provide a comprehensive overview of each theory. Based on these key features, I divide the
theories into three major categories: (1) derivational grammars; (2) constraint-based
grammars; and (3) OT. I will highlight some important differences among these approaches, and illustrate how these differences have influenced the interpretation of
judgment data. I will show that while there is a consensus that acceptability judgments
can reflect a variety of different factors, some approaches tend more toward formal
syntactic explanations, while other approaches tend more toward non-syntactic explanations. I will argue that these tendencies are due to two main factors: (1) the degree of
isomorphism between and semantics/pragmatics that is built into the theory; (2) the
nature of constraint application as either categorical or probabilistic/stochastic. After
discussing each category of generative theories, I will also discuss one of the prominent
functionalist theories: the Usage-based Theory as proposed by Bybee and McClelland (2005) and Bybee (2010). Within this theory, the distinction I have been making
between formal syntactic and non-syntactic explanations no longer makes sense. Instead, acceptability judgments are interpreted with respect to notions of frequency and
familiarity.

2.1 Derivational grammars

Although as mentioned above, derivational theories include all of the approaches
closely associated with Noam Chomsky, including the highly influential Government and Binding Theory (Chomsky 1981), I restrict my discussion here to those

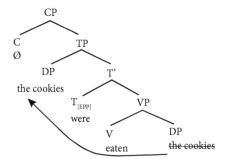

Fig. 2.1 A basic Minimalist analysis of an English passive sentence

Source: Adapted from Radford (2009: 257).

approaches in current use which identify themselves with Chomsky's Minimalist Program (Chomsky 1995; 2000). Shared among the current Minimalist approaches is the notion of 'derivation'—a process of structure building that includes two main operations: Merge and Move.[2] Merge is the generative engine of Minimalism—the process that combines words together to create novel phrases and sentences. It is an iterative process that combines two constituents together at each step, operating from the bottom up. This means that the last word of a sentence is the first to undergo merger with an immediately left-adjacent constituent. Merge continues to operate in this manner until the entire sentence is formed. The resulting structure is hierarchical and binary branching, meaning that Merge never combines more than two constituents at the same level. Move is a process which allows displaced constituents to be interpreted similarly to corresponding non-displaced constituents. Technically, it allows features which occur higher in the structure to attract constituents that occur lower in the structure to be moved up (or more precisely, copied and merged into to a higher position), meaning that movement is always in a leftward direction. For example, in forming a passive sentence such as *The cookies were eaten* in (1a), the subject *the cookies* originates as the complement of *eaten*, where it receives its semantic role (allowing it to be interpreted as the theme argument, just as in the corresponding active sentence *Someone ate the cookies*), and moves up to a higher specifier position where is can satisfy the EPP features of the clause (Radford 2009: 257). The EPP features express the requirement for an overt grammatical subject in a finite clause, as initially formulated in Chomsky's (1982) EPP (Extended Projection Principle). An unpronounced copy or trace is left behind in the original position. Radford (2009), a popular textbook in Minimalist theory, depicts a simple passive sentence as in Figure 2.1, before introducing a more elaborate argument structure representation with split verbal projections in later chapters.

In sum, the movement shown in Figure 2.1 satisfies the requirement for an overt subject, while also allowing predicates such as *eat* to assign semantic roles in a

---

[2] In some versions of Minimalism, movement is understood as Internal Merge, whereby a constituent that is a subpart of the original constituent is remerged into a higher position. The operation that combines two distinct constituents is called External Merge (rather than simply Merge) in this version of the theory (Chomsky 2004).

uniform way across active and passive sentences. If movement does not apply, the EPP features of the clause cannot be satisfied, and the result is an ungrammatical sentence, as in (1b).

(1)   a. The cookies were eaten.
      b. *Were eaten the cookies.

2.1.1 Form–meaning correspondences in derivational grammars

Of particular relevance to the interpretation of judgment data is the degree of iso-morphism assumed to hold between syntax and semantics and between syntax and discourse information structure. In current Minimalist approaches, the answer to this varies somewhat among different authors, but in general there is assumed to be a high degree of isomorphism. By isomorphism, I mean that the syntactic phrase structure representation is in close alignment with semantic argument structure and discourse information structure (Culicover and Jackendoff 2005).[3] This is possible despite mis-alignments between surface word order and meaning, due to the presence of various covert elements (e.g. traces of movement, null pronouns, and covert functional pro-jections), in the phrase structure. In our previous example, repeated in (2a), a local relationship between the predicate *eat* and its theme argument *the cookies* is main-tained by assuming that *the cookies* originates from a position adjacent to the verb, and leaves behind a trace in the canonical object position as it moves to the subject (Spec TP) position. As a result of this underlying isomorphism between structure and meaning, semantic and pragmatic distinctions can be taken to reveal important struc-tural differences. For example, the sentences in (2a–b) display the same word order, and yet they show a contrast in acceptability.

(2)   a. The cookies were eaten.
      b. ?The cookies have eaten.

This contrast is clearly related to the choice of auxiliary and, correspondingly, the semantics of passive vs. active clauses. Cookies can be eaten, but they cannot eat! However, a key component of the derivational account is an underlying difference in the structural position of semantic role assignment. The active sentence in (2b) is semantically anomalous because the NP *the cookies* originates in a specifier position where it must receive an agent role. In contrast, the passive sentence in (2a) is seman-tically well-formed because *the cookies* is able to receive an appropriate theme role in the object position, before movement applies.[4] In this way, the semantic contrast between (2a) and (2b) may be understood as a symptom of, and therefore evidence for, underlying structural differences between active and passive clauses. In other

---

[3] Here and throughout the book, I use the term isomorphism as synonymous with Culicover and Jackendoff's (2005: 47) term Interface Uniformity.
[4] The agent role is, in this case, suppressed, by whatever mechanism designates the passive participle as having intransitive (unaccusative) properties.

words, because the sentence in (2b) lacks the abstract structure required to license *the cookies* as a theme argument, *the cookies* must instead be (implausibly) construed as an agent. Here I will consider two additional brief examples. The first example further illustrates the standard assumption of form–meaning isomorphism, while the second example shows that derivational approaches are not strictly bound by this assumption.

Following the general approach of Hale and Keyser (1993), who propose that predicate–argument relations are directly represented as positions in syntactic structure, Embick (2004) explores the difference between two types of predicates as realized by the contrast in (4a–b).

(3)   a. The package remained opened.
      b. The package remained open.

(4)   a. The package remained carefully opened.
      b. *The package remained carefully open.   (Embick 2004: 363)

The lack of contrast between (3a–b) shows that the verb *remain* allows either *open* (an adjective) or *opened* (a past participle) as its complement. However, (3a) receives a slightly different interpretation than (3b), with (3a) implying that there had been a prior event of opening. The contrast in (4a–b) (which is supported on the basis of informal judgments) is used as a diagnostic test to distinguish between these two types of stative predicates: pure statives, such as *open*, and resultatives, such as *opened*. Embick notes that this difference is not always morphologically transparent, since the word *closed* can be interpreted like either (3a) or (3b). Embick reasons that the addition of the adverb *carefully* induces an eventive reading, thus excluding the possibility of a pure stative predicate such as *open*. This, along with similar diagnostics, is used to argue for a syntactic difference between sentences like (3a) and (3b). This difference is reflected in terms of the presence or absence of the null verbal head (little *v*) in the structure: "The absence of *v* and its eventivity is responsible for the ungrammaticality of the adverbial" (Embick 2004: 363). On the face of it, the lower acceptability of (3b) appears to be due to semantic incompatibility between the adverb *carefully* and the adjective *open* (note that other adverbs, such as *slightly*, could be used to modify *open*). However, according to Embick (2004), a sentence such as (2b) is missing the abstract *v* head that is required to license an eventive interpretation, resulting in a semantic anomaly when an adverb such as *carefully* is inserted. In this way, the contrast in acceptability in (3a–b) is taken as evidence for an underlying difference in syntactic structure—a difference which is not (fully) reducible to lexical semantics. According to Marantz (2013: 160–1), current Minimalist approaches do not encode all semantic distinctions related to predicate–argument relations in the syntactic representation. Rather, some aspects of meaning are contributed by the root morphemes and not reflected in the structure. However, Embick's (2004) analysis is typical of Minimalist analyses in following Hale and Keyser's (1993) approach and assuming a high degree of isomorphism between structure and meaning.

Given the strong assumption of form–meaning isomorphism, Minimalist analyses tend to avoid purely semantic or pragmatic explanations for contrasts in acceptability. However, it is important to acknowledge that derivational analyses are not strictly bound by this assumption. For example, in his book *Syntactic Islands*, Boeckx (2012), who generally favors formal syntactic explanations for island effects (constraints on long-distance dependencies), believes that semantic and pragmatic accounts of certain weak island phenomena are more convincing (e.g. Abrusán 2011; Fox and Hackl 2006; Kroch 1989; Szabolcsi and Zwarts 1997). For example, Boeckx (2012: 47) considers examples such as (5a–b), which display an apparent contrast in acceptability. Under the standard assumptions, both (5a) and (5b) violate the Subjacency condition, since movement of the question phrase must cross over a clause-initial position which is already filled by the interrogative adverb *whether*.

(5)   a. Which glass of wine do you know whether you should poison __?
       b. *How much wine do you know whether you should poison __?

(Boeckx 2012: 47)

Boeckx first discusses a formal syntactic analysis proposed by Rizzi (1990), which considers (5a) as exceptional in that the phrase *which glass of wine* licenses a special long-distance binding relation with the gap, exempting the sentence from the usual conditions on movement. According to this account, (5b) is ungrammatical because standard movement has applied, in violation of the Subjacency condition. Boeckx seems more convinced, however, by Kroch's (1989) pragmatic account, which says that both (5a) and (5b) are syntactically well-formed, but (5b) is merely pragmatically odd. In (5b), there is no uniquely identifiable quantity of wine that should be poisoned, and therefore asking *how much wine* is not a felicitous question to ask. This analysis predicts that such a sentence could be improved given an appropriate context in which some particular portions of wine (one liter, two liters, etc.) are known in advance, and this indeed appears to be the case. Such contextual amelioration is typical of arguments for pragmatic accounts of apparently syntactic phenomena, as seen in Chapter 1 with the example of outbound anaphora (Ward, Sproat, and McKoon 1991).

2.1.2 Processing-based explanations in derivational grammars

While accepting some semantic and pragmatic explanations for weak island effects, Boeckx (2012) is not convinced by accounts of island effects that appeal to general processing mechanisms. For example, Boeckx does not accept Kluender and Kutas's (1993) position that some island effects are due to general constraints on processing capacity. In this respect, Boeckx is typical of derivational theorists, as becomes clear from examining the contributions by such theorists in a recent volume showcasing experimental studies of island effects (Sprouse and Hornstein 2013). Why should this be? It is certainly not the case that derivational theorists deny any influence of processing factors on acceptability. Processing accounts are, in fact, often welcome when examining contrasts in acceptability involving sentences that are assumed to be grammatical. For example, using an acceptability judgment task which tested sentences like those in (5a–d), Sprouse (2007a: 61) found that long-distance object questions as in (6b) were rated as less acceptable than short-distance subject questions as in (6a). Similarly, short-distance subject questions containing an interrogative complement clause, as in (6c) were rated as less acceptable than short-distance subject questions containing a declarative complement clause, as in (6a). Given that sentences (6a–c) are predicted to be fully grammatical, Sprouse (2007a: 53) believes that these differences in acceptability are likely due to processing factors.

(6) a. Who __ thinks that John bought a car?
     b. What do you think that John bought __?
     c. Who __ wonders whether John bought a car?
     d. What do you wonder whether John bought __?

Where Sprouse disagrees with the approach of Kluender and Kutas is in the interpretation of judgments found for sentences like (6d), which are standardly assumed to violate the Subjacency condition. Sprouse found that these island-violating sentences were judged as less acceptable than would be expected if one were simply adding up the two effects shown in the comparisons of the grammatical sentence types (i.e. the effect of dependency distance and the effect of the interrogative complementizer). He calls this type of interaction a superadditive effect, as opposed to an additive effect. Following up on this finding, Sprouse et al. (2012) tested whether the acceptability of island-violating sentences varied with individual working memory capacity. If participants with lower working memory capacity were to show a bigger superadditive effect, this would support an account based on processing capacity. To test this hypothesis, they conducted two acceptability judgment tasks which examined four different types of island effects, and correlated those results with individual participants' scores on two working memory tests. Although the expected superadditive effects were found for all four types of islands, these effects did not vary systematically among individual participants based on their working memory scores. This null result led Sprouse et al. to conclude that a grammatical account of island effects is more plausible than a processing-based account. It is notable that Boeckx (2012: 46) agrees with the conclusions of Sprouse et al. (2012), while at the same time preferring a pragmatic explanation for certain weak island effects. There is no inconsistency in this view, since neither a syntactic constraint nor a pragmatic effect would be predicted to vary according to individual working memory capacity, and so either type of explanation would be compatible with the null results of Sprouse et al. (2012). The interpretation of effects due to working memory capacity will be taken up again in Chapter 4.

Other scholars who work in constraint-based theories, especially Hofmeister et al. (2012; 2013), have challenged the methods and conclusions of Sprouse et al. (2012), and the question of whether certain island effects can receive a processing-based account remains an issue of active research and debate. What we can see from reviewing the positions of derivational theorists, to the extent that they consider processing-based accounts, is a high standard of evidence required for considering such an account preferable to a syntactic account of island effects. As such, the empirical work testing the possibility of a processing-based explanation has involved carefully controlled experiments correlating judgments with other types of cognitive measures. In contrast, acceptability judgments alone (whether formally or informally obtained) are often presented as evidence in favor of a syntactic explanation for island effects. In short, a processing-based explanation is often welcome to explain contrasts in acceptability between fully grammatical sentences which differ according to some measure of processing complexity (e.g. dependency distance), but tends to be seen as a last resort to explain contrasts in acceptability which receive a principled explanation in terms of some constraint on syntactic structure. I will consider some possible reasons for this in Section 2.2.3.

2.2 Constraint-based grammars

In contrast to Minimalism, which assumes a procedural (step-by-step) derivation for forming a sentence, most of the alternative generative theories posit *unification* as a generative mechanism for combining pieces of prefabricated structure (including both lexically specified elements and unspecified variables) together in a non-procedural (simultaneous) fashion and checking those pieces for compatibility (Jackendoff 2011: 276–7).[5] These theories share in common a relatively simple, surface-oriented, phrase structure representation, and a more central role for semantics and pragmatics in the explanation of traditionally syntactic phenomena. They also share an expanded role of the lexicon as an interface between different types of linguistic information, and a reduced role for purely syntactic processes. These constraint-based theories differ, however, in terms of the centrality of the linguistic sign and, consequently, the extent to which different types of information are segregated into separate levels or modules. Based on this difference, these theories can be divided into two main groups: level-mapping grammars and sign-based grammars. Level-mapping grammars include Lexical-Functional Grammar (Bresnan 2000; Kaplan and Bresnan 1982), Automodular Grammar (Sadock 1991; 2012; Yuasa 2005), Role and Reference Grammar (Van Valin 2005; Van Valin and LaPolla 1997), and Simpler Syntax (Culicover and Jackendoff 2005). Sign-based grammars include Head-Driven Phrase Structure Grammar (Pollard and Sag 1994), Sign-Based Construction Grammar (Sag 2012), Berkeley Construction Grammar (Fillmore, Kay, and O'Connor 1988), Cognitive Construction Grammar (Goldberg 1995; 2006), Fluid Construction Grammar (Steels 2013), and Radical Construction Grammar (Croft 2001). While level-mapping

---

[5] In Cognitive Construction Grammar, Goldberg (2006: 215) does not adopt the feature-based unification formalism used in some constraint-based theories such as Head-Driven Phrase Structure Grammar (Pollard and Sag 1994) and Sign-Based Construction Grammar (Sag 2012). However, she accepts an informal notion of unification, which she also calls integration (2006: 221), as a mechanism by which language users combine constructions together to form utterances during online production and comprehension. "Constructions are combined freely to form actual expressions as long as they are not in conflict. Unresolved conflicts result in judgments of ill-formedness" (Goldberg 2006: 10).

grammars and sign-based grammars are similar in most respects, the distinction we have been making between formal syntactic and semantic or pragmatic explanations of variable acceptability is somewhat more straightforward for level-mapping grammars. I will discuss level-mapping grammars first and sign-based grammars in the following section.

2.2.1 Form–meaning correspondences in level-mapping grammars

Level-mapping grammars make use of separate but parallel representations of different types of linguistic information, with each level having its own set of categories and well-formedness conditions. These parallel representations, which I am calling levels, are connected to each other via mapping rules and via lexical entries for morphemes, words, and constructions. The exact levels differ depending on the theory, but typically include phrase structure, grammatical function structure, semantic role structure, discourse information structure, and phonological structure. Although the level of phrase structure includes familiar categories such as VP (verb phrase) and PP (preposition phrase), it lacks most of the more abstract elements (e.g. empty categories, functional projections) used in Minimalist phrase structure representations. To the extent that similar abstract information is used, it is distributed across different levels such as semantic role structure (which encodes semantic roles such as agent and theme) and grammatical function structure (which encodes grammatical relations such as subject and direct object). For example, in a passive sentence in English, such as (1a) *The cookies were eaten*, the theme argument, *the cookies*, is directly mapped to the canonical subject position in phrase structure. Because level-mapping theories do not require uniformity of semantic role assignment, there is no need for syntactic movement, and therefore arguments originate in their surface positions in phrase structure. The verb itself takes on a morphologically passive form and a reduced transitivity, usually by means of a lexical rule specifying the relationship between the passive verb form and its active counterpart. Various mapping rules determine how semantic roles map onto grammatical functions and phrase structure positions in a language-specific manner, with different level-mapping theories having somewhat different analyses of the non-canonical mappings involved in passive sentences. As an example, Figure 2.2 shows schematic phrase structure and semantic role structure representations for a simple passive sentence in English in Automodular Grammar (Sadock 2012: 80). Essentially, Sadock's analysis says that in a passive sentence, the agent role is represented by a syntactically defective element, <<AGT>>, which receives only a conceptual representation and no syntactic realization. Assuming a standard hierarchy of semantic roles, the next highest ranked argument, the theme (or patient, in Sadock's terminology), must be mapped onto the subject position in syntax.[6]

---

[6] Figure 2.2 simplifies Sadock's analysis by omitting the combinatoric semantic level of F/A (function-argument structure). The F/A level maps straightforwardly to the syntax for both active and passive sentences, capturing the semantic differences between active and passive sentences with respect to predication and quantifier scope.

Syntax

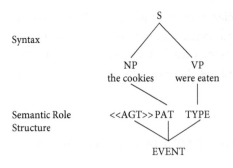

Semantic Role
Structure

<<AGT>> PAT   TYPE

Fig. 2.2 A basic Automodular analysis of an
English passive sentence
Source: Adapted from Sadock (2012: 80).

As alluded to in the discussion of Minimalism above, level-mapping theories assume a
lesser degree of isomorphism between phrase structure and semantic argument structure than is assumed in Minimalism, resulting in a greater tolerance for 'mismatch'
between syntax and semantics (Francis and Michaelis 2003). This, in turn, results in
the more common occurrence of semantic and pragmatic explanations for observed
contrasts in acceptability. For example, according to the analysis of passive sentences
sketched here, the sentences in (2a) and (2b) (*The cookies were eaten/?The cookies have
eaten*) share the same syntactic constituent structure, but differ in the semantic role
associated with the NP *the cookies*. The semantic anomaly in (2b) thus arises from the
difficulty of construing cookies as willful agents (as it also does in the derivational approach), but crucially, it is not taken as evidence for the absence of the relevant abstract
structure (object-to-subject movement) for licensing a theme argument.

As an additional example, let us turn again to Embick's (2004) examples in (4a–b),
repeated as (7a–b). Within a level-mapping approach such as Automodular Grammar
(Sadock 2012), the sentences in (7a–b) would be assumed to share the same simple
phrase structure, and the difference in acceptability would not be taken to reflect any
abstract structural differences. Rather, the observed difference in acceptability would
be understood in terms of the compatibility (or lack thereof) between the lexical semantic features of the predicate (*opened* vs. *open*) and those of the adverb *carefully*. In
short, without the assumption of strict form–meaning isomorphism, evidence of a semantic anomaly need not be taken as evidence of an underlying structural difference.

(7)   a. The package remained carefully opened.
      b. *The package remained carefully open.   (Embick 2004: 363)

Does this mean that, within a level-mapping approach, differences in acceptability are
never caused by a purely syntactic difference? Not at all. To take a simple example,
consider the passive sentences in (8a–d):

(8)   a. Whether to go was debated.
      b. It was debated whether to go.
      c. The cookie was eaten.
      d. *It was eaten the cookie.

In (8a), the passive verb *debated* takes a clausal subject *whether to go* as its argument. In (8b), the meaning is the same as (8a), but the clausal argument is extraposed (i.e. occurs in the sentence-final position) and is replaced with expletive *it* (a semantically empty pronoun) in the subject position. Why, then, does a similar alternation not work in (8c–d)? An explanation consistent with Sadock's analysis is quite simple. A passive participle such as *debated* is intransitive, and so cannot select an NP complement (2012: 83). As a result, even though there is no semantic anomaly in (8d), the sentence becomes less acceptable due to a syntactic subcategorization error.[7] Notably, such an explanation is substantially similar to the proposal common to many derivational analyses which says that passive participles cannot assign abstract accusative case to an NP complement (Radford 2009: 257). That is, both the level-mapping approach and the derivational approach provide a purely syntactic explanation for the lower acceptability of (8d) as compared with (8b) and (8c).

In sum, within level-mapping approaches, contrasts in acceptability are given a non-syntactic explanation in cases where a constraint is said to apply in semantics, discourse information structure, or some other level. Because less information overall is represented in phrase structure, and because phrase structure can be mapped onto other levels in a relatively flexible manner (i.e. without any requirement for strict isomorphism), non-syntactic explanations for apparently syntactic phenomena are more common for level-mapping analyses as compared with Minimalist analyses. However, because there remains a well-defined level of syntactic structure, it is still possible to distinguish formal syntactic explanations for contrasts in acceptability from other types of explanations. As we will see, this distinction between syntactic and semantic explanations is still present but somewhat less clear for sign-based theories.

2.2.2 Form–meaning correspondences in sign-based grammars

While early transformational analyses (Chomsky 1965; Ross 1967) posited numerous construction-specific rules to account for apparently idiosyncratic grammatical patterns, more recent work in Minimalism has aimed to reduce idiosyncrasy in grammatical representations while increasing the coverage of linguistic generalizations. Specific transformations such as Passive and Raising have been replaced by highly general operations such as Merge and Move. In contrast, sign-based grammars continue to include idiosyncratic properties of language-specific constructions in their grammatical descriptions, together with broader generalizations. They do so by eschewing traditional syntactic rules and conceiving of grammar instead as a set of partially specified phrasal constructions which are learned (just as words are learned) and stored in the mental lexicon together with words and morphemes. Normally, constructions are specified for syntactic, semantic, and pragmatic information, and may include specific

---

[7] A subcategorization error does not occur in in (8b) because, according to Sadock (2012: 84), any verb that selects a semantic proposition as its argument can by default realize this argument as a clausal complement. In the absence of any additional arguments, expletive *it* occurs in the canonical subject position.

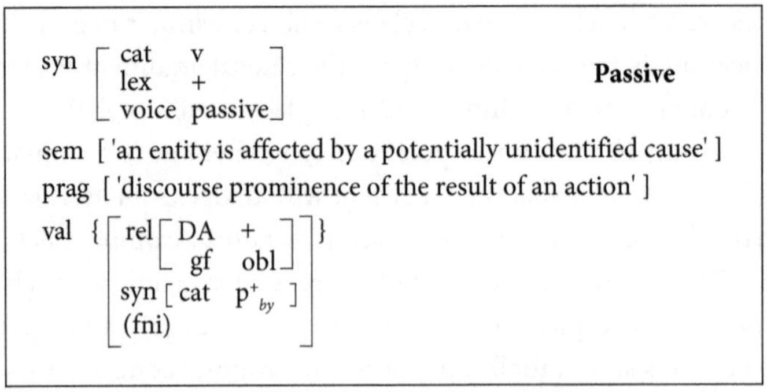

$$
\begin{array}{ll}
\text{syn} & \begin{bmatrix} \text{cat} & \text{v} \\ \text{lex} & + \\ \text{voice} & \text{passive} \end{bmatrix} \qquad\qquad \textbf{Passive}
\end{array}
$$

sem ['an entity is affected by a potentially unidentified cause']

prag ['discourse prominence of the result of an action']

$$
\text{val} \ \left\{ \begin{bmatrix} \text{rel} \begin{bmatrix} \text{DA} & + \\ \text{gf} & \text{obl} \end{bmatrix} \\ \text{syn} \ [\ \text{cat} \quad p^+_{by} \ ] \\ \text{(fni)} \end{bmatrix} \right\}
$$

Fig. 2.3 A basic Construction Grammar analysis of the English passive

Source: Reproduced from Fried and Östman (2004: 49) by permission of John Benjamins.

lexical content as well. As in level-mapping theories, syntactic category, valence, and constituency information is specified, but many of the more abstract features (syntactic movement, null pronouns, null functional projections) as used in Minimalism are absent. A basic analysis of the passive linking construction in English is shown in Figure 2.3 from Fried and Östman (2004: 49).[8] In this example, syntactic information is divided into SYN, which specifies the syntactic category of the passive verb form, and VAL, which indicates the syntactic category of the arguments that may unify with the verb, in this case an optional *by*-phrase. SEM and PRAG specify the semantic and pragmatic functions of the construction, here given in prose rather than formal notation. Essentially, this analysis is similar to that of the level-mapping approach. The theme role is directly mapped to the syntactic subject function, without any underlying movement. Therefore, an explanation of the semantic anomaly in (1b) (*The cookies have eaten*) would make no reference to the presence or absence of object-to-subject movement and would instead refer to the distinct mappings of semantic roles to syntactic functions in the transitive construction as opposed to the passive construction.

Constructions may be highly general (e.g. the transitive construction, which specifies the basic structure and schematic meaning of a transitive clause), or highly specific (e.g. the *let alone* construction, which specifies idiosyncratic syntactic and semantic properties associated with the conjunction *let alone*). Because constructions are arranged within a taxonomic hierarchy, more specific constructions are said to 'inherit' syntactic, semantic, and/or pragmatic properties from more general constructions, allowing for cross-constructional generalizations. For example, an idiom such as *kick the*

---

[8] Fried and Östman's (2004) analysis of the passive linking construction was based on a similar analysis in Fillmore and Kay's (1993) Construction Grammar textbook. As Laura Michaelis (p.c.) points out, this analysis views the passive as a bare-bones construction which is underspecified and essentially a more schematic version of the information in the lexical entry of a passive verb. This particular example was chosen to be consistent with the examples of English passive in the earlier sections on derivational and level-mapping theories.

bucket (meaning 'die') inherits most of its syntactic properties from the transitive construction, while being semantically specified as having a special non-compositional meaning. As Michaelis (2009: 6) puts it: "we do not sacrifice linguistic generalizations by stipulating idiosyncratic properties of constructions, because detailed constructions are instances of more abstract constructions." This idea of a structured hierarchy of constructions is shared with many level-mapping approaches as well (Culicover and Jackendoff 2005; Van Valin 2005; Yuasa 2005), and in fact these two types of theories differ relatively little from each other. In sign-based theories, however, the modularity of individual levels is reduced. All grammatical information is stated in terms of what is called the interface in level-mapping theories—i.e. the lexical entries of words and constructions. Thus, while linguistic information is still segregated into different types (e.g. phrase structure, phonology, grammatical functions, semantic roles), it is represented in the form of signs—multiple information types bundled together within a feature matrix—and grammatical constraints are stated as constraints on the unification of lexical signs and constructions.

When grammatical constraints are understood as constraints on the unification of signs, it can become more difficult to distinguish between what we have been calling formal syntactic as against non-syntactic explanations of contrasts in acceptability. However, I maintain that we can still make this distinction. For example, the syntactic anomaly in (8d) (*It was eaten the cookie*) can be understood in a similar manner to the level-mapping approach. Because the VAL (valence) specification of the passive construction does not allow for an NP complement, the argument of a passive clause cannot be realized as an extraposed NP. This qualifies as a purely syntactic explanation, in that there is no need to refer to any semantic information about the verb or its arguments.

To take a more challenging example, Goldberg (2006: 53–4) discusses the highly specific $GoVP_{bare}$ construction, in which the verb *go* or *come* is followed by a bare VP. The construction expresses a meaning of 'move to express an action' (2006: 54), as in (8a).

(9)   a. She should come sit with me.
      b. *She came/comes sit with me.
      c. She should help write the proposal.
      d. She helped/helps write the proposal.

Goldberg observes that a sentence such as (9b), in which the first verb is tensed, is unacceptable, and she attributes this to a syntactic requirement of the construction. Namely, the first verb position of the construction can only unify with a bare form of the verb *come* or *go*. Because the construction comes with a particular meaning, and the syntactic restriction on verb form is construction-specific, it is still possible to have a similar sequence (tensed verb + bare VP) in other constructions that express a different meaning. Although Goldberg does not discuss such examples, the acceptability of (9c–d) suggests that the syntactic restriction applying in (9b) is construction-specific.

When dealing with restrictions on the combination of signs, our previous distinction between formal syntactic and semantic explanations becomes less clear. Although a restriction on verb form is apparently a syntactic restriction, it cannot be understood without reference to the construction as a whole, including its meaning. I would argue, however, that a restriction such as the one applying in (9b) is in fact a formal syntactic restriction in that the failure of unification is due to a syntactic feature of the verb and not due to any semantic anomaly. This becomes clear when we observe that auxiliary *do*, which carries the tense (and sometimes a contrastive focus) but (unlike modal auxiliaries such as *should*) contributes no lexical meaning of its own, can occur with this construction. In (10a), two synonymous answers are given to the question asked, only one of which violates the syntactic restriction. In (10b), a paraphrase of the same question using a different construction (with the conjunction *and* added) shows no such restriction.

(10)   a. Did she come sit with you? Yes, she did come sit with me. /
           *Yes, she came sit with me.
       b. Did she come and sit with you? Yes, she did come and sit with me. /
           Yes, she came and sat with me.

These examples suggest that the unacceptability of (9b) is not due to any semantic anomaly, but rather the result of a syntactic restriction. Conversely, we can identify semantic restrictions on this construction that make no reference to syntactic features.

(11)   a. She should come help me.
       b. *She should come resemble me.
       c. She has come to resemble me.

Example (11b) is unacceptable because the stative VP *resemble me* is not easy to construe with a meaning of 'move to express an action', while the VP *help me* in (11a) can readily be construed with this meaning. The VP *resemble me* can, however, be used in a different construction with the verb *come*, as in (11c), to express a different meaning that does not involve motion. Because there is no necessary structural correlate to the semantic anomaly in (11b), we can provide a purely semantic explanation for the contrast between (11a) and (11b) based on the semantic requirements of the construction. In this way, we can maintain a distinction between syntactic and semantic explanations for acceptability contrasts, even though the domain of explanation is in this case restricted to a single construction.

Just like level-mapping theories, sign-based theories have no requirement for strict isomorphism between syntax and semantics. Although syntactically and semantically related constructions are linked to each other within a structured hierarchical network, the relationship between meaning and syntactic form is many to many. This implies that synonymous or nearly synonymous constructions may have different syntactic properties, as we see in the difference between (10a) and (10b). Similarly, syntactically similar constructions may have different semantic and pragmatic properties. Because of this many-to-many relationship between meaning and syntactic form, evidence for a semantic or pragmatic restriction on the use of a construction is not taken as evidence of a formal syntactic constraint applying at an abstract level of structure. In this way, both level-mapping theories and sign-based theories are amenable to purely semantic or pragmatic explanations of acceptability contrasts to a greater extent than Minimalist approaches are.

2.2.3 Processing-based explanations in constraint-based grammars

We have seen that level-mapping theories and sign-based theories are similar but not identical with respect to their treatments of the syntax–semantics–pragmatics interfaces. With respect to processing-based explanations of acceptability contrasts, level-mapping theories do not differ in any systematic way from sign-based theories, although individual authors may have somewhat different approaches to this issue. Therefore, in discussing processing-based explanations of traditionally syntactic phenomena, I will not attempt to distinguish between these two types of theories and will refer to them jointly as constraint-based theories.

Similar to the situation within derivational approaches, linguists working in constraint-based theories have typically focused on grammatical description and theoretical explanation, without emphasizing processing-based explanations. Furthermore, supporters of constraint-based theories have traditionally relied on informally collected acceptability judgments as the primary data source, obviating any compelling need to explore extra-grammatical factors that might affect speakers' judgments. However, some proponents of constraint-based theories have made this issue a major focus of their research, and have advocated for processing-based approaches to phenomena traditionally considered to be syntactic. In particular, one group of researchers, led by Ivan Sag from Stanford, conducted a series of experimental studies supporting a processing-based approach to certain types of island constraints (Hofmeister et al. 2013; Hofmeister and Sag 2010). These studies are to a large extent theory-independent in that their arguments do not hinge on any particular design features of constraint-based grammars. On the contrary, constraint-based grammars have the necessary formal tools to represent island constraints in terms of syntactic (or semantic) restrictions, and have in fact done so, at least for certain types of island constraints (e.g. Culicover and Jackendoff 2005; Pollard and Sag 1994). However, it is not coincidental that Sag was a leading architect of two closely related sign-based theories—Head-Driven Phrase Structure Grammar (Pollard and Sag 1994) and Sign-Based Construction Grammar (Sag 2012)—and at the same time an advocate for processing-based explanations of certain island constraints. Like all constraint-based theories, these theories reduce the scope of syntactic explanation, making more room for semantic and pragmatic explanations of traditionally syntactic phenomena. In the same spirit, processing-based explanations can also reduce the size and scope of syntax, in this case by removing certain patterns of judgments from the realm of grammatical explanation altogether.

Hofmeister and Sag (2010) begin with the observation that judgments of island-violating sentences vary widely in acceptability, and that this variation is difficult to understand in terms of grammatical constraints alone. Following similar proposals by Deane (1991) and Kluender and Kutas (1993), among others, they set forth a research program for systematically relating variation in acceptability judgments with ease or difficulty of processing. They do so by performing experiments which measure both acceptability (e.g. on a rating scale) and processing ease (e.g. word-by-word reading time) of the same stimulus sentences, and which manipulate "non-structural" aspects of the sentences. By nonstructural, they do not mean that the manipulations change no aspects of the sentence structure, but rather that these manipulations (at least arguably) do not affect the crucial syntactic properties that are assumed to determine whether a sentence violates an island constraint or not. They reason that if acceptability can be shown to depend on factors that are independently shown to alter processing difficulty, then one can reasonably conclude that island constraints do not need to be specified in the grammar. Instead, they suggest, the unacceptability of many island-violating sentences in English may result from an accumulation of factors, some of which can be ameliorated by altering the context and/or the lexical content, which conspire to increase processing difficulty. For example, it was hypothesized that bare filler phrases (e.g. *who*) are more difficult to hold in memory and more susceptible to interference from intervening NPs than complex filler phrases (e.g. *which employee*). Thus complex fillers should facilitate processing at the retrieval site (the main verb) as compared to bare filler phrases (e.g. *who*). One of their experiments tested this hypothesis using *wh*-islands, as in (12a–b) (Hofmeister and Sag 2010: 394).

(12) a. Who did Albert learn whether they dismissed ___ after the
         annual performance review? (bare filler)
      b. Which employee did Albert learn whether they dismissed ___
         after the annual performance review? (complex filler)
      c. Who did Albert learn that they dismissed ___ after the annual
         performance review? (baseline, non-island)

Results for reading time and acceptability were correlated, in that the complex filler sentences as in (12b) received both higher acceptability ratings and shorter reading times at the main verb than the bare filler sentences as in (12a). In addition, non-island sentences as in (12c) did not differ from island-violating sentences as in (12b) in terms of reading time. Hofmeister and Sag (2010) argue that a processing-based explanation for the variation they found in both reading time and acceptability is more plausible than a grammar-based explanation, given that the same factor (i.e. filler complexity) affected both acceptability ratings and reading times in a similar manner.

The conclusions of Hofmeister and Sag (2010) have been challenged by linguists who assume a derivational approach to grammar. As I discussed in Section 2.1.2, these linguists accept the possibility of processing-based explanations for contrasts in acceptability, but generally tend to favor formal syntactic explanations for island effects

(Dillon and Hornstein 2013; Phillips 2013b). Indeed, linguists are divided largely along theoretical lines in the debate over where island effects come from, as is evident from the contributions in Sprouse and Hornstein's (2013) volume *Experimental Syntax and Island Effects*. However, it is important to note that there is nothing about the architecture of constraint-based theories that necessitates a processing-based approach to island constraints. Nor is there anything about the architecture of derivational theories that necessitates a formal syntactic approach to island constraints. For either type of theory, a processing-based approach would simplify the syntactic analysis of filler–gap dependencies such that (certain) island effects would not need to be associated with any grammatical constraint. I have suggested here that because constraint-based theories already assume a simpler syntactic component (putting more of the explanatory burden on the semantic and pragmatic components), it seems natural for users of such theories to be looking for non-syntactic explanations even outside the grammar itself. Perhaps for this reason, linguists working in constraint-based theories, to the extent they have weighed in on this debate at all, have often been more sympathetic to the types of arguments put forth by Hofmeister, Sag, and colleagues than their counterparts working in Minimalism have been. This ongoing debate over the relative contributions of grammar and processing to island effects will be explored in more detail in Chapter 4.

2.3 OT

I am using the term OT to refer to a family of theories unified by the idea of competition within the grammar among possible candidate forms. Although most widely used as an approach to phonology (McCarthy and Prince 1995; Prince and Smolensky 2004), OT has been applied to morphology (Wunderlich 2001) and syntax (Grimshaw 1997; Legendre, Grimshaw, and Vikner 2001) as well. I will focus here exclusively on its application to syntax.

The generative component of an OT grammar, called GEN, takes as its input an abstract representation of the meaning and lexical content of an expression (a representation which is assumed not to vary among languages) and generates a set of candidate forms for the syntactic realization of this content. The syntactic representations of the GEN component are borrowed from other major theories of syntax, most commonly Government and Binding (Grimshaw 1997), Minimalism (Legendre, Smolensky, and Wilson 1998), and Lexical-Functional Grammar (Bresnan 2000; Kuhn 2000). Once the candidate forms have been generated, the candidates are evaluated (through a process called EVAL) according to a set of ranked or weighted constraints, and the most 'optimal' candidate is chosen as the output form. Importantly for our purposes, the 'winner' of such a competition can still violate certain constraints, as long as those constraints are lower-ranked than the constraints violated by the other candidate forms. Thus, a sentence can be grammatical (and fully acceptable) while still violating some constraints.

To take a basic example, Kuhn (2003: 35) discusses the generalization that finite clauses in English require an expletive subject with verbs like *seem*, while finite clauses in Italian have no such requirement, as shown in (13).

(13)   a. It seems that John has left.
          b. *Seems that John has left.
          c. Sembre che Gianni è andato.
             seems that Gianni is gone
             'It seems that Gianni has gone.'

Following the analysis of Grimshaw and Samek-Lodovici (1998), Kuhn (2003) captures this generalization in terms of the interaction of two constraints called Subject and DEP-IO (Dependence Constraint on Input–Output Correspondence). The Subject constraint states that the clausal subject position must be overtly filled, while the DEP-IO constraint states that elements in the output should correspond to elements in the input. The input representation is assumed to be the same for both English and Italian, while the ranking of the two constraints differs: the Subject constraint is ranked higher in English, while the DEP-IO constraint is ranked higher in Italian. Kuhn (2003: 36) represents this constraint interaction graphically in the form of an OT tableau (Figure 2.4), in which the constraint ranking is indicated across the top, and the candidate forms are shown in the first column. The winning candidate is indicated by a pointing finger.

In English, for which the winning candidate is the expletive subject form, the Subject constraint is satisfied by the presence of the pronoun *it*, but the DEP-IO constraint is violated due to the (presumed) absence of any semantic content corresponding to *it* in the input. Conversely, in Italian, for which the winning candidate has no overt subject, the DEP-IO constraint is satisfied, while the Subject constraint is violated. Although this example only uses two constraints, it illustrates the basic logic of OT, which has been used to capture various cross-linguistic differences in syntax (Aissen 2003). The most important observation for our purposes is that any well-formed sentence will usually violate one or more lower-ranked constraints while satisfying the highest-ranked constraint.

Input: ⟨ seem(x), x = ⟨ leave (y), y = John ⟩⟩	SUBJECT	DEP-IO (FULL-INT)
a. seems [that …]	*!	
b. ☞ it seems [that …]		*

Input: ⟨ sembra(x), x = ⟨ andare (y), y = Gianni ⟩⟩	DEP-IO (FULL-INT)	SUBJECT
a. ☞ sembra [che …]		*
b. *expl* sembra [che …]	*!	

Fig. 2.4 OT constraint interaction in English (top) and Italian (bottom)

Source: Reproduced from Kuhn (2003: 36) by permission of CSLI Publications.

2.3.1 Form–meaning correspondences in OT

In OT approaches to syntax, the semantic argument structure (including functional features such as tense and aspect) and lexical content of a sentence form an abstract input representation, while GEN creates the candidate forms for realizing this content via particular syntactic structures (Legendre 2001). Faithfulness constraints ensure that the syntactic structure of a sentence is transparently related to its semantic and lexical content, while structural (or markedness) constraints allow for various types of form–function mismatch. The relative ranking of constraints varies for different languages, and the constraints that are active in a competition may differ for different sentence types within the same language. In this way, cross-linguistic and within-language variation are modeled without reference to the Principles and Parameters notion of parameter settings (i.e. universal constraints that are switched on or off for a particular language). Faithfulness to the input will always be represented in the syntactic structure of some candidate forms. However, the syntactic structure of the winning ('optimal') candidate may deviate from the input, violating one or more of the faithfulness constraints. For the example discussed in (12a–c), the DEP-IO constraint is a kind of faithfulness constraint, since it helps ensure that only the meaningful elements in the input are realized overtly in the output. In English, where this constraint is systematically violated in sentences like (12a), the optimal candidate includes an expletive pronoun *it* with no meaningful lexical content. Importantly, those (losing) candidate forms which are more faithful to the input (e.g. *Seems that John has left*), do not affect the syntactic representation of the optimal candidate form. Rather, the degree of isomorphism between form and meaning depends on which theoretical framework is adopted to generate the candidate forms. Kuhn (2003) uses a GEN component based on Lexical-Functional Grammar, which assumes a direct mapping between the input representation (f-structure) and the phrase structure (c-structure) of each candidate form, generally allowing for phrase structure representations which bear a non-isomorphic relationship to the input.[9]

Regardless of which type of syntactic representation is assumed, the acceptability of a sentence such as (13a) can be interpreted in one of two ways within a standard OT analysis: (1) as the result of a constraint interaction that favors this form over other candidates; (2) as the result of some non-syntactic factors that make an ungrammatical sentence seem relatively acceptable. Conversely, the unacceptability of a sentence such as (13b) can be interpreted either as the result of violating a high-ranked constraint or as the result of some non-syntactic factors that make a syntactically well-formed sentence seem less acceptable. In this respect, the problem of interpreting acceptability judgments within OT is fundamentally similar to that of derivational and constraint-based theories. However, when we consider other variations on OT which adopt a

---

[9] The choice of theoretical framework in fact makes little difference in this case, since derivational theories require no covert structural elements to represent an expletive subject. However, it could affect how certain semantic anomalies (e.g. *The cookies have eaten*) are treated with respect to the syntax, as discussed in the previous sections on derivational and constraint-based theories.

stochastic (probabilistic) architecture, a very important difference emerges: the possibility of gradient grammaticality. The following section elaborates on this idea and its importance for interpreting gradient acceptability judgments.

2.3.2 Stochastic OT, gradient grammar, and processing-based explanations

We have seen that the relationships between meaning and syntactic form vary among different implementations of OT syntax. For this reason, it is impossible to make any broad generalizations about the form–meaning interface in OT and its implications for the interpretation of acceptability judgments. Rather, OT approaches to syntax are similar to constraint-based approaches when they adopt a version of Lexical-Functional Grammar to generate the candidate forms, but similar to derivational approaches when they adopt a Government and Binding or a Minimalist grammar to generate the candidate forms. Within either type of approach, if a sentence is judged as unacceptable or marginally acceptable, this can be attributed either to the violation of a high-ranked syntactic constraint or to the influence of some non-syntactic factor. More generally, I have been assuming throughout the chapter that syntactic constraints (regardless of how they are specified within a particular theoretical framework) apply in a categorical fashion, but interact with various non-syntactic factors, resulting in gradient acceptability judgments. Such an assumption does not hold true, however, for versions of OT that adopt a *stochastic* approach to grammatical constraints. In such an approach, syntactic constraints apply in a probabilistic fashion, such that violating even a high-ranked constraint may result in a well-formed sentence a certain proportion of the time. Such constraints are often referred to as 'soft constraints' since they may be violated during language use without resulting in ungrammaticality and without being considered performance errors.

One example of a purported soft constraint is the tendency in English for transitive VPs that include prepositions to show V–NP–PP order, as opposed to V–PP–NP order. Wasow (2009) observes that although both orders are possible and apparently synonymous with each other, the V–NP–PP order as in (14a) is much more frequent in usage and typically judged as more acceptable.

(14)   a. Olson brings a great deal of experience to the table.
        b. Olson brings to the table a great deal of experience.

A traditional, non-stochastic theory must say either that both options are grammatical, with differences in usage or acceptability being due to non-syntactic factors, or that the V–PP–NP order is actually ungrammatical, despite its regular occurrence in language use. The first of these possibilities appears quite plausible. As Hawkins (2004: 26) observes, the preference for V–NP–PP order relates to the well-attested processing-based preference for ordering shorter phrases before longer phrases. Such an ordering benefits production, since shorter phrases are generally more accessible than longer phrases (Arnold et al. 2000), and comprehension, since such an ordering creates shorter dependencies between the head words of phrases (Hawkins 2004: 103). Since direct object NPs are typically shorter than PPs, it makes sense that V–NP–PP order would be generally preferred, while V–PP–NP order should be favored in cases where the NP is longer than the PP. However, Wasow (2009) points out that the preference for V–NP–PP order is stronger than would be predicted by constituent length alone. A performance account based purely on constituent length predicts that there should be no clear preference for one order over the other when the NP and the PP are of equal lengths. However, Wasow's (2009) sample of about 10,000 items from the Brown corpus shows that speakers rarely produced V–PP–NP order when the two phrases were of equal length, and only started to prefer this order over the canonical V–NP–PP order when the PP was at least five words longer than the NP. Wasow argues that although the relative length of the two constituents clearly affects speakers' choice of which order to use, this factor cannot fully explain speakers' avoidance of V–PP–NP order. He concludes that there is plausibly a 'soft constraint' in the grammar which specifies the V–PP–NP order as less preferred.

What does it mean for a grammar of a language to include soft constraints? Manning (2003: 327–9) describes one particular implementation within OT known as Stochastic OT (Boersma and Hayes 2001; Bresnan and Aissen 2002). This approach is similar to standard OT as described above, except that each constraint is specified with a particular numeric value to indicate its strength, rather than simply being ranked relative to the other constraints. In addition, each output undergoes a stochastic evaluation, which randomly perturbs the values of the constraints, resulting in a unique constraint ranking for every evaluation. In this way, constraints can be re-ranked so that the same input results in different outputs on different occasions. This is in contrast to standard OT, according to which there can be only one winning output for any given input for a particular language or dialect. Thus, standard OT and Stochastic OT model optionality (i.e. competition among alternate syntactic forms that express the same meaning) in different ways. In standard OT, each possible sentence type must have a unique input, meaning that syntactic variants do not compete with each other directly within the grammar. Any competition among related grammatical sentence types occurs instead during language use. In contrast, Stochastic OT models competition among related sentence types directly in the grammar, making it less likely that gradient judgments or gradient frequency distributions will be given a purely performance-based explanation. It should be noted here that other variants of OT, including Linear OT (Keller 2006; Sorace and Keller 2005) and the Decathlon Model (Featherston 2008; 2019) also incorporate soft constraints directly into the grammar, although they implement them somewhat differently.[10]

---

[10] Linear OT (Keller 2006; Sorace and Keller 2005) and the Decathlon Model (Featherston 2008; 2019) take judgment data to be the primary data source for revealing soft constraints in grammar, while Stochastic OT analyses typically derive soft constraints from frequency of use. There are, in addition, technical differences with regard to constraint weightings, constraint interaction, and cumulativity of constraints which distinguish these two approaches from each other and from Stochastic OT.

For the purposes of a basic illustration, consider the previous example from Wasow (2009). Using a Stochastic OT approach based on Heidinger's (2015) analysis of Spanish postverbal constituent order, we can suppose that there are two constraints that are most relevant for determining the choice between V–NP–PP and V–PP–NP word order in English: DO-Adjacent and Heavy-Last. The first constraint, DO-Adjacent, penalizes structures in which the verb is separated from its direct object, while the second constraint, Heavy-Last, penalizes structures in which longer constituents precede shorter ones. To accommodate Wasow's observations of corpus frequency, we can assume that the strength value of DO-Adjacent exceeds that of Heavy-Last, meaning that normally, the canonical V–NP–PP order is preferred both when the two constraints are in alignment (i.e. when the PP is longer than the NP in the input) and when the two constraints are opposed (i.e. when the NP is longer than the PP in the input). However, the stochastic evaluation can reverse the usual ranking, resulting in legitimate outputs (as opposed to speech errors) instantiating V–PP–NP order in cases such as (14b).

You may have noticed something odd about our proposed constraint of Heavy-Last: grammatical rules traditionally do not refer to processing-related factors like constituent length! This is in fact an important feature which distinguishes Stochastic OT from other generative theories, including both derivational and constraint-based theories. Advocating for a Stochastic OT approach, Bresnan and Aissen (2002: 83) argue that grammatical constraints do not need to be stated in terms of purely structural representations. Rather, constraints that are grounded in language processing or discourse function can still be considered grammatical constraints, provided that the strength value is conventional to a particular language or dialect. For example, they point out that one of the discourse functions of the passive across many languages is to help maintain topic continuity across grammatical subjects in the discourse. However, they note that this pressure to avoid noncontinuous subjects varies in its strength across languages in a manner not predictable from principles of discourse information structure alone, resulting in different frequency distributions in different languages. For example, corpus analyses of the tendency to passivize in continuous vs. noncontinuous contexts suggest that this discourse pressure is roughly twice as strong in Bella Coola as in English. While not traditionally thought of as being within the domain of syntax, such a tendency can be represented in Stochastic OT as a grammatical constraint (e.g. Avoid Noncontinuous Subjects) with a language-specific strength value (Bresnan and Aissen 2002: 83).

Going back our previous example, Wasow's (2009) corpus data suggest that the strength values of Heavy-Last and DO-Adjacent are conventional to English. Thus, Heavy-Last, although grounded in processing, can be considered a grammatical constraint within a Stochastic OT analysis. One problem for such an analysis is that it becomes very difficult to distinguish grammatical constraints from the direct effects of performance factors during language use. For example, Wasow (2009) found that rate of V–PP–NP order increased *gradually* as the length of the NP increased. A gradual effect of NP length is predicted on a purely production-based account that recognizes the difficulty of planning and producing increasingly longer phrases early in a sentence

(Arnold et al. 2000). Under such an account, there is no need to specify phrase length as a continuous variable in the statement of a constraint such as Heavy-Last. However, this solution leaves us with the problem from which we started: the language-specific preference for adjacent order (V–NP–PP) over shifted order (V–PP–NP). One solution might be to assume that performance factors (e.g. relative weight/accessibility of NP and PP) are directly involved in determining speakers' choice of structure during language planning, in addition to interacting with soft constraints such as DO-Adjacent and Heavy-Last. As Clark (2005: 215) suggests, such an interaction could be implemented in Stochastic OT by allowing performance factors to systematically (rather than randomly) perturb the value of the relevant constraints during the stochastic evaluation. Thus, Clark (2005) conceptualizes the competence–performance distinction as a distinction between the grammatical constraints, which are specified for a certain strength value, and the stochastic evaluation, a dynamic process that interacts with performance factors to perturb the strength values and determine the final output during production planning. While such a mechanism has not been worked out in any detail, it remains a possibility within a Stochastic OT approach.

Although it is possible to distinguish between soft constraints and performance factors in the way that Clark (2005) describes, this distinction tends not to be a feature of Stochastic OT analyses. Rather, analyses start with frequency distributions or gradient acceptability judgments and use these as the basis for determining the relevant grammatical constraints and their strength values. For example, Heidinger (2015) uses the frequency distributions from an elicited production task and a forced-choice preference task to determine the relative strengths of different factors that affect postverbal constituent order in Spanish. These factors include the tendency to place shorter constituents before longer ones, the tendency to place discourse focus on the final constituent, and the tendency for verbs to occur adjacent to their direct objects and other phrasal dependents. These factors are characterized as soft constraints (similar to our Heavy-Last and DO-Adjacent) that overlap with each other in their ranges of application, allowing for variation in word order, but which have different strength values that determine speakers' preferences given an input specification with particular characteristics. Heidinger (2015) does not consider whether some aspects of the results from the experiments might be better understood using performance mechanisms instead of, or in addition to, grammatical constraints. In this way, practitioners of Stochastic OT can deal with gradient data while still proposing grammar-based explanations. This is achieved by allowing for probabilistic constraints and by incorporating semantic, discourse, or processing-related elements (e.g. animacy, discourse focus, constituent length) in the statements of these constraints. In this way, Stochastic OT expands the scope of grammar-based explanations in comparison with standard OT.

In summary, researchers working within Stochastic OT tend to start with gradient data from corpus frequencies, production tasks, or judgment tasks and develop an analysis of constraint interaction based on such data. Rather than ignoring gradient data where it is theoretically inconvenient, or relegating it entirely to the performance system, Stochastic OT embraces gradient data and incorporates it directly into the competence grammar. While, as Clark (2005) suggests, there is room within such an approach to maintain a separation between syntactic and discourse or processing-based explanations for distributional patterns in language, the tendency has been to avoid such explanations in favor of functionally grounded grammatical explanations.

2.4 Gradient grammaticality in derivational theories: a look back

As discussed in the preceding section, OT-style approaches, including Stochastic OT (Bresnan, Dingare, and Manning 2001; Manning 2003), Linear OT (Keller 2006; Sorace and Keller 2005), and the Decathlon Model (Featherston 2008; 2019), have been developed within the last 20 years to model gradience within the grammar itself. However, there were important precedents for this idea of gradient grammaticality dating back to Chomsky's early work (1964, 1965). It is true that linguists who favor derivational theories have typically approached gradient acceptability from the perspective of multiple interacting syntactic and non-syntactic factors (Newmeyer 2003; Schütze 1996). However, the concept of gradient grammaticality has played a significant role in certain syntactic analyses within derivational frameworks, especially with respect to 'strong' and 'weak' island constraints and 'squishy' syntactic categories. In this section, I will briefly review some of these earlier proposals to encode gradience directly within the syntactic component of grammar.

In a discussion of selectional restrictions in Chapter 1, I briefly touched upon Chomsky's (1965: 153) idea that we must, in some cases, recognize "degrees of grammaticalness" to account for different degrees of acceptability. Here, I repeat Chomsky's example (Chomsky 1965: 152), which I also discussed in Chapter 1. I have added '*' and '?' notation to indicate the decreasing degrees of acceptability of (15a–d):

(15) a. *Sincerity may virtue the boy.   (lexical category error)
     b. ??Sincerity may elapse the boy.   (strict subcategorization error)
     c. ?Sincerity may admire the boy.   (selectional restriction error)
     d. Sincerity may frighten the boy.   (fully grammatical sentence)

Chomsky proposed a hierarchy of feature dominance to account for the observed differences in acceptability: "features introduced by strict subcategorization rules dominate features introduced by selection rules, and...all lexical features are dominated by the symbols for lexical categories. Furthermore, deviation from selectional rules involving high-level features is apparently more serious than deviation from selectional rules involving lower-level features" (1965: 153). In his paper "Degrees of Grammaticalness," Chomsky (1964) similarly proposed a hierarchy of categories to account for these same types of examples. He explains: "The degree of grammaticalness is a measure of the remoteness of an utterance from the generated set of perfectly well-formed sentences, and the common representing category sequence will indicate in what respects the utterance in question is deviant" (1964: 387).

For example, sentence (15b) is well-formed at the level of lexical categories, but deviant with respect to the subcategory of the verb *elapse* (an intransitive verb here used in a context that normally requires a transitive verb). Although the paper only offers a brief sketch, Chomsky expressed hope that such a hierarchy, when properly worked out, would "increase the power of the grammar to mark distinctions among utterances" (1964: 387).

Following on from Chomsky's (1964) suggestion, John Robert "Haj" Ross offered several similar proposals for dealing with gradient acceptability (Ross 1973a; 1973b; 1987). I will mention just one representative example here. Ross (1973a) proposed a "Fake NP Squish" to distinguish among different members of the category NP in English. He observed that although almost all NPs can occur in certain highly permissive constructions (e.g. in subject position of a simple declarative or interrogative clause), some constructions are relatively 'choosy' about what types of NPs can occur in them. He further argued that different types of NPs seem to form a cline of acceptability with respect to each of these choosier constructions, and that the constructions themselves form a cline with respect to just how limited they are in the range of possible NP types they accept. Tentatively, he proposed a hierarchy of 12 NP types (going from perfectly ordinary to highly defective) and a cline of 19 constructions (going from highly permissive to highly choosy), and classified each combination of NP type and construction as to its acceptability, according to his own judgments. For example, Ross (1973a: 106) noted the gradient acceptability of different types of NPs with respect to so-called Being Deletion, as shown in (16), and Tough Movement, as shown in (17). Examples are given with Ross's original '*' and '?' notation.

(16)   a. **Hinswood** in the tub is a funny thought.
       b. ?**The existence of Las Vegas** provable is a funny thought.
       c. ??**This tack** taken on filibustering is a funny thought.
       d. *****Close tabs** kept on Kissinger is a funny thought.
       e. *****Little heed** paid to public apathy is a funny thought.

(17)   a. **This tack on racism** is tough to take.
       b. ?**Noticeable headway** is tough to make on problems of this complexity.
       c. *****Close tabs** are really impossible to keep on Kissinger.
       d. *****Sufficient heed** is not easy to pay to a real kvetsch.

In the end, Ross (1973a) was less optimistic than Chomsky about the possibility of a strongly predictive theory of gradient grammar. He noted a number of inconsistencies within the proposed hierarchy of NP types with respect to his own judgments, and conjectured that other people's judgments would be likely to show considerable individual variation. He concludes that the differences shown among different types of NPs should be considered part of the core of grammar, and thus should be high on the research agenda of generative linguists, but that "it would seem premature to attempt to quantify categories until a far wider range of squishes is available for comparison" (1973a: 12).

Although Ross's proposed hierarchy of NP types was similar in spirit to Chomsky's (1964) proposed hierarchy of feature dominance, it is important to note that the source of the observed gradience was different. For Chomsky (1964), different degrees of ill-formedness were said to result from violating different types of syntactic restrictions. For Ross (1973a), different degrees of ill-formedness were said to result from syntactic and semantic variation among members of the category NP. While the first approach to gradience is evident in some subsequent work by Chomsky and other derivational theorists (as I discuss directly below) and has inspired OT-style theories that distinguish between soft and hard constraints (Featherston 2019; Keller 2006), the second approach has inspired cognitive theories that admit gradient categories (prototype and radial categories) (Lakoff 1987; Taylor 2003). Both of these approaches include gradience within the grammar and both have implications for interpreting acceptability judgments. However, following the dominant debates within experimental syntax, I focus on the first approach when dealing with potential examples of gradient grammaticality in the current work.[11]

In his 1986 book *Barriers*, Chomsky again takes up the idea of gradient grammaticality, this time with respect to island constraints. Chomsky (1986a) proposed that different constraints on *wh*-movement incur different degrees of syntactic deviance when they are violated, resulting in gradient acceptability. He discusses the examples in (18) and (19), to which I have added indications of acceptability based on the discussion in the text (1986a: 34–7).

(18)   a. *Which book did John meet a child who read __?

(strong Subjacency violation)

   b. ?Which book did John hear a rumor that you had read _?

(weak Subjacency violation)

(19)   a. ??To whom did you wonder what John gave __?

(weak Subjacency violation)

   b. ?To whom did you wonder what to give __?

(weaker Subjacency violation)

   c. *How did John tell you when to fix the car __?

(strong ECP + weak Subjacency)

   d. ?Which car did John tell you how to fix __?

(weakest Subjacency violation)

The sentence types shown in (18) both involve extraction from within a complex NP, and thus fall under Ross's (1967) Complex NP constraint. However, Chomsky claims that (18a) involves extraction across two barriers (CP and NP), while (18b) only involves extraction across one barrier (CP). As a result, speakers judge (18a) as less

---

[11] For a perspective on category gradience outside the cognitive tradition, Aarts (2007) presents a detailed proposal to account for gradience within categories (Subsective Gradience) and between categories (Intersective Gradience) in formal syntactic terms.

acceptable than (18b). He claims that this distinction is due to the status of a relative clause as a non-subcategorized adjunct in (18a), which causes the NP to 'inherit'
a barrier status from the CP (1986a: 34). In contrast, because the CP complement of
the noun has the status of an argument in (18b), the CP does not pass on barrier status
to the NP, and thus there is only one barrier crossed. To sum up, crossing one barrier
is said to be more acceptable than crossing two barriers, even though both types of
sentences in (18a–b) are assumed to be syntactically deviant.

The sentences in (19) all involve *wh*-island configurations, in which it was assumed
that a *wh*-phrase undergoes a long movement across another *wh*-phrase, incurring a
Subjacency violation due to movement across a clausal boundary. Although these examples all involve only one barrier crossing, the syntactic deviance is said to be weakest
when the embedded question is nonfinite, as in (19d), and strongest when the Subjacency violation is combined with an ECP (Empty Category Principle) violation, as in
(19c). (In this case, an ECP violation is incurred when a non-subcategorized adverbial such as *how* or *when* undergoes long movement across another *wh*-phrase. The
technical details need not concern us here.) The deviance is intermediate in a case like
(19a) in which the embedded question is finite, but the *wh*-phrase is subcategorized
(i.e. acts as an argument of the verb). We can thus identify two orthogonal dimensions
of deviance in (19): (1) ECP effect: barrier crossing by a subcategorized argument (e.g.
who, what) is more acceptable than barrier crossing by a non-subcategorized adjunct
(e.g. *how, when*); (2) finiteness effect: barrier crossing over a nonfinite clausal boundary is more acceptable than barrier crossing over a finite clausal boundary. Because
the ECP violation is perceived to be so strong, a floor effect is observed, and the finiteness distinction is apparently neutralized within ECP-violating sentences so that no
gradations of acceptability can easily be observed.

Chomsky's (1986a) gradient approach to island constraint violations was influential
in subsequent works on the topic, in that ECP-violating-sentences like (19c) and relative clause islands like (18a) came to be known as 'strong islands' while *wh*-islands like
(19b) and (19d) came to be known as 'weak islands' (Szabolcsi 2006). For example,
Rizzi (1990: 88) similarly discussed the distinction between the sentence types in
(19c–d) as involving a difference between a weaker Subjacency violation (19d) and
a stronger ECP violation (19c). His approach to why those two constraints differ in
strength was rather different than Chomsky's, however. Instead of proposing that certain phrase boundaries are barriers to movement, Rizzi (1990) proposed a principle
of Relativized Minimality, which "blocks government of some kind across an element
which could bear a government relation of the same kind" (1990: ix). Thus, the relevant
locality conditions on movement are more akin to the traditional binding conditions
on anaphoric dependencies than they are to the structural barriers that Chomsky
(1986a) proposed. However, the idea of different levels of structural deviance for ECP
vs. Subjacency violations was essentially the same as what Chomsky (1986a) proposed.
Similar distinctions between ECP and Subjacency violations, as well as further distinctions among the so-called weak islands, have been discussed by Cinque (1990), Kiss
(1993), Postal (1998), and Szabolcsi (2006), among others. The general upshot is that

there have been a number of proposals that assume different levels of strength for different syntactic constraints, resulting in gradient grammaticality. However, no general theory of gradient grammaticality has been proposed within this tradition. Furthermore, most of these proposals regarding strong and weak islands have yet to be tested experimentally. One exception is McDaniel and Cowart (1999), who conducted an acceptability judgment task showing that among *wh*-island-violating sentences, ECP-violating sentences with a gap in the subject position of an embedded interrogative clause were judged as significantly less acceptable than similar non-ECP-violating sentences with a gap in object position, in accordance with the predictions of Chomsky (1986a) and others. The authors consider both sentence types to be ungrammatical, but to differ in terms of the strength of the violation.

Besides McDaniel and Cowart (1999), Kluender (1998) also used experimental methods to test certain predictions regarding strong vs. weak islands. Kluender (1998) used a speeded acceptability judgment task and an ERP (event-related potentials) experiment to test for differences among various types of *wh*-islands. While the results showed evidence of gradient acceptability in the expected direction, Kluender accounted for it not in terms of different types of syntactic constraints but rather in terms of the interaction of semantic, pragmatic, and processing factors that apply more generally, as shown through the inclusion of a yes–no question condition in which there were no movement violations but clear semantic and processing effects. Thus, Kluender (1998) does not contribute to any refinement of earlier theoretical proposals regarding strong and weak islands, but rather seeks to eliminate these effects from the syntax proper. As discussed in Section 2.3.2, more recent OT-style analyses involving soft constraints have been proposed to account for gradient acceptability in terms of gradient grammaticality, and these approaches are, in my view, the most clearly in line with Chomsky's (Chomsky 1964; 1986a) thinking on gradient grammaticality. Although the core phenomena of strong and weak islands have not yet been tackled within OT-style frameworks, there has been promising work on a number of other syntactic phenomena, including other types of extraction constraints (e.g. Superiority, *that*-trace effects), in work by Keller (2000), Sorace and Keller (2005), and Featherston (2005a; 2005b; 2011). Unlike earlier proposals by Chomsky (1964; 1986a), Ross (1973a), and Rizzi (1990), these OT-style proposals incorporate an explicit quantitative component into the grammar to model the cumulative effects of soft constraints and the relative strength values of different constraints. As I noted in my discussion of Stochastic OT above, these approaches tend to put any measurable differences in acceptability into the syntax, in contrast to processing-based approaches like Kluender (1998), which attribute the variation in judgments to extra-syntactic factors. I will argue in this book that we need both types of explanations within our toolkit: (1) soft constraints in the grammar; and (2) grammar-external processing constraints.

This section has acknowledged the important contributions of Chomsky, Ross, Rizzi, Cinque, and other derivational theorists to developing the ideas of gradient grammaticality and gradient constraint strength—ideas which have been taken up more formally and systematically in OT-style analyses that include a quantitative component (Featherston 2008; Sorace and Keller 2005). Let us now turn to a very different approach to gradient acceptability that has been developed outside the generative tradition within usage-based functionalist frameworks.

2.5 Usage-based approaches: grammar as a complex adaptive system

The label 'usage-based' applies to a family of theoretical approaches that take language users' repeated experiences producing and understanding spoken, written, and/or signed language as central for understanding the nature of language. These approaches, which have grown out of the functionalist tradition in linguistics, have often focused on the role of usage-based factors in child language development (Bates and MacWhinney 1989; Christiansen and Chater 2016; Elman et al. 1996; Tomasello 2003) and language change (Bybee 2010). In keeping with the goals of the current chapter, however, I will focus here on how such approaches have dealt with the implications of gradient linguistic data for understanding synchronic grammar (keeping in mind that there is no strict division between synchronic and diachronic phenomena within the usage-based approaches).

As Diessel and Hilpert (2016: 1) state: "In the usage-based approach, grammar is a dynamic system consisting of fluid categories and variable constraints that are shaped by frequency of occurrence." Some of the most influential usage-based theories of grammar are Cognitive Grammar (Langacker 1987), Cognitive Construction Grammar (Goldberg 2006; 2019), Fluid Construction Grammar (Steels 2013), and Usage-based Theory (Bybee 2006; 2010; Bybee and McClelland 2005). These theories are similar to the constraint-based theories that we have already discussed in adopting a surface-oriented view of syntax and a construction-based architecture. In fact, Cognitive Construction Grammar (Goldberg 2006), Fluid Construction Grammar (Steels 2013), and Cognitive Grammar (Langacker 1987) may be considered as constraint-based (therefore generative) and usage-based (therefore functionalist) at the same time. However, some constraint-based theories are not usage-based in orientation (e.g. Automodular Grammar), while others are partially usage-based while retaining an autonomous level of syntactic structure (e.g. Simpler Syntax). In this section, I will first introduce the Usage-based Theory of Joan Bybee and colleagues (Bybee 2006; 2010; Bybee and McClelland 2005) because this approach represents a major departure from generative grammar and provides the clearest contrast with the more traditional constraint-based theories. I will then consider how similar generalizations have been framed within Cognitive Construction Grammar.

In her Usage-based Theory, Bybee (2010: 9) adopts a construction-based architecture: synchronic grammar consists of an inventory of symbolic constructions linked together within a structured network. In this respect, Bybee's approach is similar to that of the original Construction Grammar, now known as Berkeley Construction Grammar (Fillmore, Kay, and O'Connor 1988; Kay and Fillmore 1999; Michaelis and

Lambrecht 1996). Her idea of what a construction is differs, however, from that of Berkeley Construction Grammar, in such a way that even my use of the word 'inventory' may be misleading here. While traditionally, constructions, as well as other units of structure including words and morphemes, have been thought of as having a relatively fixed representation, Bybee (2010: 28) adopts an exemplar-based model of linguistic knowledge in which each experienced instance of a word, morpheme, or construction affects how it is represented in the mind of a language user. She gives the example of a corpus study by Boas (2003) that examined the use of the special resultative construction in English exemplified by the expression: *It drives me crazy*. She points out that while the lexeme *drive* is deeply entrenched in the representation of the construction, other parts of the construction show varying degrees of specificity and schematicity. For example, the subject can be instantiated by almost any NP, but the words *it* and *that* are most commonly used. Similarly, the object can be any animate NP, but most commonly is instantiated as a personal pronoun with a human referent. Bybee claims that both general and specific information about the form, meaning, and usage of the construction are encoded in its mental representation, which itself is constantly evolving each time a language user produces or experiences a new instance. Thus, units and categories of language structure are gradient and fluid, despite the convenience of referring to them using a fixed notation.

While some other theories, such as Cognitive Grammar (Langacker 1987), also admit gradient categories, the Usage-based Theory goes beyond most other generative and functionalist theories, including other usage-based theories, in the degree to which grammatical representations are viewed as dynamic. According to this approach, grammar is "the cognitive organization of one's experience with language" (Bybee 2006: 2). More specifically, it can be thought of either as a network of exemplar clusters (Bybee 2006; 2010) or as connection weights within a distributed neural network (Bybee and McClelland 2005; McClelland 2015) that are constantly being updated with new information. In each instance of language use, a pattern-matching process relates new information to previously experienced information, while also incorporating the new information into a revised mental representation. An important consequence of this view is that grammar is no longer generative in the traditional sense. That is, there is no process such as Merge or unification that operates over symbolic units to combine words and phrases together. How, then, can such an approach account for language users' ability to generate novel utterances? Jackendoff (2007: 352) interprets the usage-based approach of Bybee and McClelland (2005) as having no combinatoric mechanism at all. McClelland and Bybee (2007: 441) rebut Jackendoff's characterization of their view. They explain that they are not denying that language has combinatoric mechanisms, but rather they are claiming that generative operations such as unification are unnecessary to account for compositionality. Rather, they argue that the ability to produce novel utterances derives from properties of the nonlinguistic conceptualization of events (2007: 442). For example, they note that tense tends to be a highly productive inflectional category because of the relative independence between the time of an event and its (other) conceptual content. It is not clear from their description what mechanism (if not some form of unification) accounts for conceptual compositionality, nor how concepts are mapped onto linguistic forms. Setting aside these matters, let us consider the implications of the Usage-based Theory for the main issues with which this chapter is concerned: the interpretation of gradient judgment data.

Because the Usage-based Theory incorporates language users' continuous experience into a dynamic model of grammar, researchers have relied primarily on data from corpora of spontaneous discourse, from which they are able to derive information about frequency of use and change of linguistic forms and meanings over time. However, some studies within this framework have examined acceptability judgments in addition to corpus frequencies. For example, examining data from a large corpus of Spanish, Bybee and Eddington (2006) investigated the distribution of verbs of 'becoming' (*quedarse, ponerse, hacerse, volverse*) in combination with different predicative adjectives, finding that the verb–adjective combinations formed clusters of exemplars. For some of the verbs (*quedarse, ponerse*), a single high-frequency exemplar served as the prototype for the exemplar cluster (e.g. *quedarse inmovil* 'become immobile'), from which a number of semantically related adjectives were productively extended (e.g. *quedarse atrapado* 'become trapped'). In addition, each verb was used with some adjectives that were semantically unrelated to the most frequent adjective (e.g. *quedarse sorprendido* 'to be surprised'). To isolate the effects of frequency and semantic similarity, the authors conducted an acceptability judgment task in which participants were asked to rate various sentences taken directly from the corpus. The results showed that high-frequency items were rated higher in acceptability than low-frequency items. Perhaps more surprisingly, low-frequency items that were semantically related to a high-frequency exemplar (e.g. *quedarse atrapado*) were rated significantly higher than other low-frequency items that were not semantically related to any high-frequency exemplar (e.g. *quedarse sorprendido*). Bybee and Eddington take this as evidence that both frequency of particular exemplars and semantic similarity with respect to frequent exemplars contribute to the mental representations of BECOME + ADJ constructions in Spanish, thus supporting an exemplar-based model of grammar.

As this Spanish example illustrates, the inherent variability found in corpus frequencies and acceptability ratings is conceptualized in a different way within the Usage-based Theory as compared with other theories we have considered so far. Such variability is understood not in terms of performance factors interacting with grammatical constraints, as in derivational theories, constraint-based theories, and standard OT. Nor is it understood in terms of functionally grounded grammatical constraints that apply in a probabilistic fashion, as in Stochastic OT. Although the Usage-based Theory shares with Stochastic OT the desire to explain gradient grammatical phenomena as arising from functional motivations, the idea of grammar itself is rather different. Because Stochastic OT assumes fixed representations, it is still possible (if not always easy in practice) to distinguish between syntactic constraints and other factors that affect language use. In contrast, it makes no sense within the Usage-based Theory to distinguish between syntactic and non-syntactic explanations for gradient patterns of judgments. Instead, acceptability judgments are understood to reflect a combination of frequency and similarity. Frequency is the number of times the same expression (e.g. the phrase *quedarse inmovil*) has been previously experienced, while similarity is the extent to which an expression is similar (in some respect) to other expressions that have been frequently experienced. As similarity and frequency decrease, acceptability ratings should decrease as well. There is no distinction drawn between sentences that are unacceptable due to low frequency and lack of similarity to a frequent exemplar, as in Bybee and Eddington's (2006) study, and those that are unacceptable due to violating a grammatical constraint (whether of the 'hard' or 'soft' variety). Rather, the traditional notion of 'ungrammatical' is reduced to a notion of 'unfamiliar': we perceive certain sentences as unacceptable because they are unfamiliar and not (specifically) because the competence grammar fails to license them. There is, in fact, no competence grammar in the traditional sense.

It is notable that, in many usage-based studies of grammar, the criteria for determining frequency and similarity refer to fixed representations. This boils down to the fact that corpus examples are recorded using a fixed notation system (usually orthography, with words separated by spaces) and coded for linguistic features along a variety of dimensions (syntactic category, morphological class, semantic role, phonological form, etc.). This makes it possible that frequency can be calculated based on the number of matching strings, while similarity can be calculated based on matching of linguistic features. If we take seriously the idea of grammar as a complex adaptive system, however, there are, in reality, no fixed linguistic units or features, but only "continuous-valued parameters" (McClelland 2015: 53). As Bybee and McClelland (2005: 298) state in a discussion of category change: "there is no analysis into units at any level or set of levels that will ever successfully and completely capture the realities of synchronic structure or provide a framework in which to capture language change." While recognizing that traditional linguistic categories and features are helpful tools for conducting usage-based linguistic analyses, Bybee and McClelland (2005) reject the traditional notion of a competence grammar in favor of a much more fluid system. Ideally, they prefer models of linguistic knowledge such as distributed neural networks which can generalize over input from unannotated text corpora or even continuous auditory or articulatory signals (Bybee and McClelland 2005: 404).

It seems that the Usage-based Theory, due to its fundamentally dynamic and emergent view of grammar, cannot be used to address the major issue with which this book is concerned: identifying the syntactic and non-syntactic factors that contribute to gradient acceptability. Nevertheless, studies framed within this theory and within other usage-based approaches offer many insights that we can use to help address this issue. In particular, usage-based studies have shown that language users are sensitive to frequency of use, both for specific lexical items or collocations and for more schematic constructions, and that language users are able to productively generalize from exemplars. As I will argue in Chapters 5–8, such considerations are important for understanding some of the variability that we find in acceptability judgments. Furthermore, I note that these types of insights can be captured in hybrid models which combine symbolic units and rules with information about frequency of use, thus capturing usage-based generalizations while maintaining a more traditional notion of competence grammar. Usage-based computational models which include the grammatical categories and constraints of Lexical-Functional Grammar (Bod 2000), Head-Driven Phrase Structure Grammar (Arnold and Lindardaki 2007), Cognitive Construction Grammar (Barak and Goldberg 2017; Goldberg 2019), Fluid Construction Grammar (Steels 2011; 2013), and Harmonic Grammar (Cho, Goldrick, and Smolensky 2017) have been proposed, among others. Typically, such models have been applied to problems of language learning, language change, and parsing. While the details of these models are beyond the scope of the current work, I will briefly highlight one of them here, as it directly pertains to interpreting gradient acceptability judgments.

Barak and Goldberg (2017) use the results from a learning simulation to bolster previous experimental findings on the acceptability of verb–argument constructions. Building on theoretical proposals from Cognitive Construction Grammar and related psycholinguistic studies, they develop a computational model of the partial productivity of constructions using a Bayesian clustering analysis to simulate exemplar-based verb and construction learning. The input corpus for this model includes a large number of 'usage events' which contain bundles of prespecified lexical, syntactic, and semantic information. These usage events represent instantiations of verbs used in specific argument structure constructions. Their frequency distributions in the input are based on natural corpus data but manipulated to test specific hypotheses. The authors show that their model is successful in simulating several findings from psycholinguistic experiments which distinguish between the novel extensions of a construction that participants find relatively acceptable and those that they find unacceptable. For example, in one simulation, the model estimated the likelihood of a verb with specific semantic features being used in a new syntactic pattern (e.g. the verb *fall* in *Fell the lamp*). It was shown that the estimated likelihood of using the new syntactic pattern was lower in cases where the verb had been frequently encountered with a different syntactic pattern to express a similar meaning (e.g. *The lamp fell*). This simulation was therefore consistent with acceptability judgment experiments showing that participants found novel verb–construction pairings less acceptable when there was a frequently used paraphrase available to express the same meaning (Robenalt and Goldberg 2015). I will discuss these experimental findings from Robenalt and Goldberg (2015) in more detail in Chapter 5 when I discuss the relationship between corpus frequency and acceptability judgments.

In Chapters 6–8, I will argue that soft constraints within the grammar are sometimes needed to account for gradient patterns of acceptability judgments. Following the approach in my own previous work with Laura Michaelis (Francis and Michaelis 2014; 2017) and in recent work by Barak and Goldberg (2017) and Goldberg (2019), I will suggest that soft constraints can be understood as preferred constructional subtypes—abstractions over well-attested clusters of exemplars with overlapping forms and meanings. Sentences which deviate from the preferred subtype may result in degraded acceptability even when they are otherwise well-formed, depending on factors such as variability within the cluster and the existence of a well-attested alternative syntactic form for expressing the same meaning. While I will not attempt to justify a particular implementation of soft constraints in this book, I will sketch out a usage-based constructionist approach as a possible alternative to OT-style theories which view soft constraints as competing within the grammar to select a winning candidate form.

2.6 Conclusions

Among generative linguists, there is a consensus that many factors in addition to syntactic constraints can affect the responses obtained in an acceptability judgment task. Such factors include semantic, pragmatic, and prosodic constraints as well as general cognitive mechanisms that affect language processing. Despite this consensus, each theoretical approach comes with certain assumptions and traditions that influence how linguists working within that approach tend to interpret judgment data. In this chapter, I have identified two main factors that can affect how judgments are interpreted: (1) the degree of isomorphism between syntax and semantics/pragmatics that is built into the theory; and (2) the nature of constraint application as either categorical or probabilistic/stochastic.

In derivational theories, the strong assumption of isomorphism between syntactic structure and meaning (especially meaning associated with event structure) leads to a wide range of acceptability contrasts that are interpreted as fundamentally syntactic in nature, despite having semantic or pragmatic correlates. In contrast, constraint-based theories lack this strong assumption, leading to a narrower range of acceptability contrasts that are interpreted as syntactic in nature, and correspondingly, a wider range of contrasts that are interpreted as semantically or pragmatically driven. I have also observed that linguists working within constraint-based theories have often been more amenable to processing-based explanations for apparently syntactic phenomena than linguists working within derivational theories. In this case, the architecture of the theory is not the crucial issue, since both types of theory allow for processing-based explanations. Rather, I have suggested that perhaps the smaller and simpler syntactic component of constraint-based theories has encouraged researchers to be more accepting in general of non-syntactic explanations for contrasts in acceptability.

Besides the degree of form–meaning isomorphism, the nature of constraint application as either categorical or gradient is another important factor affecting how judgments are interpreted. Within derivational theories, hierarchies or rankings of constraints have occasionally been proposed to account for the certain patterns of gradient acceptability as associated with syntactic categories (Chomsky 1964; Ross 1973a) and syntactic islands (Chomsky 1986a; Cinque 1990; Rizzi 1990). OT-style theories with a quantitative component, including Stochastic OT (Bresnan, Dingare, and Manning 2001), Linear OT (Keller 2006; Sorace and Keller 2005), and the Decathlon Model (Featherston 2008; 2019) have taken this idea a step further and developed more systematic models of gradience which include constraints of varying strength values. Because such theories tend to expand the scope of the competence grammar in a way that potentially obscures the role of performance factors, they may not be ideal for distinguishing among the different grammatical and performance-based factors that affect acceptability judgments. However, in my discussion of certain cases of gradient acceptability in Chapters 6–8, I will defend the general idea of soft constraints as crucial for capturing the full range of conventional linguistic knowledge that can affect judgments.

Finally, I have considered a prominent functionalist approach: the Usage-based Theory of Bybee (2006; 2010). Because this theory rejects the generative notion of a competence grammar, it makes little sense to distinguish between syntactic and non-syntactic explanations within this theory. However, the empirical studies that have been used to support usage-based approaches offer important insights into the effects of linguistic experience on language use and on acceptability judgments. Several of these studies and their implications for understanding judgment data will be considered in Chapter 5. In addition, I have suggested that a constructionist approach which combines usage information with a symbolic representation provides a useful way of understanding soft constraints within the grammar. I will elaborate on how this type of approach can be applied to specific cases in Chapters 6–7.

By considering the interpretation of gradient judgment data from the perspective of different theoretical approaches, I hope to encourage other linguists to do the same. As I argue throughout the book, the theoretical assumptions we bring to the task of data interpretation are important but often unacknowledged. Theory comparison thus raises one's awareness of these assumptions and of different possible approaches to the same problem. In addition, by considering multiple theoretical perspectives, we might occasionally gain insights into a linguistic phenomenon that would remain obscure if viewed through the lens of just one theoretical framework. As Kertész and Rákosi (2014: 45) state: "The pluralism of linguistic theories is fruitful because it allows linguists to examine linguistic phenomena from different perspectives and must not give way to the absolutist defense of particular theories."[12] Readers will no doubt notice that my own background and training have led me to favor constraint-based theories. However, my aim in this book is not to promote a particular theoretical framework. Rather,

---

[12] Kertész and Rákosi (2014) take this position as a component of a novel metatheoretical framework that they propose for understanding how generative linguists construct arguments on the basis of evidence, and how such argumentation can be improved. This framework is elaborated more fully in a book-length work (Kertész and Rákosi 2012). In addition to their perspective on the value of multiple theoretical perspectives, I would like to acknowledge two additional ideas from their model which converge with my own ideas in this book: (1) that there are often different ways of resolving apparent contradictions between different sources of evidence; and (2) that converging data from different sources (e.g. acceptability judgments, corpus analyses, psycholinguistic experiments of various kinds) can lend a higher plausibility value to a given analysis. I am grateful to an anonymous reviewer for making me aware of Kertész and Rákosi's theory, and of noting the similarities between my approach and theirs. I hope to explore this convergence in future works.

I intend to promote a constructive dialogue among linguists from different theoretical backgrounds and between linguists and colleagues in closely related fields, with a view toward better situating theoretical linguistics within an integrated approach to cognitive science. As this goal is quite ambitious, I also aim for the more modest goal of elucidating the pervasive phenomenon of gradient acceptability from the perspective of a few major theories and in relation to some of the ongoing debates in experimental syntax.

In the following two chapters, I discuss how syntactic effects on acceptability can be distinguished from effects of other aspects of linguistic knowledge and from the effects of processing-related factors, again highlighting the importance of certain theoretical assumptions for interpreting gradient variation in acceptability judgments.

3

On distinguishing formal syntactic constraints from other aspects of linguistic knowledge

As we have seen, acceptability judgments are only an indirect measure of grammatical competence. Even a well-designed judgment task cannot provide us with an absolute rating below which a sentence may be considered 'ungrammatical'. At best, such a task provides information about perceived differences among minimally contrasting pairs/sets of sentences. The task of the linguist is then to isolate the reason or reasons for the observed differences. The previous chapter discussed how the assumptions and traditions associated with different theoretical approaches tend to affect linguists' interpretations of such contrasts. With this discussion in mind, let us now turn to the ongoing debate within experimental syntax concerning the validity of different types of evidence for distinguishing among the factors that affect acceptability judgments. This debate has played out most prominently in the last decade or so of experimental research on island constraints—constraints on long-distance dependencies such as those found in interrogative constructions and relative clauses. A basic example of the phenomenon in question is given in (1–2), in which the (a) examples are grammatical while the (b) examples are said to violate island constraints.

(1) a. **Who** did she claim that she had met__?
     b. *__**Who** did she make the claim that she had met __?

(2) a. **Who** is it likely that she had met __?
     b. *__**Who** is that she had met __ likely?

Contrasts in acceptability as illustrated in (1a–b) and (2a–b) have traditionally been understood as syntactic in nature. In his groundbreaking dissertation, Ross (1967) proposed that sentences like (1b) and (2b) involve structural configurations that are 'islands' to movement. That is, although operators such as question words can undergo long-distance movement in sentences such as (1a) and (2a), they cannot be moved out of certain structural configurations. Specifically, sentences like (1a) violate the Complex Noun Phrase Constraint (a constraint on movement out of noun—complement configurations), while sentences like (2b) violate the Sentential Subject Constraint (a constraint on movement out of clausal subjects). While the formulation of the constraints has changed over the years, it remains the dominant view in derivational approaches to grammar that contrasts as in (1a–b) and (2a–b) involve the application

Gradient Acceptability and Linguistic Theory. Elaine J. Francis, Oxford University Press.
© Elaine J. Francis (2022). DOI: 10.1093/oso/9780192898944.003.0003

of syntactic constraints. However, this view has occasionally been challenged by studies which have proposed pragmatic (Erteschik-Shir and Lappin 1979; Kuno 1987; Van Valin 1993) or processing-based explanations (Kluender and Kutas 1993; Pritchett 1991) (see Newmeyer (2016) for an overview). The more recent debate in experimental syntax has developed out of this earlier literature on non-syntactic explanations for island constraints, most of which, with the exception of Kluender and Kutas (1993) and related works, had been based on corpus examples or informally collected acceptability judgments.

Building on these earlier works, Hofmeister and Sag (2010) inspired a renewed interest in non-syntactic approaches to island constraints when they presented experiments showing that acceptability judgments improved and reading times got faster for island-violating sentences when certain factors (which they assumed to be irrelevant to any syntactic constraints on islands) were manipulated. On one side of the current debate are those researchers who typically favor pragmatic and/or processing-based explanations and align themselves with constraint-based theories of syntax (Ambridge and Goldberg 2008; Chaves 2012; Culicover 2013; Goldberg 2013; Hofmeister and Sag 2010; Hofmeister et al. 2013). On the other side are those researchers who usually favor syntactic approaches to island constraints and who align themselves with the Minimalist Program in syntax (Dillon and Hornstein 2013; Phillips 2013b; Sprouse 2008; Sprouse, Schütze, and Almeida 2013; Sprouse, Wagers, and Phillips 2012). An alternative to both of these is represented in the work of Sam Featherston (2005b; 2005a; 2007; 2011), who generally favors syntactic approaches to island constraints, but works within a theory called the Decathlon Model—a gradient approach to grammar similar to Stochastic OT (Boersma and Hayes 2001) and Linear OT (Keller 2000; Sorace and Keller 2005). For Featherston, island constraints can be either hard or soft constraints in the grammar, with constraint strength potentially varying across languages. Cross-cutting these various approaches, Chaves and Putnam (2021) argue that there are several different types of island constraints within and across languages, with different constraints reflecting different syntactic, semantic, pragmatic, or processing factors or in some cases, combinations of factors.

While the current debate within experimental syntax centers on the interpretation of island effects, the problem of identifying and parceling out the factors that affect acceptability judgments is a more general one. In the current chapter, I discuss experimental research on both island and non-island phenomena bearing on one aspect of this general problem: how syntactic effects on acceptability can be distinguished from effects of other aspects of linguistic knowledge, including semantics, pragmatics, and prosody. The related issue of how to distinguish syntactic effects from extra-grammatical factors that affect language processing will be taken up in the next chapter, Chapter 4.

The main arguments for distinguishing between the effects of syntax and other aspects of linguistic knowledge have come from amelioration effects. The basic idea is that reduced acceptability due to non-syntactic factors can be ameliorated by changing the discourse context or by changing syntactically irrelevant aspects of the sentence.

For such cases, it is argued that there is no need to posit any syntactic constraint to account for the reduced acceptability. Specifically, reduced acceptability due to a semantic or pragmatic anomaly can be ameliorated by changing the lexical content and/or manipulating the context in which a sentence occurs. Similarly, reduced acceptability resulting from inappropriate prosody can be ameliorated by changing the prosodic contour of the sentence. While the interpretation of amelioration effects can be complicated by theoretical disagreements over what counts as a non-syntactic manipulation, arguments in favor of semantic, pragmatic, or prosodic effects on acceptability can be strengthened with reference to attested examples from spontaneous language use and through correspondences between patterns of acceptability judgments and patterns of performance on additional tasks that specifically target semantic, pragmatic, or prosodic features. In the following sections, I will discuss experimental evidence from outbound anaphora and factive islands in English, word order variation in Czech, and split intransitivity in German. For the first three cases, I will claim that the authors make substantial arguments for eliminating a proposed syntactic constraint based on evidence from amelioration, but I will point out ways in which their arguments could potentially be strengthened with additional data. Finally, for the case of split intransitivity in German, I will show that contrasts in acceptability can only be fully attributed to semantic factors within a theoretical approach that does not require strict isomorphism between event semantics and syntactic structure. Although the authors of this study provide compelling evidence that semantic factors determine speakers' acceptability ratings, they do not go so far as to propose a purely semantic account of split intransitivity in German.

3.1 Outbound anaphora in English

In Chapter 1, I briefly introduced arguments in favor of a pragmatic account of outbound anaphora. Let us now consider this case in a bit more detail. Recall that outbound anaphora refers to a phenomenon in which a pronoun takes a word-internal element as its antecedent. In (3a–b), for example, the pronoun *them* takes the first part of the compound word *bicycle thefts* as its antecedent. Based on the reduced acceptability of sentences similar to (3b), outbound anaphora had been claimed to violate a syntactic constraint on pronoun–antecedent relations (Postal 1969). However, Ward et al. (1991) found examples from actual language use showing that outbound anaphora is apparently felicitous when the referent of the antecedent NP is made accessible by some aspect of the context. In the attested example in (3a), for example, the topic of 'bicycle thefts' is introduced in the first clause, making the referent 'bicycles' sufficiently accessible.

(3)　a. Officials in the Danish capital believe they've found a way to stop **bicycle**
　　　　thefts—let people use **them** for free.　　　　(Ward et al. 1991: 452)
　　b. ***Bicycle thefts** deter the use of **them**.

Thus, the presence of a supportive context as in (3a) ameliorates the unacceptability shown by decontextualized sentences such as (3b). Based on examples such as these, along with a careful discussion of the various factors that make the pronoun's referent sufficiently accessible in cases where outbound anaphora is attested, Ward et al. (1991) argue that outbound anaphora is syntactically well-formed but pragmatically restricted.

Ward et al. (1991: 458–61) provide additional evidence for their pragmatic account of outbound anaphora from a comprehension experiment that was originally reported in McKoon et al. (1990). In the experiment, sentences containing outbound anaphora (i.e. a pronoun with part of a compound noun as its antecedent) and minimally distinct sentences containing regular anaphora (i.e. the same pronoun with a full NP as its antecedent) were embedded within contexts that were either topical (facilitating accessibility of the pronoun's referent, but without providing a direct antecedent) or non-topical. Sample stimuli are given in Figure 3.1. In this sample, the target antecedent for the pronoun *they* was the word *deer*, which was presented either as the first part of the compound noun *deer hunting* (outbound anaphora) or the object of the verb *hunting* (regular anaphora). The topical context shown here describes fishing, hunting, and small game, while the non-topical context describes outdoor activities that are unrelated to deer.

Topical Context
Sam likes the outdoor life. Having grown up in rural Kentucky, he Knows a lot about nature and is an expert at fishing and shooting. He goes on hunting trips as often as he can. He used to hunt just small game, like rabbit and quail. However, lately he's taken up
[**deer** hunting /hunting **deer**].

And he thinks that **they** are really exciting to track.

Non-Topical Context
Sam has many interests in the outdoors. He's an avid skier, and each winter he takes about a month off from work to ski in Colorado. In the summertime, he visits his parents in Montana, where he has a chance to do some mountain climbing. Lately, he' s taken up
[**deer** hunting/ hunting **deer**].

And he thinks that **they** are really exciting to track.

Fig. 3.1 Sample stimuli for reading comprehension of outbound and regular anaphora in topical and non-topical contexts

Source: Republished with permission of the Linguistic Society of America from Ward et al. (1991: 457); permission conveyed through Copyright Clearance Center, Inc.

Participants were presented with one line of text at a time, and their reading times were measured when they pressed a button to proceed to the next line. The primary dependent measure was the reading time for the final line of text containing the pronoun. Results showed that in the non-topical context, reading times were slower for outbound anaphora than for regular anaphora. In the topical context, however, reading times were faster overall and did not significantly differ for outbound anaphora vs. regular anaphora. Ward et al. (1991) interpret these results to mean that although the referent of a pronoun is generally less accessible when its antecedent is a modifier within a compound noun (outbound anaphora) than when its antecedent is an independent NP (regular anaphora), this difference disappears in a sufficiently supportive context. They argue that this result supports their analysis based on attested examples: outbound anaphora is syntactically well-formed but pragmatically restricted to contexts that facilitate identification of the referent. Further support for this conclusion could come from acceptability judgments on the same or similar stimuli as were used in the reading task. In particular, if judgments were to mirror reading times in showing higher ratings for regular anaphora in the non-topical condition, but no difference between outbound and regular anaphora in the topical condition, such a result would verify the amelioration effect (previously observed informally in corpus examples) for sentence sets that are fully matched for lexical content. On the other hand, it is possible that acceptability judgments would show some residual effect that was not shown in the reading times, such that, for example, the difference in acceptability between outbound and regular anaphora does not completely disappear in the topical context. Such a residual effect would not contradict the evidence in favor of a pragmatic constraint, but would require a separate explanation of some kind. Later in Section 3.3, I will discuss a study of word order variation in Czech in which such a residual effect is actually found (Šimík and Wierzba 2015). Let us now turn to a conceptually similar study on island effects in long-distance questions in English, with a more elaborate experimental design in which distinct measures of sentence acceptability and degree of backgroundedness were directly compared.

3.2 Factive islands and manner-of-speaking islands in English

Similar arguments from acceptability judgments in conjunction with additional experimental tasks have played a part in the current debate over sources of island effects. Ambridge and Goldberg (2008) and Goldberg (2006; 2013) have argued that some island effects result from a clash between the discourse prominence of 'extracted' phrases such as question words and the typically backgrounded nature of certain types of constituents, including complex NPs, factive VPs, and clausal subjects. In support of this argument, Ambridge and Goldberg (2008) investigated the acceptability of *wh*-questions with clausal complements, as in (4a–c). They hypothesized that the greater acceptability of (4a) as compared with (4b) and (4c) is a kind of amelioration effect arising from discourse factors. That is, by changing the main verb, it is possible to change the degree to which the complement clause is perceived as backgrounded (i.e. not part of the main assertion of the sentence), thus improving or degrading the acceptability of long-distance questions with the same syntactic structure. Specifically, Ambridge and Goldberg (2008) hypothesized that the lower acceptability of sentences like (4b–c) as compared with (4a) is due to the fact that clausal complements of manner-of-speaking verbs such as *whisper* and factive verbs such as *realize* are understood as backgrounded to a greater degree than complements of bridge verbs like *think* and *say.*

(4)   a. **What** did Jess think that Dan liked__?
      b. ?**What** did Jess whisper that Dan liked__?
      c. ?**What** did Jess realize that Dan liked__?
      d. Jess didn't realize that Dan liked fish.

The greater acceptability of (4a) is not necessarily an effect of backgrounding, however. Another possible interpretation is that (4b) and (4c) have a different underlying syntactic structure than (4a). For example, Baltin (1982) claimed that structures as in (4b) are ungrammatical because the complements of manner-of-speaking verbs are not really complements but are instead adjuncts, and adjuncts are islands to extraction. Similarly, Kiparsky and Kiparsky (1970) claimed that structures as in (4c) are ungrammatical because the complement of a factive verb is a really headed by a covert NP 'the fact.' Thus, sentences like (4c) violate the Complex Noun Phrase Constraint (Ross 1967), which was later subsumed under the Subjacency condition (Chomsky 1973).

To obtain evidence bearing on their hypothesis, Ambridge and Goldberg (2008) conducted two judgment tasks. The first task asked for acceptability ratings of sentences like (4a–c) and their declarative counterparts, while the second task assessed the degree of 'backgroundedness' of the complement clause. Both tasks included 12 verbs split evenly among three categories (bridge, manner-of-speaking, and factive). Backgrounded status was operationalized as the degree to which negation of the main clause was interpreted to imply the negation of the complement clause in sentences like (4d), as judged by participants using a 7-point scale. It was assumed that if the complement clause (*that Dan liked fish*) is perceived to hold true (i.e. if the negation of the main clause does not imply the negation of the complement clause), the complement clause is backgrounded and therefore not part of the main assertion of the sentence. Conversely, if the negation of the main clause is perceived to imply the negation of the complement clause, the complement clause is understood to be part of the main assertion to a greater extent. Thus, a higher score on the negation test implies a lesser degree of backgrounding. Examining the scores for individual verbs, Ambridge and Goldberg (2008: 376) indeed found a strong negative correlation between the acceptability ratings of interrogative sentences and the backgrounded status of the complement clause as determined by the negation test (Figure 3.2). Sentences with the factive verbs *know* and *realize* showed the strongest dispreference for interrogative structure (quantified in terms of a 'difference score' between the interrogative and declarative versions of the same sentence) and the lowest scores on the negation test (i.e. the highest degree of backgrounding), while sentences with the bridge verbs *think* and *believe* showed the weakest dispreference for interrogative structure (i.e. the lowest difference scores) and the highest scores on the negation test. Sentences with the manner-of-speaking verbs *whisper* and *mutter* were intermediate on both measures.

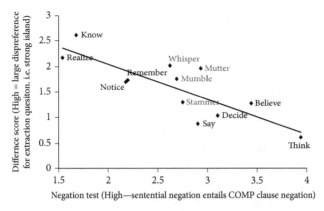

Fig. 3.2 Correlation between difference in acceptability and negation test scores

Source: Republished with permission of Walter de Gruyter and company from Ambridge and Goldberg (2008: 376); permission conveyed through Copyright Clearance Center, Inc.

The authors take these results to mean that participants were sensitive to the clash in discourse information structure between focused constituents (question words) and backgrounded constituents (factive clauses), causing them to rate interrogative sentences as less acceptable (relative to the corresponding declarative version of the same sentence) depending on the perceived degree of backgrounding. This is the simplest explanation for the findings, they argue, since a syntactic account requires covert syntactic structures to distinguish among sentences such as (4a–c) and also fails to predict that gradient differences in acceptability among verbs should be correlated with gradient differences in degree of backgrounding (2008: 377).

Choice of verb covaried with backgrounded status in these experiments, leaving open the possibility that the underlying reason for the variation in acceptability has to do with the verbs themselves rather than backgrounded status. Under such an account, backgrounded status would simply be a correlate, not a cause, of the variation in acceptability. In a recent study, Liu et al. (2019) tested this possibility. They hypothesized that the lower acceptability of interrogatives with factive and manner-of-speaking verbs was due to the frequency with which each verb occurs with a finite complement clause, combined with a general preference for declarative over interrogative sentences. They first replicated the two experiments from Ambridge and Goldberg (2008) using the same procedures but an expanded set of 24 verbs. Applying the same analysis, they found a weaker and statistically insignificant negative correlation between difference in acceptability and negation test scores, thus failing to replicate the strong negative correlation shown in Ambridge and Goldberg (2008) (Figure 3.2). In an additional post hoc analysis, they found a significant positive correlation between the acceptability ratings for *wh*-questions and verb frame frequency (defined as frequency of the verb with a *that*-clause complement in the Google Books corpus), and a similar correlation between acceptability ratings of declarative sentences and verb frame frequency. They followed up with a second experiment which tested a larger set of 48 verbs and which used a binary (acceptable/unacceptable) judgment task instead of a 5-point rating scale. The results of a mixed-effects logistic regression analysis showed that declarative sentences were rated as 'acceptable' more often than interrogative sentences, indicating a general effect of extraction. In addition, for both interrogative and declarative sentences, ratings of 'acceptable' were significantly more likely as the verb frame frequency of the matrix verb increased. The authors conclude that frequency effects best account for their participants' judgments of interrogative and declarative sentences with a finite complement clause. However, they leave open the possibility that discourse-related factors might independently contribute to the acceptability of these types of sentences, in ways that their experiments did not detect, and they agree with Ambridge and Goldberg (2008) that a purely syntactic account fails to predict the observed gradience in judgments.

Following on from Liu et al. (2019), Richter and Chaves (2020) also tested for the effects of verb frame frequency on the acceptability of interrogative sentences with clausal complements. Instead of estimating verb frame frequency based on the frequency of the verb with a *that*-complement, they used a Sentential Complement Ratio, which was calculated by dividing the number of instances of a particular verb with a finite complement clause (with or without *that*) by the total number of instances of that verb in the corpus. Their acceptability judgment experiment, in which participants were asked to rate interrogative sentences on a 7-point scale, used a larger set of 75 verbs, including all of the verbs from Liu et al. (2019). Sentential Complement Ratio was calculated separately from two corpora (VALEX and Corpus of Contemporary American English) and used as an independent variable in separate ordinal mixed-effects regression analyses of the acceptability ratings. Results showed a significant effect of SCR on acceptability for both corpora. Sentences with high SCR verbs were given higher ratings than sentences with low SCR verbs, as expected. However, additional statistical analyses showed SCR was a poor predictor of acceptability within each verb class: "Manner verbs vary widely in their acceptability, yet are clustered within low SCR values. Factive verbs, meanwhile, show the opposite: they mostly all have relatively high acceptability ratings, yet vary wildly in SCR value" (Richter and Chaves 2020: 1775). Richter and Chaves (2020) surmise that this variation within verb classes was likely due to pragmatic factors, as hypothesized by Ambridge and Goldberg (2008) and others. Using a computational model to estimate sentence probability for each of the stimulus items in their experiment, they found a significant correlation between sentence probability as calculated by the model and acceptability ratings from their judgment experiment. They take this finding as preliminary evidence in favor of a pragmatic account, assuming their estimate of sentence probability is related to "the probability of the event, and the likelihood that the content of the embedded clause is at-issue" (Richter and Chaves 2020: 1776). They acknowledge that additional studies are needed to test for pragmatic effects more directly.

If pragmatic factors can in fact help account for variation in acceptability over and above any effects of verb frame frequency, acceptability should vary when choice of verb is held constant and backgrounded status is varied through context alone. Goldberg (2013: 233) cites a study by Kothari (2008) which bears on this question to some extent. Kothari (2008) measured reading times for interrogatives with bridge verbs (e.g. *say*) and manner-of-speaking verbs (e.g. *mumble*) in different contexts. In contexts such as (5), for which the manner of speaking had already been mentioned, Kothari found that reading times were just as fast for verbs like *mumble* as for verbs like *say*.

(5) The students **spoke unintelligibly**, managing to convey that the party was a lot of fun. The residential fellow overheard what the freshman **mumbled** that he had drunk at the party.

However, in neutral contexts with no prior mention of the manner of speaking, reading times were slower for verbs like *mumble* than for verbs like *say*. Although Kothari did not measure acceptability judgments for different contexts, these reading time measures suggest that context can alleviate the processing difficulty associated with interrogative sentences like (4b). Goldberg (2013: 233) goes a step further to argue that Kothari's (2008) results support the hypothesis that backgrounded constituents resist extraction. Setting up a context in which the manner of speaking is already known allows the complement clause to become part of the focus domain, and therefore backgrounded to a lesser degree. Additional support for this interpretation is lacking, but could come from a follow-up study using measures similar to what Ambridge and Goldberg (2008) used (acceptability and negation test scores), but varying context rather than (or in addition to) choice of verb. If it were shown that both acceptability and backgrounded status vary according to context and independently of verb choice, this could be taken as relatively strong evidence in favor of Ambridge and Goldberg's original hypothesis. Any account that appealed to syntactic structure would then need to show that sentences like (4b–c) are actually structurally ambiguous.

In Chapter 5, I will discuss the effects of corpus frequency on acceptability with respect to studies of various syntactic constructions in English, German, and Polish. Some of these studies are like Liu et al. (2019) in showing a systematic relationship between corpus frequency and acceptability, while others are like Richter and Chaves (2020) in showing variation in acceptability which is not predictable from frequency.

3.3 Word order and prosody in Czech

While Ward et al. (1991) and Ambridge and Goldberg (2008) argue that the phenomena they examine can be fully understood in terms of pragmatic factors, Šimík and Wierzba (2015) explore a similar line of argumentation in their study of prosodic factors affecting word order variation in Czech. Similar to these other studies, they show that prosodic constraints make more accurate predictions of acceptability ratings than syntactic constraints as proposed in Kučerová (2012) do. However, they also find a residual effect of definiteness on word order that is not predicted by either the prosodic constraints (as in their own proposal) or the syntactic constraints (as proposed by Kučerová). In the remainder of this section, I elaborate on a few of the authors' key findings.

Šimík and Wierzba's (2015) study examines a number of variables that affect the word order of declarative sentences in Czech. The basic word order of a declarative sentence is subject–verb–object, and this order is generally preferred when the object represents new information. However, the basic order becomes less acceptable, and an alternative subject–object–verb ordering is preferred, in cases where the object NP represents discourse-given information. In (6), which is from Šimík and Wierzba's stimuli, the object *potkana* 'rat' represents given information and occurs most naturally in the scrambled (object-fronted) word order, as in (6a) (2015: 29). The same sentence with basic word order, as in (6b), is judged as unacceptable in this context.

(6)   Context: 'I don't know how long we will tolerate this. We have to get rid of that rat in the cellar.'
   a.   No, volal mi   Jirka,   že   prý   právě   potkana objevil.
        well called me.DAT   Jirka.NOM   that allegedly just   rat   found
        'Well, Jirka called and said that he has just found the rat.'
   b.   * No, volal mi   Jirka,   že   prý   právě   objevil potkana.
        well called me.DAT   Jirka.NOM   that allegedly just   found   rat

Kučerová (2012) analyzed the scrambled word order as in (6a) as the product of a syntactic movement operation which is necessary to prevent an ungrammatical ordering of new information before given (specifically, presupposed) information. As an alternative, Šimík and Wierzba (2015) proposed two prosodic factors to account for the scrambled word order: (1) default sentence stress occurs on the final constituent; (2) given information must not be stressed. According to this account, the basic word order with stress on the final constituent produces an ill-formed prosodic structure when the object represents given information. As a result, a sentence like (6b) is judged as unacceptable when default stress is applied (see Kitagawa and Fodor (2006) for a discussion of how written stimuli prompt readers to apply default prosody in the absence of other cues). Speakers can avoid this by fronting the object to a position before the verb, as in (6a), and placing the stress on the verb. While both proposals relate discourse given status to word order, the prosody-based explanation relates them only indirectly.

To distinguish between the predictions of the syntactic and prosodic approaches, Šimík and Wierzba (2015) compared alternative ways of formulating a declarative sentence with a given direct object, manipulating patterns of definiteness, word order, and stress in spoken stimuli. The first experiment included items with the basic word order in which the stress was shifted forward to occur on the verb instead of the object (e.g. placing stress on *objevil* 'found' in 6b). In general, stress shift is limited in its application but can be used for placing emphasis on a nonfinal constituent. However, since stress shift does not change the syntactic structure, the prediction of the syntactic theory is that the stress-shifted version of the basic order should be unacceptable, just like the stress-final version. On the other hand, the prosodic theory predicts that shifting the stress should improve the acceptability of the sentence. As shown in Figure 3.3, the results supported the prosodic theory.

For the basic order (VO) sentences, the stress-shifted version with stress on the verb was significantly more acceptable than the stress-final version in both the definite and indefinite object conditions (see VO column on the right in Figure 3.3), although still less acceptable than the scrambled (OV) version with final stress on the verb (top left condition in Figure 3.3). The authors attribute this intermediate result to two separate OT-style constraints, one of which specifies that sentence-final stress is generally preferred, and the other of which specifies that given NPs should not carry stress. The scrambled sentences with final stress on the verb conform to both constraints, while the stress-shifted version of the basic order conforms to only the second one.

Their second experiment included items in which the basic word order was used to express given information in the object (thus violating the syntactic constraint), but stress on the object was avoided in a different way—this time by including an additional PP at the end to take up the stress. The results of this experiment provided further evidence in favor of the prosodic theory. The sentences with stress on the final PP (where the PP represented new information) were highly acceptable despite violating the purported syntactic constraint.

Although the results of the experiments appear to support the predictions of the prosodic theory, a residual effect of definiteness was also shown in both experiments. Definiteness of the object was included as a factor because Kučerová's syntactic approach predicts an effect such that basic word order should be preferred with indefinite objects, while scrambled order should be preferred with definite objects (where both types of objects are discourse-given but only the definite ones are presupposed to exist). Results of Experiment 1 showed that the scrambled word order was

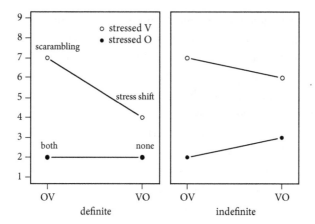

Fig. 3.3 Effects of word order, stress, and definiteness on the acceptability of Czech transitive clauses

Source: From Šimík and Wierzba (2015: 34).

in fact strongly preferred for both definite and indefinite objects, failing to confirm Kučerová's predictions with regard to indefinite objects (Figure 3.2). However, there was a significant effect of definiteness in the expected direction: indefinite objects were significantly more acceptable than definite objects in the basic (VO) word order, even though they were still less acceptable than either type of object in the scrambled (OV) order. In Experiment 2, which only tested the basic word order, definite objects were found to be more acceptable preceding a PP than indefinite objects. This result was contrary to Kučerová's prediction that indefinite objects should be more acceptable in the basic word order than definite objects. Šimík and Wierzba proposed a possible explanation for both of these results: "A non-presupposed expression does not linearly precede a presupposed expression" (2015: 63). Possibly, this residual effect of definiteness is syntactic in nature, meaning that the patterns of judgments that Šimík and Wierzba elicited can be mostly but not fully reduced to prosodic factors. However, the authors conclude that more data are needed to make any firm conclusion regarding the definiteness effect. Most importantly for our purposes, this example illustrates some of the subtleties and complexities involved in teasing apart the various factors that affect acceptability judgments. In short, Šimík and Wierzba (2015) showed that the acceptability of non-scrambled (VO) sentences that express given information in the object NP can be improved by manipulating the prosodic contour of the sentence, either by shifting the stress to the verb or by adding an extra adjunct phrase to the end of the sentence. They conclude based on these findings that the purported syntactic constraint makes the wrong predictions, and that a prosodic explanation for the observed patterns of judgments is preferable. However, they also found a small effect of definiteness that was predicted by neither the syntactic account nor the prosodic account. Residual effects that apparently defy a fully non-syntactic explanation are not uncommon in these types of studies.

3.4 Auxiliary selection and impersonal passives in German

While evidence from amelioration effects might not be definitive, the arguments in favor of eliminating certain syntactic constraints from the grammar were relatively straightforward in the first two cases of outbound anaphora and factive islands. In the case of word order and prosody in Czech, there was the minor complication of a residual difference in acceptability that was not eliminated through the prosodic manipulation. When considering phenomena at the interface between syntax and event semantics, such arguments become even trickier to make. Because event semantics has been so integral to the syntactic representations that have been proposed within derivational theories, semantic evidence and syntactic evidence essentially become one and the same. As we will see in a discussion of Keller and Sorace's (2003) study of German, a purely semantic account becomes possible only by abandoning these central theoretical assumptions.

Keller and Sorace (2003) examine the notoriously complex issue of split intransitivity in their experimental study of auxiliary selection and impersonal passivization in German. Split intransitivity refers to the cross-linguistic tendency for different semantic classes of intransitive verbs, commonly known as 'unaccusative' and 'unergative' (Burzio 1986; Perlmutter 1978), to display distinct syntactic distributions. Roughly speaking, unaccusative verbs denoting concepts such as 'arrive' and 'fall' tend to express telic events (i.e. events with a defined endpoint) and select a patient-like argument, while unergative verbs denoting concepts such as 'talk' and 'dance' tend to express atelic events and select an agent-like argument. Various grammatical constructions which appear to be sensitive to split intransitivity have been identified across different languages and typologically diverse language families. Within derivational theories of syntax, these various constructions are commonly understood to incorporate a uniform underlying syntactic distinction. The precise details vary according to different authors' analyses, and need not concern us here, but the basic idea is that the subject of an intransitive clause is licensed in a different underlying position depending on whether the predicate is unaccusative or unergative (Borer 1994; McClure 1995; Ramchand 2013). The surface similarity between the two types of intransitive clauses is achieved via syntactic movement.

Sorace (2000) observed on the basis of informal judgment data from several Romance and Germanic languages that those subclasses of intransitive verbs which are semantically intermediate in terms of agentivity and/or telicity tend to display more variation across different languages/dialects and across different constructions within the same language as compared with those subclasses that encode core unaccusative or core unergative semantic properties. In addition, Sorace (2000) found that the semantically intermediate subclasses were more likely to display intermediate levels of acceptability when occurring in a construction identified as diagnostic of either unaccusative or unergative predication. To test these generalizations experimentally, Keller and Sorace (2003) conducted two acceptability judgment experiments examining split intransitivity in German. They tested eight semantically defined subclasses of intransitive verbs occurring in three syntactic contexts: (1) active clause with auxiliary *sein* 'be'; (2) active clause with auxiliary *haben* 'have'; and (3) impersonal passive construction. These three contexts are illustrated here in (7a–c) using examples from Keller and Sorace (2003). While the first context is associated with core unaccusative verbs (7a), the second and third contexts are associated with core unergative verbs (7b–c).

(7) a. Der Gefangene   ist/*hat   schnell entkommen.
         the prisoner   is/has   quickly escaped
         'The prisoner has quickly escaped.'   (unaccusative verb with *sein*)
     b. Die Lehrerin   hat/*ist   dauernd geredet.
         the teacher   has/is   continuously talked
         'The teacher has talked continuously.'   (unergative verb with *haben*)

    c. Es wurde dauernd   geredet.
        it was continuously talked
        'There were people talking continuously.' (unergative verb in
        impersonal passive)

Two magnitude estimation tasks with written stimuli were administered to 120 German-speaking participants from two dialect groups. Overall, the results of the experiments confirmed that the semantically intermediate subclasses of verbs were indeed subject to greater cross-constructional and cross-dialectal variation in German as compared with the core subclasses. Furthermore, they showed that verbs belonging to these intermediate subclasses display gradient variation in acceptability, depending in part on the context in which they occur. Since it will not be possible to consider the full set of results from this intricate study, I will focus here on a few key findings in light of the following questions as pertinent for the current chapter. Can acceptability judgments of intransitive sentences with *sein*, *haben*, and impersonal passivization be predicted from semantic properties of the sentences? If so, can the commonly assumed syntactic distinction between unaccusative and unergative predicates be dispensed with? I will argue that the answer to the first question is a tentative 'yes', while the answer to the second question depends on one's theoretical approach. I will confine my remarks to a subset of the findings from Experiment 2, as shown in Figures 3.4 (impersonal passives) and 3.5 (auxiliary selection).

Continuation of state verbs such as *andauern* 'last' and *anhalten* 'continue' were identified in this study as semantically intermediate in interpretation. Although they express atelic events, as is typical of core unergatives, they select arguments that are low in agentivity, as is typical of core unaccusatives. As shown in Figure 3.4, continuation of state verbs (fourth bar from left) received low acceptability ratings in impersonal passives, in a similar manner to typical unaccusative (change of state) verbs such as *welken* 'wilt' and *blühen* 'bloom' (second bar from left). However, the same continuation of state verbs behaved similarly to core unergative verbs with respect to auxiliary selection. As shown in Figure 3.5, continuation of state verbs (fourth bar from left) were far more acceptable with *haben* than *sein*, in a manner similar to typical unergative (controlled process) verbs like *arbeiten* 'work' and *reden* 'talk' (rightmost bar). The authors propose that the impersonal passive is more sensitive to the agentivity of the subject, whereas auxiliary selection is more sensitive to telicity. As additional evidence of this, they observe that continuation of state verbs with impersonal passives received intermediate ratings in Experiment 1 (not shown) but low ratings in Experiment 2 (Figure 3.4, fourth bar from left). The difference between the two experiments was that the stimulus sentences had animate subjects in Experiment 1 and inanimate subjects in Experiment 2. Thus, volitionality of the subject (as implied by animacy) improved ratings of continuation of state verbs with impersonal passives. In contrast, animacy made no difference for auxiliary selection. The auxiliary *haben* was highly acceptable and strongly preferred over *sein* in both experiments, suggesting that atelicity might be the more important factor.

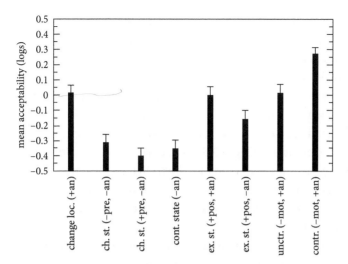

Fig. 3.4 Acceptability of impersonal passives by verb class

Source: From Keller and Sorace (2003: 96); reproduced with permission from Cambridge University Press.

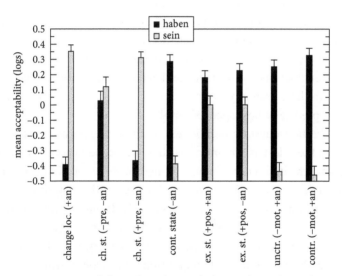

Fig. 3.5 Acceptability of auxiliaries *haben* and *sein* by verb class

Source: From Keller and Sorace (2003: 95); reproduced with permission from Cambridge University Press.

Considering all of the verb classes together, there is further support for the idea that impersonal passives may be more sensitive to agentivity of the subject, whereas auxiliary selection may be more sensitive to telicity. The results of Experiment 2 showed that impersonal passives received lower ratings for the four verb classes with inanimate subjects as compared with the four verb classes with animate subjects (−an/+an in Figure 3.4). In contrast, the animacy of the subject showed no apparent correlation with auxiliary selection. For example, change-of-state verbs (second bar from left in

Figure 3.5) with inanimate subjects were more acceptable with *sein*, while continuation of state verbs with inanimate subjects (fourth bar from left in Figure 3.5) were more acceptable with *haben*, even though both classes of verbs were incompatible with impersonal passives. Instead, the five verb classes that were more acceptable with *haben* (the five rightmost classes in Figure 3.5) express unchanging (atelic) states or processes. As further evidence of the importance of telicity, acceptability ratings for change-of-state verbs with *haben* were only slightly lower than for *sein* and this difference was not statistically significant (Figure 3.5, second bar from left). However, with the addition of a telicity-inducing verbal prefix, which changes the emphasis from the process of change to the result of change (e.g. *blühen* 'bloom' →verblühen 'finish blooming'), the acceptability of *haben* with change-of-state verbs was greatly reduced (Figure 3.5, third bar from left).

Overall, these experiments showed gradient variation in acceptability for different semantic subclasses of verbs across contexts with *haben*, *sein*, and impersonal passives. Impersonal passives were apparently more sensitive to agentivity of the subject, while auxiliary selection was apparently more sensitive to telicity. In addition, results showed that some subclasses were construed differently depending on the animacy of the subject (in the case of impersonal passives) or the inclusion of a telicity-inducing prefix (in the case of auxiliary selection). Now let us return to our two questions most relevant for this chapter. Can acceptability judgments of intransitive sentences with *sein*, *haben*, and impersonal passivization be predicted from semantic properties of the sentences? If so, can the commonly assumed syntactic distinction between unaccusative and unergative predicates be dispensed with?

To answer the first question definitively, additional experiments that further refine and isolate the relevant semantic variables would be needed. The authors note, for example, that the differences shown among change of location verbs and change-of-state verbs indicate a need for a finer-grained semantic analysis of predicates that express spatial and nonspatial transitions with or without a definite endpoint or resultant state (Keller and Sorace 2003: 101). Additional experiments could be designed to probe the effect of transitions independently of telicity. Even based only on these results, however, the answer to our first question is plausibly affirmative, with the stipulation that the semantic factors affecting acceptability are construction-specific. This observation is in line with findings from other studies (Bentley and Eythórsson 2004; Sorace 2000) but not a trivial one, given that unaccusative and unergative predicates are widely assumed to show a uniform underlying distinction in event structure across different languages and constructions.

Assuming an affirmative answer to the first question, the answer to the second question depends mostly on the theoretical approach. For those who use a derivational architecture with strong form–meaning isomorphism, semantic differences with respect to thematic role assignment and telicity are reflected transparently in the syntactic structures of unaccusative and unergative predicates, and indeed, such semantic differences (or at least a subset thereof) are considered to be a symptom of the underlying syntactic differences (Borer 1994; McClure 1995). On the other hand, for those who use a constraint-based architecture with relatively flexible form–meaning mappings, such semantic distinctions might not be reflected in the syntactic representation at all. For example, Sadock (2012) isolates the semantic factors underlying various manifestations of split intransitivity within a level of conceptual semantics that he calls role structure. On Sadock's account, these semantic factors are somewhat variable across languages and constructions. Specifically in regard to German, Sadock (2012: 109) states: "I submit that the [semantic] entailments that figure in auxiliary selection are not precisely the same as those that determine whether a verb can occur in an impersonal passive." In this respect, Sadock agrees with the approach of Keller and Sorace (2003). His approach differs from theirs, however, in that the semantic properties relevant for auxiliary selection and impersonal passivization are confined to the level of conceptual semantics and specified independently of syntactic constituent structure. Syntactic structure, by contrast, is assumed to be simple and uniform across unaccusative and unergative predicates. Such an approach does not obviate the need for a precise specification of the relevant semantic factors, but does pave the way for a fully semantic account of the gradient acceptability judgments obtained by Keller and Sorace (2003). The authors themselves take a more moderate view, in which construction-specific semantic factors drive the acceptability ratings shown in their study, but a uniform syntactic distinction between unaccusative and unergative predicates is maintained in order to capture generalizations across languages and constructions (Keller and Sorace 2003: 62).

3.5 Conclusions

In this chapter, I have examined how the effects of syntactic factors can be distinguished from the effects of other types of linguistic knowledge when interpreting gradient patterns of acceptability judgments. I have argued that evidence from amelioration—improvement in acceptability due to a semantic, pragmatic, or prosodic manipulation—can be used to argue successfully in favor of a semantic, pragmatic, or prosodic explanation for a purportedly syntactic phenomenon. I have further argued that such evidence can be strengthened with data from spontaneous speech and from other types of psycholinguistic experiments. For example, in their study of pragmatic constraints on outbound anaphora, Ward et al. (1991) combined a close analysis of attested examples in context with data from a reading time experiment that probed the effects of discourse context in a tightly controlled manner. Similarly, in their study of factive and manner-of-speaking islands, Ambridge and Goldberg (2008) conducted separate but parallel experiments measuring the acceptability of long-distance questions with different main verbs and the degree to which non-interrogative versions of the same sentences were perceived as backgrounded. For both of these studies, I have argued that the evidence presented by the authors makes a compelling case for dispensing with the syntactic constraints on outbound anaphora and factive and manner-of-speaking islands in English that had been proposed in earlier work.

A purely pragmatic explanation for the observed patterns of acceptability can in this way simplify the syntactic component of the grammar. In considering Ambridge and Goldberg's (2008) analysis of factive and manner-of-speaking islands, I described two more recent studies on this topic. Liu et al. (2019) found that verb frame frequency appears to influence the acceptability of interrogative sentences with clausal complements (including factive and manner-of-speaking islands) and their declarative counterparts. In a similar experiment that also examined the effects of verb frame frequency, Richter and Chaves (2020) found variation within each verb class which was not due to verb frame frequency and which they believe indicates an effect of pragmatic factors. While additional studies are needed to demonstrate whether pragmatic effects apply independently of frequency effects, the available evidence from these studies suggests that the variation in acceptability among interrogative sentences with clausal complements is unlikely to be caused by differences in syntactic structure among different classes of verbs.

In the second half of the chapter, I have pointed to two possible reasons why a non-syntactic explanation might not be warranted, even when the semantic, pragmatic, or prosodic manipulation is successful. The first reason has to do with residual differences in acceptability that are not fully neutralized by manipulating the meaning, context, or prosody. Šimík and Wierzba (2015) found such a residual effect in their study of word order and prosody in Czech. Although they were able to account for most of the variation in judgments with their prosodic manipulation on auditory stimuli, they found a residual effect of definiteness which received no obvious explanation. The second reason why a non-syntactic explanation might not be warranted has to do with the theoretical approach that is adopted. Within derivational theories, the assumption of form–meaning isomorphism is so integral to the analysis of verbal event structure that syntax and semantics can hardly be considered separately. Rather, semantic factors that affect acceptability judgments are often considered to be symptomatic of underlying syntactic differences. Keller and Sorace (2003) provide a detailed and careful account of construction-specific semantic factors that affect German speakers' judgments of intransitive verbs with *sein*, *haben*, and impersonal passives. From this, they argue that the semantic basis of split intransitivity cannot be uniform across languages and constructions. However, they do not go so far as to propose a purely semantic explanation for their findings because they believe that the traditional syntactic analysis of unaccusative and unergative predicates is useful for maintaining broader generalizations. In fact, a purely semantic account of the German data only really makes sense within an approach that rejects the assumption of form–meaning isomorphism. As an example of this alternative approach, Sadock (2012) outlines a purely semantic account of auxiliary selection and impersonal passivization in German whereby distinct, construction-specific semantic representations are mapped to a simple syntactic structure which is the same for unaccusative and unergative predicates. I will return to this theme of form–meaning isomorphism again in

Chapter 6, in the context of interpreting various constraints on relative clause extraposition in English and German. For now, I will continue to explore the ongoing debate within experimental syntax over how to parcel out the different factors that affect acceptability judgments. In the following chapter, I discuss the major criteria that have been proposed in the literature for distinguishing between syntactic constraints and grammar-external processing constraints.

4

On distinguishing formal syntactic constraints from processing constraints

In Chapter 3, we considered several cases in which a semantic, pragmatic, or prosodic infelicity resulted in reduced acceptability for what were (arguably) syntactically well-formed sentences. Likewise, certain types of complexity can make a sentence harder to process, similarly resulting in reduced acceptability. For example, as part of a larger study on resumption and island effects in English, Greek, and German, Alexopoulou and Keller (2007) found differences in acceptability among different types of fully grammatical sentences. The interrogative sentences in (1), which are from their stimuli for the English experiment, vary in terms of depth of embedding of the gap.

(1) a. **Who** will we fire __ ?   (no embedding)
     b. **Who** does Mary claim we will fire __?   (single embedding)
     c. **Who** does Jane think Mary claims we will fire __?   (double embedding)

Results showed that sentences like (1a) with no embedding were judged as significantly more acceptable than sentences like (1c) with double embedding. Sentences like (1b) with single embedding were intermediate in acceptability, although they did not differ significantly from sentences with no embedding (2007: 119). Pointing to previous studies of the processing of long-distance dependencies, including Frazier and Clifton (1989) and Kluender and Kutas (1993), the authors interpret these differences in acceptability as effects of processing difficulty (2007: 136). Such a conclusion is relatively uncontroversial, given that sentences with the structural characteristics of (1b–c) can be found in corpora and have never been argued to be ungrammatical. Contrasts as in (2a–b), also from Alexopoulou and Keller's (2007) stimuli, have been more controversial, however.

(2) a. **Who** does Mary claim that we will fire __ ?   (single embedding, *that*)
     b. ?**Who** does Mary wonder whether we will fire __ ?
                                                          (single embedding, *whether*)
     c. *__**Who** does Mary meet the people that will fire __ ?   (single embedding, RC)

Alexopoulou and Keller (2007) found that sentences like (2b) were judged as significantly less acceptable than sentences like (2a). This contrast, which was noted by Chomsky (1973), has been well documented in other studies, and is now commonly

Gradient Acceptability and Linguistic Theory. Elaine J. Francis, Oxford University Press.
© Elaine J. Francis (2022). DOI: 10.1093/oso/9780192898944.003.0004

known as a *wh*-island effect. In a *wh*-island, a long-distance dependency is blocked by the presence of a *wh*-phrase (in this case, *whether*) in between the filler and the gap. A popular theoretical explanation says that this type of dependency violates the Subjacency condition, which bans movement across more than one bounding node (Chomsky 1981). Because *whether* occupies the usual landing site for cyclic movement, the word *who* must illegally cross two bounding nodes (here, clause boundaries) to form a sentence like (2b). Kluender and Kutas (1993) offered an alternative processing-based explanation. They argued that this difference in acceptability was due to the relative difficulty of processing the semantic content associated with *whether* vs. *that* at a clause boundary—a claim they also supported with data from online measures (specifically, ERP). Alexopoulou and Keller (2007) attempt to combine these two views by taking a gradient grammar perspective. They propose that (2b) in fact violates a grammatical constraint; however, they claim that the constraint in question is a 'weak island' (a type of soft constraint) which is grounded in processing difficulty. In support of their argument, they point to an additional result: the acceptability of *whether* questions as in (2b) was affected by depth of embedding in a manner similar to the fully grammatical sentences in (1a–c), and in contrast with strongly ungrammatical relative clause islands, as in (2c), which were equally unacceptable regardless of embedding.

How might we begin to distinguish between these alternative interpretations of contrasts such as (2a–b)? While the answer remains controversial, several types of arguments have figured prominently in the ongoing debates. Effects that have been claimed to favor a syntactic explanation include overgeneration of ungrammatical sentence types, cross-linguistic differences, resistance to repeated exposure effects, and resistance to individual differences in working memory capacity. Effects that have been claimed to favor a processing-based explanation include amelioration effects, isomorphism between acceptability ratings and online measures such as reading time, repeated exposure effects, and effects of individual differences in working memory capacity. Drawing on experimental work on island effects, subject–verb agreement, missing VP illusions, and Superiority effects, I will consider each of these arguments in turn. Where relevant, I will relate these arguments to the assumptions of different syntactic theories. While the concept of form–meaning isomorphism was important for interpreting certain semantic effects on acceptability as discussed in Chapter 3, the concept of gradient grammaticality will be significant for interpreting possible processing-based effects as described in the current chapter.

4.1 Amelioration and isomorphism

Similar to what we have seen in Chapter 3 with respect to pragmatic or prosodic manipulations, sentences that are grammatical but hard to process can often be made easier by manipulating the lexical content and/or the discourse context, resulting in improved acceptability ratings. In the context of island constraints, numerous examples of such amelioration effects, which are often characterized as 'exceptions' to island constraints, have been observed in the literature. I will focus on just one class of examples here: Complex NP Constraint violations. Complex NP configurations, as in (3a), involve a long-distance dependency within a clausal modifier or complement of a noun. Similar to *wh*-islands, Complex NP islands are standardly assumed to violate Subjacency (Chomsky 1981), since the *wh*-phrase must move across two bounding nodes (here, NP and IP, where IP refers to the clause excluding the complementizer *that*). While agreeing that sentences like (3a) are unacceptable, Hofmeister and Sag (2010) argue that this might be due to general processing factors rather than a syntactic constraint. They note that there are a few things that make the long-distance dependency difficult to process in a sentence like (3a). One is that readers or listeners must process three referential NPs (*the newscaster, reports, the legislature*) while holding the filler phrase in memory. Any of these NPs could potentially interfere with the retrieval of the filler at the gap site (Gibson 1998; Vasishth and Lewis 2006). They hypothesize that processing difficulty of this type can be alleviated by using a semantically richer filler phrase to increase activation of the filler, and by making the intervening NPs highly accessible first or second person pronouns. As initial evidence in favor of this hypothesis, they note that sentences like (3b) are "quite acceptable" (2010: 386). In our terms, the intuitive contrast between (3a) and (3b) is an example of an amelioration effect.

(3)   a. **Who** did the newscaster read reports that the legislature had impeached __ ?
      b. **Which politician** did you read reports that we had impeached __ ?

What might such an amelioration effect mean? If one assumes a categorical (as opposed to gradient) view of grammar, there are at least three possibilities. The first is that both sentences are ungrammatical due to a syntactic constraint, but (3b) is easier to process, giving the illusion of grammaticality. A second option is that both sentences are grammatical, but (3a) is more difficult to process, giving the illusion of ungrammaticality. Yet a third possibility is that (3a) is ungrammatical, but (3b) is grammatical due to an underlying difference in structure. With evidence from reading time and acceptability judgment tasks on the same stimuli, Hofmeister and Sag (2010) argue in favor of the second option. Their argument hinges not only on amelioration effects, but also on evidence of systematic correspondences between acceptability judgments and reading times—a type of evidence which Phillips (2013a: 162) refers to as isomorphism (not to be confused with form–meaning isomorphism, as discussed in Chapters 2–3).

I will limit the discussion here to three of the seven conditions that were tested in one of the two experiments, as illustrated in (4a–c). It was hypothesized that sentences like (4b) with a more complex filler phrase (*which convict*) should show faster reading times and higher acceptability ratings than sentences like (4a) with a bare pronoun (*who*) as the filler phrase. Non-island-violating sentences like (4c) were included as a baseline.

(4) a. I saw **who** Emma doubted reports that we had captured __ in the nationwide
     FBI manhunt.   (bare, island)
  b. I saw **which convict** Emma doubted reports that we had captured __ in the
     nationwide FBI manhunt.   (*which*, island)
  c. I saw **which convict** Emma doubted that we had captured __ in the
     nationwide FBI manhunt.   (*which*, non-island)

Results showed that reading times at the main verb (retrieval site for interpreting the
filler in context) were slower for sentences like (4a) with a bare filler phrase than for
sentences like (4b) with *which*+N. However, there was no effect of island status on
reading time: sentences like (4b) were read just as quickly as fully grammatical sentences like (4c). These results invite the authors' conclusion that both (4b) and (4c)
are grammatical, and by extension, (4a) is grammatical as well, albeit more difficult to
process. However, the results of the judgment task on the same stimuli complicate this
picture somewhat. Similar to the reading time results, island-violating sentences with
a bare filler phrase were judged as less acceptable than similar sentences with a complex filler phrase. However, both types of island-violating sentences were judged as
less acceptable than the grammatical baseline condition as in (4c). The authors argue
that this was likely due to a difference in semantic and pragmatic complexity which
affected acceptability judgments after the entire sentence was read, but which did not
affect first-pass reading times. In support of their conclusion, they point to evidence
from response times on the comprehension questions that came at the end of each
trial, which were significantly slower (but equally accurate) for the island-violating
sentences than for the baseline sentences.

Phillips (2013a: 162–9) argues that such evidence from amelioration and isomorphism is helpful, but ambiguous. Arguably, Hofmeister and Sag's (2010) data are still
consistent with the first and third options mentioned above. For example, the improvement in acceptability of (4b) over (4a) might mean that the sentences with more
complex fillers are easier to comprehend (hence the difference in reading times), even
though they are still ungrammatical. According to this account, the lower acceptability
of the island-violating sentences compared to the baseline reflects a difference in grammaticality. Alternatively, the higher acceptability of (4b) compared with (4a) could
mean that (4b) is actually grammatical because the more complex filler phrase changes
the structure in such a way as to circumvent the island violation. Such an account,
known as D-linking, has been proposed for other types of island violations, including
Superiority (Pesetsky 1987) and *wh*-islands (Rizzi 2004). Under such an account, the
slower readings times for bare filler sentences like (4a) would be due to the relative
difficulty of processing an ungrammatical dependency. As Goodall (2015: 6) notes,
however, Complex NP islands as in (10a–b) have been considered 'strong islands'
(Szabolcsi 2006), which unlike 'weak islands' (e.g. *wh*-islands) should not be subject
to D-linking effects under standard assumptions.

Data from two additional studies give us reasons to doubt the validity of the D-
linking account, which says that sentences like (4a) and (4b) differ in grammaticality.

Hofmeister and Sag (2010) cite reading time data from Hofmeister's (2007) dissertation showing an apparent D-linking effect even for fully grammatical *wh*-questions.
Hofmeister (2007) found faster reading times at the main verb (here *record*) for questions with complex fillers, as in (5a), as compared with similar questions with bare
fillers, as in (5b).

(5)   a. **Which album** did the musician that Robert saw record __ with two popular
         blues guitarists?
      b. **What** did the musician that Robert saw record __ with two popular blues
         guitarists?

Hofmeister and Sag (2010) argue that such a difference in reading time is unexpected
if D-linking is a device for saving an ungrammatical sentence, but is fully expected
under a processing-based account. Goodall (2015) provides further evidence along the
same lines from acceptability judgments of island-violating and non-island-violating
sentences. Four of Goodall's six experimental conditions are given in (6a–d).

(6)   a. **What** do you believe the claim that he might buy __ ?
      b. **Which of the cars** do you believe the claim that he might buy __?
      c. **What** do you believe that he might buy __?
      d. **Which of the cars** do you believe that he might buy __ ?

Goodall found a significant effect of filler type for both Complex NP islands, as in
(6a–b) and grammatical non-islands, as in (6c–d). For both pairs of conditions, complex fillers were rated as more acceptable than bare fillers. This is shown in Figure 4.1
by the dark and light bars in the CNPC (left) and *that*-clause (right) conditions.

  As Goodall argues, these results lend further support to the idea that D-linking
is a processing effect. In addition, there was an effect of island status, such that
non-island questions (6c–d) were more acceptable than island-violating questions
(6a–b). Goodall interprets this to mean that despite the amelioration effect of filler
type, island-violating sentences like (6b) are still ungrammatical. This interpretation
depends on a subtle and controversial argument, which says that if the lower acceptability of island-violating questions were due to processing difficulty, there should
have been a bigger effect of filler type for island-violating questions (6a–b) than for
non-island questions (6c–d). This assumption depends on the resource capacity theory of Kluender and Kutas (1993), which says that when different processing demands
combine together to exceed a certain threshold of working memory capacity, superadditive effects on acceptability (i.e. a larger effect than would be expected by simply
adding two independent factors together) can occur. A similar superadditive effect is
predicted by the D-linking approach: there should be a bigger effect of filler type for
the island-violating conditions, since these are the only conditions in which D-linking
is expected to apply at all. However, the results showed that there was no interaction
between filler type and island status, and hence no superadditive effect at all. Rather,
the two factors (filler type and island status) showed a simple additive effect. Goodall

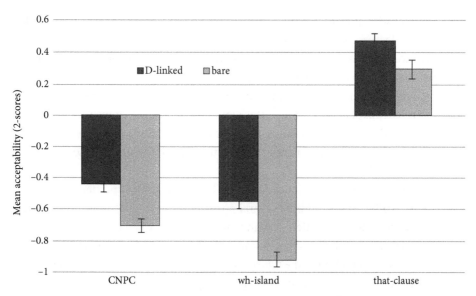

Fig. 4.1 Mean acceptability ratings of bare and D-linked *wh*-questions in CNPC island, *wh*-island, and non-island (*that*-clause) conditions

Source: From Goodall (2015: 5).

(2015) tentatively concludes that such an outcome is likely due to a processing effect of filler type combined with a grammatical constraint on island configurations. However, an equally plausible explanation for the additive effect would be that both effects (filler type and island status) are due to processing costs, but the combination of those processing costs does not exceed the resource capacity threshold. Such an interpretation receives some support from the fact that participants in Hofmeister and Sag's (2010) study were able to answer the comprehension questions about the stimulus sentences just as accurately for Complex NP islands as for non-island baseline sentences (2010: 391).

To sum up, Hofmeister and Sag (2010) argued in favor of a processing account of Complex NP islands, based on evidence from amelioration due to filler complexity as well as isomorphism between acceptability ratings and reading times. However, we noted following Phillips's (2013b) approach that these results are ambiguous among at least three possible interpretations. Goodall's (2015) similar results from acceptability judgment tasks can help us rule out the grammar-based D-linking account, which says that the complex filler is a device to circumvent the syntactic island constraint. However, it appears that the results are still ambiguous with respect to the source of the island effect itself. While Hofmeister and Sag (2010) attribute this effect to processing factors, Goodall (2015) attributes it to a grammatical constraint. Both explanations appear to be compatible with the assumptions of the resource–capacity theory of Kluender and Kutas (1993). Further complicating the issue, there is also the possibility of a gradient grammar approach. As noted in the introduction to this chapter, Alexopoulou and Keller (2007) attributed the lower acceptability of *whether*-islands in comparison with non-islands to a 'weak island' (soft constraint) that is grounded in processing factors. This was part of a three-way distinction between embedded questions (non-islands), *whether*-islands (weak islands), and relative clause islands (strong islands) shown in their study. The lower acceptability of Complex NP islands as compared with non-islands shown by Hofmeister and Sag (2010) and Goodall (2015) could be similarly explained, although this would go against the conventional wisdom that Complex NPs are 'strong islands' (Szabolcsi 2006). In any case, there seems to be little evidence available from these studies to identify the ultimate source of the observed island effect.

What types of additional evidence might be helpful here? Hofmeister et al. (2013) and Phillips (2013a; 2013b) address several possibilities, including repeated exposure effects, effects of individual differences in working memory capacity, overgeneration of ungrammatical sentences, and cross-linguistic differences. In the remainder of this chapter, I provide a sampling of the types of arguments that have used these data types to support either a syntactic or a processing-based perspective. I refer the reader to the chapters in Sprouse and Hornstein (2013) for a more detailed overview.

4.2 Syntactic satiation

As summarized in a recent handbook chapter by William Snyder (2020), numerous studies have shown that at least in some cases, acceptability judgments of unacceptable or marginally acceptable sentences improve following repeated presentations of stimuli with the same syntactic structures, but distinct lexical content (Chaves and Dery 2014; Francom 2009; Hofmeister et al. 2013; Luka and Barsalou 2005; Snyder 2000). This phenomenon, known as 'syntactic satiation' (Snyder 2000), is an instance of the more general phenomenon of 'structural priming'—a facilitation effect in production and/or comprehension due to repeated exposure to the same grammatical structures. The most commonly reported structural priming effects involve the tendency to produce structures that have been recently heard or read (Pickering and Ferreira 2008). Syntactic satiation effects are relevant in the current context because they have been used as evidence in the debate over syntactic vs. processing-based accounts of island constraints.

Sprouse (2007b: 119–23) argued that syntactic satiation in judgment tasks can help distinguish between sentences that are ungrammatical and those that are grammatical but difficult to process. He hypothesized that representations of grammatical sentences can be constructed during language processing, but representations of ungrammatical sentences cannot be so constructed. Since structures must be represented in memory in order to be recognized during processing as similar to previously encountered structures, he predicts that only grammatical sentences should display repeated exposure effects. He recognizes that this prediction goes against earlier data from Snyder (2000), who found satiation effects for *wh*-islands and Complex NP islands in English. However, he attributes Snyder's finding to a confound in the design of the judgment task (an unbalanced item set). Sprouse's (2007b) own judgment tasks, which eliminate this confound, are consistent with this hypothesis. For four different types of syntactic islands in English (Subject islands, *wh*-islands, Complex NP islands, and Adjunct islands), Sprouse found that acceptability judgments did not significantly change following repeated exposures. He takes this as evidence in favor of the hypothesis that ungrammatical structures do not show repeated exposure effects.

Sprouse's (2007b) proposal that only grammatical sentences should show syntactic satiation effects was an exciting one for experimental syntax because it seemed to provide a straightforward way to distinguish between grammatical and ungrammatical sentences of equal acceptability. However, subsequent studies, as discussed by Hofmeister et al. (2013) and Snyder (2020), cast doubt on the validity of satiation effects as a test for grammaticality. Some additional studies have shown repeated exposure effects for three of the four island types that Sprouse (2007b) tested: *wh*-islands (Crawford 2012; Francom 2009; Snyder 2018), Complex NP islands (Goodall 2011), and Subject islands (Chaves and Dery 2014; 2018; Francom 2009). Strikingly, Snyder (2018) found significant repeated exposure effects for *whether*-islands which persisted long after the experiment was over. Fifteen participants completed a judgment experiment and came back four weeks later for a second experiment. In the first experiment, participants started with an average acceptance rate of 26.7% for *whether*-islands and by the end of the session showed a 66.7% acceptance rate. In the second experiment four weeks later, the same participants started the experiment with a mean acceptance rate of 73.3%, and none of them reverted to the lower acceptance rate shown at the beginning of the first experiment (Snyder 2018; 2020). Although the grammatical status of *whether*-islands remains controversial, these findings suggest that satiation is a form of learning.

Because the status of island effects is controversial to start with, experiments showing repeated exposure effects in island structures have been interpreted differently by different authors, and have failed to provide definitive evidence regarding the grammatical status of these structures. More informative are findings from Hofmeister et al. (2013) showing that ungrammatical sentences with jumbled word order, as in (7a), still showed satiation effects. The authors conjecture that through repeated exposure, participants learned to rely less on word order to construct meaningful interpretations, causing acceptability to rise during the course of the experiment. Contra Sprouse's (2007a) hypothesis, it appears there does not need to be a preexisting syntactic representation available in order for structures to receive a representation (presumably a provisional one, in this case) and prime each other. Conversely, Hofmeister et al. (2013) showed that sentences with multiple center embeddings, as in (7b), did not show any amelioration with repeated exposure. Such sentences are generally assumed to be grammatical but difficult to process (see Miller and Chomsky 1963).

(7)   a. Iran has gun-control strict laws that bar private citizens carrying from firearms.
      b. The cheerleader who the quarterback who was on the team dated snubbed the teammates although this hurt her reputation.

Following Francom (2009), Hofmeister et al. (2013) suggest that interpretability (i.e. ease with which a sentence can be parsed and assigned a meaning) may be an important factor in determining whether acceptability ratings will show satiation effects or not. More importantly for the goals of experimental syntax, it appears that satiation is affected by multiple factors and therefore not a litmus test for grammaticality.

On a more hopeful note, repeated exposure effects have been used successfully in conjunction with other types to data to support syntactic or processing-based accounts of particular structures. To conclude this section, I will consider exemplary studies by Goodall (2011) and Chaves and Dery (2018). Goodall (2011) set out to test whether repeated exposure effects would apply similarly to unacceptable *wh*-questions in Spanish and their English equivalents. Acceptability judgment tasks with binary (yes–no) response options were conducted in Spanish with Spanish-speaking participants from Mexico and in English with English-speaking participants from the United States. Goodall included several types of unacceptable questions, but was particularly interested in questions with no inversion of the auxiliary in English as in (8a), or of the main verb in Spanish as in (8b), both of which are generally assumed to be ungrammatical.

(8)   a. *What Maria will say?   (compare: What will Maria say?)
      b. *Qué María dijo?   (compare: Qué dijo María?)
         what María said

Although the unacceptable questions in (8a–b) are similar, the overall distribution of inversion in the two languages is rather different. Goodall points out that some syntactic analyses have treated inversion in Spanish as essentially similar to English (i.e. as involving T-to-C movement), while others have claimed that what appears to be inversion in Spanish actually involves some other syntactic operation. Yet a third possibility, which Goodall had proposed in earlier work (2010), is that sentences like (8b) do not violate any syntactic constraints at all, but rather they are unacceptable because the subject intervenes between the *wh*-phrase and the verb, making the filler–gap dependency more difficult to process. Goodall (2010) supported this view with experiments showing that acceptability ratings of no-inversion questions varied depending on the complexity of the intervening subject and the nature of the interrogative phrase. Results of Goodall's (2011) yes–no acceptability judgment tasks showed that Spanish speakers rated no-inversion questions as acceptable significantly more often following repeated exposures, while English speakers showed no changes in their responses to no-inversion questions following repeated exposures. Based on these results, Goodall (2011) argues that the unacceptability of (8b) most likely derives from a different source than that of (8a), possibly reflecting the application of different grammatical principles, or possibly reflecting a processing-based effect in the case of Spanish. A third possibility that Goodall did not consider is that no-inversion questions in Spanish violate a soft constraint, while no-inversion questions in English violate a hard constraint. This would be consistent with Sorace and Keller's (2005) proposal, which says that soft constraints are subject to contextual variation in acceptability, while hard constraints are not. Using Linear OT, they model this difference in terms of contextually variable vs. stable constraint weightings for the two kinds of constraints. Goodall (2011) concludes that satiation effects in Spanish provide one type of evidence against a unified syntactic analysis of inversion in Spanish and English and, in conjunction with other types of evidence, help support a processing-based account of the constraints on verb position in Spanish interrogatives. More generally, he shows that there is a useful distinction to be drawn between structures which do not show repeated exposure effects and those that do. In such cases, the source of unacceptability is unlikely to be exactly the same.

As a final example of how satiation effects can be used effectively as part of a larger argument, let's briefly consider the case of Subject islands in English. Subject islands are configurations in which a *wh*-phrase is extracted from a position within the subject, as shown in (9b) (Chaves and Dery 2018: 484).

(9)   a. **Which country** does the King of Spain resemble the President of __?
      b. **Which country** does the President of __ resemble the King of Spain?

Subject islands are known to vary in acceptability depending on the lexical content and the type of phrase extracted from, but they are most commonly analyzed as ungrammatical due to a syntactic violation (Chomsky 1986a; Rizzi 1990). However, Chaves (2013) presents an alternative view which says that Subject islands are not ungrammatical, but rather they are less acceptable in contexts where the gap position is less expected. He supports this view with evidence from amelioration effects due to semantic, pragmatic, and prosodic manipulations which provide additional cues for interpreting the gap location. Chaves and Dery (2018) use evidence from repeated exposure effects in support of Chaves's (2013) proposal. Their position is tricky to defend, since previous studies had failed to consistently show repeated exposure effects for Subject islands. While Chaves and Dery (2014) and Francom (2009) found that Subject islands became more acceptable following repeated exposures, Crawford (2012), Goodall (2011), Snyder (2000), and Sprouse (2007b) found no effects of repeated exposures for this structure. To distinguish their design from that of previous studies that found no effects, Chaves and Dery (2018) constructed the stimuli to be semantically felicitous by including a common noun within the *wh*-phrase which was closely related to the head noun and also relevant for the main predication of the sentence, as in (9b). Also unlike previous studies, they used reversible predicates such as *resemble* so that the meaning of the Subject island sentence was almost the same as that of the corresponding grammatical control sentence (9b), and they conducted a norming task to ensure that the declarative versions of sentence pairs such as (9a–b) were equally plausible. Results of a scalar acceptability judgment experiment showed that Subject island sentences like (9b) started out as less acceptable than grammatical control sentences like (9a), but within eight exposures, the two sentence types were rated as equally acceptable. (The acceptability of control sentences like (9a) did not change with repeated exposures.) The authors take these findings as evidence in support of the view that Subject islands are syntactically well-formed: "Subject Island effects (and certain other phenomena) are instead due to probabilistic knowledge about the distribution of gaps: if the correct location of a gap is syntactically, semantically, or pragmatically highly unlikely in that particular utterance, then it is less likely for the sentence to be acceptable" (Chaves and Dery 2018: 479).

Importantly, Chaves and Dery (2018) present corroborating evidence for this proposal from one other acceptability judgment experiment and two self-paced reading experiments. For example, one of the self-paced reading experiments tested the same type of Subject island sentences as in (9b), but with an adverb inserted before the main verb to induce a temporary garden path reading. Stimuli were presented in two blocks, such that the first block consisted of 15 Subject island sentences and 30 distractor sentences for one group of participants, and 45 distractor sentences for the second group of participants. The second block, which was the same for both participant groups, consisted of 10 Subject island sentences and 20 distractor sentences. Results for the Subject island sentences in the second block showed that the participants who had read Subject island sentences in the first block showed faster reading times at the main verb region (the disambiguation point) than participants who had read only distractor sentences. This finding suggests that the subject-internal gap was less surprising to the participants who had recently read similar sentences, and is consistent with their hypothesis that Subject islands are less acceptable and more difficult to process to the extent that a within-subject gap is unexpected. In conclusion, both Goodall (2011) and Chaves and Dery (2018) show how repeated exposure effects in acceptability judgments can be used along with other types of evidence to help determine the grammatical status of unacceptable sentence types, even though they cannot be taken on their own as a test for grammaticality.

4.3 Working memory capacity

Satiation effects have been claimed to target only grammatical sentences that present some processing difficulty, the idea being that repeated exposure facilitates processing, but only for licit structures that can be constructed by the grammar and activated during processing. Similar arguments have been put forth regarding individual differences in working memory capacity (Phillips 2013a; Sprouse et al. 2012). The idea is that individuals with a higher capacity should find grammatical but hard-to-process sentences more acceptable than individuals with a lower capacity. In contrast, working memory capacity should not affect participants' ratings of ungrammatical sentences, since the application of syntactic constraints apparently does not depend on working memory capacity. When applied to sentences of controversial grammatical status, such as island-violating sentences, an effect of working memory capacity on acceptability ratings can then be taken as evidence in favor of a processing-based analysis and against an analysis that says such sentences are ungrammatical.

The first major study of acceptability judgments in relation to working memory capacity tested various types of island-violating sentences and showed a null effect, which the authors interpreted to support a syntactic account of island constraints. Sprouse et al. (2012) tested participants on four different types of island-violating sentences in an acceptability judgment task. For each of the four island types, they manipulated two factors: island status (whether the sentence contained an island configuration or not) and gap position (whether the gap functioned as subject of the matrix clause or as a complement within the embedded clause). An example of the four Complex NP island conditions is given in (10a–d). Of the four conditions, only the island embedded condition, as in (10d) actually violates the Complex NP Constraint. The remaining conditions in (10a–c) are fully grammatical according to both syntactic and processing accounts of islands.

(10) a. **Who** __ claimed that John bought a car?   (non-island, matrix)
       b. **What** did you claim that John bought __?   (non-island, embedded)
       c. **Who** __ made the claim that John bought a car?   (island, matrix)
       d. **What** did you make the claim that John bought __?   (island, embedded)

It was expected that due to the general difficulty of processing long-distance dependencies, embedded conditions would be less acceptable than matrix conditions. It was further expected that this difference between matrix and embedded conditions would be greater for the island sentences. In other words, the acceptability ratings should show a superadditive effect of embedding within the island conditions (10c–d). Results showed the expected superadditive effect for each island type. As shown in Figure 4.2, matrix questions like (10a) and (10c) (left) were equally acceptable, embedded questions like (10b) (top right) were significantly less acceptable than the matrix questions, and island-violating embedded questions like (10d) (bottom right) were least acceptable of the four conditions (Sprouse et al. 2012: 97).

Similar results were reported for the other three island types. To achieve a measure of the size of the superadditive effect for each individual participant within each island type, the authors calculated a DD (differences-in-differences) score based on the z-transformed acceptability ratings. Essentially, this score measured the difference

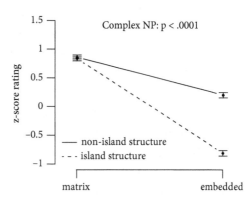

Fig. 4.2 Mean acceptability ratings for island and non-island Complex NP questions

Source: Republished with permission of the Linguistic Society of America from Sprouse et al. (2012: 97); permission conveyed through Copyright Clearance Center.

between the non-island embedded question and the island-violating embedded question (10b–d), and then subtracted from that the difference between the two matrix conditions (10a–c). Thus, a larger DD value represents a stronger island effect.

Sprouse et al. (2012) also tested each participant in two memory tasks: serial recall and *n*-back. For each trial in the serial recall task, participants listened to eight words and then attempted to recall all of the words in the same order. The same eight words were used in all of the trials, but the order of items was different for each trial. For each trial of the *n*-back tasks, participants viewed one of eight possible letters on the screen and were asked if the same letter appeared *n* trials prior to the current trial. Three *n*-back tasks were given in order of increasing difficulty: two-back (n = 2), three-back (n = 3), and four-back (n = 4). Results showed that as expected, participants varied across a range of working memory capacities. However, individual scores on the memory tasks did not show any systematic relationship with individual scores (DD scores) in the judgment task. Although they considered several possible explanations for the null result, the authors ultimately conclude that participants rated the sentences in the island-violating conditions as less acceptable because such sentences were grammatically ill-formed and not because they were more difficult to process.

In their reply to Sprouse et al. (2012), Hofmeister et al. (2012) argue against the conclusion that the null result favors a syntactic account of island constraints. Although they criticize the study and its conclusions on several grounds, I will focus on just one main criticism here. Hofmeister et al. (2012) argue that Sprouse et al. (2012) did not first establish any baseline for interpreting the data from controversial sentences involving island constraints. That is, they did not demonstrate how participants with different working memory scores respond to fully grammatical sentences of different levels of processing difficulty. To address this issue, Hofmeister et al. (2013: 55–6) examined grammatical (non-island) sentences that are difficult to process for well-understood reasons. They tested short *wh*-dependencies (11a–b) and long *wh*-dependencies (9c–d). All stimuli also included a relative clause containing either a subject (11a, c) or object (11b, d) dependency.

(11)   a. Someone figured out **which politician** __ wrote that Robert bribed a
          reporter that trusted Nancy without thinking about it.   (short-SRC)
       b. Someone figured out **which politician** __ wrote that Robert bribed a
          reporter that trusted Nancy without thinking about it.   (short-ORC)
       c. Someone figured out **which politician** a reporter that trusted Nancy wrote
          that Robert bribed __ without thinking about it.   (long-SRC)
       d. Someone figured out **which politician** a reporter that Nancy trusted wrote
          that Robert bribed __ without thinking about it.   (long-ORC)

To test for effects of individual differences in working memory capacity, Hofmeister et al. (2013) included a reading span task. Similar to the serial recall task that Sprouse et al. (2012) used, this task required participants to read a list of sentences and then recall the last word of each sentence in the correct order. The results showed that short *wh*-dependencies produced the expected correlation between working memory capacity and acceptability judgments: participants with higher reading span scores rated sentences like (11a–b) as more acceptable than participants with lower scores did. However, for the conditions with long *wh*-dependencies, there was no relationship between reading span score and acceptability. The authors suggest that the more difficult sentences possibly showed a floor effect, such that even high-capacity individuals could not process them efficiently and so did not rate them more highly than low-capacity individuals did. In this light, Hofmeister et al. (2013) suggest that the null results shown by Sprouse et al. (2012) could similarly be a floor effect, indicating that the island-violating sentences were just too difficult for working memory capacity to make much difference. Some possible support for this explanation comes from Sprouse et al.'s own data (2012: 116–17). In an analysis that specifically targeted the dependency length effect in non-island sentences, as in (10a–b), Sprouse et al. (2012) found a significant difference between the low- and high-capacity groups as defined by their performance in the three-back task. (No group differences showed up for the serial recall task.) However, this difference only showed up in the easiest condition: the non-island matrix condition (10a). The high-capacity group rated these sentences as more acceptable than the low-capacity group did and as a result, showed a greater effect of dependency distance. Non-island embedded sentences were rated as lower than non-island matrix sentences by both groups, but there was no difference between the two groups in judgments of the non-island embedded sentences (10b). Since it is assumed that both types of non-island sentences are grammatical but difficult to process, but only the easier matrix condition showed any difference attributable to working memory capacity, it is possible that the non-island embedded sentences showed a floor effect similar to what Hofmeister et al. (2013) describe for non-island sentences like (11c–d). At the least, the lack of any difference in acceptability due to working memory capacity for non-island embedded sentences casts some doubt on the premise that grammatical but difficult-to-process sentences should generally show such differences. Thus, it can be argued that the lack of relationship between working memory capacity and acceptability of island-violating sentences does not rule out the possibility that such sentences are grammatical. More research is needed to understand how working memory capacity affects acceptability judgments for different types of (uncontroversially) grammatical and ungrammatical sentences.

4.4 Overgeneration of ungrammatical sentences

Phillips (2013a) argues that evidence from isomorphism between acceptability judgments and online measures such as reading time is often ambiguous with respect to the source of the isomorphism. He is more optimistic, however, when there is a lack of isomorphism: "it is particularly informative when we encounter situations where on-line processes construct representations that are judged as unacceptable in off-line tasks" (Phillips 2013a: 170). Phillips is referring here to *overgeneration*: cases in which apparently ungrammatical representations are produced or accepted under limited circumstances. For example, he points out that English speakers sometimes produce or accept sentences with subject–verb agreement errors, especially in cases where a plural noun that is not the head of the subject NP triggers a plural verb form, as in: *The key to the cabinets are on the table.* This phenomenon, known as agreement attraction, is widely recognized as a type of grammatical error that sometimes occurs during online production and comprehension (Bock and Cutting 1992; Eberhard, Cutting, and Bock 2005; Franck, Vigliocco, and Nicol 2002; Thornton and MacDonald 2003). This type of error qualifies as overgeneration in Phillips's sense, since such sentences are generally rated as unacceptable in untimed judgment tasks. Pertinent to the issue of distinguishing between grammatical and processing-based explanations, Phillips (2013a: 175) discusses more controversial cases such as (10), in which plural number marking on the verb within a relative clause matches the plural marking on the head noun rather than matching the singular marking on the clause-internal subject. This is in contrast to the ordinary pattern, as shown in (12b), in which the same verb agrees with its clause-internal subject.

(12) a. *The **drivers** who the runner **wave** to each morning honk back cheerfully.
      b. The drivers who the **runner waves** to each morning honk back cheerfully.
      c. *The **driver** who the runner **wave** to each morning honk back cheerfully.

Phillips (2013a) observes that sentences like (12a) are accepted more often than comparable sentences such as (12c), even though both sentence types are normally understood to be ungrammatical. He argues based on reading time and judgment data from Wagers et al. (2009) that agreement attraction of the type illustrated in (12a) is the result of faulty memory retrieval mechanisms which all speakers share. This explanation is in contrast to that of Kimball and Aissen (1971), who characterize sentences like (12a) as showing a well-formed agreement pattern from a nonstandard dialect. For Phillips (2013a), (12a) involves agreement attraction, but (12c) does not. This is because in (12c), the first noun is singular, and only plural nouns have been shown to induce this type of effect. For Kimball and Aissen (1971), (10a) is actually a permissible form (although perhaps not the preferred form) in some dialects of American English. The status of (10c) as an ungrammatical sentence (regardless of dialect) is not controversial.

Although the precise mechanisms that cause agreement attraction have been a matter for debate (Eberhard et al. 2005; Staub 2009; Tanner et al. 2014; Wagers et al. 2009), Phillips (2013a) argues convincingly that an overgeneration account is more plausible than an account in which (12a) is grammatically licensed in some dialects and not others. Primarily citing results from Wagers et al. (2009), he discusses three main types of evidence in favor of this conclusion. One is that this effect is not limited to a particular regional dialect, but rather is observed across speakers of different dialects of English. Second, the data from acceptability judgments show a different profile than what we find with grammatically licensed agreement patterns. Speakers accepted sentences like (12a) much more often than they accepted similar ungrammatical sentences like

(12c) in speeded judgment tasks. Similarly, sentences like (12a) showed less disruption from the agreement violation during self-paced reading than sentences like (12c) did. Most importantly for distinguishing this from a non-standard dialect, the amelioration effect on acceptability was much weaker for untimed judgments than for timed judgments. According to Phillips, such a difference between timed and untimed judgments suggests that participants' acceptance of this structure was only fleeting, and therefore more likely to be detected in a timed task. In contrast, a grammatically licensed agreement pattern should show a more stable level of acceptance across different types of judgment tasks. Finally, data from timed judgments and reading times showed asymmetries between grammatical and ungrammatical sentences and between singular and plural attractors that are characteristic of uncontroversial cases of agreement attraction, suggesting that the higher acceptance rate of (12a) as opposed to (12c) is in fact a type of agreement attraction.

While some of the characteristics of this example in (12a–c), such as the asymmetry between singular and plural attractors, appear to be specific to agreement attraction, Phillips provides two main diagnostics that can be applied more generally to identify cases of overgeneration: (1) overgeneration effects should not systematically vary according to the dialect or language background of the participant; (2) overgeneration effects should be relatively fleeting, resulting in a discrepancy between online and offline measures. Specifically, untimed judgments should show less of an amelioration effect than timed judgments, reading times, or other online measures. In support of the latter diagnostic, we find this type of pattern in uncontroversial cases of overgeneration, such as the so-called missing VP illusion. For example, Gibson and Thomas (1999) investigated the acceptability of sentences as in (13a–b). According to Miller and Chomsky (1963), among others, sentences like (13a) are fully grammatical but difficult to process due multiple center embeddings. Sentences like (13b), however, are clearly ungrammatical, because the second VP is missing. That is, there is no verb to accompany the subject NP *the graduate student* in (13b). Although VP ellipsis is possible in English, the elided VP must have an antecedent to receive an interpretation. There is no such antecedent in (13b).

(13)   a. The ancient manuscript that the graduate student who the new card catalog had confused a great deal was studying in the library was missing a page.
       b. *The ancient manuscript that the graduate student who the new card catalog had confused a great deal was missing a page.
       c. *The ancient manuscript that the graduate student who the new card catalog was studying in the library was missing a page.

Using an untimed questionnaire, Gibson and Thomas (1999) found that participants' complexity ratings of ungrammatical sentences like (13b) did not differ from their ratings of grammatical sentences like (13a). In contrast, their ratings of ungrammatical sentences such as (13c), in which the first VP is missing, were rated as higher in complexity than the grammatical sentences. In a subsequent study that investigated similar

sentences, Christiansen and MacDonald (2009) used a word-by-word self-paced reading procedure which did not allow participants to reread any words before giving their
judgment. Participants were instructed to read the sentences as quickly as possible,
and to reject the sentence at the point where it was perceived as ungrammatical. At
the end, they gave an acceptability rating for the sentence. The results showed that
ungrammatical sentences like (13b) were rated as significantly higher in acceptability
than grammatical sentences like (13a). Consistent with Phillips's (2013a) prediction
that overgeneration should result in a discrepancy between untimed judgments and
online measures, Christiansen and MacDonald (2009) found what appears to be a
stronger amelioration effect for missing VP sentences in a word-by-word reading task
than what Gibson and Thomas (1999) found for the same sentences in an untimed
judgment task.

Although Christiansen and MacDonald (2009) used a subset of the same stimulus
sentences used in Gibson and Thomas (1999), it is not clear what effect the difference
in instructions (complexity ratings vs. acceptability ratings) or the difference in procedure (the possibility to reject the sentence as ungrammatical before reading all of it
in Christianson and MacDonald's study) might have had on the results. We can, however, find some further corroboration for a difference between timed and untimed
judgments for similar missing VP sentences in German. According to Bader (2016:
10), a conference presentation by Bader et al. (2003) reported the results of a speeded
judgment task that examined German sentences such as (14a–b). The task required
participants to read the sentence and choose between two options ('grammatical' and
'ungrammatical') as quickly as possible.

(14) a. Heute morgen ist das Programm,   das den Programmierer,
         today morning is the program   that the programmer
         der die Dokumentation erstellen musste,   geärgert hat, abgestürzt.
         who the documentation compile must   bothered has crashed
         'This morning, the program that had bothered the programmer who had to
         compile the documentation crashed.'
      b. *Heute morgen ist das Programm,   das den Programmierer,
         today morning is   the program   that the programmer
         der die Dokumentation erstellen musste,   abgestürzt.
         who the documentation compile must   crashed
         'This morning, the program that the programmer who had to compile the
         documentation crashed.'

Bader et al. (2003) found that participants accepted complete grammatical sentences
as in (14a) 76% of the time, while still accepting missing VP sentences as in (14b) 57%
of the time. A follow-up study by Häussler and Bader (2015: 9) found similar results for
the same sentences in an untimed judgment task. While this task also asked for binary
grammaticality judgments, items were presented on a written questionnaire, and participants were allowed to take as much time as they needed to make a decision. In line

with Phillips's (2013a) diagnostic, the results showed a bigger difference between the grammatical and ungrammatical sentences for the untimed task than for the speeded judgment task. Participants accepted complete sentences with no missing VP at a rate of 81%, while accepting sentences in which the second VP was missing at a rate of 33%. Since the improved acceptability of ungrammatical sentences like (14b) is a clear case of overgeneration (nobody disputes that missing VP sentences are ungrammatical), this difference between the two task types supports Phillips's (2013a) diagnostic. More generally, by identifying overgenerated forms, we can reasonably hypothesize the existence of some grammatical constraint (e.g. an elided VP cannot be licensed without an appropriate antecedent) that normally rules out such forms.

As with other metrics proposed to distinguish grammatical constraints from other types of constraints, we should be cautious in interpreting an observed difference between timed and untimed tasks as necessarily due to overgeneration of ungrammatical forms. For example, such a pattern could potentially emerge for a grammatical sentence type that is difficult to process, but which is temporarily parsed as a different sentence type that is easier to process. A potential source of such an effect could be cleft sentences in English. Previous research has shown that object cleft sentences, as in (13a), are more difficult to comprehend that subject cleft sentences, as in (13b), due to the noncanonical ordering of semantic roles (Patient–Agent–Verb) in object clefts. In a decision task that asked participants to listen to a sentence and then identify either the Agent or Patient of the action, Ferreira (2003) found that participants commonly interpreted object cleft sentences, as in (15a), as though they were subject clefts, as in (15b). However, subject clefts were rarely misinterpreted.

(15)   a. It was the man who the woman visited.

                    (Agent = the woman; Patient = the man)

       b. It was the man who visited the woman.

                    (Agent = the man; Patient = the woman)

Ferreira (2003: 186) reported that the Agent argument was misidentified in 21% of trials for items similar to (15a), but only for 2% of trials for items similar to (15b). Similarly, the Patient argument was misidentified in 22% of trials for items similar to (15a), but in only 5% of trials for items similar to (15b). Ferreira attributed this pattern of results to a shallow processing strategy ('good-enough processing') by which participants interpreted the ordering of arguments according to a simple heuristic (Agent–Verb–Patient) rather than computing the full syntactic structure. While this heuristic works for identifying the semantic roles of a subject cleft or an ordinary transitive clause, it does not work for identifying the semantic roles of an object cleft.

It is possible that such shallow processing strategies could be reflected in judgment tasks, leading participants to accept object cleft sentences less often in untimed tasks (where they would be more likely to compute the full syntactic structure) as compared with timed tasks (where they would be more likely to use the Agent–Verb–Patient heuristic). Another possibility, of course, is that object clefts would show equally high acceptability (a ceiling effect) in both types of tasks. The main point here is that if any difference between timed and untimed judgment tasks were to show up for fully grammatical sentences that are infrequent or hard to process (as opposed to overgenerated ungrammatical sentences), it would most likely show up in the context of shallow parsing.

4.5 Cross-linguistic differences: Superiority effects in Czech, English, German, and Russian

The final criterion to be considered in this chapter for distinguishing between the effects of grammar and processing involves cross-linguistic comparison. Cross-linguistic differences in constraint application have sometimes been used to argue in favor of grammatical over processing-based accounts of island effects. Some studies have observed cases in which a particular island effect is clearly observable in one language, but apparently fails to occur in another language. For example, Stepanov (2007: 90–1) discusses cases of Sentential Subject Constraint violations (extraction from a clausal subject) which are unacceptable in English, but acceptable in Russian, Hungarian, and other languages. This is an example of what Phillips (2013b) calls *deep variation*, since the languages have comparable constructions for expressing filler–gap dependencies, and yet show distinct patterns of judgments for SSC-violating sentences. Phillips (2013b: 97–8) argues that such differences can be more readily explained in terms of grammar (different grammatical constraints or parameter settings) than in terms of processing.[1]

Similarly, Featherston (2005a) observes that languages may differ in terms of the strength with which an island effect shows up, meaning that a particular island effect may be very easy to detect in one language, but harder to detect in another. Similar to Phillips (2013b), he argues such differences reflect underlying grammatical differences. Such an analysis is possible even when both languages show the relevant island effects because Featherston assumes that grammatical constraints may be gradient in nature. According to Featherston's Decathlon Model (Featherston 2008; 2019), two languages or dialects may differ with respect to the strength value of a particular grammatical constraint, or with respect to the number of constraints that are violated in a cumulative fashion. Such an analysis would be unavailable under the standard conception of grammatical constraints as categorical (non-gradient) in nature. However, there is another possible analysis of this type of effect which does not require gradient grammatical constraints. Häussler et al. (2015) argue that at least for some cases, island effects of different strengths may have different sources (grammar, processing) in different languages. Such an analysis is also consistent with Phillips's (2013b) proposal in that languages may vary as to whether a particular island constraint is encoded in the

---

[1] I am excluding any discussion of what Phillips (2013b) calls *surface variation*. In such cases, constructions which resemble an island-violating structure but which show no island effects have been plausibly analyzed as having some other non-island-violating structure.

grammar or not. However, to accommodate more subtle cross-linguistic differences, the approach of Häussler et al. (2015) invokes processing constraints to understand (what appear to be) weak island effects, while invoking grammatical constraints to understand stronger island effects. Under this conception, stronger island effects are grounded in processing factors, but conventionalized in language such that they apply on the basis of structural conditions, regardless of the level of processing difficulty associated with any particular token of use (see Hawkins 2004; 2014).

Although cross-linguistic differences have been used as evidence in favor of a grammatical constraint being applicable in at least one of the languages, Arnon et al. (2006) argue that a processing-based approach may still be preferable. In a discussion of multiple *wh*-questions in English, German, and Russian, they claim that processing factors alone may account for cross-linguistic differences, once differences in the available cues for interpretation, such as case-marking, are taken into account. In the remainder of this section, I will discuss these different approaches to the problem of cross-linguistic variation by focusing on alternative approaches to understanding constraints on multiple *wh*-questions in English, Russian, German, and Czech.

In languages that require the fronting of one *wh*-phrase to form a question, questions that include multiple *wh*-phrases within the same clause may display what are known as Superiority effects (Chomsky 1973; Kuno and Robinson 1972). English shows robust Superiority effects when the *wh*-phrase takes the form of a bare pronoun (i.e. in the absence of D-linking, as discussed with respect to other types of *wh*-dependencies in Section 4.1). For sentences like (14b–c), it is unacceptable for the direct object or PP complement to occur in the fronted position when the subject is also a question phrase. Multiple *wh*-questions are high in acceptability, however, when subject itself occurs in the fronted position, as in (16a).

(16) a. Who said what to whom?
     b. *What did who say to whom?
     c. *To whom did who say what?

Overlooking the details of specific theoretical proposals, this pattern of acceptability has typically been interpreted as the result of a syntactic Superiority constraint—a syntactic constraint on *wh*-movement that prevents derivations as in (16b–c).

Interestingly, such an effect appears to be absent in Russian, even though questions are formed in a manner similar to English. Fedorenko and Gibson (2008) conducted two acceptability judgment tasks comparing native speakers' responses to comparable stimuli in English and Russian. The first task examined multiple *wh*-questions in embedded contexts. Here, I will only highlight the crucial contrasts between subject-first and object-first orderings with bare *wh*-words, as in (17a–d). Participants were first given a context sentence, and then asked to rate the acceptability of a sentence containing an embedded question. The Russian stimuli were the same as the English stimuli in word order and content, except that subject-first sentences as in (15c) had the more natural subject–object–verb (SOV) order within the embedded clause, rather than subject–verb-object (SVO) order.

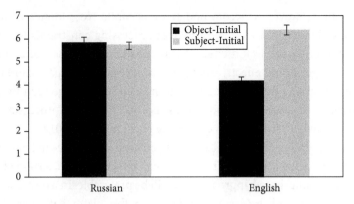

Fig. 4.3 Mean acceptability ratings for multiple *wh*-questions in English and Russian
Source: From Fedorenko and Gibson (2008: 28).

(17) a. Helen tried to figure out who ordered what.   (subject-first)
      b. Helen tried to figure out what who ordered   (object-first)
      c. Elena staralas'   razobrat'sia kto chto zakazal.   (subject-first)
         Elena tried   to figure out who what ordered
      d. Elena staralas'   razobrat'sia chto kto zakazal.   (object-first)
         Elena tried   to figure out what who ordered

The results of this experiment showed that English speakers rated subject-first sentences as significantly more acceptable than object-first sentences—the expected Superiority effect. However, Russian speakers rated subject-first and object-first orders as equally acceptable (Figure 4.3).[2]

To facilitate cross-linguistic comparison, the authors included two baseline experiments. The first baseline experiment compared Russian and English speakers' responses to sentences that form relative clause islands—interrogative dependencies for which the gap is contained inside a relative clause. The results showed the expected island effect in both languages, with no differences in the magnitude of the effect. The second baseline experiment compared Russian and English speakers' responses to center-embedded relative clauses—a structure that is known to be difficult to process but generally assumed to be grammatical. Again, both groups of participants behaved similarly. Sentences with two levels of embedding were rated significantly less acceptable than sentences with one level of embedding by both groups. Taken together, these baseline experiments suggest that the two groups of speakers were responding similarly to the judgment tasks. Thus, the authors conclude that between-group differences shown in the Superiority experiment are likely related to linguistic experience rather than idiosyncrasies of the materials or populations tested.

---

[2] This finding concurs with linguistic studies of Russian (Rudin 1988; 1996), although it differs from Meyer (2004), who found that Russian speakers rated subject-first sentences higher than object-first sentences in a magnitude estimation task.

Perhaps the most obvious interpretation of Fedorenko and Gibson's (2008) findings is that English has a syntactic Superiority constraint, which Russian lacks. This would then be a case of what Phillips (2013b) calls deep variation in island constraints. While problematic for claims that Superiority is a universal constraint (Featherston 2005a), such an explanation accords well with the experimental findings. However, this is not the interpretation given by Fedorenko and Gibson (2008), nor by Arnon et al. (2006) in reference to the same findings. Both authors attempt to relate this cross-linguistic difference not to any specific syntactic constraint, but rather to other differences between Russian and English that affect how multiple *wh*-questions are processed. For Fedorenko and Gibson (2008), the relevant difference relates to the relative flexibility of word order in a basic declarative clause. In English, SVO order is highly dominant in transitive clauses, and so is the expected order in a full-sentence answer to a multiple *wh*-question. It is further assumed that English speakers should expect to find parallel word order between multiple *wh*-questions and their full-sentence answers. Thus, multiple *wh*-questions with object-first order defy this expectation for parallelism, causing participants to rate object-first questions as less acceptable. In contrast, because Russian has a more flexible ordering of subject, verb, and object in a declarative clause, Russian speakers should have no strong expectation for subject-first order in answers to questions. In effect, there is no penalty for object-first order in multiple *wh*-questions. A judgment experiment reported in the same paper asked English-speaking participants to rate the appropriateness of the answer in question–answer pairs involving one *wh*-dependency (subject vs. object questions). Results showed that English speakers generally preferred answers to questions in the form of a basic transitive clause with SVO order, regardless of question type. In addition, there was a preference for parallelism in word order between question and answer whenever answers took a noncanonical form (subject cleft, object cleft, or topicalized object). Although the authors take these findings to support a non-syntactic account of Superiority effects in English, they do not provide a clear link between Superiority effects and perceived appropriateness of question–answer pairs in English. In particular, the results of the question–answer task showed that question–answer parallelism was only preferred when the answer was in a noncanonical form. However, their explanation for the Superiority effect depends on the idea that answers in the *canonical* form should negatively influence the acceptability of object-first multiple *wh*-questions. While the results of the question–answer task are not incompatible with this explanation, they appear to provide no positive support for it either.

Arnon et al. (2006) offer an alternative explanation for the observed difference between English and Russian. They claim that in English, Superiority effects are caused by processing difficulties associated with understanding multiple *wh*-dependencies within the same clause. Such difficulties are enhanced when filler–gap distance is greater (object-first questions show a longer dependency distance than subject-first questions) and when accessibility of the *wh*-phrases is lower (bare pronouns are said to be less accessible than *which*+N phrases). Their experiments on English showed that object-first multiple *wh*-questions were more acceptable and showed faster reading times when the *wh*-phrases took the form of *which*+N (i.e. the D-linked form) as compared with the bare form. They did not include subject-first questions as a control in their experiments, leaving open the possibility that there might have been a residual Superiority effect. However, Fedorenko and Gibson (2008) directly compared subject-first and object-first questions with bare and D-linked forms, finding that the Superiority effect (i.e. a preference for subject-first order over object-first order) only showed up in the bare pronoun conditions, and was completely neutralized when the intervening subject took the D-linked form. In addition, they found no effect of D-linking in the subject-first conditions, all of which showed a high level of acceptability. Thus, these results from Fedorenko and Gibson (2008) suggest that D-linking neutralizes the Superiority effect, and are consistent with Arnon et al.'s (2006) claim that D-linking facilitates comprehension of multiple *wh*-questions which are grammatical but hard to process. However, such results do not rule out the possibility that multiple *wh*-questions with bare pronouns are subject to a syntactic superiority constraint, but D-linking changes the structure of the sentence in such a way that the Superiority constraint no longer applies.

Referring to the data from Fedorenko and Gibson's study, Arnon et al. (2006) extend their processing-based approach to account for the lack of any Superiority effects in Russian. They point to the greater availability of case-marking on Russian question words, which, when present, makes it easier for readers/listeners to quickly identify the grammatical role of a *wh*-phrase. Citing reaction time data from an Agent decision task (Kempe and MacWhinney 1999), they propose that the greater reliability of case-marking in Russian possibly mitigates the difficulty involved in processing multiple *wh*-questions.[3] As support for this hypothesis, they present corpus data showing that case is unambiguously marked on 35% of the question words in the Uppsala corpus of Russian (Boguslavsky et al. 2002). While this is lower than the availability of case-marking on nouns as found by Kempe and MacWhinney (1999) for a different corpus, it is still higher than the availability of case-marking on German questions words, which were unambiguously marked in only 11% of tokens from the TIGER and NE-GRA corpora. German is relevant to their discussion, since Featherston (2005a) found a Superiority effect for German using an acceptability judgment task, albeit a weaker effect than he found for English. Arnon et al. argue that since the relative availability of case-marking on *wh*-phrases correlates with the relative strength of Superiority effects in Russian, German, and English (where case-marking is only rarely marked using the pronoun *whom*), it is possible that the availability of case-marking mitigates the processing difficulty that otherwise gives rise to Superiority effects. Fedorenko and Gibson (2008) point out a problem with this line of reasoning, however. The word *chto* 'what', which was used to express the object role in the Russian Superiority experiment,

---

[3] Kempe and MacWhinney (1999) showed that the presence of overt case-marking resulted in faster response times for Agent decisions by both Russian and German participants, but that this effect was stronger for Russian. They suggest that this difference results from the overall greater reliability of case-marking as a cue for identifying the grammatical role of the noun in Russian as compared with German, as evident from corpus data from both languages.

bears no overt case-marking. Thus, it is hard to see how the availability of case-marking could have facilitated processing of the object-first questions. The inanimate feature of *chto* could of course help participants identify *chto* as the object, but the same would be true for the corresponding questions with *what* in English. Possibly, the nominative case on the following pronoun *kto* 'who' helped disambiguate the grammatical role of *chto* 'what.' However, English speakers can also reliably identify *what* as the object based on the following word: the two interrogative pronouns are only adjacent when the first one is the object (e.g. *what who said* vs. *who said what*). Furthermore, Russian does not differ from German in the case-marking of *who* (unambiguous) and *what* (ambiguous), but Superiority effects (albeit in a weaker form than in English) have been shown for German (Featherston 2005a; Häussler et al. 2015). All of this seems to point back to our original idea that multiple *wh*-questions are subject to some kind of grammatical constraint in English (which becomes weaker or inactive in D-linking contexts), but not in Russian (where object-first questions are equally acceptable to subject-first questions and there are no effects of D-linking). Based on the data discussed so far, it is impossible to draw any firm conclusion.

So far, we have seen some of the difficulties involved in supporting a processing-based account of Superiority in English in the face of cross-linguistic differences between English and Russian. Judgment data from additional languages both clarify and complicate our understanding of Superiority. The picture that emerges from comparative research on several European languages is that there appears to be a continuum of variation in Superiority effects, with some but not all of the effects being due to processing-related factors that are independent of any specific syntactic constraints on multiple *wh*-questions. While it will be impossible to give a full treatment of the topic here, I will close this section by briefly discussing some additional data on Superiority effects in German (Featherston 2005a; Häussler et al. 2015) and Czech (Häussler et al. 2018).

Featherston (2005a) was the first study to report a formal judgment task comparing Superiority effects in English and German. While previous theoretical studies had reported a lack of any Superiority effect in German (Fanselow 2001; Haider 1993; Lutz 1996), Featherston's results from a magnitude estimation task showed a clear preference for subject-first questions in both English and German when the interrogative subject was left in situ, for sentences as in (18a–b) and (18c–d).

(18) a. Who showed the patient what? (subject-first)
    b. What did who show the patient? (object-first)
    c. Wer   hat dem Patienten was   empfohlen? (subject-first)
       who.NOM has the   patient   what recommended
       'Who has recommended what to the patient?'
    d. Was   hat wer   dem Patienten empfohlen? (object-first)
       what   has who.NOM   the patient   recommended
       'What has who recommended to the patient?'

In addition, Featherston tested a number of other sentence types, including multiple *wh*-questions in which the direct object was extracted, the indirect object left in situ, and the subject expressed as a non-interrogative NP, as in (19a–b).

(19)   a. Who did the dentist show what?
      b. Wem   hat Der Zahnarzt was empfohlen?
         who.DAT   has the dentist   what recommended
         'To whom has the dentist recommended what?'

The two language groups showed very similar patterns of judgments across most of the conditions. The main difference was in the size of the effect for contrasts as in (18a–b), which was stronger for English than for German. (However, note that Featherston did not include any control experiment to provide a baseline for comparing the two groups of speakers.) A further difference was that sentences with a fronted indirect object and an in situ direct object, as in (19a), were less acceptable in English than sentences with an interrogative subject in the initial position, as in (18a). No such difference was found for German. Featherston suggests that perhaps English has two constraints on multiple *wh*-questions (a constraint against in situ interrogative subjects, and a constraint against nonsubject-initial questions), both of which are violated in (18b), resulting in a cumulative degradation in acceptability. In contrast, German only has a constraint against in situ interrogative subjects, which is violated in (18d), but no corresponding constraint against nonsubject-initial questions. He offers this as a possible reason for the larger Superiority effect for English as compared with German (Featherston 2005a: 695).

More generally, Featherston favors a gradient view of grammar in which cross-linguistic differences in effect size can result either from a difference in the number of constraints violated in the two languages (with cumulative degradations in acceptability), or a difference in the strength value of the same constraint. For example, instead of having a different number of constraints in each language, there could instead be a single constraint (e.g. a constraint against in situ subjects in multiple *wh*-questions) that has a stronger weighting in English as compared to German. There is another possible way to accommodate these types of gradient effects, however. Cross-linguistic differences may result from different *types* of constraints in different languages. In a similar study of Superiority effects in English and German, Häussler et al. (2015) offer an explanation of this kind. The results of an acceptability rating task for multiple *wh*-questions in embedded contexts showed similar effects to what Featherston (2005a) found: a stronger Superiority effect for English as compared with German. That is, the English participants showed a much stronger preference for subject-first over object-first multiple *wh*-questions than German participants did, but German participants still showed a significant difference between the two conditions.

In this study, Häussler et al. (2015) followed Fedorenko and Gibson's (2008) approach by including two control experiments to establish a baseline for comparing the two groups. The first control experiment included relative clause island violations (e.g. *What did Thomas accuse the student who copied?*). Results showed that both groups similarly rated such island-violating sentences as highly unacceptable. The second control experiment compared subject and object questions with only one *wh*-dependency. Again, the English and German groups showed similar patterns of judgments. Although object questions have a longer dependency distance than subject questions, there were no significant differences in acceptability due to question type for either language group. Based on the results of the Superiority experiment and the two control experiments, Häussler et al. argue that the cross-linguistic differences shown in the Superiority experiment cannot be reduced to general differences in how speakers of English and German process interrogative dependencies. Rather, they argue that the relatively stronger Superiority effects in English were due to a language-specific grammatical constraint, while the relatively weaker effects in German were due to processing-related factors. They further argue that because Superiority effects have shown up reliably in English across multiple studies, even for very simple six-word sentences (Clifton et al. 2006), and because English, unlike German, showed no differences due to the animacy of the interrogative object (which they take to indicate a processing effect, as detailed below), the Superiority effect was mostly likely due to a grammatical constraint in English.

The argument for a processing effect in German (as opposed to a grammatical constraint against in situ interrogative subjects, as proposed by Featherston) hinges on a difference due to the animacy of the two interrogative pronouns. The verbs used in the Superiority experiment (e.g. *discover, mention, describe, praise*) require an animate subject and allow for either an animate or inanimate object. Thus, the authors were able to manipulate the animacy of the object (*what/who* in English; *was/wen* in German), while keeping the subject constant. Results of the Superiority experiment are shown in Figure 4.4. Similar to Featherston's findings, the German group showed a weaker Superiority effect (i.e. a smaller penalty for object-first order) than the English group across both animacy conditions. However, the German group showed a relatively stronger effect when both subject and object were animate (*wer* 'who'/*wen* 'whom'), and a relatively weaker effect when the subject was animate and the object was inanimate (*wer* 'who'/*was* 'what'). In contrast, the English group showed an equally strong Superiority effect regardless of the animacy of the object. Häussler et al. argue that in German, there is no specific grammatical constraint affecting multiple *wh*-questions, but readers may have experienced processing difficulty when the object was animate, since the object then became more easily confusable with the subject. This may have been because *was* 'what' in initial position was easily interpreted as the object, since all of the verbs in their stimuli required an animate subject (Häussler et al. 2015: 247). On the other hand, the animate pronoun *wen* 'whom' can semantically function as either the agent or undergoer of the action, and is morphologically similar to the subject form *wer* 'who'. This morphological and semantic similarity between *wen* and *wer* possibly created a temporary interpretive problem for readers when *wen* 'whom' was used in the less-expected object-first position.

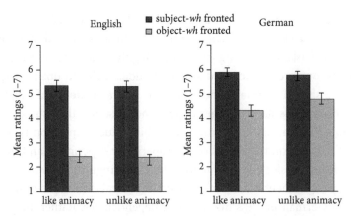

Fig. 4.4 Mean acceptability ratings for multiple *wh*-questions in English and German

Source: Republished with permission of John Wiley & Sons from Häussler et al. (2015: 243); permission conveyed through Copyright Clearance Center.

Extending the findings of Häussler et al. (2015), Häussler et al. (2018) examined similar Superiority-violating sentences in five additional languages (Czech, Dutch, Icelandic, Swedish, Spanish) and compared these findings with the results from the 2015 study. For purposes of exposition, I will consider only the findings for Czech here. Häussler et al. (2018) found no significant difference between subject-first and object-first questions in Czech when the object was inanimate. This finding was similar to what Fedorenko and Gibson (2008) found for Russian—a closely related Slavic language with similar word order and case-marking properties. However, when the object was animate, Czech speakers showed a small but significant preference for the subject-first order.[4] Interestingly, Czech showed a similar pattern to German, except that German showed a small Superiority effect even in the inanimate object condition. The authors speculate that this residual effect for inanimate objects in German may be due to pragmatic factors that disfavor leaving a focal subject in situ (Erteschik-Shir 2006). However, they do not address the issue of why Czech exhibits no evidence for such a pragmatic effect.

To sum up, Häussler et al. (2015) and Häussler et al. (2018) argue that Superiority effects as manifested in patterns of acceptability judgments indicate the presence of a grammatical constraint on the formation of multiple *wh*-questions in English, whereas they appear to be reducible to processing factors, possibly in combination with pragmatic constraints, in Czech and German. These conclusions are in contrast to those of Featherston (2005a), who proposed on the basis of similar data that Superiority effects in German are due to a syntactic constraint against in situ interrogative subjects. Stronger effect sizes in English were attributed to the presence of additional constraints which apply in a cumulative fashion. Although Featherston's (2005a) explanation is distinctive in assuming a gradient model of grammar, both explanations

---

[4] Since Fedorenko and Gibson's (2008) study only tested inanimate objects, it is unknown whether the Russian speakers who participated in that study would have shown a Superiority effect for animate objects.

are consistent with Phillips's (2013b) idea that cross-linguistic differences in patterns of acceptability reflect cross-linguistic differences in grammatical constraints. This is in contrast to Arnon et al. (2006), who claimed that Superiority effects can be explained without appealing to any special grammatical constraints. Rather, cross-linguistic differences are due to differences in the availability and reliability of interpretive cues such as overt case-marking.

It is not easy to decide among these options based solely on judgment data, since marginal and low acceptability can be associated with both grammatical and ungrammatical sentence types. Furthermore, both grammatical and ungrammatical sentences can be pragmatically infelicitous and/or difficult to process. The most compelling argument given by Häussler et al. (2015) was that low acceptability on very short, simple, easily interpretable sentences, as they found for English, is unlikely to be due to processing difficulty. This conclusion is strengthened by the finding that acceptability ratings did not improve for object-first sentences with inanimate as compared with animate objects. Both were equally unacceptable, unlike in Czech and German, where ratings were higher for inanimate objects. As Häussler et al. (2015) argue, the difference between inanimate and animate objects in German and Czech is plausibly due to processing factors. However, they also found a residual Superiority effect in German, even for object-first sentences with inanimate objects, replicating a similar effect found by Featherston (2005a). Both authors agree that German shows a constraint against in situ subjects in multiple *wh*-questions. However, their interpretations of this effect are slightly different. Featherston (2005a) proposed a syntactic account framed within a gradient approach to grammar, while Häussler et al. (2015) suggested a possible pragmatic account of the same contrast. What other evidence might help us decide? Corpus data showing that Superiority violations are relatively frequent in German and Czech, but rare in English, might tip the scales in favor of Häussler et al.'s explanation. Such a pattern, if found, would provide positive evidence that Superiority-violating sentences in Czech and German are sometimes used when pragmatic conditions are favorable, and that they are generated often enough that they are unlikely to be the result of overgeneration. Alternatively, an experimental task (such as a judgment task or completion task) that manipulates the pragmatic conditions for multiple *wh*-questions could be used to support or refute a pragmatic account. In the next chapter, I will explore the relationship between acceptability and production, and how data from corpus frequencies can better inform our theoretical conclusions.

4.6 Conclusions

In this chapter, we have considered how to distinguish between grammatical constraints and general cognitive factors that affect language processing. Effects that have been claimed to identify the presence of a grammatical constraint include overgeneration (as identified by a discrepancy between online and offline measures), cross-linguistic differences, lack of repeated exposure effects, and lack of any effects attributable to individual differences in working memory capacity. While all of these effects (and non-effects) must be interpreted carefully, evidence from overgeneration and from cross-linguistic differences can support a grammar-based explanation. For example, with regard to cross-linguistic differences, Fedorenko and Gibson (2008) found a clear Superiority effect for English, but no effect for Russian. This can be taken, at least cautiously, to suggest a difference in the grammatical constraints affecting question formation in English and Russian. On the other hand, evidence from the absence of repeated exposure effects or the absence of individual differences due to working memory capacity seems less promising, since these patterns may only indicate that the stimulus sentences used in the experiments were difficult to process. Effects that have been claimed to favor a processing-based explanation include amelioration effects, isomorphism between acceptability ratings and online measures such as reading time, repeated exposure effects, and effects of individual differences in working memory capacity. As Phillips (2013a) points out, amelioration and isomorphism do not provide definitive evidence, since even ungrammatical sentences can be made easier to interpret by manipulating the lexical content and discourse context. Hofmeister et al. (2013) point out similar problems with interpreting data from repeated exposure effects and from effects of individual differences in working memory capacity. However, when combined with corpus data showing that the structure in question occurs in natural production, all of these types of evidence can point toward a processing-based explanation for gradient variation in judgments. In the next chapter, I will examine the relationship between corpus frequency and acceptability, shedding further light on the problem of how to interpret variability and gradience in acceptability judgments.

5

On the relationship between corpus frequency and acceptability

As discussed in Chapter 1, most studies of syntax in the generative tradition have relied heavily on data from acceptability judgments, including both formal experiments and informally collected judgments, with the major exception being for languages that lack living speakers. In contrast, studies of syntax within the functionalist traditions have more often (although by no means exclusively) relied on observational data, such as from corpora of spontaneous speech or written texts. This methodological difference has resulted in part from the different research goals within these traditions. While generative linguists have primarily aimed to identify structural conditions that constitute knowledge of grammar, functionalist linguists have focused more on understanding the semantic, pragmatic, and social functions of syntactic constructions within a broader communicative context. This has sometimes been characterized as a division of labor between the study of competence and the study of performance (Newmeyer 2003). However, it is more precise to say that functionalists see themselves as studying both competence and performance, where competence is more broadly defined as the knowledge one accumulates over a lifetime of linguistic performance. I will not attempt to argue for or against a particular view of competence in this chapter. However, we have seen in Chapter 4 that even if one assumes a narrow generative view of competence, the effects of competence and performance are not always so easily separated from each other. Furthermore, we have seen that acceptability judgments—themselves a type of metalinguistic performance—are not a direct window into competence. For these reasons, I believe that it is to our advantage to examine additional data sources when attempting to determine the source of a particular contrast in acceptability. In this chapter, I will survey the existing empirical evidence regarding the relationship between acceptability judgments and corpus frequency, and I will argue that corpus data can in fact provide valuable information for generative linguists, including those who take a very narrow view of competence.

In an article based on his 2003 presidential address to the Linguistic Society of America, Newmeyer (2003) defends a traditional generative view on grammar, usage, and linguistic methodology. Newmeyer sees the different theoretical traditions (generative and functionalist) and their preferred methods (judgment data and observational data) as complementary to each other. He claims that while corpus data are valuable for studying language in its communicative context, they provide only limited

Gradient Acceptability and Linguistic Theory. Elaine J. Francis, Oxford University Press.
© Elaine J. Francis (2022). DOI: 10.1093/oso/9780192898944.003.0005

evidence about competence. Although he acknowledges that corpus data can provide useful information about the major constructions of a language (e.g. constituent orderings in phrases and clauses, morphological inflections), he argues that they provide little or no information about the syntactic constraints that are relevant for forming more complex sentence types, especially those that are rarely used. He contends that judgment data are more informative in this regard, citing experimental studies of subtle syntactic phenomena, including Subjacency, *that*-trace effects, and binding effects (Cowart 1997). In these studies, participants provided consistent acceptability ratings distinguishing between complex sentence types and ungrammatical structures that differ minimally from these complex sentence types. For example, Cowart (1997) found that participants reliably rated rare sentence types like (1a) as more acceptable than (purportedly) ungrammatical sentence types like (1b).

(1)   a. I wonder who you think likes John.
       b. *I wonder who you think that likes John.

Newmeyer (2003: 691) interprets such results to mean that speakers have consistent and reliable intuitions that reflect their knowledge of grammar, despite the (apparent) paucity of relevant data from language use.

   Newmeyer (2003) is also critical of newer generative frameworks such as Stochastic OT (Bresnan et al. 2001; Manning 2003) which incorporate quantitative information about usage, as gleaned from corpus frequencies, into the competence grammar. Instead, he argues for a strict division between grammar (competence) and usage (performance), and suggests that data from corpus frequencies primarily bear on the latter. First, he understands competence to reflect the knowledge of individual speakers, whereas corpus data reflect the combined usage of many speakers over different genres of discourse. However, if one accepts the basic premise of experimental syntax that acceptability ratings of isolated sentences as averaged over multiple speakers can provide valuable evidence about competence (Cowart 1997; Schütze 1996), as Newmeyer (2003) himself appears to do in his discussion of Cowart's (1997) studies, then this argument seems to lose much of its force. More convincing are his arguments that corpus frequencies can be understood as arising from a combination of cognitive constraints on language use, real-world knowledge, and intended meanings. For these reasons, he argues that it is not necessary to include frequency information in the competence grammar. He cites the following example from Manning (2003: 307):

(2)   a. It is unlikely that the company will be able to meet this year's revenue
          forecasts.
       b. That the company will be able to meet this year's revenue forecasts is
          unlikely.

Manning (2003) observes that sentences like (2a) are much more frequent in corpora of English than sentences like (2b), and argues that this type of frequency information forms a part of speakers' grammatical competence. However, Newmeyer (2003) provides an alternative explanation: that (2b) is less common because sentences with heavier subjects are harder to produce, and thus speakers tend to avoid using them. Along the same lines as Manning (2003), Wasow (2002: 133) has argued that frequency information about a verb's subcategorization frames forms a part of competence. For example, he notes that intransitive uses of *walk*, as in (3a), are much more frequent than transitive uses of the same verb, as in (3b), and claims that speakers have robust intuitions about these frequency differences.

(3)   a. Sandy walked (to the store).
      b. Sandy walked the dog.

Newmeyer argues instead that such frequency differences can be derived entirely from speakers' real-world knowledge, and need not form an aspect of speakers' grammatical competence. Simply put, walking of one's own volition is a more common activity than walking some other creature, and as a result, people talk about walking somewhere more often than they talk about walking something. Finally, Newmeyer (2003: 697) argues that "probabilities may be more a function of the meaning that one wants to convey than of some inherent property of the structure itself." He points out that syntactically distinct constructions that are paraphrases of each other may express subtle differences in meaning, and that this can help explain why one syntactic variant is used more often than the other. Although Newmeyer does not elaborate on this point, the idea can be supported with a basic example. In most genres of speech and writing in English, active clauses (e.g. *Someone ate all the pie*) are used more often than passive clauses (e.g. *All the pie was eaten*). One reason for this is that the subject position is generally used to express topical information, and Agent arguments tend to be used as topics more often than Patient arguments (Givón 1993: 47). Newmeyer (2003: 698) concludes that frequency information drawn from corpora is "all but useless for providing insights into the grammar of any individual speaker."

Schütze (2011) takes a view of grammatical competence very similar to that of Newmeyer (2003), but he is more optimistic about the potential contributions of corpus data to the goals of generative syntax. Similar to Newmeyer (2003), Schütze (2011) argues that judgment data are more informative than corpus data for gaining information about sentence types that are rare or unattested in language use: "speakers can consistently distinguish well-formed from ill-formed strings among those whose probabilities are zero, based on past occurrence. This is not to deny that speakers, if asked, can detect probability/frequency differences among many sentence types; the claim is that grammaticality cannot be wholly reduced to such factors" (Schütze 2011: 207).

While preferring judgment data for such cases, Schütze (2011) also points out some ways in which corpus data can positively inform our understanding of the competence grammar. First, he acknowledges that lexical and structural frequencies, as measurable in corpus counts, are among the various factors that can affect acceptability judgments. Regardless of whether frequency information is predictable from other factors such as intended meaning and real-world knowledge (as Newmeyer argues), language users have been shown to be sensitive to lexical and structural frequency in judgment tasks and other types of psycholinguistic experiments. In this sense, lexical and structural frequency are psychologically real. Corpus counts therefore provide valuable information for constructing well-controlled sentence materials for judgment experiments. Second, for sentence types that have been judged as unacceptable and then claimed to be ungrammatical on that basis, corpus data can sometimes be used to show that those same sentence types actually occur in natural production. For example, Schütze (2011) cites Bresnan and Nikitina (2010), who showed that manner-of-speaking verbs, which had been described by some authors as ungrammatical in the ditransitive construction (i.e. lacking the subcategorization frame for this construction) based on examples like (4a) (Levin 1993), sometimes do occur with ditransitive syntax in actual language use. This is shown using corpus examples like (4b–c) (Bresnan and Nikitina 2010: 8).

(4)   a.   *Susan whispered/yelled/mumbled/barked/muttered… Rachel the news.
       b.   The shepherd-dogs, guardians of the flocks, **barked him a welcome**, and the sheep bleated and the lambs pattered round him.
       c.   I still can't forget their mockery and laughter when they heard my question. Finally a kind few (three to be exact) came forward and **whispered me the answer.**

If a particular sentence type is attested in language use, and occurs in contexts that tend to improve its acceptability, we can reasonably conclude that the grammar must license these sentence types. The lower acceptability of sentences like (4a) must then be explained in terms of additional factors such as discourse context, lexical content, plausibility, ease of production/comprehension, and/or low frequency of occurrence. In short, Schütze (2011) maintains that corpus data can provide valuable information about lexical and structural frequency, which can help linguists develop well-controlled sentence materials for judgment tasks. Furthermore, they can provide a fuller picture of the range of structures that are licensed by the grammar, allowing linguists to eliminate unnecessary syntactic rules from their models of grammar and better describe the discourse contexts that permit those structures.

In contrast to Newmeyer (2003) and Schütze (2011), who view frequency information as separate from grammatical competence, functionalist linguists who identify as usage-based in orientation, including Bybee and Eddington (2006) and Diessel and Hilpert (2016), view frequency information as an essential aspect of grammatical knowledge, where such knowledge is understood to be based on an individual's experience using language over a lifetime. For usage-based linguists, frequency of use is not viewed merely as a potential confound for interpreting judgment data, but rather it is understood to be one of the most significant factors affecting judgments. As Bybee and Eddington put it: "grammaticality or acceptability judgments are heavily based on familiarity, that is, the speaker's experience with language in use. Sequences of linguistic units that are of high frequency or resemble sequences of high frequency will be judged more acceptable than those that are of low frequency or do not resemble frequently used structures" (2006: 349).

Similarly, generative linguists who take a probabilistic view of grammar incorporate frequency information directly into the grammar. In Stochastic OT (Bresnan, Dingare, and Manning 2001; Manning 2003), for example, frequency information is used to determine the constraint weightings for competing forms. While the constraints themselves are stated as structural conditions similar to those found in standard OT and other generative theories, frequency of use is encoded in the constraint weightings, thus allowing cross-linguistic and cross-dialectal differences in speakers' preferences to be modeled as differences in the constraint weightings. Incorporating frequency information into the constraint weighting also allows the model to predict how likely a certain form is to be chosen over competing forms under different conditions, and similarly, how acceptable speakers will judge it to be in relation to those competing forms. As in usage-based approaches, a close correlation between probability (as derived from corpus frequencies) and acceptability is generally assumed (Bresnan 2007).

We have seen that linguists from different traditions have professed different views on the relative importance of judgment data and corpus data for developing theories of grammatical knowledge. Similarly, while everyone recognizes frequency of use as a factor to which language users are sensitive, there is disagreement as to how it relates to acceptability. While proponents of usage-based and probabilistic theories have tended to emphasize the close correlations between frequency and acceptability, proponents of traditional derivational and constraint-based theories have tended to place more importance on cases in which acceptability judgments differ among low-frequency or zero-frequency structures. To date, the precise relationship between frequency of use and acceptability is rather poorly understood. However, a few studies have directly examined this relationship. Both scenarios described above—close correlations between frequency and acceptability, and mismatches in which low-frequency items are relatively acceptable—have been reported. In this chapter, I discuss some of the key literature on this topic, with a view toward identifying ways in which linguists can use corpus data to supplement and enrich their interpretations of judgment data. Throughout the chapter, I take Schütze's (2011) view that corpus data and judgment data are mutually informative, and that both types of data can lead us to a fuller understanding of grammatical competence, even if one takes a narrow view of what competence entails.

5.1 Evidence from close correlations: acceptability mirrors corpus frequency

Dąbrowska (2008) examined the acceptability of long-distance *wh*-questions in English from a usage-based perspective. An analysis of the spoken portion of the British National Corpus had shown that 70% of long-distance questions conform to one of two lexically specified templates, as illustrated in (5a–b). The first template, as in (5a), begins with a *wh*-phrase and specifically includes the words *do you think*. The second template, as in (5b), begins with a *wh*-phrase and includes *did NP say* (where NP stands for any noun phrase). Both templates end with a single embedded clause containing a gap.

(5)   a. What do you think Brian'll say?
      b. What did they say it meant?

In addition, the corpus analysis showed that only 6% of long-distance questions in the corpus departed from these templates in more than one respect (for example, using another matrix verb besides *think* or *say*, or a different auxiliary than *do*). Dąbrowska (2008) hypothesized that English speakers' acceptability judgments of long-distance questions would mirror these preferences as shown in the corpus data. Since similar preferences were not shown for declarative sentences in the corpus, she further hypothesized that declarative sentences with matching lexical content should not differ in acceptability or should at least show a smaller difference. Her sentence materials included questions that conformed to the templates, questions that departed from the templates in just one respect (e.g. choice of verb), and questions that departed from the templates in several respects (verb other than *think* or *say*, auxiliary other than *do*, lexical subject NP, presence of a complementizer, and additional embedded clause). The two extremes of prototypical and non-prototypical long-distance questions are given in (6a–b). Note that the additional *if*-clause was added to the prototypical question in (6a) to maintain a constant sentence length. Declarative controls, as in (6c–d), and ungrammatical controls, as in (6e–f), were also included.

(6)   a. What do you think the witness will say if they don't intervene?
      b. What would Claire believe that Jo thinks he said at the court hearing?
      c. But you think the witness will say something if they don't intervene.
      d. Claire would believe that Jo thinks he said something at the court hearing.
      e. *What did you say that works even better? (*that*-trace violation)
      f. *What did Claire make the claim that she read in a book?
         (Complex NP island)

The results of a judgment task supported Dąbrowska's main hypotheses. First, prototypical questions like (6a) were judged significantly higher in acceptability than non-prototypical questions like (6b). In addition, the latter did not differ from ungrammatical *that*-clause sentences like (6e). For declarative sentences like (6c–d), the difference was in the same direction as for (6a–b), but much smaller, suggesting that specific lexical content may have had some effect on the acceptability of long-distance questions. Dąbrowska concludes with the observation that long-distance questions are only fully acceptable when they conform to certain lexically specified templates, as derived from the most frequently used corpus tokens, suggesting that the widely held assumption that questions are formed through highly general movement rules might need to be reexamined. More generally, the results of this study suggest that corpus frequencies of partially lexically specified sequences show a relatively direct relationship to acceptability, in the case of long-distance questions in English.

In her study of the English dative alternation, Bresnan (2007) provides additional evidence in favor of a tight relationship between corpus frequency and acceptability. Instead of using corpus frequencies to identify lexically specified templates for a single construction type, Bresnan (2007) instead used corpus frequencies to compute the probability of a speaker using the ditransitive construction, as in (7a), or its prepositional dative paraphrase, as in (7b), in any given instance. These probabilities were based on the findings of an earlier corpus analysis, in which Bresnan et al. (2007) coded 2,360 instances of dative and ditransitive sentences in the Switchboard Corpus for a number of variables, including verb class, information status, phrase length, animacy, pronominality, and definiteness (Bresnan 2007: 75). They entered these variables into a logistic regression model, from which they were able to compute the probability of a particular form (dative or ditransitive) based on the combination of values for each variable. They report that the model achieved about 94% accuracy when used to predict the occurrence of dative vs. ditransitive sentences in a different corpus.

(7)   a. Who gave you that wonderful watch?
       b. Who gave that wonderful watch to you?

Bresnan (2007) sought to test whether these probability values for a sample of items from the corpus could predict participants' judgments of these same items. For one experiment, she randomly sampled a selection of dative and ditransitive sentences from the corpus across a range of probability values, and presented them to participants together with the preceding context and an alternative paraphrase, as shown in Figure 5.1.

Instead of being asked to rate each item on a Likert scale or express a binary preference, participants were asked to rate the naturalness of each alternative by distributing 100 points between the two options given at the end of the paragraph. Results showed that the predictions of the corpus model strongly correlated with the participants' ratings, as shown in Figure 5.2. In addition, participants' responses matched the original corpus items 76% of the time on average. Bresnan (2007) takes this to mean that probabilities derived from corpus frequencies form a part of speakers' implicit knowledge of language, which they can then use to predict the syntactic choices of other speakers to a relatively high degree of accuracy (2007: 91).

```
-----------------------------------------------------------------
Speaker:

About twenty-five, twenty-six years ago, my brother-in-
law showed up in my front yard pulling a trailer. And
in this trailer he had a pony, which I didn't know he
was bringing. And so over the weekend I had to go out
and find some wood and put up some kind of a structure
to house that pony,

(1) because he brought the pony to my children.
(2) because he brought my children the pony.
-----------------------------------------------------------------
```

Fig. 5.1 Sample item from the judgment task

Source: Republished with permission of Walter de Gruyter and Company from Bresnan (2007: 80); permission conveyed through Copyright Clearance Center.

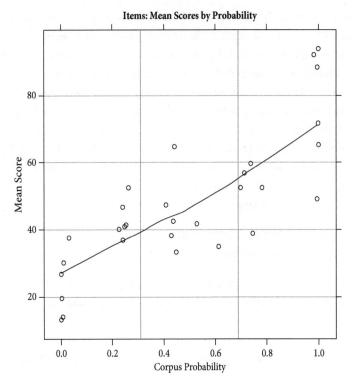

Fig. 5.2 Mean rating of prepositional dative option by corpus probability

Source: Republished with permission of Walter de Gruyter and Company from Bresnan (2007: 81); permission conveyed through Copyright Clearance Center.

5.2 Evidence from mismatches: differences in acceptability among low-frequency forms

As a critic of usage-based and probabilistic approaches to grammar, even Newmeyer (2003) acknowledges that "language users and hence their grammars are sensitive to frequency" (2003: 697). Given this, results such as those of Dąbrowska (2008), in which corpus frequency correlates with acceptability, are not particularly surprising. Crucial for generative linguists, however, is the distinction between possible and probable forms. Possible forms are licensed by the grammar, even if they are improbable and hardly ever occur in everyday language use. Newmeyer (2003: 691) further assumes that acceptability judgments of complex sentence types, although not a perfect window into competence, tend to show stable patterns in experimental tasks, which can potentially be used to distinguish between rare but possible forms and ungrammatical forms. In this section, I consider three studies that examined differences in acceptability judgments among sentences types that were either very rare or failed to occur at all in a corpus sample. I discuss possible reasons for these discrepancies from the point of view of usage-based and generative theories.

Kempen and Harbusch (2008) compared acceptability judgments and corpus frequencies for various word order variations in German declarative clauses. For example, Figure 5.3 shows the ratings (left) and corpus frequencies (right) for six different permutations of subject, direct object, and indirect object in a verb-final subordinate clause. The rating data were taken from an earlier study by Keller (2000), while the corpus data were collected from NEGRA and TIGER treebank corpora of written German and from the VERBMOBIL corpus of spoken German. The authors' main observations were as follows: "On the one hand, linear orders that receive similarly high grammaticality ratings may have very different but at least moderate corpus frequencies. On the other hand, linear orders whose corpus frequency is (virtually) zero, may nevertheless elicit variable grammaticality ratings, although at best moderate ones" (2008: 1).

The latter observation is shown clearly in Figure 5.3 for permutations 3, 4, 5, and 6. The corpus data (right) show that these variants were never used, and yet the judgment data (left) show that they varied from moderate to low acceptability.

Kempen and Harbusch (2008) claim that only the configurations with at least moderate frequency are clearly encoded in the grammar and accessible to language users during production. In this case, only the two most frequent orders (1–2) are grammatical and accessible to production, while the four zero-frequency orders are ill-formed. Why, then, do these four orders (3–6) differ in acceptability? Following a similar suggestion by Schütze (1996), Kempen and Harbusch (2008) claim that these differences can be attributed to the degree of deviance from the "ideal delivery" version of the sentence. For example, the position of the subject correlated with acceptability. For sentences with full NPs, subject-first orders were rated highest, while subject-last orders were rated lowest. Similarly, for sentences in which one of the three arguments was pronominal, the pronoun-first orders were more acceptable than other orders. The authors take this to mean that participants were comparing the marked word orders to an ideal word order, and computing the degree of deviance to come up with a judgment of the sentence. Notably, this distinction depends on the assumption in generative linguistics that familiarity and grammaticality are different things. For some

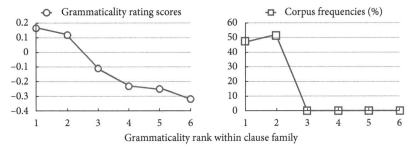

Fig. 5.3 Acceptability ratings (left) and corpus frequencies (right) for six word order permutations in German clauses

Source: Republished with permission of Walter de Gruyter and Company from Kempen and Harbusch (2008: 5); permission conveyed through Copyright Clearance Center.

usage-based linguists such as Bybee, familiarity and grammaticality are not clearly distinguished.

In two studies on German, Bader and Häussler (2010) examined argument ordering preferences in relation to case-marking and animacy, as well as linearization preferences in verb clusters. They compared corpus frequencies with data from two types of acceptability judgment tasks: a magnitude estimation (ME) task and an offline grammaticality judgment (OGJ) task with binary yes–no response options. Here, we will be most concerned with the mismatches between corpus frequency and acceptability, and will not attempt to address the minor differences between the results of the two types of judgment tasks. Figure 5.4 summarizes the results for both argument order and verb clusters. The percentage scale is shown in the left y-axis pertains to the percentage of items in the corpus belonging to each sentence type as well as the percentage of sentences judged as grammatical in the forced-choice judgment task. The right y-axis shows the normalized rating on the ME task. Regarding these data, the authors identify two types of mismatches between frequency and acceptability, which they call Ceiling Mismatch and Floor Mismatch. Their definitions are given in (8a–b), from Bader and Häussler (2010: 136).

(8)   a. **Ceiling Mismatch**
         When perceived well-formedness is at ceiling, two syntactic structures may differ in terms of frequency despite being perceived as equally well-formed.
      b. **Floor Mismatch**
         If frequency is at floor, two syntactic structures may differ in terms of perceived well-formedness despite both occurring with zero or near-zero frequency.

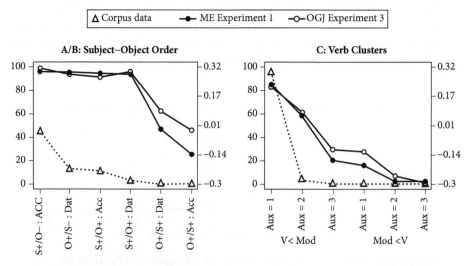

Fig. 5.4 A comparison of corpus frequency, Magnitude Estimation judgments, and binary grammaticality judgments

Source: From Bader and Häussler (2010: 314); reproduced with permission from Cambridge University Press.

Ceiling Mismatch is most apparent in the data from argument order, as presented on the left side of Figure 5.4. Although the four highest-frequency argument orders greatly varied in absolute frequency in the corpus, they were all rated at ceiling, as highly acceptable, while only the two lowest-frequency orders were rated lower. Floor Mismatch is most apparent in the data from verb cluster linearization, as shown in the right side of Figure 5.4. Corpus data showed that only one of the six possible orders of verb clusters was frequent in the corpus, and this is the order that the authors had identified in advance as the only prescriptively correct order in Standard German. Similar to what Kempen and Harbusch (2008) found, they found that the five low-frequency structures, although all rated below ceiling, varied widely in acceptability from moderately high to very low. Looking in particular at the four rightmost verb cluster orders in Figure 5.4, which all showed zero or near-zero frequency, the two orders which deviated most strongly from the normal (highest-frequency) word order were rated lower than the two orders which partially resembled the normal word order. In particular, they identified two parameters of deviance from the expected order of auxiliary–verb–modal: (1) verb before modal; and (2) auxiliary in second or third position instead of first. The two orders with both of these deviations were rated lowest. The authors do not discuss any specific mechanism which might explain this pattern of judgments, but their observations imply that speakers may have used a similarity-based metric similar to what Kempen and Harbusch (2008) proposed to account for similar data. If such an analysis is applied, the four orders which were never or very rarely used would all be considered ungrammatical and therefore inaccessible to production, with differences in acceptability due to their perceived similarity to the grammatically licensed form. A usage-based account would be very similar, except that there would be no need to determine the status of these rarely used structures as either grammatical or ungrammatical.

Building on these previous studies by Kempen and Harbusch (2008) and Bader and Häussler (2010), Divjak (2017) examined variation in acceptability among a particular low-frequency sentence type in Polish: sentences in which the matrix verb takes a *that*-clause complement, where *that*-clause is defined in this paper as a finite clause beginning with a form of the complementizer *żeby* 'that'. In general, most verbs that select a clausal complement either only allow an infinitival complement, or optionally allow either an infinitival or a *that*-clause complement, with the infinitival complement generally being the preferred option. Only a few verbs (five in the PELCRA reference corpus of Polish) showed a preference for a *that*-clause complement over an infinitival complement. For the acceptability judgment task, in which participants rated each item on a 5-point Likert scale, Divjak (2017) selected 95 verbs that allow a clausal complement (infinitival and/or *that*-clause) and for each verb constructed a stimulus sentence containing a *that*-clause complement. For 69 of the 95 verbs, the stimulus sentence was based on a modified version of an attested corpus example that already contained a *that*-clause. For the remaining 26 verbs, no example with a *that*-clause complement was found in the corpus. For those verbs, the stimulus sentences were instead based on attested examples with an infinitival complement, which the author then converted into a *that*-clause paraphrase. Two additional lexicalizations of each of the 95 verbs were also constructed in order to vary the lexical content. Although a large number of filler sentences were also included in the design, this task was unusual in only including one sentence type (*that*-clause) among the test sentences. This was done in order to include dozens of variables related to choice of verb.

Divjak (2017) administered the judgment task to 285 native speakers of Polish, and analyzed the results with respect to a number of different independent variables falling into three general categories: (1) information derived from corpus frequencies; (2) information about morphologically related words; (3) semantic information. Interestingly, none of the semantic variables showed any statistically reliable relationship to acceptability judgments. In fact, although dozens of variables were tested, only two of them turned out to be significant predictors of acceptability ratings: morphological transparency (a measure of similarity) and reliance (a measure of conditional probability). Morphological transparency was quantified for each verb in terms of the degree to which the verb is similar to another derivationally related word in terms of its morphological form and word class. Results for the 69 verbs that were attested in the corpus with a *that*-complement showed that a low degree of morphological transparency predicted lower acceptability ratings. Divjak describes this finding as follows: "The effect suggests that verbs that are visibly part of a morphological family are (considered) constructionally more versatile: Speakers appear to assume a wider variety of constructional options for words that are part of morphological families" (2017: 368). Reliance was a measure of how likely a *that*-clause complement was to occur following a particular verb, regardless of the overall frequency of that verb. For example, a verb that occurred 200 times in the corpus would have high reliance if it occurred with a *that*-complement 180 times. By contrast, a verb that occurred 2,000 times in the corpus would have a low reliance if it occurred with a *that*-complement 180 times. Due to limitations of the statistical model, reliance was only calculated for the 69 verbs that actually occurred in the corpus at least once with a *that*-clause. Interestingly, reliance was a strong predictor of acceptability only for those verbs within the second and third quartiles (middle 50%) of overall frequency. For the verbs in the lowest quartile of overall frequency, morphological transparency was a stronger predictor.

Overall, these results show that even for a relatively infrequent construction, participants in the judgment experiment were sensitive to the conditional probability of a *that*-clause complement coming after the verb. Notably, this was a more fine-grained measure of frequency than had been applied in previous similar studies. For those verbs with the fewest *that*-clause tokens in the corpus, however, participants appeared to rely more on morphological transparency, a measure of similarity to other existing word forms. This is reminiscent of the similarity-based metric that participants in the studies by Kempen and Harbusch (2008) and Bader and Häussler (2010) apparently applied in judging rarely occurring sentence types. For reasons that are not clear, the opposite trend was shown for those 26 verbs that were completely unattested with *that*-complements: higher transparency was associated with lower acceptability. Overall verb frequency also affected the ratings of sentences containing those 26 unattested verbs: the ones that were in the bottom quartile of overall frequency were found to be slightly more acceptable than the ones with a higher overall frequency. Divjak (2017) notes that this finding is in line with Ambridge (2013), who found the children were more accepting of low-frequency verbs occurring in an unexpected construction as compared with high-frequency verbs. What can explain these results for the unattested verbs? Some recent studies on statistical preemption, to which we now turn, suggest a possible answer.

5.3 Evidence from statistical preemption: judgments of unusual verb-construction combinations

So far, we have seen that the frequency with which a particular construction is encountered together with particular lexical content (Dąbrowska 2008), as well as its similarity to related but higher-frequency constructions (Bader and Häussler 2010; Kempen and Harbusch 2005), can affect speakers' acceptability judgments. Furthermore, Bresnan (2007) showed that in cases where a construction exists alongside a close paraphrase, the probability of encountering that construction as opposed to its paraphrase (as determined by factors such as verb class, phrase length, and animacy) can predict acceptability ratings. More probable uses of a construction were generally rated higher. Similarly, Divjak (2017) showed that there can be competition among constructional paraphrases at the level of individual verb. The more frequently a particular subcategorizing verb occurred with a *that*-clause complement (in proportion to the infinitival complement) in the corpus, the more acceptable participants in the experiment found that verb with a *that*-clause complement to be.

Divjak's (2017) data displayed a slightly different type of competition that occurred for completely novel verb-construction combinations. Based on Divjak's other results, we might expect verbs that are unattested with a *that*-clause (i.e. verbs which always occur with an infinitival complement) to be uniformly low in acceptability when used with a *that*-clause complement. However, they were not. Divjak (2017) found that verbs that were in the bottom quartile for overall frequency were more acceptable with a *that*-clause than those with a higher overall frequency. In other words, novel verb-construction combinations were more likely to be deemed unacceptable when the verb itself was frequently encountered in the alternative infinitival construction. As Divjak (2017) acknowledges, this result is consistent with previous findings on "statistical preemption"—the idea that verbs can be extended for use in new constructions more easily when the new construction is not in direct competition with another synonymous construction. Or as Goldberg (2016: 373) puts it: "a new coinage will be inhibited to the extent that there already exists a readily available alternative formulation that serves the requisite function; in this case, the alternative will statistically preempt the coinage." In the remainder of this section, I will discuss one additional study (among several) which supports this idea of statistical preemption for novel verb-construction combinations in English.

Robenalt and Goldberg (2015) set out to test the idea of statistical preemption against an alternative interpretation which they call 'conservatism via entrenchment'. The idea of conservatism via entrenchment is that speakers will be less accepting of a novel verb-construction combination to the extent that the verb is frequently encountered in other constructions. Thus, higher-frequency verbs should be less readily accepted in a novel construction than lower-frequency verbs. This differs from the idea of statistical preemption in that the other constructions need not have the same meaning or function as the novel construction. If statistical preemption is at play (and not merely conservatism via entrenchment), participants should *only* prefer novel combinations with lower-frequency verbs when there is another competing construction which is a close paraphrase of the novel construction. The authors designed an acceptability judgment task which compared pairs of verbs with high and low frequency in three types of sentences: (1) familiar sentence types, as in (9a–b); (2) novel sentence types without any clear alternative paraphrase, as in (9c–d); (3) novel sentence types with a clear alterative paraphrase, as in (9e–f). In the case of (9e), the competing paraphrase would have an *-ing* complement (*contemplated giving her a raise*), and in (9f), the paraphrase would be the prepositional dative construction (*recited the answer to Zach*).

(9) a. Will <u>slept/napped</u> on the sofa.
  b. The family <u>considered/contemplated</u> going to Disneyland.
  c. Jeff <u>slept/napped</u> the afternoon away.
  d. The shopkeeper <u>shouted/hollered</u> the teenagers out of the building.
  e. Kayla's boss <u>considered/contemplated</u> to give her a raise.
  f. Amber <u>explained/recited</u> Zach the answer.

Results from an acceptability rating task with 108 participants showed that familiar verb-construction combinations, as in (9a–b), were rated highest among the three types of verb-construction combinations, and within this condition, higher-frequency verbs were rated higher (Figure 5.5). This result was consistent with both conservatism via entrenchment and statistical preemption. However, the results also showed a difference between novel verb-construction combinations based on whether there exists a readily available paraphrase. Those that have a readily available paraphrase (9e–f) were rated lower overall than those that do not (9c–d). Furthermore, there was only an advantage for low-frequency over high-frequency verbs for those sentences with a competing paraphrase. The authors argue that these two key results favor statistical preemption over conservatism via entrenchment. The latter hypothesis predicts a preference for low-frequency verbs in both cases, and predicts no difference between the two types of novel combinations.

Robenalt and Goldberg (2015) explain their results as follows. When a verb fits the semantic and discourse requirements of a construction but is never or very rarely encountered in that construction, speakers learn to avoid using the verb in that

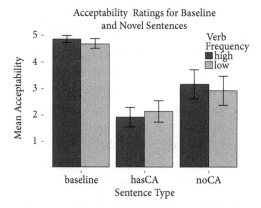

Fig. 5.5 Acceptability ratings for familiar and novel sentence types, with and without a competing alternative

Source: Republished with permission of Walter de Gruyter and Company from Robenalt and Goldberg (2015: 481); permission conveyed through Copyright Clearance Center.

construction. This results in lower acceptability for the verb in that construction, and such an effect is enhanced to the extent that the verb is more frequently encountered in the alternative construction. In contrast, speakers are relatively more willing to accept novel combinations when there is no obvious competing paraphrase. As noted previously, this is similar to Divjak's (2017) finding that novel verb-construction combinations were judged less acceptable in the *that*-clause construction for verbs that were frequently encountered in the alternative infinitival construction. In this way, the idea of statistical preemption can help explain certain cases of what Bader and Häussler (2010) call Floor Mismatch: differences in acceptability among sentence types that are never or very rarely used.

5.4 Evidence from machine learning: deriving acceptability judgments from corpus patterns

Most studies that attempt to relate acceptability judgments to corpus frequencies have taken a fine-grained approach by examining the frequency with which specific constructions occur with specific lexical content, and then testing to what extent those frequencies can predict speakers' acceptability judgments of the same sentence types. The studies discussed so far in this chapter have been of this type. However, there is a new line of research that takes a much coarser approach to the same problem. In a series of experiments, Lau and colleagues (Lau et al. 2017) used machine learning techniques to compute the probabilities of various surface patterns (i.e. sequences of words) found in corpora of naturally occurring language, which in turn they used to predict speakers' acceptability judgments of grammatically deviant sentences. While a review of machine learning studies is well beyond the scope of this chapter, I will briefly discuss the experiments reported in Lau et al. (2017). I will then consider the follow-up experiments conducted by Sprouse et al. (2018). Although the experiments conducted by the two research groups were similar, their interpretations of the data are rather different. I will conclude (weakly) that while machine learning studies have the potential to offer valuable insights into the factors affecting acceptability judgments, the results of these recent studies remain rather obscure to interpretation.

Lau et al. (2017) trained several types of probabilistic models on large unannotated English texts from the British National Corpus and Wikipedia. These models included various types of N-gram models, Bayesian Hidden Markov models, and recurrent neural network models. They then used the trained models to infer the probabilities of test sentences of varying degrees of deviance. Many of the deviant sentences were created using round-trip machine translation—automatically translating English sentences taken from a corpus into Norwegian, Spanish, Chinese, or Japanese, and then back into English using Google Translate. The different languages were used to generate different degrees of deviance, with Japanese tending to produce the most distortion (Lau et al. 2017: 1210). Importantly, the test sentences were not part of the original input. The probability value assigned to each test sentence was then normalized to take into account the effects of sentence length and lexical frequency, which are known to affect acceptability judgments independently of sentence type. Finally, the normalized probability values were correlated with the mean ratings obtained in a judgment task in which English speakers rated the same test sentences for naturalness using the Pearson correlation coefficient. The idea was to test how successfully the probability values derived from the trained models could be used to predict the actual mean acceptability ratings of the participants.

Results varied between different models, different test sets, and different normalization formulas, but in general showed positive correlations between the normalized probability values from the trained models and the participants' ratings. In most cases, the RNN models, which are capable of extracting generalizations across longer distances, outperformed the more limited N-gram models, which only extract sequences of N words at a time. For example, for one of the machine translation test sets, the values derived from the RNN model showed a 0.64 correlation with the participants' acceptability ratings, while the values derived from the 3-gram model showed a 0.53 correlation (Lau et al. 2017: 1227). The authors take these positive correlations to mean that "enriched probabilistic models predict observed human acceptability judgements to an encouraging degree of accuracy" (1236). More controversially, they claim that the results provide "initial, if tentative support for the view that human grammatical knowledge can be probabilistic in nature" (1236). Their claim is thus generally compatible with both usage-based theories, which assume that grammar is reducible to something analogous to connection weights in a neural network, and with stochastic versions of OT, which posit a traditional rule-based competence grammar that is enriched with probabilities. They do not take a stand on which of these approaches would be preferable for understanding

grammatical knowledge, but instead contrast their probabilistic view with the categorical view of grammar that is commonly assumed in generative syntax. They concede
that in principle, a categorical grammar could be used in combination with gradient performance factors to predict gradient acceptability judgments, but note that
no such model has yet been developed. They further suggest that such a grammar
may not be necessary if acceptability judgments can be successfully predicted without
one. For reasons of economy, then, they favor a probabilistic model of grammatical
knowledge.

Following up on Lau et al.'s (2017) study, Sprouse et al. (2018) tested two of the
same models (3-gram and RNN) with a different training corpus, different test sets,
different groups of human raters, and some additional evaluation metrics. They were
interested in the implications of Lau et al.'s (2017) findings for theories of grammatical
knowledge. In particular, they were skeptical of the claim that probabilistic models
could potentially replace traditional syntactic theories for understanding patterns of
acceptability judgments. As such, their goal was to compare the success of the 3-gram
and RNN models against the success of a simplified categorical grammar in predicting
participants' acceptability judgments of the test sentences. I will focus here only on
their results for the RNN model with one of the three test sets which they refer to
as Adger. This set consisted of eight constructed tokens each of 230 sentence types
taken from Adger's (2003) textbook *Core Syntax*. For one set of analyses, Sprouse et al.
(2018) used the same type of evaluation metric as the one used by Lau et al. (2017).
They call this the gradient metric, since the gradient probability values derived using
this metric help to capture gradient variation in acceptability judgments. In general,
their results using this metric showed a similar range of correlations to those reported
in the original study. For example, they found that for the Adger test set, the probability
values derived from the RNN model achieved a 0.55 correlation with the acceptability
ratings obtained in a judgment task. Interestingly, this particular analysis showed a
stronger correlation than what Lau et al. (2017) found using the same RNN model, a
similar test set from Adger, and a different group of participants.

Sprouse et al. (2018) then conducted analyses on the same test sets using
two additional evaluation metrics, which they call the categorical metric and the
experimental-logic metric. The categorical metric measures the correlation between
a binary classification of each sentence (i.e. as either grammatical or ungrammatical)
and the mean acceptability ratings obtained in the judgment task. As the authors put
it, "The categorical metric assumes that the grammar should be able to predict an
ordering relationship among the sentences: grammatical sentences should be more
acceptable than ungrammatical sentences" (2018: 591). To estimate the binary classification of a simple categorical grammar, they used the diacritics reported in Adger's
textbook, since these diacritics are taken to represent the output of the syntactic derivation of each sentence (as either well-formed or not) according to a set of internally
consistent syntactic principles. For comparison with the Adger grammar, the authors
also used the RNN model as a binary classifier for each sentence. To do this, they chose
a particular probability value as a threshold, below which a sentence was classified as

ungrammatical, and above which a sentence was classified as grammatical. The threshold was determined by trial and error by testing 100 possible thresholds and choosing the one that resulted in the strongest correlation with the acceptability judgments. Results for the Adger test set showed stronger correlations for the categorical grammar (as estimated from Adger's diacritics) than for the RNN model: the former showed an *r* value of 0.87, while the latter showed an *r* value of 0.52. From this, the authors argue that the sentence classifier based on Adger's grammar does a better job accounting for speakers' gradient acceptability judgments than the sentence classifier based on probabilities from the RNN model does.

The third evaluation metric, which they call the experimental-logic metric, measures the ability of each model to predict a difference between pairs of sentences that are matched for lexical content and differ only with respect to a single syntactic variable. Within each pair, one of the sentences is claimed to be grammatical while the other is claimed to be ungrammatical, for some principled reason. Specifically, an adequate model should be able to predict that the grammatical sentence will be judged as more acceptable (to some unspecified degree) than the ungrammatical sentence. Sprouse et al. (2018) operationalize this idea by comparing the accuracy of the Adger grammar (i.e. the grammaticality contrasts as indicated in the Adger textbook) with the accuracy of the RNN-derived probability values for predicting which sentence in each pair will be judged as more acceptable. For the Adger grammar, the prediction is considered accurate when the sentence marked as grammatical is rated higher in the judgment task than the sentence marked as ungrammatical. For the RNN model, the prediction is considered accurate when the probability value derived from the model is higher for the sentence from each pair that is given the higher rating in the judgment task. Results showed that the Adger grammar achieved 100% accuracy, meaning that for all of the sentence pairs in their data set, participants rated the putatively grammatical sentence higher than the putatively ungrammatical sentence. By contrast, the RNN model achieved 88% accuracy in predicting which sentence in each pair would be rated higher. From this, the authors conclude that the RNN model is overall less successful than the Adger grammar in predicting contrasts in acceptability of the type that are typically used in syntactic argumentation.

What do these additional results imply with regard to Lau et al.'s (2017) claim that grammatical knowledge may be probabilistic in nature? Sprouse et al. suggest that while the probability-based models capture some gradient patterns in the judgment data that categorical grammars cannot possibly capture, they do so at the expense of empirical coverage: "Anyone wishing to pursue LCL's models as competitors with existing syntactic theories must therefore either be satisfied with these tradeoffs, or modify the models to capture the phenomena that are not currently captured" (2018: 597). In their reply to Sprouse et al. (2018), Lappin and Lau (2018) disagree with this interpretation. They argue that neither the categorical metric nor the experimental-logic metric offers a suitable categorical grammar with which to compare the performance of their RNN model. Rather, they emphasize that the grammar used for comparison with the RNN model is based on linguists' acceptability judgments of the same sentence types that the participants judged.[1] In contrast, the RNN model was trained on unrelated sentences. Sprouse et al. (2018) acknowledge that using linguists' judgments as a predictor of participants' judgments is "a bit circular" but interpret the correlation obtained by the categorical metric as "a measure of how well a comprehensive binary grammar built from the diacritics… would capture the gradient judgment data" (Sprouse et al. 2018: 589). Lappin and Lau (2018) do not specify what a sufficiently formalized, noncircular categorical grammar should look like, but note that no such has thing has yet been attempted.

Regardless of how the categorical metric is interpreted, the same limitations apply to the experimental-logic metric, since it also relies on linguists' judgments to represent the output of the categorical grammar. It is, however, instructive to look at the accuracy results obtained using the experimental-logic metric more closely. Sprouse et al. (2018) report that the RNN model achieved 88% accuracy in predicting which sentence in each pair should be judged as more acceptable, whereas the Adger grammar achieved 100% accuracy for the same data set. The authors were then able to examine which sentence pairs the RNN model got right and which ones it got wrong. They found that sentence types involving constraints on long-distance dependencies, ellipsis, subject–verb agreement, argument structure, and polarity items—construction types traditionally described with reference to complex dependencies within hierarchical structures—were misclassified (2018: 595). These error patterns are in line with studies that have explored the ability of RNN models to learn specific aspects of syntactic structure (Pater 2019). For example, Linzen et al. (2016) trained an RNN model on corpus data, with no specific grammatical supervision, and then tested which present tense verb form (singular or plural) the model predicted to be more probable in a number prediction task which required the model to predict the verb number (singular or plural) as a continuation of a subject NP preamble (e.g. *The keys to the cabinet__*). The model achieved an overall accuracy rate of 93%, but performed worse than chance on sentences with one or more nouns intervening between the subject and the verb. In contrast, two other RNN models that were trained with some explicit grammatical information (verb number or presence/absence of an agreement violation), but nothing explicitly identifying the subject noun or indicating hierarchical sentence structure, performed much better on such sentences, with only around 20% error rates. Thus, Linzen et al. (2016) showed that with some minor supervision, their RNN models were able to learn structural generalizations that involve nonlocal dependencies. However, the models still posited agreement with a nonsubject in some difficult cases, and apparently used heuristics for identifying the subject noun that differ from the hierarchical syntactic structures posited by linguists.[2]

---

[1] Lappin and Lau (2018) observe that the categorical metric is similar to one of their own analyses reported in Lau et al. (2017), in which the judgments of a single participant were correlated with the mean judgments of all the participants. Similar to the categorical metric, this analysis showed a strong correlation of 0.78 for the Adger test set. The authors take this as an estimate of an upper bound on the performance of any model.

[2] Linzen et al. (2016) note that human participants also make errors involving agreement with a nonsubject during real time production and comprehension, and (to a lesser extent) in judgment tasks. In a follow-up study,

Although they acknowledge that current machine learning models often benefit from direct supervision (i.e. explicit grammatical information coded in the training corpus) and fall short of accurately imitating human performance, Lappin and Lau (2018) take the results of Linzen et al. (2016) and other similar machine learning studies as encouraging evidence for the plausibility of probabilistic models of abstract grammatical knowledge. In contrast, Sprouse et al. (2018) are more skeptical, emphasizing the limitations of these models and the need to develop more direct comparisons against categorical theories of syntax. Returning to the theme of the current chapter, let us set aside this debate over the nature of grammatical knowledge and consider a somewhat more practical question. What do these studies by Lau et al. (2017) and Sprouse et al. (2018) tell us about the relationship between frequency information extracted from corpora and acceptability judgments? The observed correlations tell us that there is in fact a systematic relationship of some kind. Because the RNN models were trained on unannotated texts, however, and because the patterns they detect are hidden, we do not know which linguistic patterns the probability values derived from the models were based on. Thus, the observed correlations remain obscure to interpretation at a fine-grained level. This is in contrast to a more traditional corpus-based study such as Divjak (2017), as discussed earlier in this chapter. In this study, the conditional probability of encountering a *that*-complement given a particular verb (a measure they call Reliance) was computed and then correlated with the acceptability ratings. In this case, the relationship between the probability values derived from the corpus and participants' acceptability judgments was relatively straightforward to interpret: a positive correlation indicates that participants are sensitive to the likelihood of a particular verb–complement combination when they rate these types of sentences for acceptability. Whether this sensitivity belongs in the competence grammar or not is debatable, but at least the nature of the correlation is clear enough. The correlations observed in the studies by Lau et al. (2017) and Sprouse et al. (2018) are, however, more difficult to interpret. Comparisons across different test sets and different types of models, as well as patterns of errors, offer some clues as to what the RNN model has learned and failed to learn, but do not tell us the precise basis for assigning a higher or lower probability to a given sentence.

While the results of studies by Lau et al. (2017) and Sprouse et al. (2018) show that there is a systematic relationship between probabilities derived from corpus frequencies and acceptability judgments, they are rather inconclusive with respect to the nature of that relationship. However, this line of research may give us more

---

Linzen and Leonard (2018) directly compared the performance of RNN models against that of human participants. They conducted two RNN simulations using the verb prediction task from Linzen et al. (2016) and two parallel experiments in which human participants read the subject NP of a sentence and had to choose between the verb forms *is* and *are*. Results showed that both the RNNs and the human participants made more errors for items where the subject noun was singular and the attractor noun was plural than for the reverse situation. An interesting difference was that the RNNs were unable to reliably detect the end of a relative clause within the subject NP, and made significantly more errors on items that included an attractor noun within a relative clause as compared with a PP. By contrast, human participants showed slightly more errors when the attractor noun was within a PP.

specific answers to these questions in the future, when enhanced with additional techniques for interpreting patterns of neural activation. In his review of the intersections between generative linguistics and neural network research, Pater (2019) is indeed optimistic about the potential contributions of machine learning research on language to generative grammar and vice versa. With respect to the problem of determining what linguistic generalizations a model has learned, Pater notes that "one can inspect the values of connection weights and the activation patterns produced for particular inputs to gain insight into the representations they have constructed" (Pater 2019: 25). While such techniques go back to early work by Elman (1990), their numerical inputs and outputs have been difficult to interpret conceptually. Pater points to more a recent study by Palangi et al. (2017), who develop something called Tensor Product Recurrent Networks. Like the models used by Lau et al. (2017), these models were also trained on unannotated texts. However, the internal representations were converted into a set of discrete symbols and roles, which the model then organized into distributional categories during the learning process. The authors were then able to interpret these categories by comparing them with standard lexical and grammatical categories. Following detailed analyses, Palangi et al. (2017) claim that the categories the models learned from unannotated texts during a question–answering task (a task applied in various machine learning applications) were similar to standard linguistic categories such as lexical semantic features, parts of speech, phrase types, and grammatical roles. Such a technique involves building discrete symbolic structures into the model, and thus cannot be considered as purely unsupervised learning. However, the categories derived from those symbolic structures are learned entirely from unannotated texts. This technique, along with several others as reviewed by Linzen and Baroni (2021), can help researchers interpret the grammatical patterns learned by a neural network model, potentially shedding light on correlations between the model's predictions and the responses of human participants to the same stimuli.

5.5 Conclusions

Various studies that have correlated quantitative corpus data with acceptability have demonstrated that more probable uses of a construction are typically given higher acceptability ratings than less probable uses of the same construction (Bresnan 2007; Dąbrowska 2008; Divjak 2017). Such a positive correlation indicates that speakers are sensitive to frequency information during the judgment process, but what exactly this means has been interpreted differently within different theoretical traditions. To the extent that generative linguists have acknowledged the effects of frequency, they have tended to interpret frequency effects as a nuisance variable: something which affects judgments and should therefore be controlled for in designing an experiment, but which has no direct bearing on the theory of grammar (Schütze 2011). If a construction is possible, it should be generated by the grammar, regardless of whether it occurs frequently or infrequently in language use. In contrast, linguists working in the usage-based tradition have tended to interpret such correlations between frequency and acceptability as favoring a gradient or probabilistic notion of grammar, whereby frequency information is encoded directly in the grammatical representation of a construction (Diessel and Hilpert 2016). Similarly, generative linguists working with stochastic models of grammar have interpreted such correlations as indicating the relative strength of different 'soft constraints' in the grammar.

A crucial argument in favor of the traditional generative approach has been that controlled judgment tasks can reveal significant differences among forms that rarely or never occur in language use. If extremely rare but grammatical sentences are judged as more acceptable than ungrammatical sentences under controlled conditions in which the two sentence types are lexically matched, this is taken as evidence that grammaticality is, in principle, independent of frequency of use (Newmeyer 2003). Indeed, several studies have shown differences in acceptability among rarely occurring or non-occurring forms. However, the results of these studies fail to provide definitive evidence in favor of this approach. For example, in their study of German word order variants, Kempen and Harbusch (2008) found that four of the six variants that they tested failed to occur in the corpus, and yet differed from each other in acceptability. They interpreted these results as meaning that none of these zero-frequency orders was actually grammatical, but that participants rated them differently due to their perceived similarity to the most frequent word order. The authors' interpretation is in contrast to the situation described by Newmeyer (2003), in which differences in acceptability among rare or non-occurring forms may be taken to reflect differences in grammaticality. Indeed, the results of Kempen and Harbusch's (2008) judgment task could be given this alternative interpretation. It is in fact difficult to see how these two possible interpretations could be distinguished in any noncircular way. Proponents of a usage-based approach avoid this issue by eschewing any discrete notion of grammaticality. However, they must still explain the observed differences in acceptability among zero-frequency forms. In this case, a similarity-based metric like what Kempen and Harbusch (2008) proposed appears plausible, and is compatible with both generative and usage-based theories.

Recent studies of machine learning put the debate over how frequency information relates to acceptability into a broader perspective. Rather than focusing on the frequency and acceptability of specific constructions, these studies instead demonstrate a general correlation between probability values derived from corpus-trained models and acceptability ratings of a range of grammatical and ungrammatical sentences of different types. Taking a usage-based perspective, Lau et al. (2017), take such correlations to demonstrate the plausibility of a probabilistic model of grammatical knowledge. In contrast, Sprouse et al. (2018) defend a traditional generative approach, arguing that these models are less successful than categorical grammars in accounting for speakers' judgments, especially in the case of certain complex sentence types. Both groups of authors agree, however, that studies of supervised and unsupervised machine learning have the potential to shed light on these foundational issues.

In the following two chapters, I will continue to explore the implications of correlations and mismatches between corpus frequency and acceptability. In Chapter 6, which examines cases of relative clause extraposition and PP extraposition in English and German, I will review two studies that include corpus data (Francis and Michaelis 2014; Strunk and Snider 2013). While both studies show the expected correlations between corpus frequency and acceptability, they also provide evidence that some lower-frequency forms may be subject to grammatically specified 'soft constraints' which are not fully reducible to grammar-external factors. I will again return to similar issues in Chapter 7, in a discussion of resumptive pronouns in Hebrew, English, and Cantonese. For example, I will relate corpus data from conversational Hebrew (Ariel 1999) to experimental data from acceptability judgments (Farby et al. 2010) and elicited production (Fadlon et al. 2019). In the case of resumptive pronouns in Hebrew object relatives, an apparent mismatch between low corpus frequency and high acceptability will be explained with reference to additional data from elicited production which more closely matches the judgment data. This discussion will underline the importance of understanding the linguistic properties of the experimental stimulus items which may not be present in the corpus data.

6

Relative clause extraposition and PP extraposition in English and German

Extraposition from NP refers to the rightward displacement of a noun-modifying phrase to a position that is nonadjacent to the head noun. In English, the displaced phrase can be either a PP (1b) or a relative clause (1d), and displacement can occur from either a subject NP (1b, 1d) or an object NP (1f) (sentences adapted from Guéron and May (1984: 1)).

(1) a. <u>Many books about language and linguistics</u> have been published recently.
     b. <u>Many books</u> have been published recently <u>about language and linguistics</u>.
     c. <u>Many books which I've enjoyed reading</u> have been published recently.
     d. <u>Many books</u> have been published recently <u>which I've enjoyed reading</u>.
     e. They have recently published <u>many books which I've enjoyed reading</u>.
     f. They have published <u>many books</u> recently <u>which I've enjoyed reading</u>.

Since the distributions of extraposed relative clauses and PPs are somewhat different, I will use the terms relative clause extraposition (henceforth, RCE) and preposition phrase extraposition (henceforth, PPE) to refer to specific cases. In addition, since some constraints on extraposition are sensitive to the position of the antecedent NP, I will note for each case under discussion whether the antecedent NP functions as subject (as in 1d) or object (as in 1f). It is noteworthy that RCE and PPE typically have only a subtle effect, if any, on the interpretation of the sentence. In (1a–b) and (1c–d) the adjacent and extraposed variants are close paraphrases that can be used to describe the same scenario. However, the two variants are not always interchangeable. The distribution of RCE and PPE is generally more limited than that of the corresponding adjacent ordering, due to various syntactic and discourse constraints. At the same time, there are some contexts in which RCE or PPE is strongly preferred over the adjacent ordering (Francis and Michaelis 2014).

The current chapter will primarily be concerned with RCE in English, but will also refer to data from PPE in English, as well as data from the related RCE and PPE constructions in German. In the literature on these constructions in English and German, there is a broad consensus that a speaker's choice between extraposed and adjacent orderings depends on a number of factors, any of which can also affect acceptability judgments. These factors include formal syntactic constraints (e.g. locality conditions on rightward displacement), constraints on discourse information status (e.g. the tendency for RCE with a subject antecedent to apply in presentational focus contexts),

Gradient Acceptability and Linguistic Theory. Elaine J. Francis, Oxford University Press.
© Elaine J. Francis (2022). DOI: 10.1093/oso/9780192898944.003.0006

and general processing constraints (e.g. short-before-long bias in production). Beyond this broad consensus, however, there has been little agreement on how to characterize the syntactic structure of RCE and PPE (Baltin 2006). Furthermore, the status of certain contrasts in acceptability as being syntactic, discourse-based, or processing-based has also been controversial. For these reasons, studies of RCE and PPE provide a valuable testing ground for applying the theoretical and methodological concepts introduced in Chapters 2–5. I should emphasize that the studies discussed in this chapter are only loosely connected with respect to the linguistic phenomena they investigate. All of them involve either RCE or PPE, but the constraints being tested are different in each case. Moreover, the corresponding constructions in English and German are not quite the same. For example, extraposition of an object-modifying phrase over a clause-final verb is common in German, but impossible in English (Strunk 2014). Despite their differences, however, the various studies on RCE and PPE are connected by two major themes (and a few minor ones) at the metatheoretical and methodological levels. The first theme is that theoretical assumptions matter. Specifically, we will consider the consequences of theoretical assumptions regarding form–meaning isomorphism and gradient grammar for interpreting the results of several experimental studies of RCE and PPE. The second theme is that multiple data sources can often give a clearer picture of a phenomenon and help decide among competing theoretical interpretations. In particular, we will consider studies that have incorporated reading time measures (Levy et al. 2012), elicited production tasks (Francis and Michaelis 2017), and corpus data (Francis and Michaelis 2014; Lee 2017; Strunk and Snider 2013). Minor themes include the following: the markedness of extraposition relative to adjacent order, the interpretation of additive vs. superadditive effects, the relative resistance of ungrammatical sentences to manipulations of processing ease, and the interaction of constraints that are in partial conflict with each other.

The chapter is organized into four main sections. In the first section, I discuss an experimental study of NPI licensing in RCE in English (Overfelt 2015), focusing on the consequences of theoretical assumptions about form–meaning isomorphism for interpreting the observed contrasts in acceptability. The second and third sections examine experimental studies which claim to show that certain syntactic constraints that have been proposed in the literature can be understood as processing effects. Hofmeister et al. (2015) investigate English PPE sentences involving extraction out of the extraposed constituent in interrogative sentences. Such structures have been claimed to be ungrammatical due to a Freezing constraint, but the authors argue that their experimental results are more consistent with a grammar-external, processing-based account. Similarly, Strunk and Snider (2013) examine subclausal locality conditions on rightward displacement in English and German RCE constructions. Reporting both experimental and corpus data, they do find evidence for syntactic locality effects, but these effects turn out to be gradient in nature. The authors interpret their data to be most consistent with either a processing-based account or a gradient grammar approach that incorporates soft constraints. I consider which of these options appears to be better supported, and how it might be possible to decide between them. Finally, the fourth main section considers studies of RCE in English that investigate what I am calling the Predicate Constraint and the Name Constraint. The Predicate Constraint limits what types of matrix predicates occur with RCE, while the Name Constraint limits the types of subject NPs that occur with RCE. Although it is agreed that these constraints are interpretive in nature and are related to discourse conditions on RCE with a subject antecedent, their status with respect to the syntax has been debated. I will begin this section by discussing judgment data from Walker (2013; 2017) as interpreted within different theoretical approaches. I will then discuss how additional data from corpus studies (Francis and Michaelis 2014; Lee 2017), and elicited production (Francis and Michaelis 2017) can help us decide between competing analyses of these constraints. I will conclude the section by arguing in favor of a construction-based approach which incorporates soft constraints and which does not require strict form–meaning isomorphism.

6.1 NPI licensing in RCE as evidence for syntactic structure?

In terms of their distribution, extraposed relative clauses behave in some ways as though they are ordinary adjuncts occurring in the surface position, and in some ways as though they are ordinary relative clauses occurring in the canonical position adjacent to the head noun. Thus, an ongoing controversy in studies of RCE syntax is whether the extraposed relative clause is directly generated in its surface position, or whether it is adjacent to the head noun at some more abstract level of structure (Baltin 2006). Overfelt (2015) reports an acceptability judgment task that tested this question by investigating whether NPIs (negative polarity items) can be licensed by the quantifier *every* when occurring within an extraposed relative clause. NPIs such as *any* and *at all* are polarity-sensitive, in the sense that they occur most readily in negative, interrogative, or conditional contexts, or in the presence of certain quantifiers, including *every*. Among the sentence types that Overfelt tested are those in (2a–d).

(2)   a. Yesterday park rangers removed <u>every</u> camper who was at <u>any</u> of the sites with significant flooding.
   b. Yesterday park rangers removed <u>some</u> campers who were at <u>any</u> of the sites with significant flooding.
   c. Park rangers removed <u>every</u> camper yesterday who was at <u>any</u> of the sites with significant flooding.
   d. Park rangers removed <u>some</u> campers yesterday who were at <u>any</u> of the sites with significant flooding.

Sentence types (2a–b) are control conditions in which a quantified noun functioning as the direct object of the main verb is modified by a relative clause containing the NPI *any* within it. Overfelt predicts that (2b) will be judged as less acceptable than (2a) because the quantifier *every* is capable of licensing an NPI, whereas the quantifier *some* is not. Based on established accounts of NPI licensing in generative grammar (Hoeksema 1986; Ladusaw 1979), this prediction is straightforward. The quantifier *every* is an NPI licensor, meaning that polarity sensitive items such as *any* and *at all* can freely occur within its scope, whereas the quantifier *some* is not. Since the NPI *any* occurs within the scope of the quantifier *every* in (2a) (where scope is defined in terms of the structural relation of *c-command*) the sentence is well-formed.[1] In contrast, *any* in (2b) is not within the scope of any NPI licensor, causing the sentence to be ill-formed. To address the question of whether a quantifier such as *every* can license an NPI within an extraposed phrase, Overfelt (2015) also tested sentences such as (2c–d), in which a relative clause that modifies the direct object is extraposed to a position following an adverbial modifier.[2] He predicted that if NPI licensing works the same way in adjacent and extraposed clauses, (2c) should be more acceptable than (2d), just as (2a) should be more acceptable than (2b). Alternatively, if *every* cannot license an NPI within an extraposed clause, (2c–d) should be equally unacceptable, since both would contain an NPI without any licensor. In addition, both (2c) and (2d) should be less acceptable than (2a).

As indicated by the dark bars in Figure 6.1, results showed that clauses containing the NPI *any* were rated as more acceptable in the presence of the NPI licensor *every*, as compared with the quantifier *some*. That is, sentence type (2a) was rated higher than (2b), while (2c) was rated higher than (2d). There was also a small but significant overall advantage for adjacent order over RCE, but no interaction between quantifier type and order when comparing the NPI conditions. That is, for the sentence types containing an NPI, *every* was rated higher than *some* to the same degree, regardless of the position of the relative clause. Overfelt (2015) interpreted these results as showing that NPI licensing with *every* works in the same way for extraposed and adjacent clauses. He plausibly suggested the small overall advantage for adjacent order over RCE in terms of markedness: RCE is an infrequently used construction that occurs in a more limited range of discourse contexts as compared with the adjacent order. Thus, participants judged RCE as somewhat less natural than adjacent order for sentences taken out of context.

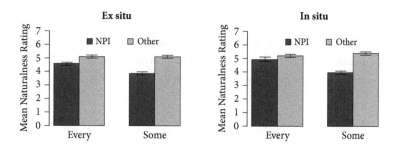

Fig. 6.1 Acceptability ratings by condition for extraposed (ex situ) and adjacent (in situ) relative clauses in English

Source: Reproduced from Overfelt (2015: 33) with permission from Elsevier.

---

[1] This analysis assumes a structure in which the quantifier is a left sister to the phrase containing the noun and its modifying clause, and therefore c-commands the other elements within the NP.

[2] Overfelt (2015: 39) predicts that the same pattern of NPI licensing should also be found in cases of RCE with a subject NP antecedent. He further suggests that his formal analysis can help explain why extraposition from a subject NP, which apparently violates a constraint on movement commonly known as the Subject Condition, is permitted at all. Late merger means that there is no rightward movement of the relative clause, and so there can be no violation of the Subject Condition.

What do these results suggest about the syntactic structure of RCE? Overfelt (2015) argues that the similar behavior of extraposed and adjacent clauses with respect to NPI licensing implies that the NPI *any* is within the scope of the quantifier in both cases. Because scope is defined in terms of syntactic c-command, this further implies that the extraposed clause must be adjacent to its head noun, at least at some abstract level of structure. Following the approach of Fox and Nissenbaum (1999), he offers one possible implementation of this idea, which says that the phrase containing [Quantifier + N] is "covertly moved" (meaning that an unpronounced copy is made) to a position right-adjoined to the VP. The overt relative clause is then "late-merged" within the covert NP. As Overfelt explains, "The extraposed material is simultaneously generated inside its host and in its extraposed position" (2015: 38). That is, the relative clause itself is generated in the extraposed position and does not need to undergo rightward movement. At the same time, it is still within (a covert copy of) its host NP, and therefore c-commanded by (a covert copy of) the quantifier *every*. This analysis is not the only possible one, but it is consistent with the results of the rating task.[3]

The debate within generative grammar over how to represent RCE syntax (e.g. as covert movement, overt movement, or base generation) is beyond the scope of the current work (see Baltin 2006 for an overview). For the purposes of the current discussion, the most important aspect of Overfelt's covert movement analysis is his assumption of strict form–meaning isomorphism, as discussed in Chapter 2. What this means in this case is that a sentence such as (2c) receives the semantic interpretation it does with respect to NPI licensing due to aspects of the underlying syntactic structure. Specifically, the quantifier *every* is able to license the NPI *any* through a syntactic c-command relation that is derived via covert movement. Notably, the same generalizations about quantifier scope and RCE can be expressed within a sign-based framework in which movement operations (overt or covert) are not needed, and strict form–meaning isomorphism does not obtain. In her dissertation on the syntax and semantics of RCE in English, Walker (2017) proposed the RCE Scope Constraint to ensure that "the quantifier of the antecedent has scope over the phrase to which the relative clause is attached" (Walker 2017: 199). Walker's analysis, which uses the HPSG framework, does not define quantifier scope in terms of syntactic c-command, and so does not require overt or covert movement in the syntax to obtain the observed semantic interpretation.

---

[3] Another possible analysis consistent with the results of the rating task would be that the relative clause originates within its host NP and undergoes rightward movement (Akmajian 1975; Baltin 1981; Guéron 1980). Under such an analysis, interpretation would then be subject to reconstruction of the original NP structure. While Overfelt's data from the judgment task are consistent with either analysis, he favors the covert movement analysis to accommodate additional patterns of judgments discussed in the literature which suggest that the relative clause behaves in some respects like an ordinary (base-generated) adjunct (Rochemont and Culicover 1990). Incidentally, Overfelt's analysis appears to better accommodate an additional contrast related to NPI licensing as observed by Guéron (1980: 650):

a. *Some customers who had any complaints weren't contacted.
b. ?Some customers weren't contacted who had any complaints.

If the apparent contrast between (a) and (b) turns out to be systematic, it could be understood within Overfelt's framework as the result of "late merger" of the relative clause into its surface position, which allows *any* to occur within the scope of negation. A rightward movement analysis with reconstruction would predict that (b) should be just as bad as (a), since the relative clause would have to be interpreted in its base position.

Instead, the RCE Scope Constraint is implemented via a semantic coindexing mechanism that relates the quantifier (which occurs within the "parts" list of the head noun) to an "anchor" feature within the extraposed relative clause. Essentially, the special form–meaning mapping that is characteristic of RCE is specified in a sign-based feature structure that combines a VP-adjoined relative clause in syntax with a semantic representation that closely resembles that of an ordinary NP-adjoined relative clause. Walker's analysis does not adhere to strict form–meaning isomorphism, since the same VP-adjunction structure is used to express very different meanings across different constructions (RCE vs. ordinary adverbial modification). Likewise, the same quantifier scope relations are expressed using two different syntactic configurations that share no common underlying syntactic structure at an overt or covert level (VP-adjunction vs. NP-adjunction).

This difference with respect to form–meaning isomorphism is not important for understanding the patterns found in Overfelt's study, since both analyses make the same predictions for quantifier scope with RCE. However, the two approaches differ in how they would accommodate evidence for new or unexpected form–meaning mappings. For example, suppose an unexpected quantifier scope relation were to show up repeatedly in a corpus sample of RCE. A sign-based analysis could accommodate this new pattern by adding a new subtype of RCE to the inventory of signs. This would be done in much the same way that a new sense of a polysemous word (e.g. *thirsty* meaning 'attention-seeking' in current youth slang) is added to the lexicon. The new subtype would reuse the same syntactic structure, modifying only the relevant semantic features as needed. To accomplish the same thing in a derivational analysis, a different syntactic derivation would be required. For example, it could be proposed that RCE involves covert movement in some cases and overt movement in others, with slightly different interpretive consequences for each option. These differences with respect to form–meaning mappings are not just in technical implementation, however. They tend to come with a difference in expectation on the part of the researcher as well. From the perspective of a sign-based framework, minor variations in form–meaning mappings are considered to be commonplace and are expected. From the perspective of a derivational theory, the default assumption is that a particular syntactic structure will be consistently associated with a particular (abstract) meaning. Thus, apparent counterexamples should, as far as possible, be subsumed under the same syntactic derivation and the same abstract meaning. Although this difference in approach is of little consequence for interpreting Overfelt's judgment data, I am bringing it up now because it will become important for understanding additional constraints on RCE in English known as the Predicate Constraint and the Name Constraint, to be discussed in Section 6.4.

6.2 Freezing effects as grammar or processing?

In the previous section, we considered the theoretical interpretation of polarity-sensitive words within extraposed constituents, which showed similar patterns of acceptability to their non-extraposed counterparts. Although there were different possible theoretical interpretations of the patterns of judgments shown in Overfelt's (2015) study, it was clear that the explanation relates to syntactic and/or semantic restrictions on the distribution of NPIs such as *any*. In other cases, however, the role of the competence grammar in understanding a pattern of judgments is less clear. Hofmeister et al. (2015) examined whether the phenomenon known as "freezing" might receive a grammar-external processing-based explanation. As they explain, "freezing refers to the idea that a constituent displaced to a noncanonical position is resistant to extraction of any of its subconstituents" (2015: 465). Ross (1967) was the first to propose such an idea. Ross's Frozen Structure Constraint ruled out extraction (e.g. via question formation) of any elements from within an extraposed PP or clause. This constraint was meant to explain the perceived drop in acceptability for questions like (3b), in which a stranded preposition occurs within an extraposed PP with a direct object antecedent, as compared with minimally contrasting questions like (3a), in which the PP is within the direct object NP but is not extraposed.

(3) a. **Who** did he see a picture of __ yesterday?
     b. ?**Who** did he see a picture yesterday of __?

Hofmeister et al. (2015) hypothesized that the lower acceptability for sentences like (3b) might be due to general constraints which affect how certain constructions are processed in real time. Both filler–gap dependencies (as in interrogative and relative clauses) and Extraposition from NP (PPE and RCE) are known to cause difficulties for parsing (Gibson 1998; Levy et al. 2012). The authors hypothesized that for sentences like (3b), which involve both filler–gap and extraposition structures, these difficulties may combine to create a perception of lowered acceptability. To test this hypothesis, they administered an acceptability rating task that included the sentence types in (4a–d), in which two factors (extraposition and extraction) were manipulated. Sentence type (4c) is a control condition, without any interrogative dependency or extraposed constituent. Sentence type (4a) involves an embedded interrogative, but no extraposition, thus isolating any effect of extraction (i.e. filler–gap dependency). Similarly, sentence type (4d) contains an embedded declarative clause with extraposition, and so isolates any effect of extraposition. Sentence (4b) combines extraction and extraposition within the same sentence. If there is a freezing constraint, it would apply to (4b), whereas the other three sentence types are assumed to be fully grammatical. For clarity, I have underlined the extraposed PPs in (4b) and (4d), boldfaced the filler phrases in (4a–b), and indicated the interrogative gaps with '__' in (4a–b).

(4) a. Kenneth revealed **which President** he overheard a nasty remark about __ earlier.
     b. Kenneth revealed **which President** he overheard a nasty remark earlier <u>about __</u>.

   c. Kenneth revealed that he overheard a nasty remark about the President earlier.

   d. Kenneth revealed that he overheard a nasty remark earlier <u>about the President</u>.

As indicated in Figure 6.2 (Hofmeister et al. 2015: 472), the results of a rating task showed independent effects of extraction and extraposition on participants' judgments. Sentence type (4b), which combines interrogative and extraposition structures, was rated no lower than would be expected from adding up the penalties incurred by (4a) (extraction without extraposition) and (4d) (extraposition without extraction) relative to (4c) (the control condition). In fact, (4b) was slightly *more* acceptable than would be expected by simply combining the two effects together (a simple combination of factors would have resulted in the bottom line being parallel to the top line in Figure 6.2). Thus, the effect of the two factors is additive (or more precisely, underadditive) rather than superadditive.

The authors acknowledge that their results are compatible with multiple interpretations, as is generally the case for both additive and superadditive effects (see Staum Casasanto, Hofmeister, and Sag 2010). However, they argue that a grammatical freezing constraint is not needed, and would unnecessarily complicate the interpretation of the data. Since independent effects of extraction and extraposition were manifested even for the grammatical sentence types in (4a) and (4d), they argue that there is no need to invoke a special grammatical constraint to understand the combined effects of these two factors. Rather, all of the effects shown can be attributed to the complexity involved in processing filler–gap dependencies and/or extraposition structures.

This seems to be a plausible interpretation, since both filler–gap and extraposition structures are independently known to cause comprehension difficulty, as shown by slower reading times around the point where the gap (Frazier and Clifton Jr. 1989) or extraposed constituent (Levy et al. 2012) is encountered. For a sentence like (4b) that combines both structures, a reader must integrate the extraposed PP with its antecedent (the noun *remark*), and in addition, interpret the filler phrase *which President*

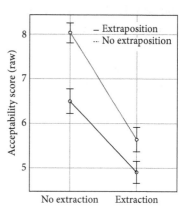

Fig. 6.2 Acceptability ratings for English interrogative and non-interrogative clauses, with and without extraposition

Source: Reproduced from Hofmeister et al. (2015: 472) by permission from John Wiley & Sons.

as the object of the preposition *about*. The authors further address the logic of their conclusion using an analogy. If two known grammatical constraints (e.g. agreement violations and head-complement order violations) were to combine to produce an additive effect on judgments, there would likewise be no need to invoke an *additional* grammatical constraint to understand the results (Hofmeister et al. 2015: 476). In such a case, the additive effect could be interpreted as the combined effect of two separate grammatical constraints. Thus, the interpretation of an additive (or underadditive) effect depends on what is being added and does not require any additional mechanism such as a grammatical constraint that specifically targets certain combinations of structures.

The authors' argument in favor of a processing-based account of freezing effects is generally persuasive, and constitutes part of a larger research program on the processing basis for freezing effects. In more recent papers by the same group, Culicover and Winkler (2018) and Konietzko et al. (2018) present similar arguments based on experiments on extraction with Heavy NP Shift in English and on the *was–für* 'what–for' split in German, both of which have been previously analyzed in terms of grammatical freezing. The design and results of the Heavy NP Shift experiments are similar to those of Hofmeister et al. (2015) in showing additive effects of extraction and shifting, and the authors' arguments in favor of a processing-based analysis are also similar. The *was–für* split experiments add an additional element of context, showing that extraction of *was* from a (purportedly) frozen subject NP shows improved acceptability when embedded in a discourse context that allows the subject to be interpreted as part of the discourse focus. Culicover and Winkler (2018) argue that these results can be best understood in terms of discourse constraints and parsing complexity, and that no special grammatical freezing constraint is needed. By the same token, it is worth asking how context effects might be used to support or refute the processing-based analysis of sentences like (4a–d) as proposed by Hofmeister et al. (2015). One possibility would be to take the approach of Levy et al. (2012) and test whether the comprehension difficulty associated with PPE can be neutralized in contexts where a PP is strongly expected to occur. In their study of RCE in English, Levy et al. (2012) found that sentences with RCE showed slower reading times at the first four words of the relative clause as compared with the corresponding sentences with adjacent order, indicating a localized processing cost for RCE. However, this effect was neutralized when the head noun was premodified by *only those*, inducing a strong expectation on the part of the reader that a relative clause should be coming up. For example, one experiment showed that sentences with RCE, as in (5a), were read just as quickly at the first four words of the relative clause as sentences with adjacent order, as in (5b).

(5)   a. The chairman consulted <u>only those executives</u> about the company <u>who were highly skilled and experienced in the industry</u>.

   b. The chairman consulted only those executives about <u>the company which was acquired recently by an aggressive rival firm</u>.

When *only those* was replaced by the determiner *the*, which comes with a weaker expectation for a relative clause to follow, RCE sentences were read slower at the critical region than sentences with an adjacent relative clause.[4]

A similar approach could be taken to follow up on the findings from Hofmeister et al. (2015). A set of sentences similar to (4a–d) could be modified as in (6a–d) to create a strong expectation for a PP following the head noun. Here, I have changed the head noun to *reliance*, which creates a strong expectation for the preposition *on* to follow.[5]

(6)   a. Kenneth revealed **whose money** he fostered an unhealthy reliance on __ earlier.

   b. Kenneth revealed **whose money** he fostered an unhealthy reliance earlier on __.

   c. Kenneth revealed that he fostered an unhealthy reliance on Phil's money earlier.

   d. Kenneth revealed that he fostered an unhealthy reliance earlier <u>on Phil's money</u>.

If this manipulation is successful at neutralizing the processing difficulty of PPE, we would expect to find no differences in acceptability between (6a) and (6b), or between (6c) and (6d). Such a finding would further support the claims of Hofmeister et al. (2015). On the other hand, if the effect due to PPE is neutralized in (6c–d), but not in (6a–b), this could be taken as evidence in favor of a grammatical freezing constraint that applies only in contexts where an element is extracted from an extraposed constituent.[6] The idea, familiar from our earlier discussion in Chapter 4 of Superiority effects in English and German (Häussler et al. 2015), is that an ungrammatical sentence should remain relatively unacceptable even when it is made easier to process. In contrast, judgments of sentences that are grammatical but somewhat difficult to process should be more susceptible to manipulations that affect ease of processing.[7] Finally, I would note that a processing-based analysis of freezing effects could be further supported with naturally occurring corpus examples of sentences with a structure similar to that of (4b). If it could be shown that the structure occurs in spontaneous

---

[4] Tom Wasow (p.c.) points out that this weaker expectation is still greater than zero. Wasow et al. (2011: 182) found that the determiner *the* occurs more often with a following NSRC (nonsubject relative clause) than some other determiners such as *a* and *some*. This difference was correlated with a lower incidence of the relativizer *that* in NSRCs that modify an NP containing the determiner *the* as compared with *a* and *some*.

[5] A search for the noun *reliance* in the Corpus of Contemporary American English (COCA) shows that the following word is *on* in 3,388 out of 3,633 cases (93%), while the following word is *upon* in 150 out of 3,633 cases (4%). Since the following word is a preposition 97% of the time, there should be a strong expectation for an upcoming PP when encountering the noun *reliance*. This is in contrast to the actual stimulus sentence in (4). In the COCA corpus, the next word after the noun *remark* is *about* in 349 out of 1,083 cases (32%). It is a different preposition in 39 out of 1,083 cases (4%), meaning that *remark* is directly followed by a PP only 36% of the time.

[6] This is, in fact, the line of reasoning taken by Dillon (2017) to argue that the Right Roof Constraint (a clausal locality condition on extraposition) is specified as part of the grammar and not (fully) reducible to general processing factors.

[7] Recall from Chapter 4 that Häussler et al. (2015) argued on a similar basis that Superiority effects are grammaticalized in English, but not in German, since only the German group showed any differences due to the animacy of the object.

discourse, this could be taken as evidence that the structure is generally licensed by the grammar of English. This is, in fact, one of the strategies that Strunk and Snider (2013) take in their study of subclausal locality constraints on RCE, as I discuss in the following section.

6.3 Subclausal locality: hard constraint, soft constraint, or neither?

In their study of RCE in German and English, Strunk and Snider (2013) take an approach similar to that of Hofmeister et al. (2015). Based on data from two acceptability judgment experiments and a quantitative corpus analysis, they argue that extraposition from an embedded NP within the same clause is grammatical in both German and English, and therefore no syntactic locality condition is needed to rule such structures out. In this section, I will discuss the motivation and the major findings from two acceptability judgment experiments, focusing primarily on the second experiment.[8] I will then consider their corpus findings for German and English, which help support their conclusion that extraposition from an embedded NP is grammatical in both languages.

Strunk and Snider's (2013) study is motivated by previous claims in the literature stating that a noun within an embedded NP cannot be the antecedent of an extraposed phrase. For example, Akmajian (1975: 118) observed a contrast in acceptability between (7a) and (7b), leading him to characterize sentences like (7b) as ungrammatical (hence the '*' notation).

(7)   a. <u>A photograph</u> was published last year <u>of a book about French cooking.</u>
      b. *<u>A photograph of a book</u> was published last year <u>about French cooking.</u>

Assuming a rightward movement analysis of Extraposition from NP, Akmajian (1975) proposed that sentences like (7b) violate Subjacency because the extraposed phrase (the PP *about French cooking*) must move across two NP boundaries—the subject NP, and the embedded NP (*a book*). According to this analysis, sentences like (7a) do not violate Subjacency because the movement only crosses one NP boundary (the subject NP). Strunk and Snider (2013) note that similar syntactic locality conditions have been proposed by other authors. For example, Chomsky's (1986a) formulation within the *Barriers* framework is somewhat less restrictive (ruling out fewer sentence types, since embedded adjuncts block extraction but embedded complements do not), while Baltin's (1981) Generalized Subjacency formulation is more restrictive (ruling out more sentence types, since PPs as well as NPs count as barriers to extraction). However, the experimental stimuli were designed with Akmajian's (1975) Subjacency-based formulation in mind.

---

[8] The second experiment tested only German, using a simple 2×2 design (extraposed/adjacent and high/low attachment). The first experiment, which tested both German and English, used a larger number of factors and more complex stimulus sentences, making the results somewhat difficult to interpret.

The first experiment tested comparable stimulus sentences in English and German, as judged by native speakers of each language using an 8-point rating scale. Relative clause position was held constant and not included as a factor: all of the sentences contained RCE. Due to the complexity of the design, I will focus here on just two of the conditions from this experiment. For the English sentences in (8a–b) and for the German sentences in (8c–d) (Strunk and Snider 2013: 119), a Subjacency account predicts that the high-attachment conditions (8a, 8c) should be grammatical, since the extraposed relative clause modifies the head noun. In contrast, the low-attachment conditions (8b, 8d) should be ungrammatical, since the extraposed relative clause modifies an embedded noun. Unlike in Akmajian's example (7), all of the experimental stimuli used object NPs instead of subject NPs as antecedents to the extraposed relative clause. The English stimuli also differed from the German stimuli in the category of the phrase that comes between the object NP and the relative clause. In English, there was an intervening adverbial (8a), while in German, there was an intervening verb (8c). The latter sentence type is possible in German, but not in English, because nonfinite verbs in German occur in a clause-final position. Since the proposed locality conditions refer only to the embedding of the antecedent noun and not the position of the antecedent or the category of the intervening phrase, the low-attachment sentences are predicted to be ungrammatical for RCE with an object antecedent in both languages. For clarity, I have underlined the entire NP antecedent and the extraposed relative clause in each example.

(8) a. I consulted the diplomatic representative a small country with <u>border disputes</u> early today <u>which threaten to</u> cause a hugely disastrous war. (low attachment)

   b. I consulted <u>the diplomatic representative a small country with border disputes</u> early today <u>who threatens to cause a hugely disastrous war.</u> (high attachment)

   c. Ich habe eine ältere Nonne aus einem traditionellen Kloster   mit
      I   have an elderly nun   from a traditional   monastery with
      einem strengen
      a strict
      <u>Verhaltenskodex</u> interviewt <u>der große Hingabe an die täglichen Rituale</u>
      code.of.conduct interviewed which great devotion to the daily rituals
      <u>verlangt.</u>
      demands
      'I have interviewed an elderly nun from a traditional monastery with a strict code of conduct which demands great devotion to daily rituals.'
      (low attachment)

   d. Ich habe <u>eine ältere Nonne aus einem traditionellen Kloster   mit einem</u>
      I   have an elderly nun from a   traditional monastery with a
      <u>strengen</u>
      strict

<u>Verhaltenskodex</u> interviewt <u>die große Hingabe an die täglichen Rituale</u>
code.of.conduct interviewed who great devotion to the daily   rituals
<u>verlangt.</u>
demands
'I have interviewed an elderly nun from a traditional monastery with a strict code
of conduct who demands great devotion to daily rituals.' (high attachment)

Results of the rating task showed that there were no significant differences in acceptability between high and low attachment for either English (8a–b) or German
(8c–d). Thus, there was no measurable effect of subclausal locality for these stimuli. However, the authors acknowledge a possible confound related to a different
sort of locality—linear distance. In the high-attachment condition in (8d), there
are nine words intervening between the head noun and its relative clause modifier,
whereas in the low-attachment condition in (8c), there is only one word intervening.[9]
According to Gibson's (1998) Dependency Locality Theory of sentence processing,
intervening constituents, especially referring expressions, are predicted to incur additional processing difficulty. Because the high-attachment conditions contain two
additional nouns between the head noun and its relative clause modifier, participants may have found these sentences more difficult to comprehend than the low-
attachment sentences. The authors suggested that this difficulty may have offset any
advantage for the high-attachment sentences based on subclausal locality (Strunk
and Snider 2013: 133).[10] If the authors had included non-RCE (adjacent order) sentences corresponding to (8a–d) in the design, it is possible that the difficulty incurred
by the intervening nouns might have shown up as a significant advantage for low
attachment. Such a result could then have supported the authors' idea that an op-
posing effect of structural locality might have neutralized this advantage for the RCE
sentences.

To address the potential effects of subclausal locality more directly, the authors ran
a second experiment on German only. This experiment used a simple design with
two factors: relative clause position (extraposed/adjacent) and attachment (high/low).
These sentences included only one embedded (genitive-marked) noun within the
subject NP. All four conditions used the same lexical items within each lexical set,
while high and low attachment were manipulated by varying the gender marking
of the two nouns within the subject NP and the corresponding relative pronouns.
Sample stimuli for these four conditions are given in (9a–d). The high-attachment

---

[9] In a study of RCE in German, Konieczny (2000) found a significant effect of linear distance on acceptability.
However, the stimuli were not exactly the same. Linear distance was manipulated by varying the length of the
intervening VP (just the verb, verb + short PP, verb + long PP) rather than the length of the noun complements.
Konieczny also did not include any conditions with more than one intervening noun.

[10] Note that subclausal locality is a kind of structural locality that depends on hierarchical structure rather than
linear order. In the high-attachment sentences, the head noun is "closer" to the extraposed clause in the sense that
the NP node directly dominating the head noun is higher in the structure and therefore closer to the VP node
where the clause is adjoined. In terms of linear distance, however, the head noun is farther from the extraposed
clause in the high-attachment sentences.

conditions are (9a–b), where (9a) shows adjacent order and (9b) shows extraposition. The corresponding low-attachment conditions are (9c–d). As before, I have underlined the entire NP antecedent and its relative clause modifier in each example. I have also boldfaced the head noun and the relative pronoun to further indicate the intended co-reference relations, which were made clear to the participants using gender marking alone.

(9) a. Ulli hat **den Mitarbeiter** der Professorin **der** die Stelle ausgeschrieben hat
Ulli has the coworker.M of.the professor.F who.M the job advertised has
verärgert.
annoyed
'Ulli has annoyed the coworker of the professor who advertised the job.'
(high-adjacent)

b. Ulli hat **den Mitarbeiter** der Professorin verärgert, **der** die Stelle
Ulli has the coworker.M of.the professor.F annoyed who.M the job
ausgeschrieben hat.
advertised   has
'Ulli has annoyed the coworker of the professor who advertised the job.'
(high-extraposed)

c. Ulli hat **den Mitarbeiter** der Professorin **die** die Stelle ausgeschrieben hat
Ulli has the coworker.M of.the professor.F who.F the job advertised has
verärgert.
annoyed
'Ulli has annoyed the coworker of the professor who advertised the job.'
(low-adjacent)

d. Ulli hat den Mitarbeiter **der Professorin** verärgert, **die** die Stelle
Ulli has the coworker.M of.the professor.F annoyed who.F the job
ausgeschrieben hat.
advertised   has
'Ulli has annoyed the coworker of the professor who advertised the job.'
(low-extraposed)

For these stimuli, a Subjacency account predicts that RCE sentences with low attachment, as in (9d), should be ungrammatical, while the other three conditions should be grammatical. As shown in Figure 6.3, the results do appear to support such an account. First, there was an overall main effect of relative clause position on acceptability: extraposition was rated lower than adjacent order for both low-attachment and high-attachment sentences. This is consistent with Overfelt's (2015) finding, and likely reflects the general markedness of the RCE construction. More pertinent to the predictions of the Subjacency account, there was a significant interaction between relative clause position and attachment. The overall penalty for extraposition was greater in the low-attachment conditions than in the high-attachment conditions, possibly reflecting the application of a grammatical constraint that applies only to low-attachment

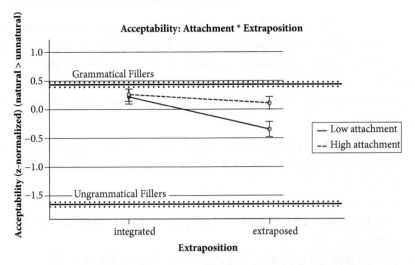

Fig. 6.3 Acceptability ratings for extraposed and adjacent (integrated) relative clauses in German, with low vs. high attachment

Source: Reproduced from Strunk and Snider (2013: 137) by permission of John Benjamins.

RCE sentences such as (9d). This is precisely the type of interaction predicted by the Subjacency account.[11]

In light of these results, the authors interpret subclausal locality as "a relevant cognitive factor" but they do not believe it to be a categorical syntactic constraint (2013: 138). Instead, they argue that it should be considered either a soft constraint (as in Stochastic OT) or a purely processing-based effect (such as that proposed for freezing effects in Hofmeister et al. 2015). One of their arguments for this position is that the ratings for low-attachment RCE sentences are closer to those of the grammatical filler sentences than to those of the ungrammatical fillers (see Figure 6.3). However, the filler sentences were not listed, and were not described in enough detail to determine what factors might have affected the ratings. A more convincing argument comes from the corpus study of German RCE reported in the same paper, as I discuss in the remainder of this section.

In their introductory discussion of Subjacency, Strunk and Snider (2013: 109–10) cited the following attested examples of Subjacency-violating sentences in English and German:

(10)   a. A wreath was placed in the doorway of <u>the brick rowhouse</u> yesterday <u>which is at the end of a block with other vacant dwellings</u>.
       b. I had a memory of <u>my dear old grandma</u> yesterday <u>who used to buy the EXACT</u> same <u>outfit in every color available (down to the shoes!)</u>.

---

[11] This difference between low and high attachment with RCE was not found in Experiment 1. This is possibly because there were two intervening nouns for the high-attachment conditions in Experiment 1, but only one intervening noun in Experiment 2. As a result, the high-attachment conditions may have posed less processing difficulty in Experiment 2, allowing the subclausal locality effect to be more easily detected.

   c. Und dann sollte ich Augenzeuge der Zerstörung <u>einer Stadt</u> werden,
     and then should I witness the.GEN destruction a.GEN city   become
     <u>die mir am Herzen lag</u>—Sarajevo.
     that me at the heart lay   Sarajevo
     'And then I was about to become an eyewitness of the destruction of a city
     that was dear to my heart—Sarajevo.' (TüBa-D/Z 16294)

   d. …es sei ihm nicht gelungen, genug   Unterstützung für die Bildung
        it be him not   succeeded enough support   for the formation
     <u>einer Übergangsregierung</u> zu bekommen, <u>die das</u>   <u>Wahlsystem</u>
     a.GEN interim.government to obtain   which the election.system
     <u>reformieren solle</u>.
     reform   should
     '… he didn't succeed in finding enough support for the formation of an
     interim government which could reform the election system.'
     (Welt Kompakt, 2008-02-05)

The apparent naturalness of these examples suggests that there is no strict syntactic constraint on subclausal locality in either English or German. However, given the significant effect of subclausal locality on acceptability shown in Experiment 2, it is possible that such structures are in fact generally avoided in language use. To examine this possibility, they conducted a quantitative corpus analysis of written German, examining the frequency with which RCE was chosen over adjacent order under different conditions of subclausal locality. They first extracted a sub-corpus of 2,789 relative clauses from the Tübingen Treebank of Written German (TüBa-D/Z) (Telljohann et al. 2006). Each relative clause was then assigned to one of three categories: extraposed, integrated, or edge.[12] Based on the existing syntactic annotation of the TüBa-D/Z, each relative clause was further coded for subclausal locality, as operationalized in terms of the depth of embedding of the antecedent noun. Each clause received a score from zero to eight, allowing for a graded measure of subclausal locality. For extraposed clauses, this measure reflects "the number of maximal projections crossed in addition to the antecedent DP during extraposition," assuming a rightward movement analysis of RCE (2013: 113). For non-extraposed clauses, this measure reflects the number of maximal projections (phrase boundaries) that would have been crossed if the clause had been extraposed. Clauses with a level of zero were similar to the high-attachment stimuli in the experiments, except that the head noun did not necessarily have any complements or modifiers after it, apart from the relative clause itself. Thus, the linear distance between the antecedent noun and the relative clause was not accounted for in this analysis. Clauses with a level of two or higher were similar to the low-attachment stimuli, in that for almost all of them, the antecedent noun was

---

[12] The 'edge' category was distinguished from the 'integrated' category because the head noun occurred at the right edge of the matrix clause in a position where extraposition would not even be possible.

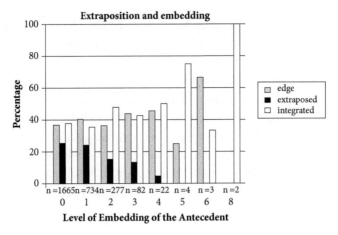

Fig. 6.4 Rate of extraposition as a function of depth of embedding of the antecedent noun

Source: From Strunk and Snider (2013: 114).

contained within an embedded NP.[13] These sentences therefore violated Subjacency as defined by Akmajian (1975). Clauses with a level of one did not always violate Subjacency, since this category included sentences in which the antecedent noun was within a PP (which counts as a phrase boundary but not as a bounding node) but not within an embedded NP.

Overall, they found more than 50 tokens of RCE with a depth of embedding of two or higher, suggesting that there can be no strict syntactic constraint ruling out sentences of this type. However, they did find a gradient effect of syntactic locality. As indicated by the dark bars in Figure 6.4 (Strunk and Snider 2013: 114), writers used RCE less often relative to their use of adjacent order (as measured by percentage of overall tokens at each level) as the depth of embedding of the antecedent noun increased to two, three, and four levels.[14] They did not use RCE at all when the antecedent was embedded more than four levels deep. This effect was confirmed statistically using a binary logistic regression analysis which included choice of structure (extraposed vs. adjacent) as the dependent variable and depth of embedding (zero to eight) as the only predictor variable. Results showed that depth of embedding was a highly significant predictor of extraposed order. The authors acknowledge that other factors known to affect the rate of RCE, such as linear distance of extraposition and relative clause length (Uszkoreit et al. 1998; Konieczny 2000), were not included in the statistical analysis because the corpus had not been annotated for these factors. However, they take these

---

[13] Strunk and Snider (2013: 116) note three exceptional cases out of 43 relative clauses at level two which did not violate Subjacency. However, they did not describe the structure of these sentences. Possibly, the antecedent noun was embedded within two PPs.

[14] The logistic regression analysis excluded the edge clauses, since there was no possibility for writers to choose RCE in such cases. If the descriptive analysis shown in Figure 6.4 had done the same, it would have shown a 40% rate of RCE (60% adjacent) for levels zero and one, a 24% rate of RCE for levels two and three, and an 8% rate of RCE for level four. These percentages are based on the raw numbers of extraposed and adjacent (non-edge) clauses reported in their table 1 (Strunk and Snider 2013: 114).

preliminary corpus findings to mean that subclausal locality is at least potentially a significant factor affecting writers' choice of structure.

Considering the findings of the two experiments and the corpus analysis together, Strunk and Snider (2013: 139) suggest two possible conclusions: (1) the effects of sub-clausal locality are entirely due to general processing factors and need not be specified in the grammar; (2) the effects of subclausal locality are due to a soft constraint in the grammar. The first conclusion would be similar to that of Hofmeister et al. (2015), as discussed in the previous section, while the second option would be consistent with a gradient view of grammar as in Stochastic Optimality Theory, as discussed in Chapter 2. Strunk and Snider consider both options to be plausible, but avoid taking any firm position on this issue. I agree with them that the data are ambiguous, but I will attempt to clarify some issues here.

The gradient effect of depth of embedding shown in the corpus study points to processing complexity as a probable factor, since other types of locality effects that are widely considered to reflect processing complexity, such as relative clause length (number of words in the relative clause) and extraposition distance (number of words intervening between the head noun and the relative clause), have resulted in similar corpus patterns for RCE in German (Strunk 2014; Uszkoreit et al. 1998) and English (Francis 2010), as well as similar gradient effects on reading time (Francis 2010) and acceptability (Francis 2010; Konieczny 2000). Given this, it is worth considering why the idea of a soft constraint comes up at all. Let's consider again the results of the second experiment, which showed that Subjacency-violating sentences like (9d), as re-peated here, were rated as less acceptable than the other three sentence types that were tested.

(9) d. Ulli hat den Mitarbeiter **der Professorin** verärgert, **die** die Stelle
        Ulli has the coworker.M of.the professor.F annoyed who.M the job
        ausgeschrieben hat.
        advertised   has
        'Ulli has annoyed the coworker of the professor who advertised the job.'
        (low-extraposed)

A key finding here was that there was an interaction which showed a superaddi-tive relationship between extraposition and low attachment. For high-attachment sentences, there was only a slight penalty for RCE in comparison to adjacent order, whereas for low-attachment sentences, there was a bigger penalty. This bigger penalty could potentially be due to the violation of a grammatical con-straint (interpreted here as a soft constraint) that applies to low-attachment but not high-attachment sentences. Alternatively, it could be due to processing fac-tors that make low attachment, as in (9d), more difficult than high attachment, as in (9b), specifically in cases where the relative clause is extraposed across a VP.

This pattern of results is different than what Hofmeister et al. (2015) found in their study of freezing. In that study, the penalty for extraposed as compared with adjacent order was not bigger for interrogatives than for declaratives. In other words, for Strunk and Snider (2013), there was something about the combination of RCE and low attachment that negatively affected acceptability judgments, whereas for Hofmeister et al. (2015), there was no penalty for combining PPE and extraction together. In the first case, a special explanation is needed for why the RCE/low-attachment sentences were rated lower than the other three sentence types, whereas in the second case, the lower ratings of the PPE/extraction sentences can be attributed to a combination of independent factors (extraposition and extraction) which are known to affect processing. It is in the context of this need for a special explanation that the idea of a soft constraint comes into play at all. Because a soft constraint is a form of conventional grammatical knowledge, its effects on acceptability judgments need not be fully predictable from independent processing factors. Since no other studies have tested how these particular sentence types are processed, not enough is known to determine which option (pure processing explanation or soft constraint) is preferable. Strunk and Snider (2013) are therefore justified in considering the soft constraint analysis as a plausible option, given their clear corpus data showing that a strict grammatical constraint cannot be maintained.

6.4 What are the Predicate Constraint and the Name Constraint?

Starting with Guéron (1980), several syntactic studies of Extraposition from NP in English have discussed examples similar to those in (11) (from Walker 2017: 54), in which a subject-modifying relative clause or PP is extraposed to a position following the VP (Guéron 1980; Guéron and May 1984; Rochemont and Culicover 1990; Takami 1992). In this section, I will focus on two particular contrasts in acceptability that have been identified in these studies. The first indicates that predicates that denote appearance, as in (11a), are more acceptable with extraposition than those that do not, as in (11b) (Guéron 1980; Rochemont and Culicover 1990; Takami 1999). The second shows that indefinite subject NPs, as in (11a), are more acceptable with extraposition than definite subject NPs, as in (11c) (Guéron 1980; Guéron and May 1984; Huck and Na 1992; Takami 1992).

(11) a. A girl arrived who was hugging a doll.
       b. ?A girl fainted who was hugging a doll.
       c. ?The girl arrived who was hugging a doll.
       d. ?The girl fainted who was hugging a doll.

Although different authors have given somewhat different accounts of these contrasts, all are agreed that these patterns exist, and that they are related to the presentational discourse function that is commonly associated with extraposition from a subject position. Avoiding any theoretical commitment to start with, I will refer to these

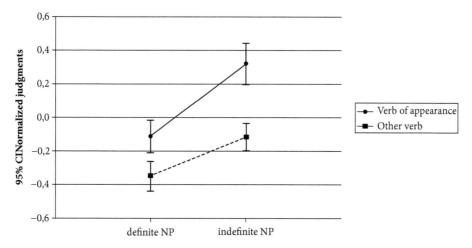

Fig. 6.5 Acceptability ratings for RCE in English according to definiteness of the subject NP and verb type

Source: Reproduced from Walker (2013: 161) by permission of John Benjamins.

patterns descriptively as the Predicate Constraint (11b), and the Name Constraint (11c).[15]

Walker (2013; 2017) was the first to investigate the Predicate Constraint and the Name Constraint using an acceptability judgment task. Sentences (11a–d) represent a subset of Walker's experimental conditions, in which verb type (appearance/nonappearance) and definiteness of the subject NP were varied. As shown in Figure 6.5 (Walker 2013: 161), the results showed that each factor (verb type and definiteness) presented gradient and cumulative effects on acceptability, such that the least acceptable sentences combined a definite subject NP with a nonappearance predicate (11d), while the most acceptable sentences combined an indefinite subject NP with an appearance predicate (11a). The other two conditions (11b–c) were intermediate in acceptability.

Since verb type and definiteness showed independent effects on acceptability, Walker (2013; 2017) takes these results to provide an empirical foundation for the Predicate Constraint and the Name Constraint. However, she interprets these constraints as soft constraints rather than as strict grammatical constraints. Walker supports this idea by noting that even the lowest-rated condition showed an intermediate degree of acceptability, about halfway between the "good" and "bad" filler sentences. As noted in Section 6.3, intermediate acceptability can have various causes, including ungrammaticality, and filler sentences typically differ from the experimental sentences along multiple dimensions. For this reason, Walker's argument based on

---

[15] Guéron (1980) used the term the Name Constraint, but the Predicate Constraint is my own descriptive term. Guéron used the term Presentation S to describe the interpretive restriction on RCE that I am calling the Predicate Constraint, while Walker (2013) used the term predicate restriction.

the acceptability of the experimental sentences relative to the filler sentences should be taken with caution. Following the approach of Sorace and Keller (2005), Walker further predicts that as soft constraints, the Predicate Constraint and the Name Constraint should be subject to variation in acceptability based on discourse context. Because the stimulus sentences were presented in isolation, the results of Walker's experiment do not tell us whether the effects of verb type and definiteness could be modulated by the context. However, both Guéron (1980) and Rochemont and Culicover (1990) have provided constructed examples suggesting that these factors do in fact vary depending on the context. For example, Rochemont and Culicover (1990: 65) note that nonappearance verbs can be made more felicitous with extraposition when embedded in a context in which the same verb has already been mentioned and therefore can more easily be construed as presentational. For example, they consider the use of the verb *scream* to be more felicitous in (12b) as compared with (12a).

(12)   a. ?A man screamed who wasn't wearing any clothes.
       b. Suddenly there was the sound of lions growling. Several women screamed. Then a man screamed who was standing at the very edge of the crowd.

If the effects of verb type and definiteness are variable according to context, as Rochemont and Culicover (1990) suggest, does this support Walker's idea that the factors affecting participants' judgments are best understood as soft constraints? Not necessarily. Gradient judgments of acceptability which vary according to context can still be understood as involving strict grammatical constraints. I explore this possibility here in the context of Guéron's (1980) analysis of the Predicate Constraint and the Name Constraint.

Guéron's (1980) approach adheres to a categorical notion of grammaticality and strict form–meaning isomorphism, as discussed in Chapter 2 and earlier in the current chapter (Section 6.1). According to Guéron, the syntactic movement associated with RCE can only be grammatically licensed when certain interpretive conditions are met. These conditions require that the subject NP must denote a nonspecific referent (the Name Constraint) and the sentence must have a presentational function of introducing the subject NP into the world of discourse (the Predicate Constraint). Importantly, they are not directly tied to any specific morphology (e.g. verbs of appearance, indefinite determiners). Therefore, it is possible to use extraposition felicitously with various verbs and even definite determiners, given an appropriate supporting context, as Rochemont and Culicover (1990) also suggested. Nevertheless, it is clear from the following passage that Guéron intends to follow to a categorical notion of grammaticality and strict form–meaning isomorphism: "The claim made here is that although people may differ on whether they accept a particular PP Extraposition output (there is in fact little difference among speakers), no one will both accept PP Extraposition from subject and interpret the S as a predication" (1980: 654). By "interpret the S as a predication" she is referring to a non-presentational reading in which the VP expresses an assertion about a topical subject NP. Later in the paper, she illustrates this point with the example in (13) (example 96 in the original paper).

(13)   a. A book by Chomsky hit the newsstand.
         b. A book hit the newsstand by Chomsky.

Guéron states: "(96a) [13a] is ambiguous between a literal meaning and an idiomatic 'appearance' meaning. But (96b) [13b] has only the 'appearance' meaning" (1980: 664).

The claim here is that the literal meaning of "hit the newsstand" strongly biases the reader to interpret the VP as making an assertion about a particular book. On the other hand, the idiomatic meaning of "hit the newsstand" (meaning simply that a book came out) is easy to construe in a presentational reading. Because the PP is extraposed in (13b), only the idiomatic meaning is available. This line of reasoning implies that if a sentence does not receive the required presentational reading, extraposition is ungrammatical.

Applying Guéron's (1980) approach to interpret Walker's (2013) judgment data, the gradient and cumulative effects of verb type and definiteness can plausibly be interpreted to reflect the ease with which participants were able to construe the isolated stimulus sentences in the required presentational reading. The easiest case would be the combination of an indefinite subject NP and a verb of appearance, as in (11a), while the most difficult case would be the combination of a definite subject NP and a non-appearance verb, as in (11d). According to this analysis, grammaticality is categorical: extraposition is either licensed or not, depending on whether the relevant structural and interpretive conditions are met. However, the construal of a particular sentence as having met or failed to meet these conditions may be gradient, possibly varying across participants and according to context.

It appears that Walker's (2013) gradient judgment data are compatible with both 'soft' and 'hard' interpretations of the relevant constraints. To determine which type of analysis is better supported, we will need more data. In the remainder of this section, I will discuss recent corpus studies of RCE in English (Francis and Michaelis 2014; Lee 2017) which provide additional empirical support for some version of the Predicate Constraint and the Name Constraint, but which also show that RCE occurs in a wider range of discourse functions than what Guéron (1980) predicted. In addition, I will discuss an elicited production study (Francis and Michaelis 2017) showing that speakers were sensitive to the low probability of occurrence of a definite subject NP when speaking a sentence with RCE. I will argue that the Predicate Constraint and the Name Constraint are better understood as soft constraints than as categorical grammatical constraints, while strict form–meaning isomorphism cannot be maintained.

Francis and Michaelis (2014) collected a small sample of 53 RCE sentences from the International Corpus of English Great Britain (ICE-GB), and Lee (2017) followed up with a larger sample of 597 RCE sentences from the Corpus of Contemporary American English (COCA) and the British National Corpus (BNC). Both studies specifically examined cases in which a relative clause was extraposed from a subject position, as in (10) and (11). The results were largely consistent with the previous studies of RCE that used constructed examples. Both corpus studies showed that most instances of RCE from a subject position occur with an indefinite subject NP and a limited range of passive and intransitive verbs. For example, in Lee's (2017) sample, 89% of subject NPs were indefinite, and 96% of verbs were either passive (84%) or intransitive with a presentational meaning related to existence or appearance (12%). Examples of verbs in the latter category include *come along, take place, arise, pass, happen, occur,* and *come* (Lee 2017: 19). The remaining 4% were a form of copula *be* followed by an adjective (e.g. *are available*). Similarly, in Francis and Michaelis's sample, 81% of subject NPs were indefinite, while 70% of the verbs were either passive (46%) or intransitive with a presentational meaning (24%). The remaining verbs were divided among several categories, including copula *be* plus an adjective, intransitive verbs with a non-presentational meaning (e.g. *get in touch, get caught up*), and in just two cases, transitive verbs (e.g. *reestablish, face*). Typical examples from the COCA and BNC as reported in Lee (2017: 27: 40), are shown in (14a–d).

(14)   a. <u>Several articles</u> have been written <u>which focus primarily on</u>
    <u>identifying specific psychological factors related to athlete alcohol use.</u>
    (COCA, 1995)
    b. In the next chapter, <u>an area of the world</u> is introduced <u>in which diarrhea</u>
    <u>remains a</u> <u>common illness.</u> (BNC, 1985)
    c. All her life, <u>things</u> had happened <u>which she had not arranged.</u>
    (BNC, 1975–84)
    d. Meanwhile across the Atlantic Ocean <u>an event</u> had taken place
    <u>which was destined to have the most far-reaching consequences.</u> (BNC, 1991)

In each case, the subject NP is indefinite and is used to introduce new information. The verb is either passive (14a) or intransitive (14b–d). These examples are consistent with a presentational reading, just as Guéron (1980), Rochemont and Culicover (1990), and others predicted.

In addition to generally confirming the presentational function of RCE, Francis and Michaelis (2014) also found evidence for gradient and cumulative effects of verb type and definiteness which are consistent with the acceptability judgment results from Walker (2013). In an analysis that compared RCE sentences with comparable non-RCE (adjacent order) sentences from the corpus, they found that RCE occurred most frequently relative to adjacent order when the subject NP was indefinite and the verb was either passive or presentational (intransitive with a presentational meaning), and least frequently when the subject NP was definite and the verb was neither passive nor presentational (Figure 6.6). Also as in Walker's (2013) study, the other two combinations of definiteness and verb type showed an intermediate rate of RCE usage. These corpus data showed that in addition to affecting acceptability of RCE sentences, the factors definiteness and verb type also affected rate of usage of RCE. This can be taken to support some version of the Predicate Constraint and the Name Constraint. Similar to Walker's study, which found that even the lowest-rated condition was still relatively acceptable in comparison to the ungrammatical filler sentences, Francis and Michaelis (2014) found that even the most unfavorable combination of linguistic features was still used with RCE in a few instances (Figure 6.6).

While judgment data are inherently ambiguous with respect to grammaticality, corpus data should be somewhat more definitive, since attested examples demonstrate that people are actually using the constraint-violating sentence type. In the previous section, for example, we saw how Strunk and Snider (2013) were able to eliminate subclausal locality as a hard constraint in German based on examples from the corpus showing that RCE occurs quite naturally in low-attachment contexts. Does this then suggest that we are dealing with soft constraints as per Walker's suggestion? Again, not necessarily. Since the categories used for the corpus analysis were operationalized in terms of linguistic form (definiteness marking, passive voice, etc.), the apparent counterexamples may still be compatible with Guéron's (1980) proposal. Since Guéron (1980) defines these constraints more abstractly in terms of nonspecific reference (the Name Constraint) and a presentational discourse function (the Predicate Constraint), it becomes somewhat more challenging to identify counterexamples. It may still be possible, however. Let's explore this idea a bit further.

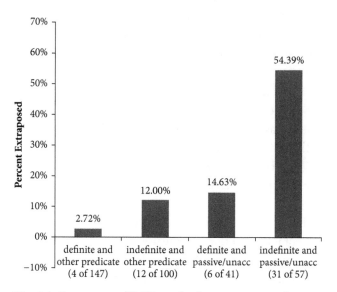

Fig. 6.6 Percentage of RCE use for four categories of definiteness and verb type

Source: From Francis and Michaelis (2014: 79).

Some of the corpus examples collected by Francis and Michaelis (2014) and Lee (2017) suggest that RCE sometimes can be used even when the matrix VP is used to express an assertion about a topical subject NP (and are consistent with focal stress falling within the VP), contrary to Guéron's (1980) prediction that such sentences should be ungrammatical. Consider these examples in (15a–c) from Francis and Michaelis (2014: 84) and in (15d) from Lee (2017: 19).

(15)   a. <u>Various people</u> did get in touch with me <u>who had done informal trials with addicts in clinics and had found that if they gave strenuous and regular exercise regimes, the addicts did get better and did not relapse</u>. (ICE-GB)
b. As you can imagine <u>the first few days</u> will be a bit hectic <u>during which time I will be ringing you and every client personally to invite you into my office</u>. (ICE-GB)
c. <u>The best singer</u> is this Olaf Bergh <u>that I've seen</u>. (ICE-GB)
d. If this were the sole criterion of success in economic policy, then <u>those critics</u> would be right <u>who argue that our nation is captive to the ideology of possessive individualism that elevates pursuit of individual satisfactions over a larger common good</u>. (COCA 1992)

Francis and Michaelis (2014) maintain that such exceptional cases are not an aberration or the result of production errors, but rather reflect the application of additional constraints affecting the use of RCE, which may sometimes override the Predicate Constraint and the Name Constraint when these constraints are in conflict. As noted in the introduction to this chapter, an important constraint affecting RCE and various other syntactic alternations (e.g. dative shift, Heavy NP Shift, particle shift, noun–genitive ordering) is the short-before-long preference in language production (Arnold et al. 2000; Francis 2010; Lohse, Hawkins, and Wasow 2004; Rosenbach 2005; Stallings, MacDonald, and O'Seaghdha 1998). In a logistic regression analysis that included RCE sentences and comparable non-RCE sentences from the ICE-GB corpus, Francis and Michaelis (2014) found that the ratio of VP length (in words) to relative clause length was the strongest predictor of RCE. For example, 91% of the sentences for which the relative clause was at least five times the length of the VP showed extraposition, while less than 3% of the sentences for which the relative clause was the same length or shorter than the VP did so (Figure 6.7). Definiteness and predicate type were also significant predictors, but their effects were only visible within a limited range of length ratios.

For the examples in (15a–b) and (15d), the relative clause was much longer than the VP, creating favorable conditions for the use of RCE despite the apparent violation of the Predicate Constraint. The example in (15c) cannot be understood in this way, however, since the length ratio should be more favorable to the adjacent order. Francis and Michaelis (2014: 84) suggested that the speaker (this particular example is from speech) may have added the relative clause as an afterthought, in order to qualify the strong claim made about the singer.

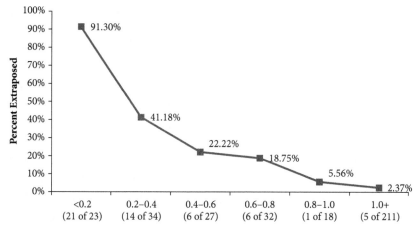

Fig. 6.7 Percentage of RCE use for increasing ratios of VP to relative clause length

Source: From Francis and Michaelis (2014: 80).

In both types of cases, then, the late production of the relative clause is apparently related to production planning. RCE offers the speaker or writer a grammatical means of postponing a phrase to allow additional time for planning of a long or complex constituent, or to allow the speaker to qualify their previous statement. Based on exceptional cases such as these, Francis and Michaelis (2014) conclude that there is no strict constraint on the discourse function associated with RCE, but rather discourse function (as manifested in such linguistic features as definiteness and verb type) is one of several factors affecting its use. Assuming a version of Construction Grammar, they briefly suggest an analysis in which the exceptional cases instantiate a minor subtype of the RCE construction which shares the syntactic properties of the basic construction but which does not share its discourse profile (2014: 87). Thus, they reject strong form–meaning isomorphism in favor of constructional polysemy, whereby the syntactic form of RCE has been extended for use in non-presentational contexts. The association of multiple meanings with a single phrasal sign type is an expected state of affairs in a construction-based theory, in which constructions mean what they mean in the way that words do: by convention rather than by a compositional syntactic derivation (Michaelis 1994; Perek 2014).

If we take the examples in (15a–d) as genuine counterexamples to Guéron's (1980) proposed constraints, it would appear that the Predicate Constraint and the Name Constraint should not be analyzed as strict grammatical constraints. One alternative would be to interpret them instead as soft constraints, as Walker (2013: 2017) suggested, while another option would be to say that these constraints are not really specific to the grammar of RCE at all, but perhaps can be understood in terms of general principles of information flow in discourse. Let's first consider the latter option.

One general principle which has been shown to apply across many languages is the tendency to express given/presupposed/topical information earlier in the sentence than new/asserted/focal information (Birner and Ward 1998; Chafe 1994; Gundel 1988). This given-before-new principle could help explain why RCE is relatively rare in language use, since a focal NP in subject position is generally much less common than a topical NP in subject position. Consistent with this tendency, Francis and Michaelis (2014) found that RCE was used only 15% of the time in sentences with a subject-modifying relative clause. In addition, these general principles could help explain why when a focal NP does occur in the subject position and is modified by a relative clause, that relative clause tends to be postponed to the end. Since the relative clause itself is part of the new information associated with the subject, RCE allows the speaker to express some of that new information later in the sentence, in accordance with the given-before-new principle.

While principles of information flow are relevant for understanding why speakers use RCE, I believe that the more specific soft constraint analysis is a more promising option for understanding the patterns of data we have seen. First, the corpus examples of RCE from Francis and Michaelis (2014) and Lee (2017) indicate that the presentational function of the VP is more specific in meaning than a general given-before-new principle would predict. In addition, the studies by Walker (2013; 2017) and Francis and Michaelis (2014) showed that English speakers were sensitive to certain linguistic cues (definiteness and verb type) which they associated directly with RCE. This would again appear to indicate the presence of language-specific, construction-specific knowledge. This idea of construction-specific knowledge is further supported by data from elicited production. Francis and Michaelis (2017) used a sentence construction task to elicit RCE and non-RCE sentences which varied according to phrase length and definiteness of the subject NP. In this task, participants were presented with three phrases (subject NP, VP, and relative clause) in a scrambled order and asked to put them together into a sentence and speak the sentence. They could respond freely using either RCE or adjacent order. As expected, participants used RCE more often when the subject NP was indefinite than when the subject NP was definite: 50% of indefinite subjects occurred with RCE vs. 24% of definite subjects. When they did use RCE with a definite subject NP, they were slower to initiate their spoken responses as compared to when they used RCE with an indefinite subject NP (Francis and Michaelis 2017: 357). In contrast, the non-RCE sentences did not show any difference in initiation time due to definiteness of the subject NP. These results suggest that speakers were sensitive to the definiteness cue *specifically in relation to the use of RCE*. Following MacDonald's (2013) Production–Distribution–Comprehension theory, Francis and Michaelis (2017: 363) proposed that frequently used linguistic plans (which we can think of here as well-attested subtypes of the RCE construction) are easier to retrieve from memory and therefore more accessible and easier to produce than infrequently used plans. Since RCE with an indefinite subject is an example of a frequently used plan, participants were faster to produce RCE sentences of this type. Although Francis and Michaelis did not put it in exactly these terms, their proposal is essentially a soft constraint analysis. We can think of the Name Constraint as a soft constraint which specifies an indefinite subject NP (or possibly something more abstract that is cued by indefiniteness, such as focal status) as a component of the preferred or prototypical subtype of the RCE construction. This constraint affects how often speakers use RCE, how quickly they produce a sentence with RCE, and how acceptable they judge such a sentence to be.

In this section, I have argued that both the Predicate Constraint and the Name Constraint are empirically supported, but do not hold up as strict grammatical constraints on RCE in the sense that Guéron (1980) intended. To be fair, it would still be possible to account for the apparent counterexamples in (15) in a different way, perhaps as production errors, or perhaps as having a different syntactic derivation than the typical RCE sentences. The latter option would allow us to maintain strict form–meaning isomorphism by establishing a different underlying syntactic form for those sentences that fail to conform to the usual interpretive constraints. However, if we understand the examples in (15) as actual instances of RCE but relax the requirement for strict form–meaning isomorphism, it then becomes straightforward to interpret the Predicate Constraint and the Name Constraint as soft constraints. For the sake of concreteness, I assume here a Construction Grammar style analysis as proposed by Francis and Michaelis (2014; 2017). This departs slightly from the idea of soft constraints in Stochastic OT and related theories, as discussed in Chapter 2. In Stochastic OT, a set of weighted constraints competes within the grammar to select the output form with the least violation cost. Although the constraint weightings are specified in the grammar, a random stochastic evaluation allows for somewhat different rankings on different occasions, resulting in the selection of the more costly (less-preferred) output form some proportion of the time. Here, I understand soft constraints instead in terms of the lexical, syntactic, semantic, and discourse characteristics of the preferred or prototypical subtype of the RCE construction. Speakers and writers are sensitive to these characteristics when they choose between RCE and adjacent order during real-time language use, and will typically use RCE more often when the preferred characteristics are present. However, they will sometimes use the RCE structure when these conditions are not met, thus violating the Name Constraint and/or the Predicate Constraint. Often, the choice to violate a soft constraint will be motivated by some other factor, such as the tendency to postpone long constituents for easier production. The effects of these constraint violations on acceptability judgments of isolated sentences, as shown in Walker's (2013; 2017) study, are also understood to be derivative of this preferred subtype of RCE.

The soft constraints I have described in this section can be implemented as a competition among weighted constraints (as in Stochastic OT, Linear OT, or the Decathlon Model), or as a set of characteristics defining the preferred subtype of a construction, as in the approach I outlined briefly above. The first approach is well established in the literature on soft constraints and has been applied successfully to different types of syntactic phenomena in different languages (Bresnan et al. 2001; Featherston 2005a; Sorace and Keller 2005), while the second approach has not been worked out in any detail. However, I believe that the second approach is a viable alternative which can be extended in interesting ways using Goldberg's (2019) usage-based theory of the partial productivity of constructions. Although the goals of Goldberg's theory are not framed in relation to soft constraints, the concepts are applicable here because the theory makes specific predictions about the acceptability of items which extend a construction to be used in an unconventional way. In the discussion above and in Francis and Michaelis (2017), we emphasized the greater accessibility of frequently used plans (MacDonald 2013) as a way to understand the slower initiation time in elicited production and degraded acceptability of RCE sentences that violate the Name Constraint. Goldberg (2019) recognizes the importance of this factor, which she calls simple entrenchment, for predicting acceptability judgments.[16] Beyond simple entrenchment, however, Goldberg provides an account of why speakers find some novel extensions of a construction relatively acceptable and others less so. According to this approach, constructions are learned incrementally through experience with individual exemplars consisting of information specified along multiple dimensions of form and meaning. As new exemplars are encountered, they are assigned to an existing cluster of previously witnessed exemplars and stored in memory in a partially abstract form. To the extent that a new exemplar fits within a well-attested cluster based on formal and functional similarity along multiple dimensions, it is typically judged as acceptable (Goldberg 2019: 63). Goldberg observes that clusters with a wider range of lexical, phonological, and semantic variability within them (a wider 'coverage' in her terms) tend to encourage productivity because there is a wider area in which the new exemplars can fit. In addition, she identifies an important role for competition among related constructions. As I discussed in Chapter 5, novel verb-construction pairings may be subject to statistical preemption (blocking) by a competing alternative construction when the verb has been frequently encountered in that construction to express the same meaning.

Barak and Goldberg (2017) proposed a computational model of the partial productivity of verb-argument constructions following this exemplar-based clustering approach. Through learning simulations based on input involving naturalistic (corpus-based) frequency distributions of verbs in different constructions, they were able to predict the likelihood of a particular syntactic pattern given a verb and an intended meaning.[17] In each instance, the verb had occurred in the input in one or more syntactic patterns but not the pattern of interest. Encouragingly, the predictions of the simulations were shown to correspond closely to acceptability judgments of novel verb-construction combinations obtained in Robenalt and Goldberg's (2015) experiments with human participants. In particular, the simulations predicted that

---

[16] At least implicitly, the idea of simple entrenchment also motivates the soft constraints of Stochastic OT, which are based on frequency distributions mediated by a learning algorithm (Boersma and Hayes 2001).

[17] The input consisted of a series of 'usage events' simulating the use of a particular verb in a particular construction. Each verb was specified for lexical semantic features and argument-selection properties, and each construction was specified with a syntactic frame and a certain number of arguments (Barak and Goldberg 2017).

the unattested syntactic pattern was less likely (and should therefore be less accept-able) when the same verb was frequently attested in an alternative syntactic pattern with the same meaning (see Chapter 5, Section 5.3 for further details of these experi-ments). In the current context, a similar type of simulation could be applied to predict the acceptability of RCE with various verbs that typically do or do not occur in this construction, in order to better understand what I am calling the Predicate Constraint. Potentially, this approach could also be extended to include information in the input about discourse information status and morphological definiteness, to better under-stand the usage-based factors underlying the Name Constraint. The predictions of the simulations could then inform the design of acceptability judgment experiments to develop a more detailed and nuanced approach to the soft constraints affecting RCE in English.

6.5 Conclusions

This chapter has covered two main themes regarding the theoretical interpretation of gradient acceptability judgments, using a variety of different studies on Extraposition from NP in English and German to illustrate these themes. The first theme is that theoretical assumptions about form–meaning isomorphism and gradient grammati-cality are an important but often unacknowledged factor affecting our interpretation of judgment data. If a researcher adopts a derivational framework that requires strict form–meaning isomorphism and categorical grammaticality, this can then limit the range of possible explanations that they are likely to consider. For example, Guéron (1980) discussed some apparent exceptions to the Predicate Constraint and the Name Constraint, but only considered explanations that were consistent with strict form–meaning isomorphism and categorical grammaticality, and which assumed a single type of syntactic derivation for extraposition. If a researcher instead adopts a the-oretical approach that does not require strict form–meaning isomorphism and that allows for the possibility of gradient grammaticality, this opens up a wider range of possible explanations for gradient patterns of judgments. However, such a perspective can also lead one to interpret gradient judgments as reflecting gradient grammatical-ity even when plausible alternative explanations are available. For example, Walker (2013; 2017) interpreted her judgment data as reflecting the application of soft con-straints, even though the data also appear to be compatible with Guéron's (1980) strict interpretive constraints. A more general point here is that although gradient patterns of judgments are usually compatible with various theoretical interpretations, our preferred theoretical frameworks will naturally guide us toward certain expla-nations and away from others even when the available data are truly ambiguous. A first step in guarding against over-interpretation of the data is to gain a better awareness of these basic assumptions. A second step is to collect additional data of different types which might at least help narrow down the range of plausible explanations.

This leads to the second main theme of this chapter—the utility of examining additional data sources to supplement judgment data. For all of the cases we examined in this chapter, the judgment data were ambiguous with respect to an appropriate theoretical interpretation. In two of those cases, however, corpus data were available to help eliminate certain interpretations from serious consideration. This was clearest for subclausal locality conditions on RCE in German. Strunk and Snider (2013) found that while subclausal locality does appear to affect writers' choice between RCE and adjacent order, cases of extraposition from an embedded NP were easy to find in the corpus. On this basis, they argued that even though their second experiment showed an interaction effect consistent with a Subjacency account, there can be no strict grammatical constraint that rules out this type of structure. Furthermore, their corpus data from German showed gradient effects of subclausal locality: writers were increasingly less likely to use RCE as depth of embedding of the antecedent noun increased to two, three, and four levels. They note that this pattern is compatible with either a processing-based account of subclausal locality, or a soft constraint analysis, and they do not attempt to distinguish between these options. Corpus data were also helpful for shedding light on the Predicate Constraint and the Name Constraint as applied to RCE with a subject antecedent in English. Based on several exceptional cases from the ICE-GB corpus, Francis and Michaelis (2014) argued that RCE can be grammatically licensed even when it does not fulfill its ordinary presentational function and thus there are no strict interpretive constraints on its occurrence. Their data also showed a systematic increase in the frequency of RCE for different combinations of verb type and definiteness, which I take to be consistent with a soft constraint analysis. Lending further support to the idea of soft constraints, Francis and Michaelis (2017) found that speakers were sensitive to the definiteness of the subject NP when producing RCE sentences, but not when producing non-RCE sentences. This finding suggests that something like the Name Constraint is part of speakers' implicit linguistic knowledge about RCE, even though it does not categorically determine the form or interpretation of utterances with RCE. Based on these earlier proposals (Francis and Michaelis 2014; 2017), I sketched out a possible way of thinking about soft constraints as preferred subtypes of a construction with particular formal and functional characteristics and discussed how this approach could be extended further following Goldberg (2019) to incorporate detailed information about language use.

7

Resumptive pronouns in Hebrew, Cantonese, and English relative clauses

Resumptive pronouns bear the morphology of ordinary pronouns, and occur in a bound position within a long-distance dependency construction where a gap would otherwise go. Although these pronouns sometimes occur in several different constructions within a given language, this chapter will be concerned exclusively with their use in relative clauses. In languages that have them, resumptive pronouns typically overlap with gaps in their distributions to some degree, but also occur in some positions where gaps are prohibited. For example, Shlonsky (1992) and Meltzer-Asscher et al. (2015) observe that in Hebrew, both pronouns and gaps are permissible in the direct object function within a relative clause (1a–b), whereas pronouns but not gaps are permissible in the prepositional object function (2a–b) (Meltzer-Asscher et al. 2015: 65). The lower acceptability of (2b) is usually attributed to a preposition stranding constraint, the violation of which can be avoided by inserting a resumptive pronoun, as in (2a).

(1) a. ze   ha-iš še-   ra'iti oto
         this   the-man that   saw   him
         'This is the man that I saw him.'
     b. ze   ha-iš   še-   ra'iti __
         this   the-man that   saw
         'This is the man that I saw __'

(2) a. ze ha-iš   še   šamati   al-av
         this the-man that   heard   about-him
         'This is the man that I heard about him.
     b. *ze ha-iš   še   šamati   al __
         this the-man that   heard   about
         'This is the man that I heard about __'

As McCloskey (2006) points out, resumptive pronouns can in this way increase the expressive power of relative clauses by extending the range of grammatical functions that can be relativized: in this case, prepositional objects. More generally, they tend to extend this range to relatively more complex dependencies. Keenan and Comrie (1977) have observed that across languages, resumptive pronouns are grammatically required more often in functions that are lower on the NP Accessibility Hierarchy, such

Gradient Acceptability and Linguistic Theory. Elaine J. Francis, Oxford University Press.
© Elaine J. Francis (2022). DOI: 10.1093/oso/9780192898944.003.0007

as prepositional objects and possessors.[1] Hawkins (1999: 262–6) further extends this hierarchy to include embedded subjects and objects and certain island-violating contexts. Indeed, resumptive pronouns are used productively in embedded clauses and in island-violating contexts in some languages, including Irish and Lebanese Arabic (McCloskey 2006). In contrast, Keenan and Comrie (1977) observe that resumptive pronouns are typically excluded as subject of a simple clause. Both Keenan and Comrie (1977) and Hawkins (1999) relate these typological patterns to the idea of processing complexity. The basic idea is that the more explicit nature of the pronoun may aid in the comprehension and production of more complex dependencies, while providing no advantage over a gap (and perhaps even a disadvantage) for processing simpler dependencies. Although some of the details are disputed, descriptions of Hebrew are generally consistent with this typological pattern. Hebrew resumptive pronouns are said to be excluded from simple subjects, optionally used as direct objects, and required in prepositional object, possessive, and island-violating contexts (to the extent such contexts can be relativized at all) (Asudeh 2012). We may then tentatively claim that the grammar of Hebrew encodes a processing preference for resumptive pronouns in complex dependencies but does so in a relatively discrete manner by means of grammatical rules which require or exclude resumptive pronouns in certain grammatical functions.

In English, resumptive pronouns are used less productively than in Hebrew and are typically judged as being lower in acceptability (Polinsky et al. 2013). Nevertheless, they show a broadly similar pattern in language use: they overlap with gaps in some contexts, while also occurring in complex dependencies where gaps are generally excluded. For example, the English relative clauses in (3a) and (4a) are attested examples cited by Prince (1990). For comparison, the corresponding gapped versions of the same sentences are given in (3b) and (4b). The embedded object relative with a gap in (3b) is well-formed and fully acceptable. In contrast, the *wh*-island relative with a gap in (4b) is ill-formed and low in acceptability. This is often interpreted as meaning that (4a) represents a strategy that speakers may use to 'repair' the island violation in (4b).

(3)   a. I don't think there's a company in the world that the stockholders would
          allow a company to copy **it**.   (Prince 1990: 486)
       b. I don't think there's a company in the world that the stockholders would
          allow a company to copy ___.

(4)   a. There are always guests who I am curious about what **they** are going to say.
                                                                            (Prince 1990: 482)
       b. *There are always guests who I am curious about what ___ are going to say.
       c. There are always guests who are unpredictable. I am curious about what
          they are going to say.

---

[1] Keenan and Comrie (1977: 66) propose a Noun Phrase Accessibility Hierarchy (NPAH) as follows: Subject > Direct Object > Indirect Object > Oblique > Genitive > Object of Comparison. Based on a sample of 26 languages, they identified two implicational relations: (1) if the grammar of a language allows gaps in one position on the hierarchy (e.g. direct object), it will allow them in all other positions that are to its left (e.g. subject); (2) conversely, if the grammar of a language allows resumptive pronouns in one structural position (e.g. direct object), it will allow them in all other positions that are to its right (e.g. indirect object).

I use the word 'repair' somewhat loosely here because the difference between (4a) and (4b) may not be as striking as the difference between (2a) and (2b) in Hebrew: structures like (4a) and (4b) are still quite low in acceptability, with some studies of resumption within *wh*-islands showing a slight preference for items like (4a) (Han et al. 2012; Keffala 2011; McDaniel and Cowart 1999; Morgan and Wagers 2018). Furthermore, the grammatical status of attested examples like (3a) and (4a) is disputed. While some linguists argue that resumptive pronouns are fully licensed by the grammar of English but contextually restricted (Cann et al. 2005; Radford 2019), most assume that they are generally ungrammatical in English. Indeed, in the theoretical literature on resumption, it is conventional to distinguish between languages like English with *intrusive* resumption and languages like Hebrew with *grammatical* resumption (Asudeh 2012; Sells 1984). On this account, sentences like (3a) and (4a) are the result of overgeneration by the production system (Asudeh 2012; Morgan and Wagers 2018; Polinsky et al. 2013). Even if such sentences are not (fully) licensed by the grammar, however, it seems that their function is similar to that in Hebrew in allowing English speakers to express a wider range of ideas using a relative clause than they otherwise would. If only the gap strategy were available, for example, a sentence like (4a) would not occur and would need to be replaced with a paraphrase such as (4c). Arguably, intrusive resumption in English serves a similar function to that of grammatical resumption in Hebrew in facilitating the use of relative clauses with relatively complex dependencies (Morgan and Wagers 2018; Polinsky et al. 2013; Prince 1990). Such similarities between grammatical and intrusive resumption have been cited in support of the hypothesis that grammatical resumption, in languages that have it, is historically derived from intrusive resumption (Alexopoulou 2010; Ariel 1999; Hawkins 2004).

To conclude this brief introduction, the distribution of resumptive pronouns within a given language is unique to that language, but, in general, it is governed by a combination of syntactic, pragmatic, and processing-related factors. For languages like Hebrew with grammatical resumption, syntactic constraints on extraction (e.g. preposition stranding constraints and various island constraints) appear to determine when resumptive pronouns will be obligatorily used or excluded entirely, while pragmatic and processing factors become more important for determining their use in grammatically optional contexts. For languages like English with intrusive resumption, the role of syntactic constraints on extraction is less clear, since resumptive pronouns have more of a marginal status in the language. For these languages, processing-related factors appear to play a more direct and prominent role in determining their use.

Although the effects of these various factors are often subtle, descriptive and theoretical studies of resumption have traditionally used informal acceptability judgments to support their claims about how resumptive pronouns are licensed in obligatory and optional contexts, and why they are often excluded from the highest subject (Aoun et al. 2001; Asudeh 2012; Borer 1984; McCloskey 2006; 2011; Shlonsky 1992). However, there is a growing literature of experimental and corpus-based studies which begin to show an even more complex set of generalizations (Ackerman et al. 2018; Alexopoulou and Keller 2007; Ariel 1999; Chacón 2019; Chen and Fukuda 2018; Fadlon et al. 2019; Francis et al. 2015; Han et al. 2012; Heestand et al. 2011; Keffala

2011; Meltzer-Asscher et al. 2015; Polinsky et al. 2013; Radford 2019). In the remainder of this chapter, I will consider several studies which bear on the division of labor among syntactic, pragmatic, and processing constraints as well as the proposed distinction between intrusive and grammatical resumption.[2] In addition to examining studies of resumption in Hebrew and English, I will also discuss experimental studies of resumption in Cantonese, a language which, like Hebrew, is characterized as having grammatical resumption. As in the case of extraposed relative clauses discussed in Chapter 6, we will see that acceptability judgment experiments can shed light on the relative contributions of various factors. However, the information they provide is only partial and often ambiguous for interpretation. I will discuss how data from other types of psycholinguistic experiments can inform the analysis and help reduce this ambiguity. Throughout the discussion, I will attempt to elucidate how our theoretical assumptions affect how we tend to interpret data from these various sources. Finally, at the end of the chapter, I will offer some brief remarks on the notion of partial grammaticalization and its implications for understanding the typological distinction between grammatical and intrusive resumption.

7.1 Resumption in contexts where gaps are permitted: object relatives in Hebrew and English

Borer (1984) and Shlonsky (1992) (among others) have observed that both gaps and resumptive pronouns are used in the direct object function in Hebrew relative clauses. Although resumptive pronouns are said to be more limited in terms of their semantic and pragmatic functions, the two alternatives can often be used interchangeably, as in (5a–b) (repeated from (1a–b)).

(5) a. ze   ha-iš   še-   ra'iti oto
         this the-man that saw   him
         'This is the man that I saw him.'
     b. ze   ha-iš   še-   ra'iti ___
         this the-man that saw
         'This is the man that I saw ___'

Direct object relatives are described in contrast to subject relatives, which only permit gaps (6a–b), and prepositional object relatives, which only permit resumptive pronouns (see (2a–b)) (Borer 1984; Shlonsky 1992).

(6) *a. ze   ha-iš   še- hu ohev et   Rina
          this the-man   that he loves ACC   Rina
          'This is the man that he loves Rina.'

---

[2] For a more comprehensive overview of the current experimental literature on resumptive pronouns, I refer the reader to Meltzer-Asscher's (2021) review article.

b. ze ha-iš   še-___ ohev et   Rina
    this the-man that loves ACC   Rina
    'This is the man that ___ loves Rina.'

While these earlier accounts were based on linguists' informal judgments, Farby et al. (2010) and Meltzer-Asscher et al. (2015) have more recently tested sentences similar to (5a–b) using acceptability judgment tasks. Results from both studies appear to confirm the grammatically optional status of resumptive pronouns in direct object relatives, while at the same time showing a slight preference for gaps. In order to understand this preference for gaps as the authors of these studies have interpreted it, it is first necessary to elucidate the notion of cognitive accessibility, as proposed by Ariel (1999) on the basis of corpus data. The experiments and findings of Farby et al. (2010) and Meltzer-Asscher et al. (2015) will then be discussed in more detail.

Ariel (1999) proposed a theory of 'accessibility' to account for patterns of resumptive pronoun use in Hebrew. In an analysis of 77 relative clauses from a corpus of conversational Hebrew, Ariel (1999) found that speakers used resumptive pronouns more often to the extent that the relativized position was less accessible for integration with the head noun. While Keenan and Comrie (1977) defined their NP Accessibility Hierarchy solely in terms of the grammatical function of the relativized element, Ariel (1999) extends the idea of accessibility to include a combination of factors which apply in a cumulative fashion and which may affect both comprehension and production. These include grammatical function (following the NP Accessibility Hierarchy), linear distance between the head noun and the relativized element, length of the head NP (not including the relative clause), and status of the relative clause as either restrictive or nonrestrictive (i.e. tighter vs. looser integration between the head noun and its relative clause modifier). Of particular relevance for the current discussion, Ariel (1999) found that resumptive pronouns were rarely used in the direct object function. Only two out of 23 simple object relatives in the corpus included a resumptive pronoun. This was similar to the rate of resumption that she found for simple subject relatives (three out of 37)—a context where resumptive pronouns are generally assumed to be ungrammatical (Borer 1984; Schlonsky 1992). Breaking from the standard view that resumptive pronouns are optional in object relatives but prohibited in subject relatives, Ariel (1999) attributes the low rate of resumption in both positions to the relatively high degree of accessibility exhibited by the particular tokens that were extracted from the corpus. That is, the subject and object relatives in the corpus sample exhibited a short distance between the head noun and the relativized element, and most were restrictive modifiers of short NPs. Ariel (1999) notes that all of the examples of resumption in subject relatives (three tokens) and object relatives (two tokens) occurred in nonrestrictive relative clauses, in line with her accessibility hypothesis.

Bearing in mind Ariel's (1999) notion of accessibility and the corpus data that inspired it, let us now return to the results of the two acceptability judgments studies that examined object relative clauses in Hebrew. Using written stimuli, Farby et al. (2010) tested simple object relatives and embedded object relatives containing either a resumptive pronoun or a gap. Similar to (5a–b), agent and patient arguments were always animate. Participants were provided with a short context paragraph before reading the test sentences to ensure that the antecedent of the relativized element was highly accessible from the context. Results showed that simple object relatives were rated higher than embedded object relatives, and gaps were rated higher than resumptive pronouns (Figure 7.1). To account for the effect of embedding, they point to the added cost of processing a longer dependency. To account for the finding that gaps were more acceptable than resumptive pronouns, they invoke Ariel's (1999) idea of accessibility, which predicts that highly accessible antecedents are more compatible with gaps than with resumptive pronouns. Given the very low rate of resumption in Ariel's (1999) corpus sample, however, it is perhaps surprising that Farby et al. (2010) only found a slight preference for gaps, even in the simple object relatives. Possibly, this is an example of what Bader and Häussler (2010: 136) call a Ceiling Mismatch, as discussed in Chapter 4: two syntactic structures which differ in frequency are both perceived as well-formed. A more specific explanation will be considered below, with reference to additional data from elicited production. In any case, the authors take the relatively high ratings for both resumptive pronouns and gaps to indicate that both options are indeed grammatically licensed in Hebrew.

Comparing the simple and embedded object relatives, it is notable that the two factors (occurrence of pronoun/gap and depth of embedding) showed a simple additive effect and did not interact (Figure 7.1). Farby et al. (2010) point out that this lack

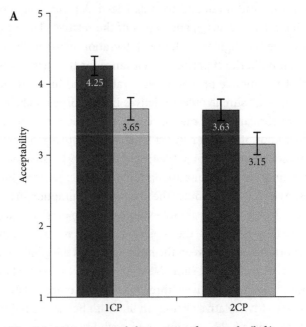

Fig. 7.1 Mean acceptability ratings for simple (left) and embedded (right) object relative clauses in Hebrew with gap (dark bar) or resumptive pronoun (light bar)
Source: From Farby et al. (2010: 13).

of any interaction is somewhat surprising, since embedded objects are less accessible than simple objects (due to depth of embedding) and might therefore have been expected to allow resumptive pronouns more freely (Ariel 1999; Hawkins 2004). They conclude that the discourse salience of the antecedent was more important than depth of embedding in determining participants' judgments (Farby et al. 2010: 13).[3]

Following on from Farby et al. (2010), Meltzer-Asscher et al. (2015) elicited acceptability ratings of embedded object relatives with a resumptive pronoun or a gap (simple object relatives were not tested). As in Farby et al. (2010), agent and patient arguments were always animate. However, the materials in Meltzer-Asscher et al. (2015) differed from those in Farby et al. (2010) in that items were presented in both written and auditory modalities.[4] In addition, materials were designed so that the relativized element was somewhat lower in accessibility according to Ariel's (1999) criteria. There was no supporting context to introduce the antecedent, and the head noun occurred within a long NP containing two additional nouns. Results for both written and spoken stimuli showed that gaps were rated slightly higher than resumptive pronouns. However, this preference for gaps was greater for the written stimuli as compared with the spoken stimuli. The first observation—the overall preference for gaps—was similar to what Farby et al. (2010) found. It was, however, somewhat less expected, given that the materials were designed to be lower in accessibility. Meltzer-Asscher et al. surmise that resumptive pronouns caused a kind of garden-path effect when they were encountered by readers or listeners: "Given that in direct object relative clauses, such as those in our experiment, the resolution of the dependency takes place on the embedded verb, the resumptive element is in fact unnecessary, and its occurrence calls for a strategy shift; the initial parse of the structure as involving movement has to be changed, and a binding strategy has to be adopted instead" (2015: 71). The authors concede that additional measures of processing ease, such as reading times, would be needed to support this type of explanation. To account for the second observation—the bigger advantage for gaps in the written modality—they give three possible explanations: (1) that resumptive pronouns are more common in speech than in writing; (2) that gaps may be slightly more difficult to interpret in the auditory modality due to decay of the antecedent from working memory; and (3) that auditory presentation made it obvious that the resumptive pronoun was unstressed, and so was more likely to be immediately understood in its intended function. They acknowledge that further research is needed to distinguish among these possibilities.

To sum up, Ariel's (1999) notion of accessibility helps account for the slight preference for gaps shown in the two acceptability judgment tasks discussed here, as well

---

[3] This type of interaction has been shown for Mandarin, a language typically classified as having grammatical resumption. For example, Chen and Fukuda (2018: 12) found that gaps were slightly more acceptable than resumptive pronouns in simple object relatives, but that difference disappeared in embedded object relatives.

[4] The materials from Meltzer-Asscher et al. (2015) also differed from those in Farby et al. (2010) in that relative clauses were tested in three different positions within the sentence: as modifiers of the subject, direct object, and indirect object. Farby et al. (2010) only tested direct object-modifying clauses. Although this manipulation showed a main effect (with subject-modifying clauses being rated higher overall), it did not show any interaction with resumption.

as the greater preference for gaps that Meltzer-Asscher et al. (2015) found for written stimuli as compared with spoken stimuli. Can a similar notion of accessibility then apply to patterns of acceptability shown in other languages? As Meltzer-Asscher et al. (2015: 71) observe, the lower acceptability of resumptive pronouns as compared with gaps in Hebrew object relatives is reminiscent of a similar effect observed for English. In separate studies, Han et al. (2012), Hofmeister and Norcliffe (2013), and Keffala (2011) found that English speakers consistently rated resumptive pronouns as lower in acceptability than gaps in both simple and embedded object relatives. Meltzer-Asscher et al. (2015) go on to suggest that a similar mechanism may be responsible for the lower acceptability of resumptive pronouns in both languages. This presents a puzzle, however. How can the similar pattern of judgments be reconciled with the widely accepted typological distinction between grammatical and intrusive resumption? More specifically, why is it that the difference in acceptability between resumptive pronouns and gaps is taken to indicate a slight preference among two grammatically licensed alternatives in Hebrew (Farby et al. 2010; Meltzer-Asscher et al. 2015), while in English, it is taken to indicate a difference in grammaticality, with resumptive pronouns being the ungrammatical option (Hofmeister and Norcliffe 2013; Keffala 2011; Morgan and Wagers 2018)? Furthermore, how does the notion of accessibility apply in each case?

As a starting point for addressing these questions, we can observe that the judgment data in fact showed different patterns in Hebrew and English. In the results from all three studies (Han et al. 2012; Keffala 2011; Hofmeister and Norcliffe 2013), English speakers showed a stronger preference for gaps over resumptive pronouns in simple object relatives, and a weaker preference in embedded object relatives. Specifically, gaps were less acceptable in embedded object relatives as compared with simple object relatives, but resumptive pronouns stayed at the same low level of acceptability in both clause types. For example, this pattern is shown in Figure 7.2 from Hofmeister and Norcliffe (2013: 230) for English sentences such as those as in (7a–b).

(7)   a. Mary confirmed that there was a prisoner who the prison officials had
        acknowledged that the guard helped (**him** / __) to make a daring escape.
                                                                    (long dependency)
        b. The prison officials had acknowledged that there was a prisoner that the
        guard helped (**him** / __) to make a daring escape.   (short dependency)

In contrast, Farby et al. (2010) found that Hebrew speakers showed a slight preference for gaps over resumptive pronouns in both simple and embedded object relatives. Both gaps and resumptive pronouns became less acceptable with embedding, and did so to the same degree (Figure 7.1).

The crucial piece of information here seems to be that in English, unlike Hebrew, there is a greater contrast in acceptability between gaps and resumptive pronouns in simple object relatives as compared with embedded object relatives. This is reminiscent of the pattern that Häussler et al. (2015) found for Superiority-violating questions in English and German, as discussed in Chapter 4. They argued that the strong contrast between Superiority-violating questions and non-Superiority-violating questions in

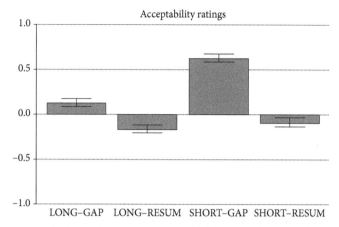

Fig. 7.2 Mean acceptability ratings for simple (right) and embedded (left) object relative clauses in English

Source: Reproduced from Hofmeister and Norcliffe (2013: 230) with permission from CSLI Publications.

English (as compared to German) was most likely due to a conventional grammatical constraint because it occurred even with simple, unambiguous clauses. Similarly, it can be argued that the relatively strong contrast in acceptability between resumptive pronouns and gaps in simple object relatives likely reflects the application of a grammatical constraint. According to such an account, the grammatical constraint still applies in embedded object relatives, but the contrast in acceptability is reduced due to a general processing cost associated with embedding. This processing cost results in lower acceptability of gaps in embedded clauses, but has no effect on resumptive pronouns, which are already less acceptable due to the grammatical constraint violation. On the contrary, in Hebrew, resumption is assumed to incur no grammatical constraint violation in object relatives. This is consistent with the finding from Farby et al. (2010) that gaps and resumptive pronouns became less acceptable to the same degree under embedding (Figure 7.1).

To further explore this cross-linguistic comparison, I will consider two elicited production studies which help elucidate the grammatical status of resumptive pronouns and the role of accessibility in production of Hebrew (Fadlon et al. 2019) and English (Morgan and Wagers 2018) relative clauses. Fadlon et al. (2019) used a series of three elicited production experiments to test how factors related to the accessibility of the relativized position affect speakers' production choices in English and Hebrew. In their first experiment, English speakers read a context scenario and then answered a question about it by typing their response. In one scenario, for example, participants were given information about a set of characters and then asked: *Who is most likely to buy the boss a nice gift for Christmas?* (Fadlon et al. 2019: 44). The question, which was paired with a prompt, was designed such that it could be answered correctly with either an object relative clause (e.g. *the day-worker that the farmer praised*) or a passivized subject relative clause with an equivalent meaning (e.g. *the day-worker*

that was praised by the farmer). In addition, the context scenarios were manipulated to force either a restrictive or nonrestrictive interpretation of the relative clause.
In the restrictive context, the correct answer had to be chosen among three characters who all fit the same description (e.g. *day-worker*) and needed to be distinguished
from each other using a relative clause. Following the question, participants received
a prompt in which they typed their answer: *The _____ that _____.* In the nonrestrictive context, the correct answer had to be chosen among three characters who
were described using different nouns (e.g. *day-worker, cowboy,* and *banker*). In this
scenario, the relative clause was not necessary to answer the question, but its inclusion
was forced by the prompt: *The _____ that, as mentioned _____.*

Building on Ariel's (1999) idea that the relativized position in a nonrestrictive relative clause is less accessible for integration with the head noun as compared with the
same position in a restrictive relative clause, Fadlon et al. predicted that restrictiveness
should affect speakers' production choices: "The idea is that as the production system
formulates the relative clause content, it should be easier to maintain a representation
of the filler if it is part of the same information unit than if it is a part of a separate information unit" (2019: 44). Because passive subject relatives have a shorter dependency
distance than active object relatives, thus mitigating the difficulty of filler retention,
Fadlon et al. (2019) predicted that English speakers should produce a higher proportion of passive clauses in the nonrestrictive context. This is in fact what they found:
57.5% of responses were passive in the nonrestrictive context, compared with 46.1%
in the restrictive context.[5] Notably, English speakers always used either an active object relative with a gap or a passive subject relative with a gap in their responses. This
is consistent with the idea that in English, resumptive pronouns are ungrammatical
and therefore not readily activated in production when a fully acceptable alternative
is available.

In their second experiment, Fadlon et al. (2019) used the same paradigm, but with
Hebrew test materials and Hebrew-speaking participants. They hypothesized that the
restrictiveness manipulation should similarly affect relative clause production in Hebrew, except that Hebrew speakers have the additional option to use a resumptive
pronoun in an active object relative clause. Following Ariel (1999), Fadlon et al. (2019)
predicted that Hebrew speakers would use resumptive pronouns in their responses
more often in the nonrestrictive context as compared with the restrictive context. They
also predicted that speakers might produce more passive subject relatives in the nonrestrictive context as compared with the restrictive context, but note that the passive
structure is less available in Hebrew than in English. The results of this second experiment confirm their first prediction. As shown in Figure 7.3, speakers produced
a resumptive pronoun in 45.2% of responses in the nonrestrictive context, compared
with 34.7% of responses in the restrictive context. The rate of the passive strategy was

---

[5] The high overall rate of passive responses was likely due to the fact that all of the arguments in the scenarios
given were animate, a factor which has been shown to increase the rate of passive responses compared with
scenarios involving an animate agent and an inanimate patient (Gennari et al. 2012).

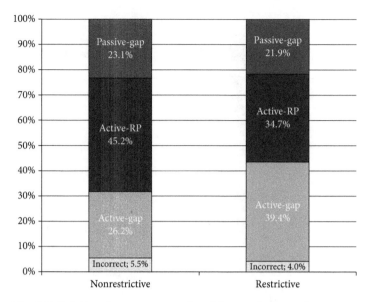

Fig. 7.3 Relative clause types produced in restrictive and non-restrictive contexts in Hebrew

Source: Reprinted from Fadlon et al. (2019: 49) with permission from Elsevier.

higher overall than the authors expected, but did not differ between the restrictive and nonrestrictive contexts.

The third and final experiment reported in Fadlon et al. (2019), which was also on Hebrew, tested a different factor which they believed would affect the accessibility of the relativized element: the animacy of the patient argument. Based on studies of similarity-based interference in sentence processing (Gennari et al. 2012), the authors hypothesized that speakers would use a resumptive pronoun more often when both the agent and the patient were animate, as compared to when the agent was animate and the patient was inanimate. The idea is that the similar animacy features of the two arguments make filler retention more challenging, possibly causing speakers to use a resumptive pronoun more often. The second experiment, discussed above, only used scenarios in which both arguments were animate, and showed relatively high rates of resumption in both conditions. However, since animacy was not manipulated, the extent of its effect was unknown. The third experiment used a question-and-answer task similar to the one in the first two experiments, except that the context was presented as a picture instead of a written scenario, and only restrictive relative clauses were elicited. As shown in Figure 7.4, the results confirm their predictions. In both the animate and inanimate patient conditions, the preferred structure was the active gap structure. However, the rate of resumption in the animate patient condition was much higher, at 27.0%, compared with 5.7% in the inanimate patient condition.

Taken together, Experiments 2 and 3 support Ariel's (1999) proposal that Hebrew speakers are more likely to use a resumptive pronoun as the accessibility of the relativized position is reduced. At 5.7%, the low rate of resumption for highly accessible

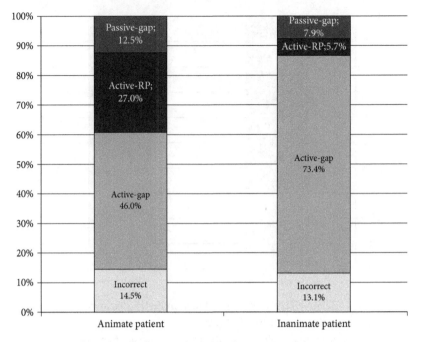

Fig. 7.4 Relative clause types produced with animate and inanimate patient
arguments in Hebrew

Source: Reprinted from Fadlon et al. (2019: 49) with permission from Elsevier.

object relatives (with a restrictive interpretation and an inanimate patient) in Experiment 3 is comparable to the low rate observed in Ariel's corpus sample. On its own,
this finding from Experiment 3 gives no clear indication of the grammatical status
of resumption. However, the significantly higher rate of resumption with animate
patients (34.7% in Experiment 2 and 27% in Experiment 3) suggests that resumption
is indeed a readily available and grammatically licensed alternative. Finally, in the least
accessible condition in Experiment 2 (animate patient and nonrestrictive interpretation), speakers used the resumption strategy even more often than they used the active
gap strategy (Figure 7.3), again consistent with the standard claim that resumption is
grammatically optional in Hebrew object relatives.

Considering these data from elicited production, we are now in a position to refine
our understanding of the judgment patterns from Farby et al. (2010) and Meltzer-
Asscher et al. (2015). I noted above that a stronger preference for gaps might have been
expected based on Ariel's (1999) corpus sample of conversational Hebrew. However,
the sentence materials in the two judgment studies were in fact more comparable to
those used in Fadlon et al. (2019), Experiment 2. In particular, both judgment studies
used animate agents and patients for constructing the sentence materials with object
relatives. The slight preference for object gaps shown in both judgment studies is consistent with the slight preference for object gaps over resumptive pronouns (about 5%)
shown in elicited production (right bar of Figure 7.3). Fadlon et al. (2019) also found

that there was a much stronger preference for gaps (about 68%) when the patient was inanimate (Figure 7.4). It is unknown whether a greater contrast might also be shown in acceptability, since similar materials have not been tested in any judgment task.

Finally, it is important to note here the contrast with English. Fadlon et al. (2019) found no instances of English speakers using a resumptive pronoun (Experiment 1), even though their sentence materials used animate agents and patients and were equivalent to the ones used for Hebrew (Experiment 2). Together with previous results from acceptability judgment tasks, as discussed above, such findings appear to support the idea that resumption is grammatically licensed in Hebrew, but grammatically restricted in English. However, it is still unclear why English speakers sometimes *use* resumptive pronouns in contexts where gaps are permitted (Cann et al. 2005; Prince 1990; Radford 2019). I will consider here a study of resumption in English which provides parallel data from acceptability judgments and elicited production, shedding light on this issue. In an acceptability judgment task with written stimuli, Morgan and Wagers (2018) found a preference for gaps over resumptive pronouns in embedded object relatives. This was in line with previous studies (Han et al. 2012; Hofmeister and Norcliffe 2013; Keffala 2011). Morgan and Wagers (2018) did not test simple object relatives, but did test doubly embedded object relatives, finding that ratings for gaps decreased while ratings for resumptive pronouns stayed at about the same low level. As a result, the preference for gaps disappeared at two levels of embedding. Morgan and Wagers (2018) interpret these findings to mean that resumptive pronouns are ungrammatical in English, thus accounting for their uniformly low ratings for different levels of embedding and for various island-violating sentence types. On the other hand, they interpret gapped relative clauses to be well-formed in both singly and doubly embedded non-islands, with acceptability decreasing as a function of processing complexity.

Using sentence materials similar to those from their judgment task, Morgan and Wagers (2018) also conducted a written production task. In this task, participants entered sentence completions into a text box based on written prompts designed to elicit different types of restrictive relative clauses. An example of a prompt for eliciting an embedded object relative clause is given in (8a–b) (Morgan and Wagers 2018: 863). Participants first read a declarative base sentence as in (8a) and were instructed to rephrase the sentence by completing a prompt as in (8b). Possible resumptive pronoun and gap responses are given in (8c).

(8) a. Base: The news that the alien dissected the woman shocked Karl.
     b. Prompt: I know the woman who the news that_____
     c. Target responses: the alien dissected (**her** / __) shocked Karl.

Among the responses for embedded object relatives as in (8c) (excluding nontarget responses), about 8% contained a resumptive pronoun and the remaining 92% contained a gap. For doubly embedded object relatives, where gaps are still considered to be a fully grammatical option, this rate went up to about 15%.[6] In island-violating contexts, for which it was assumed that no grammatical option was available, the rate of resumption increased substantially (e.g. to about 65% in *wh*-islands with an embedded object).[7] Following Asudeh (2011), they propose that resumptive pronouns are "symptomatic of a breakdown in the production of a filler–gap dependency, and the likelihood of such a breakdown is increased by low gap acceptability and by is-landhood" (Morgan and Wagers 2018: 870). This again brings us back the notion of *accessibility* that Ariel (1999) and Fadlon et al. (2019) applied to Hebrew. Fadlon et al. in fact provide a similar explanation for why their Hebrew-speaking participants pro-duced more resumptive pronouns in less accessible contexts: "we propose that since hindered filler retention impeded Hebrew speakers' ability to keep track of the well-formedness of the dependency, they cautiously opted for the safer alternative, which, in addition to satisfying local argument structure demands, is also a grammatical tech-nique for creating filler–gap dependencies in their language" (2019: 53). It is thus possible to maintain a distinction between grammatical resumption in Hebrew and intrusive resumption in English, while at the same time proposing a similar motiva-tion for producing resumptive pronouns in both languages. Crucially, this position depends on two assumptions: (1) that grammaticality is categorical, allowing for a clear-cut distinction between the two language types; and (2) that the use of a resump-tive pronoun is not a direct indication of its grammaticality, but rather depends on the presence of production difficulty when the relativized element is, for some reason, less accessible.

Importantly, the data discussed here give only a partial view of the situation, and in particular resist any firm conclusions with regard to the grammaticality of resumptive pronouns in English. For example, Cann et al. (2005) suggest on the basis of attested examples and informal judgments that resumptive pronouns are in fact grammatically licensed in English, but rarely used and often judged as unacceptable due to language-specific pragmatic restrictions. They observe that acceptability seems to improve when the resumptive pronoun is used with contrastive focus (9a), or when it is embedded in an extended context (9b) (2005: 1568–9).

(9)   a. That friend of Mary's, who even **HE** admits he needs a holiday, was
         nevertheless at the conference.
       b. Those little potato things that you put **'em** in the oven and when you take
          them out again, they've turned into mush.

These claims could be tested more systematically using judgment tasks in which supportive vs. non-supportive contexts are provided. If acceptability of resumptive

---

[6] The exact percentages are not supplied in the paper. These percentages are estimates based on the graphs.
[7] The authors believe that these findings do not indicate a 'saving' function of resumption in island contexts, since acceptability ratings were just as low for resumptive pronouns as they were for gaps in island-violating contexts. It is, however, interesting that participants consistently produced ungrammatical relative clauses with resumption, just as in a previous study by Ferreira and Swets (2005). The status of resumption in island contexts will be considered in more detail in Section 7.3.

pronouns in simple subject or object relatives were to improve to a level similar to that of gaps, such a result could be taken as evidence in favor of this proposal. Under this scenario, the low acceptability of resumptive pronouns that has been observed across multiple studies of English could perhaps be characterized as resulting from pragmatic constraints which limit the distribution of resumptive pronouns to specific contexts.

Along similar lines, Radford (2019) argues that resumptive pronouns in relative clauses are grammatically licensed in English, subject to some semantic and register-based restrictions. Radford's data set consists of 394 relative clauses with a resumptive pronoun and 50 relative clauses with a resumptive nominal, collected mostly from unscripted live radio and television broadcasts in the UK. Radford's examples show that speakers produced resumptive pronouns in a wide range of relative types, including complex island-violating structures where gaps are not permitted (10a–c), as well as simpler structures where gaps are readily permitted (10d–f) (2019: 70–5).

(10) a. Chelsea have a group of players that some of **them** are world class.
     b. We keep talking about Cesc Fabregas, who we all love the way **he** plays.
     c. They always come to a crunching end with a name that there's no way you're gonna work **it** in.
     d. He's one of those players that **he** knows where the back of the net is.
     e. We need players who we can count on **them** in a crisis.
     f. They've sent a statement through by the way, which I'll read **it** in a minute.

Overall, 43% of the items in Radford's sample showed resumption in contexts where gaps are normally not permitted, while 57% showed resumption in contexts where gaps are generally acceptable (Radford 2019: 77). In addition, most items in the sample (76%) showed relatively short dependencies, with six or fewer words intervening between the relativizer and the resumptive element (Radford 2019: 81). Radford argues from this that there is no clear evidence of accessibility effects. However, he acknowledges that because the sample did not include ordinary gapped relatives, there is no information about the proportion of resumptive pronouns vs. gaps for each type of relative clause. Possibly, simple subject relatives like (10d) are rarely used in comparison with ordinary gapped subject relatives, whereas island-violating structures like (10c) are more commonly used than similar island-violating structures with a gap. Thus, these data are not directly comparable to the findings from Morgan and Wagers's (2018) elicited production task, which showed clear effects of accessibility and island status on speakers' choices to use a resumptive pronoun or a gap. Radford's data are informative in another respect, however. Consistent with Prince's (1990) observations based on a corpus of spoken American English collected by Anthony Kroch in the early 1980s, the items with resumption were either clearly nonrestrictive, as in (10b, 10f), or they contained a kind-denoting head noun, as in (10a, 10d), or both. With respect to head nouns that are not overtly kind-denoting, Radford observes that such nouns are typically marked as indefinite and can be understood as kind-denoting.

For example, *a name* in (10c) can be paraphrased as *a type of name*, while *players* in (10e) can be paraphrased as *the kind of players*. Experimental studies, by contrast, have not directly modeled their stimulus sentences on natural corpus examples from colloquial speech. For example, in their judgment task, Morgan and Wagers (2018) used restrictive relatives with head nouns that were singular and marked with either a definite or an indefinite article. Similarly, Polinsky et al. (2013) used restrictive relatives with definite-marked singular head nouns.

Radford (2019) assumes that his example sentences, including both island and non-island structures, are acceptable in the contexts in which they were uttered, and argues that the low ratings of resumptive relatives shown in acceptability judgment tasks likely arise from the fact that the stimulus materials were not very naturalistic and were presented in a non-colloquial register (Radford 2019: 82). According to Radford, then, resumptive relatives are grammatical in English, but subject to semantic and register-based restrictions. Radford's claim thus implies that acceptability judgments of resumptive relatives could potentially be improved by modifying the task designs. Radford's position is in contrast to that of Polinsky et al. (2013), who recognize that English speakers use resumptive relatives in natural production, but argue that resumption is "a speaker-centered device for maintaining coreference" (2013: 358). For Polinsky et al., resumption serves speakers' needs even though it is intrusive in nature and not grammatically licensed, thus implying that modified task designs should do little to improve acceptability judgments.[8] However, if it were shown that acceptability judgments of resumptive relatives could be significantly improved using a modified task design, Radford's proposal that resumptive relatives are grammatical in colloquial English would be supported. Such findings would also raise the interesting questions about whether resumption in colloquial English is intrusive in nature, and how it compares with resumption in colloquial and non-colloquial registers of grammatical resumption languages like Hebrew and Irish.[9]

7.2 Resumption in contexts where gaps are not permitted: coverb stranding in Cantonese

As discussed in the previous section, it has been standardly claimed that resumption is required in Hebrew when the object of a preposition is relativized, due to a preposition stranding constraint which renders the gapped variant ungrammatical (Borer 1984; Shlonsky 1992). However, Ariel (1999) found that 10 out of the 17 examples of

---

[8] The experiments reported by Polinsky et al. (2013) showed no differences in acceptability between auditory and written stimulus presentation. However, as noted above, their stimulus sentences were not directly modeled after natural corpus examples, leaving open the question of whether more naturalistic stimuli would show improved ratings with auditory presentation.

[9] One possible difference would be that grammatical resumption languages generally lack relative pronouns (Hawkins 1999; Keenan and Comrie 1977) and instead use an invariant relativizer, whereas colloquial English allows for various forms of wh-relatives in addition to that-relatives and zero-marked relatives. Radford's corpus sample in fact contains numerous examples of resumptive relatives introduced by the relative pronouns *which*, *who*, and *where* (Radford 2019: 83).

prepositional object relatives in her corpus sample contained a gap. These exceptional tokens all involved stranding of the preposition *be* 'in/at'. She conjectures that there had been a strict preposition stranding constraint in earlier forms of Hebrew, but that the preposition *be* is leading a change in progress in the contemporary spoken language. Such a change is enabled by the fact that *be* is governed by the preceding verb, consistent with her more general finding from the corpus that verbal arguments are more likely to be realized as a gap than nonarguments. While there have been no further studies following up on this phenomenon in Hebrew, Francis et al. (2015) investigated a similar phenomenon in Cantonese in which the relativized object of a 'coverb' (a preposition-like serial verb) is variably realized as either a gap or a resumptive pronoun. In the remainder of this section, I discuss these findings for Cantonese and their implications for understanding resumption as a strategy for avoiding or mitigating grammatical constraint violations.

Although Cantonese (like Mandarin and other Sinitic languages) has prenominal rather than postnominal relative clauses, grammatical descriptions of resumption in Cantonese indicate a profile quite similar to that of Hebrew. According to Matthews and Yip (2011: 330–1), resumptive pronouns are excluded from simple subject relatives, optional in direct object relatives (with the gap option generally preferred in non-embedded contexts), and required as the object of a preposition or coverb.[10] Examples (11a–b) and (12a–b) illustrate the latter two generalizations (Francis et al. 2015: 78).[11] When the verb *bong1* is used as a main verb meaning 'help' as in (11), its direct object can be relativized using either a gap or a resumptive pronoun, with the gap being the preferred option. When it is used as a coverb meaning 'for' or 'from' as in (12), its object must be a resumptive pronoun. This restriction is generally attributed to some type of syntactic constraint on extraction. For example, Francis and Matthews (2006) characterized it as a type of adjunct island constraint, owing to the function of the coverb as a modifier of the main verb that follows. For simplicity, and to highlight its similarity to preposition stranding constraints in other languages, I will instead refer to this restriction as a coverb stranding constraint.

(11) a. ngo5   bong1   ___   go2 go3 neoi5jan2 hou2 hou2jan4
          I   help   (gap)   that CL   woman   very   kind
       'The woman who I helped is very kind.' (direct object relative)
      b. ? ngo5 bong1 keoi5   go2 go3 neoi5jan2 hou2 hou2jan4
          I   help   him/her   that CL   woman   very   kind
       'The woman who I helped her is very kind.'

---

[10] Here, the term 'coverb' refers to a grammaticalized serial verb which allows verbal morphosyntax but is used in a preposition-like function (Francis and Matthews 2006). There are a limited number of coverbs in Cantonese, most of which can also still be used with a slightly different meaning as the main verb of a simple clause. Cantonese arguably also has true prepositions which originated as verbs but no longer display verbal morphosyntax. The clearest case is the indirect object marker *bei2* 'to', which is said to require a resumptive pronoun when its object is relativized (Matthews and Yip 2011: 331).

[11] The numbers following each morpheme in the Cantonese transliteration indicate tone marks following the Linguistic Society of Hong Kong's *Jyutping* system (Tang et al. 2002).

(12) a. *ngo5 bong1   ___   maai5 ce1 go2 go3 neoi5jan2
          I   help   (gap)   buy   car that CL   woman
          hou2   hou2jan4
          very   kind
          'The woman who I bought a car from is very kind.' (coverb object relative)

      b. ngo5   bong1   keoi5   maai5 ce1 go2 go3 neoi5jan2
          I   help   him/her   buy   car that CL   woman
          hou2   hou2jan4
          very   kind
          'The woman who I bought a car from her is very kind.'

Using an acceptability judgment task and an elicited production task, Francis et al. (2015) largely confirmed Matthews and Yip's (2011) description as summarized above. Results of an acceptability judgment task with auditory presentation showed that gaps were rated as more acceptable than resumptive pronouns in direct object relatives as in (7a–b), while the reverse was true for coverb object relatives as in (8a–b) (Figure 7.5).

Similar trends were also shown in elicited production. In this task, participants listened to two simple sentences while also reading them on the screen. They were instructed to combine the two sentences together into a single sentence ending in the last three characters of the second sentence, and then speak the sentence. This procedure successfully elicited subject-modifying relative clauses, albeit not always of the exact type that was expected. Results for target productions (i.e. productions that displayed the expected relative clause type) showed that participants used a resumptive pronoun in 18% of direct object relatives and 74% of coverb object relatives

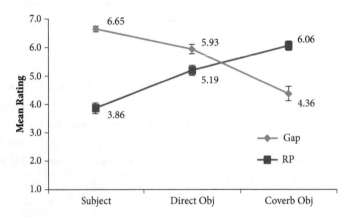

Fig. 7.5 Acceptability ratings of gaps and resumptive pronouns in subject, direct object, and coverb object positions in Cantonese relative clauses

Source: Reprinted from Francis et al. (2015: 66) with permission from Elsevier.

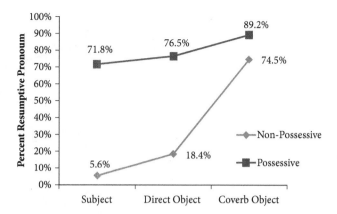

Fig. 7.6 Percent resumptive pronouns produced in subject, direct object, and coverb object positions in Cantonese relative clauses

Source: Reprinted from Francis et al. (2015: 71) with permission from Elsevier.

(Figure 7.6). Equivalently, they produced a structure with a gap in 82% of direct object relatives and 26% of coverb object relatives.

These results are mostly consistent with Matthews and Yip's (2011) grammatical description. In particular, they confirm that resumptive pronouns are possible but dispreferred in simple object relatives, and also that resumptive pronouns render coverb object relatives fully acceptable. However, these data challenge the idea that resumptive pronouns are grammatically *required* in coverb object relatives. Although there were clear preferences in the expected direction, coverb object relatives with a gap were still rated as moderately acceptable (Figure 7.5), and they were produced in 26% of the responses in which a coverb object relative was used (Figure 7.6). These results would be unexpected if a strict coverb stranding constraint had been in effect. Instead, resumptive pronouns appear to be optional in both contexts. Presumably, the preference for a resumptive pronoun in the coverb object position is related to the lower accessibility of this position in the sense of Ariel (1999) and Hawkins (2004).

In their discussion, the authors ask whether the preferences shown in the data depend entirely on the accessibility of the relativized element during comprehension and production, or whether these preferences are also somehow encoded in the grammar. In other words, is it still possible that the grammar of Cantonese encodes a coverb stranding constraint? Such an idea could be maintained, for example, if the relevant constraint is understood as a soft constraint which interacts with performance-related factors to determine choice of structure during production. Unfortunately, the tasks were not designed to answer this question, but an analysis of individual verbs offers some support for this conjecture. Results across all verbs showed that resumptive pronouns were produced more often than gaps and were judged as more acceptable than gaps in coverb object relatives. However, individual coverbs varied in acceptability and in the rate at which speakers produced a resumptive pronoun.

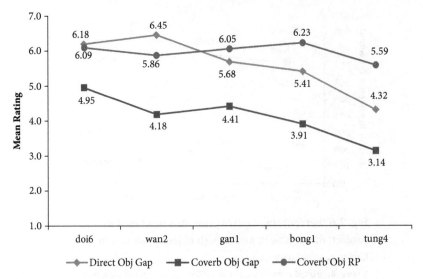

Fig. 7.7 Acceptability ratings of Cantonese relative clauses by individual verb

Source: Reprinted from Francis et al. (2015: 74) with permission from Elsevier.

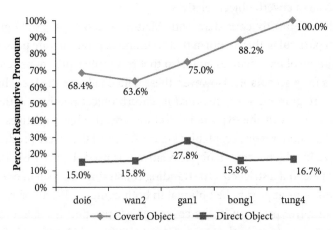

Fig. 7.8 Percentage of resumptive pronouns produced in direct object and coverb object positions in Cantonese relative clauses, by individual verb

Source: Reprinted from Francis et al. (2015: 75) with permission from Elsevier.

For example, in coverb relatives containing a gap, the coverb *doi6* 'replace' was most acceptable (mean rating 4.95), while the coverb *tung4* "with" was least acceptable (mean rating 3.14) (lowest line in Figure 7.7). Similarly, in production, the coverb *doi6* 'replace' was used with a resumptive pronoun 68% of the time, compared with 100% for the coverb *tung4* 'with' (upper line in Figure 7.8).

In sum, resumptive pronouns were produced more often when the corresponding gapped structure was less acceptable.[12] As Francis et al. (2015) point out, these differences by verb are consistent with the idea that different coverbs may be at different stages of partial grammaticalization, with *tung4* adhering to what appears to be a strict coverb stranding constraint. Based on a small-scale corpus analysis from an earlier study of coverb object relatives (Francis and Matthews 2006), they suggest that the distribution of *tung4* is possibly due to its preposition-like semantics and its overall higher proportion of use as a coverb compared with its use as a main verb. Such language-specific, verb-specific preferences are apparently not predicted from any general notion of accessibility, nor are they predicted from the application of a strict coverb stranding constraint. Rather, Francis et al. (2015) suggest that resumption has been partially grammaticalized as a strategy for mitigating an emerging coverb stranding constraint. Following the approach of the Decathlon Model (Featherston 2005a; 2008), they further suggest that this emerging constraint might be understood synchronically as a soft constraint which comes with a specified 'violation cost': "we might suggest that there is in fact an adjunct island condition which affects coverb object RCs, but its violation cost is survivable, resulting in the occasional occurrence of gaps" (Francis et al. 2015: 77). Alternatively, the emerging constraint could be understood as a preferred constructional subtype in a similar manner to the soft constraints on relative clause extraposition in English that I outlined in Chapter 6. In that chapter, I suggested that a particular constraint (the Name Constraint) could be understood as a soft constraint which specifies an indefinite subject NP as a component of the most salient, preferred subtype of the relative clause extraposition (RCE) construction in English. Similarly, the coverb stranding constraint in Cantonese could be understood as a soft constraint which specifies resumption as a component of the preferred subtype of the coverb object relative construction. Possibly, when verbs (such as *tung4* 'with') that are almost always used as coverbs (and not main verbs) occur in the construction, the constraint (framed here as a construction-specific preference for resumption) becomes especially salient to speakers and listeners, making a resumptive pronoun more likely to be selected during production, and making the corresponding structure with a gap seem less acceptable to listeners. In conclusion, I have argued that some notion of soft constraint (however it might be implemented) may be useful for capturing the type of variability shown in the Cantonese data, while still maintaining the intuition that resumption is a strategy for repairing or avoiding an illicit structure. Possibly, a similar approach could be applied to understanding the variable use of resumption in Hebrew prepositional object relatives, as observed by Ariel (1999) and mentioned at the beginning of this section.

---

[12] Note that resumptive pronoun option in the coverb construction was rated as highly acceptable for all of the verbs, and did not vary according to frequency of production (Figure 7.7). Francis et al. (2015) are also careful to point out the frequency differences shown in production were based on a relatively small sample of target responses and were not statistically significant.

7.3 Does resumption rescue islands? Evidence from Hebrew and English

In our discussion of Cantonese in the previous section, we observed that resumptive pronouns were highly acceptable in coverb object relatives across all verbs tested, whereas the corresponding gapped variants were at best moderately acceptable (Francis et al. 2015: 74). Whatever the reason for the degraded acceptability of the gapped variants (lower accessibility, coverb stranding constraint, or some combination), it was clear that resumption provided a fully acceptable alternative. Indeed, the syntactic literature highlights this 'saving' function of resumption not only in prepositional object relatives and the like, but also in more complex island configurations. For various languages with grammatical resumption, including Irish (McCloskey 2003; 2011), Lebanese Arabic (Aoun et al. 2001), and Hebrew (Borer 1984), it has been claimed that resumption can rescue otherwise island-violating structures, rendering them fully grammatical. Although the technical explanations for this vary, it is most commonly proposed that resumptive pronouns in grammatical resumption languages are base-generated, meaning that movement constraints simply do not apply (McCloskey 2006).[13] Initially, on the basis of attested examples and informal judgments, resumption was claimed to show a similar rescuing function for island-violating structures in English, at least for colloquial spoken varieties (Kroch 1981; Ross 1967; Sells 1984). This idea of a rescuing function is also consistent with the results of experimental studies which have shown that English speakers consistently produce resumptive pronouns in island-violating contexts (Ferreira and Swets 2005; Morgan and Wagers 2018) and with recent corpus data showing that speakers use resumption in island-violating structures (Radford 2019).[14] However, it is not well supported by acceptability judgment data. Several studies of island-violating constructions in English have shown either no effect at all (Alexopoulou and Keller 2007; Heestand et al. 2011; Polinsky et al. 2013), or only a subtle ameliorating effect of resumption (McDaniel and Cowart 1999; Han et al. 2012; Keffala 2011) on acceptability. From such results, it has been concluded that resumption restores the grammaticality of (certain) island-violating structures in languages like Irish with grammatical resumption, but that it does not restore grammaticality in languages like English with intrusive resumption.[15] Unfortunately, relatively little experimental evidence on resumption in island contexts

---

[13] The notion of syntactic movement is unique to derivational theories, but a similar distinction has been made in some constraint-based theories without reference to movement. For example, working within the Lexical-Functional Grammar framework, Asudeh (2012) distinguishes between filler–gap dependencies and binder–resumptive dependencies at the level of f-structure.

[14] Radford (2019: 77–9) also presents several items from the corpus sample in which speakers produced island-violating relative clauses with a gap. While it is unclear how to interpret the grammaticality of these items, Radford suggests that they call into question the idea that resumption is restricted to positions inaccessible to gap construction.

[15] There is some evidence that resumption can alleviate production difficulty (Morgan and Wagers 2018; Polinsky et al. 2013) and improve comprehensibility (Beltrama and Xiang 2016; Chacón 2019; Hammerly 2021), but such data are taken to be consistent with the view that resumptive pronouns are always ungrammatical in English. I will return to this issue later in the current section.

has been collected for languages with grammatical resumption, making it difficult to confirm or disconfirm the presumed contrast between the two language types. Furthermore, the implications of the subtle ameliorating effects that have been observed in some studies of English are not yet fully understood. In this section, I will discuss the findings of two studies of Hebrew (Farby et al. 2010; Keshev and Meltzer-Asscher 2017) and two studies of English (McDaniel and Cowart 1999; Morgan and Wagers 2018) that used acceptability judgments to examine resumption in island contexts. I will conclude that the judgment data from these studies present no obvious evidence for a typological distinction between Hebrew and English. I will also consider what additional insights can be gained from reading time, forced-choice preference, and elicited production data (Ackerman et al. 2018; Hammerly 2021; Morgan and Wagers 2018).

Farby et al. (2010) used an acceptability judgment task with written stimuli to test the acceptability of island-violating sentences in Hebrew. Their island-violating stimulus sentences contained a gap or a resumptive pronoun in a direct object position within a Complex NP (relative clause) island, as in (13a–b). Island-violating sentences were compared with non-island-violating sentences containing a gap or resumptive pronoun in the direct object position of a simple relative clause.

(13) a. Dina maskima   lifgoš et   ha-calemet   še ha-xaver
         Dina agrees   to meet ACC the photographer that the friend
         še   pagaš __   be-xeyfa   nasa le-šam be-mikre.
         that met __   in Haifa   went there by chance.
         'Dina agrees to meet the photographer that the friend that met in Haifa
         went there by chance.'
      b. Dina maskima   lifgoš et   ha-calemet   še ha-xaver
         Dina agrees   to meet ACC the photographer that the friend
         še   pagaš ota   be-xeyfa   nasa le-šam be-mikre.
         that met her   in Haifa   went there by chance.
         'Dina agrees to meet the photographer that the friend that met her in Haifa
         went there by chance.'

As given in Figure 7.9, results showed that island-violating sentences were significantly less acceptable than non-island-violating sentences.[16] Furthermore, island-violating sentences with a resumptive pronoun were quite low in acceptability (2.31 on a 5-point scale) and only slightly more acceptable than the corresponding sentences with a gap (1.85 on a 5-point scale). If resumptive pronouns were grammatically licensed in relative clause islands, as had been claimed by Borer (1984: 221), a more substantial improvement in acceptability (i.e. approaching the level of comparable

---

[16] Within the non-island sentences, gaps were slightly more acceptable than resumptive pronouns. This replicates the finding discussed in Section 7.1 from the other experiment in the same study (Farby et al. 2010).

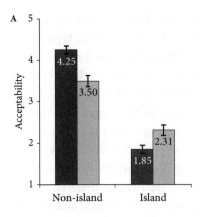

Fig. 7.9 Acceptability of gaps (dark bars) and resumptive pronouns (light bars) in island and non-island contexts in Hebrew relative clauses
Source: From Farby et al. (2010: 9).

non-island sentences) might be expected. Instead, the authors interpret these results to mean that the resumptive pronoun does not restore grammaticality. The slight improvement in acceptability is taken to reflect a general processing advantage of resumptive pronouns over gaps in less accessible positions, following the approach of Ariel (1999).

Following up on Farby et al. (2010), Keshev and Meltzer-Asscher (2017) tested the acceptability of gaps and resumptive pronouns in two types of island-violating contexts in Hebrew relative clauses: Complex NP islands (14a–b) and Coordinate Structure islands (15a–b). As in the study by Farby et al. (2010), they used written stimuli.

(14) a. Ha-šotrim hekiru et   ha-iša   še-ha-xašudim   še-takfu
         the-cops   knew ACC the-woman that-the-suspects that-attacked
         __   daxafu et
         __   pushed ACC
      ha-melcar be-mis'ada yukratit
      the-waiter in restaurant upscale
      'The cops knew the woman that the suspects who attacked pushed the waiter in an upscale restaurant.'
   b. Ha-šotrim hekiru et   ha-iša   še-ha-xašudim
      the-cops   knew ACC the-woman   that-the-suspects
      še-takfu   ota   daxafu et
      that-attacked her pushed ACC
      ha-melcar be-mis'ada yukratit.
      the-waiter in-restaurant upscale
      'The cops knew the woman that the suspects who attacked her pushed the waiter in an upscale restaurant.'

(15) a. Ha-šotrim hekiru et   ha-iša   še-ha-xašudim daxafu
         the-cops knew   ACC   the-woman that-the-suspects pushed
         et   ha-melcar
         ACC   the-waiter

ve-takfu   __   be-mis'ada yukratit.
and-attacked __   in-restaurant upscale
'The cops knew the woman that the suspects pushed the waiter and
attacked in an upscale restaurant.'

b. Ha-šotrim hekiru et   ha-iša   še-ha-xašudim daxafu
   the-cops   knew ACC   the-woman   that-the-suspects pushed
   et   ha-melcar
   ACC   the-waiter
   ve-takfu   ota   be-mis'ada yukratit.
   and-attacked   her   in-restaurant upscale
   'The cops knew the woman that the suspects pushed the waiter and
   attacked her in an upscale restaurant.'

For the Complex NP sentences, results showed a slight but statistically significant ameliorating effect of resumption. However, both resumptive pronouns and gaps were given relatively low ratings (2.77 and 1.57, respectively, on a 7-point scale) (Keshev and Meltzer-Asscher 2017: 556). This result was consistent with the findings from Farby et al. (2010), who used similar Complex NP stimuli. For the Coordinate Structure islands, which had not been tested in any previous studies, results showed no ameliorating effect of resumption: both resumptive pronouns and gaps were given low ratings (1.80 and 1.57, respectively) and showed no significant difference in acceptability.

Although the results for Complex NP islands closely mirrored those of Farby et al. (2010), Keshev and Meltzer-Asscher (2017) offer a different interpretation. They take the set of findings in their judgment experiment to mean that Coordinate Structure islands simply cannot be relativized in Hebrew, whereas Complex NP islands can be rendered grammatical by a resumptive pronoun. In contrast, recall that Farby et al. (2010) interpreted the amelioration effect in Complex NP islands as an accessibility-related effect which does not rescue grammaticality. Although Farby et al. (2010) did not collect any data on Coordinate Structure islands, their interpretation of the amelioration effect in Complex NP Islands appears to be compatible with the mean judgments shown in Keshev and Meltzer-Asscher's (2017) experiment. One could, for example, interpret the lack of any amelioration in Coordinate Structure islands as a floor effect due to the relatively greater difficulty readers might have in assigning an interpretation to such sentences. To understand why Keshev and Meltzer-Asscher (2017) interpret the amelioration effect as rescuing the grammaticality of the Complex NP sentences, it is necessary to discuss the results of their self-paced reading experiment as reported in the same paper.

In a second experiment, Keshev and Meltzer-Asscher (2017) conducted a self-paced reading task using the filled-gap paradigm (Stowe 1986). The basic logic of the filled-gap paradigm is that reading times should be higher in positions where the reader is expecting to find a gap resolving a long-distance dependency and instead finds a pronoun or NP that is not co-referential with the filler phrase. The reader must then revise their initial interpretation of the sentence. Such cases can arise when there is more than one possible subcategorizing verb or preposition to resolve the dependency, as in (16), from Keshev and Meltzer-Asscher (2017: 550):

(16) My brother wanted to know who Ruth will bring **us** home to __ at Christmas.

In this case, both the verb *bring* and the preposition *to* can potentially subcategorize for the gap in the embedded question. Because readers are actively searching for a resolution to the dependency, they initially expect to find a gap following the verb *bring*, and therefore tend to slow down at the pronoun *us*. This increase in reading time is known as a filled-gap effect. The filled-gap paradigm has been used in studies of English to show that readers exhibit no filled-gap effect in positions where an actual gap would violate an island constraint, meaning that they do not tend to posit a gap within island configurations (Pickering et al. 1994). A common interpretation of this finding has been that readers actively search for a gap only in positions where a gap is potentially licensed by the grammar. Keshev and Meltzer-Asscher extend this logic to Hebrew, a language which allows resumptive pronouns in some contexts where gaps are prohibited. They reason that Hebrew readers will tend to expect a resumptive pronoun in such contexts, potentially leading to a filled-gap effect (or more precisely, a filled resumptive pronoun effect) when a (non-resumptive) lexical NP is encountered instead. If it is the case that resumptive pronouns are grammatical in Complex NP islands, but ungrammatical in Coordinate Structure islands, this predicts that there should be a filled-gap effect in Complex NP islands but not in Coordinate Structure islands.

To test these predictions, Keshev and Meltzer-Asscher (2017) conducted a self-paced reading task that included stimuli similar to those in (14–15), but with a lexical NP in place of the gap or resumptive pronoun, and a continuation of the sentence which resolved the dependency using a resumptive pronoun within an additional adjunct clause. Results showed that as expected, readers slowed down at the lexical NP in the Complex NP sentences, but not in the Coordinate Structure sentences. Similarly, readers slowed down at the NP following the first potential subcategorizing verb outside the island context in both constructions (e.g. after *pushed* in 15a–b), confirming that these stimuli also induced a traditional filled-gap effect. The authors conclude that resumptive pronouns are indeed grammatical within Complex NP islands, despite being rather low in acceptability. However, another possible explanation is that the filled-gap effect for the Complex NP sentences was due to greater plausibility. Hofmeister et al. (2013: 47–9) argue that filled-gap effects depend primarily on the probability of finding a gap (or in this case, a resumptive pronoun) in a given position. Although this probability is generally high for grammatically licensed positions, the filled-gap effect may disappear when the relevant interpretation is semantically implausible (and therefore improbable). For example, Pickering and Traxler (2001) found that the filled-gap effect disappeared in standard object relative contexts when the preceding verb was an implausible subcategorizor (e.g *event that the coach persuaded*).

Following this line of argumentation in Hofmeister et al. (2013: 47–9), and consistent with the interpretation of Farby et al. (2010) that resumptive pronouns in

Complex NP islands are ungrammatical, it could be that the participants in Keshev and Meltzer-Asscher's (2017) self-paced reading experiment found the possibility of a long-distance dependency in the island context to be more plausible for the Complex NP sentences than for the Coordinate Structure sentences. This would then predict that readers might show a filled-gap effect even in Coordinate Structure islands if they were presented with a preceding context that would lead to a strong expectation for a resumptive pronoun in the relevant position. Such a finding would not rule out the possibility that Complex NP islands and Coordinate Structure islands differ in grammaticality. Likewise, it would not prove that the original stimuli (without any preceding context) differ only in terms of plausibility. Rather, it would simply show that factors other than syntactic well-formedness may induce or eliminate filled-gap effects.

In sum, results from two studies of Hebrew show that resumptive pronouns have a weak ameliorating effect for Complex NP islands, and no ameliorating effect at all for Coordinate Structure islands. Thus, it is clear that resumptive pronouns in these contexts do not produce the high levels of acceptability observed by Francis et al. (2015) for resumptive pronouns in Cantonese coverb relatives. Although it remains unclear whether Complex NP islands in Hebrew are grammatical with resumption, as Keshev and Meltzer-Asscher (2017) claim, it is interesting that these results from Hebrew are roughly comparable to the results from various studies of English that have investigated resumption in island contexts. As an illustration, I will discuss the findings from two acceptability judgment tasks which investigated resumption in English (McDaniel and Cowart 1999; Morgan and Wagers 2018). I will then briefly consider related findings from a production task (Morgan and Wagers 2018), a forced-choice preference task (Ackerman et al. 2018), and a self-paced reading task (Hammerly 2021).

McDaniel and Cowart (1999) set out to test whether resumptive pronouns would improve the acceptability of relative clauses with extraction out of embedded questions in English, as in (14–15). Using a version of Minimalist theory, they assume that the sentences in (14a) and (15a) both violate a movement constraint (Subjacency), while (14a) in addition violates a constraint on representation (Empty Category Principle/ECP). Setting aside the technical differences among various authors' accounts, the movement (Subjacency) violation results from a *wh*-word in a dependent clause intervening between the filler and the gap, while the representational (ECP) violation results from having a *wh*-word directly followed by a gap. McDaniel and Cowart (1999) further assume that the addition of a resumptive pronoun can 'save' the representational violation in (17a) but not the movement violation in (17a) and (18a).[17] Thus, they predict that object extraction as in (18a) should be more acceptable than subject extraction as in (17a), and that the addition of a resumptive pronoun

---

[17] McDaniel and Cowart (1999) assume that a resumptive pronoun behaves just like a gap in how it resolves a *wh*-dependency in English, and should therefore be sensitive to movement constraints in the same way. However, Alexopoulou and Keller (2007) argue that a resumptive pronoun in English creates an anaphoric dependency rather than a movement dependency. They give a different explanation for why resumptive pronouns do not improve the acceptability of island-violating interrogative sentences in their experiments.

as in (17b) should improve the acceptability of subject extraction. However, a resumptive pronoun should have no effect on the acceptability of object extraction, meaning
that (18b) should be no more acceptable than (18a).

(17)   a. That's the girl that I wonder when __ met you.   (Gap: Subjacency + ECP)
      b. That's the girl that I wonder when she met you.   (RP: Subjacency only)

(18)   a. That's the girl that I wonder when you met __.   (Gap: Subjacency only)
      b. That's the girl that I wonder when you met her.   (RP: Subjacency only)

The above predictions were supported by the results of a judgment task. McDaniel
and Cowart (1999) collected acceptability judgments using a scalable line-drawing
procedure in which participants indicated how much better or worse a sentence was
perceived to be in relation to a reference sentence. Responses were coded on a 10-point
scale and then converted to z-scores for analysis. Results showed that while sentences
in all four conditions were rated quite low in acceptability, an ECP effect was observed
(Figure 7.10): subject extraction (17a) was rated lower than object extraction (18a).
Furthermore, as predicted, adding a resumptive pronoun improved the acceptability
of subject extraction (17a–b), but not object extraction (18a–b). The authors conclude
that although all four sentence types are ungrammatical, (17a) is less acceptable than
the other three due to violating two syntactic constraints (ECP and Subjacency) instead of just one. In support of McDaniel and Cowart's conclusion, subsequent studies

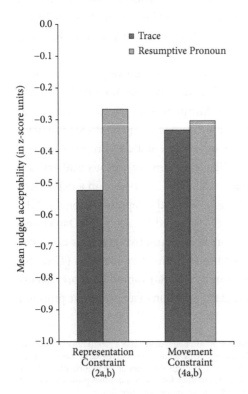

Fig. 7.10 Acceptability of gaps (dark bars)
and resumptive pronouns (light bars) in
wh-island contexts in English

Source: Reprinted from McDaniel and Cowart (1999:
B21) with permission from Elsevier.

of resumption in *wh*-islands in English have reported the same overall pattern of judgments using conventional Likert-scale ratings instead of line drawings, and the authors of these studies have provided similar explanations (Han et al. 2012; Keffala 2011; Morgan and Wagers 2018). However, it is notable that no previous studies of resumption in islands have modeled their stimuli on natural corpus examples such as those reported in Radford (2019). Possibly, the acceptability of island-violating structures would be improved in studies with more naturalistic stimuli.

To conclude this section, I will briefly consider three additional studies of English which report amelioration or facilitation effects of resumption in *wh*-islands. As mentioned in the introduction to this section, the clearest evidence for a facilitating effect of resumption in English has come from elicited production (Ferreira and Swets 2005; Morgan and Wagers 2018). For example, in a written production task (described in Section 7.1), Morgan and Wagers (2018) found that participants used a resumptive pronoun more often than they used a gap across seven island-violating sentence types, despite giving consistently low acceptability ratings for resumptive pronouns in all of these contexts. As I discussed in Section 7.1, the authors propose that using a resumptive pronoun helps alleviate production difficulty even though it cannot repair grammaticality. They further observe that the rate of resumption in production is more closely related to the acceptability of the corresponding gapped structure than it is to the acceptability of the same structure with a resumptive pronoun. This pattern is exemplified in their findings for *wh*-islands. Acceptability ratings of *wh*-island violating sentences showed the same pattern as in McDaniel and Cowart (1999): subject extraction with a gap was rated lower than the other three types of *wh*-islands tested (object extraction with a gap, subject extraction with a resumptive pronoun, and object extraction with a resumptive pronoun) (Morgan and Wagers 2018: 867). Furthermore, a similar subject-object asymmetry was shown in production. In *wh-island* contexts, participants used a resumptive pronoun about 65% of the time with object extraction, and about 80% of the time with subject extraction (Morgan and Wagers 2018: 865). This difference was predictable from participants' judgments of sentences with a gap (which showed that object extraction was more acceptable), but not from their judgments of the same sentences with a resumptive pronoun (which showed no difference between subject and object extraction).

Also of interest here is the fact that participants preferred to use a resumptive pronoun instead of a gap at a high rate (65% of the time) even in non-ECP-violating object extraction contexts. Although this was quite a strong preference, a similar preference for resumption did not show up in acceptability ratings. Is this facilitation effect in object extraction contexts then unique to production? Two recent studies of resumption in island contexts suggest that the answer is negative. Ackerman et al. (2018) used written stimuli in two types of forced-choice preference tasks. In the first task, participants directly compared two versions of the same sentence, one containing a gap and the other one a resumptive pronoun, and indicated which version was more acceptable. In the second task, a separate set of participants was presented with one sentence at a time and two possible completions, and asked to choose their preferred completion in each case. Results of both experiments showed that participants preferred the resumptive pronoun version in several types of island-violating sentences with object extraction. (Subject extraction was not tested in these experiments.) For example, for *wh*-islands in the full sentence comparison task, participants preferred a resumptive pronoun 63% of the time—nearly the same result that Morgan and Wagers (2018) found for written production of the same island type. This was in contrast to the corresponding non-island-violating sentences, for which participants preferred resumption only 13% of the time. The authors conclude that a facilitation effect of resumption in English is not limited to production, but can be similarly detected in comprehension. They argue that such an effect has not shown up in acceptability rating tasks because such tasks are simply less sensitive to certain subtle contrasts.

Hammerly (2021) provides further evidence from English for a facilitation effect of resumption in *wh*-islands, using a more implicit measure of comprehension: self-paced reading. Hammerly (2021) tested participants' reading times in *wh*-islands with either an object gap or a resumptive pronoun (19a), and in comparable non-islands (embedded object relatives) with either an object gap or a resumptive pronoun (19b). Here, the reading time regions are indicated with slashes, and the critical spiller region is in boldface.

(19)   a. Mary trained / the spy / who Beth / announced that the agency /
           had recruited {him, __} / **over the summer** / for the program. /
        b. Mary trained / the spy / who Beth / announced which agency /
           had recruited {him, __} / **over the summer** / for the program. /

As illustrated in Figure 7.11, Hammerly (2021) found a significant interaction between dependency strategy (pronoun or gap) and island status in the spillover region—the region directly following the resumptive pronoun or gap. In non-island conditions,

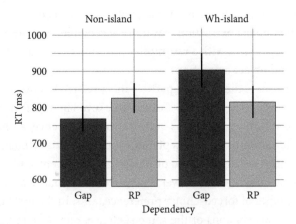

Fig. 7.11 Mean reading time for the spillover region following a gap or a resumptive pronoun in a *wh*-island or non-island sentence

Source: Reproduced from Hammerly (2021: 16) with permission from MIT Press Journals. © by the Massachusetts Institute of Technology.

sentences with a gap were read faster than those with a resumptive pronoun. Hammerly (2021) attributes this to a filled-gap effect resulting from the expectation for a gap in the position where a resumptive pronoun was encountered. Unlike for typical sentence materials in the filled-gap paradigm, the resumptive pronoun did not require a revised interpretation of the sentence. However, it still caused a slowdown in the spillover region. Conversely, in *wh*-island conditions, sentences with a resumptive pronoun were read faster than sentences with a gap. Finally, comparing the island and non-island conditions, resumptive pronouns sentences (unlike gap sentences) were read at about the same speed regardless of island status (Figure 7.11). Hammerly (2021) proposes that readers did not expect to find the tail of any long-distance dependency (gap or resumptive pronoun) within the embedded *wh*-clause, but were able to cope with such an unexpected dependency and interpret the sentence more easily when a pronoun was present.[18] Hammerly (2021) concludes that resumptive pronouns facilitate comprehension of *wh*-islands with object extraction, but hinder comprehension of comparable non-island sentences. Just like Ackerman et al. (2018), Hammerly assumes that resumptive pronouns cannot save the grammaticality of island-violating sentences in English but can make them slightly easier to understand.

Taken together, the acceptability judgment tasks discussed in the current section provide evidence that a resumptive pronoun can make long-distance dependencies into certain island-violating configurations (Complex NP islands in Hebrew, *wh*-islands with subject extraction in English) slightly more acceptable to readers/listeners, while having no effect on certain other island-violating configurations (Coordinate Structure islands in Hebrew, *wh*-islands with object extraction in English). It remains unclear, however, how to interpret these findings as bearing on the grammatical status of island-violating sentences. For example, how do we know when an improvement in acceptability indicates a shift in grammaticality? A non-syntactic approach to islands, as discussed in detail in Chapter 4 (Chaves 2013; Hofmeister and Sag 2010), attributes the low acceptability of certain types of island-violating sentences to processing complexity and/or pragmatic infelicity. From such a perspective, there would be no ungrammatical structure for a resumptive pronoun to potentially 'save' and therefore any amelioration effect would merely indicate greater processing ease or pragmatic felicity. The studies reviewed in this section view island effects as resulting from syntactic restrictions, however, allowing us to ask whether resumption can rescue grammaticality. In cases where the resumptive pronoun improves acceptability to the level of a comparable non-island-violating sentence, the answer is apparently straightforward. Resumption rescues grammaticality. We saw something like this in our previous discussion of Cantonese coverb constructions in Section 7.2. Francis et al. (2015) found that a resumptive pronoun improved the acceptability of coverb relative, making it just as acceptable as a simple object relative. Their analysis was, however, complicated by the fact that coverb relatives with a gap showed intermediate levels of acceptability,

---

[18] Interestingly, the addition of a resumptive pronoun did not affect comprehension accuracy in either island or non-island contexts, as measured by responses to the comprehension questions.

which varied depending on the verb. This finding made it less clear whether there was really any ungrammaticality to be rescued!

In cases where the resumptive pronoun improves acceptability only slightly, and not to the level of comparable non-island sentences, the answer is less clear, and seems to depend more on the availability of data from additional sources and general assumptions about the type of language under investigation. For example, Keshev and Meltzer-Asscher (2017) interpreted the slight amelioration effect of resumptive pronouns in Complex NP islands in Hebrew as an indication of grammaticality. In part, this interpretation was related to previous claims about Hebrew (Borer 1984), and general expectations about grammatical resumption languages. This interpretation was, in addition, supported by data from a self-paced reading experiment which showed a filled-gap effect for Complex NP islands. In contrast, Morgan and Wagers (2018) interpreted the minor amelioration effects in their acceptability data from English as an epiphenomenon resulting from the differing levels of *unacceptability* among island-violating sentences with gaps. Their conclusion that intrusive resumption cannot rescue grammaticality can best be understood in the context of several other judgment studies of English which have yielded similar results and similar conclusions (Han et al. 2012; Heestand et al. 2011; Keffala 2011; Polinsky et al. 2013).

Finally, in cases where resumption shows no ameliorating effect on acceptability, the answer to our question appears to be negative. Resumption does not rescue grammaticality. For example, Keshev and Meltzer-Asscher (2017) conclude that Coordinate Structure islands in Hebrew cannot be repaired. Similarly, McDaniel and Cowart (1999) conclude that the movement violation in *wh*-islands in English cannot be repaired. Again, such an interpretation may be complicated by evidence for facilitation effects in production and comprehension, as we have seen in some studies of English (Ackerman et al. 2018; Morgan and Wagers 2018). If English speakers consistently produce island-violating structures using a resumptive pronoun in elicited production tasks, rather than, for example, using a paraphrase without any island violation, is it possible that such a structure might be grammatically licensed (with resumption) after all? Moreover, what do we make of resumption in colloquial speech, as documented by Radford (2019) for both island and non-island structures? Are we justified in treating all such cases as overgeneration by the production system? One way of addressing these questions would be through systematic quantitative analyses of corpus data to ascertain when and where English speakers most often use resumption and, importantly, how often they use gaps in the same structural contexts. Corpus analyses could then be followed up with experiments that test whether the acceptability of resumption significantly improves in those contexts where it naturally tends to occur. As noted above, positive results could bolster the argument put forward by Radford (2019) that resumption is a grammatically licensed option in English, subject to semantic and register-based constraints. Whatever the outcome of such investigations might be, however, it is clear that the answer one provides ultimately depends on whether grammaticality is understood as a categorical or a gradient concept. For example, in an approach that allows for gradient grammaticality, it would not be necessary to choose between an analysis in which resumptive relatives in English are always grammatical (but subject to semantic and register-based constraints) (Radford 2019) and an analysis in which they are always ungrammatical but occur in spontaneous speech as the result of overgeneration (Morgan and Wagers 2018; Polinsky et al. 2013). Rather, it would be possible for resumptive relatives to be grammatically licensed but subject to soft constraints which may affect their acceptability even in contexts and structures where they are naturally produced. To my knowledge, such an analysis has not (yet) been put forth in the literature on resumption in English.

7.4 Gradient judgment data and the distinction between grammatical and intrusive resumption

Resumption in relative clauses has been studied experimentally in only a few languages, three of which were highlighted in the current chapter: Cantonese, Hebrew, and English. In reviewing various experimental studies of these languages, I set out to explore the relationship between acceptability judgments and theoretical interpretation, and in particular, the evidence for or against a typological distinction between grammatical resumption (Cantonese, Hebrew) and intrusive resumption (English). Although I believe such a distinction can reasonably be maintained at some level, these studies have shown that the situation is rather difficult to interpret in terms of a strict dichotomy of language types.

Several experimental studies of English have reinforced the idea that resumption is intrusive in nature (Han et al. 2012; Heestand et al. 2011; Keffala 2011; Morgan and Wagers 2018; Polinsky et al. 2013). That is, it is a production-driven phenomenon which occurs in spontaneous speech despite the fact that it is generally unacceptable and ungrammatical. For example, simple object relatives with a resumptive pronoun are very low in acceptability (Han et al. 2012; Hofmeister and Norcliffe 2013; Hitz and Francis 2016), and fail to occur in elicited production (Fadlon et al. 2019), even though they do naturally occur in spontaneous speech (Prince 1990; Radford 2019). Furthermore, earlier claims that intrusive resumption might be able to rescue the grammaticality of complex island-violating structures in English have mostly been abandoned in favor of weaker claims that resumption can help mitigate production difficulty (Morgan and Wagers 2018) and facilitate comprehension of such structures (Ackerman et al. 2018; Hammerly 2021).[19] Experimental studies of Cantonese and Hebrew have likewise reinforced the conclusion that resumption is a grammatically licensed strategy for relative clause formation in these languages. For example, simple object relatives in Hebrew are nearly as acceptable with a resumptive pronoun as

[19] Among recent studies, Radford (2019: 109) is exceptional in analyzing island-violating structures with a resumptive pronoun as grammatical in English by virtue of the fact that they do not involve syntactic movement and therefore do not violate movement constraints. Radford also presents examples from the corpus of gapped relative clauses that violate movement constraints (2019: 77–9), but presents no syntactic analysis of these sentences.

with a gap (Farby et al. 2010), and readily available in elicited production (Fadlon et al. 2019). Similarly, coverb relatives with resumption are highly acceptable in Cantonese, and also strongly preferred in elicited production (Francis et al. 2015). These basic findings from English, Cantonese, and Hebrew appear to support the traditional distinction between intrusive and grammatical resumption. The distinction becomes fuzzier, however, when considering the role of syntactic constraints on extraction. For Cantonese, Francis et al. (2015) found that the acceptability of coverb relatives with a gap varied from moderate to low acceptability depending on the verb. Although resumption is clearly available as a grammatical option for forming relative clauses in Cantonese, its status as a grammatical saving device is unclear due to the uncertain status of the purported coverb stranding constraint. Similarly, for Hebrew, Farby et al. (2010) found only a weak ameliorating effect of resumption in Complex NP islands, similar to what has been shown for some island types in English. They interpreted these results to mean that resumption does not in fact rescue grammaticality. Based on similar findings, however, Keshev and Meltzer-Asscher (2017) came to the opposite conclusion. As in Cantonese, resumption appears to be a fully grammatical option for forming some types of relative clauses in Hebrew, such as prepositional object relatives. However, its status as a grammatical saving device in island-violating contexts is unclear.

One possible way of looking at these ambiguous cases is through the lens of partial grammaticalization. Ariel (1999) and Hawkins (2004) have proposed that grammatical resumption arises historically from intrusive resumption through a conventionalization process in which a resumptive pronoun comes to be used systematically in certain positions where the accessibility of the filler phrase is relatively low. Building on this idea, Alexopoulou (2010) offers a more specific explanation of the conventionalization process. She proposes that grammatical resumption arises from a change in the syntactic features of the complementizer, to allow for an anaphoric rather than a movement-based dependency. According to this analysis, the complementizer in a relative clause (whether overt or null) is always specified for a movement dependency in languages that lack grammatical resumption. This is used to help explain the observation (as illustrated with judgment data from English in Section 7.3) that island-violating structures cannot be fully repaired with the insertion of a resumptive pronoun. Once the complementizer has been extended for use in an anaphoric dependency, however, movement constraints no longer apply, and a resumptive pronoun can then circumvent any movement violation, if indeed the structure in question can be relativized at all. This should, presumably, result in a strong ameliorating effect of resumption on acceptability in contexts where relativization is possible but movement is illicit (e.g. prepositional object relatives in Hebrew). Alexopoulou (2010) goes on to argue that this change in the function of the complementizer might or might not result in the development of a distinct morphological form. In Irish, for example, there is a special complementizer reserved for marking resumptive dependencies. It is phonologically similar but morphologically distinct from the complementizer used for marking gapped dependencies (McCloskey 2003). In Hebrew, however, the complementizer maintains the same form regardless of dependency type (Shlonsky 1992). In support of her idea that the complementizer is the primary locus of grammatical change, Alexopoulou (2010) notes that there are no known languages in which pronouns take on a special form in resumptive uses. For the purposes of this discussion, I will consider Alexopoulou's proposal as a plausible working hypothesis for how grammatical resumption might develop from intrusive resumption. In doing so, I would note that the spirit of Alexopoulou's proposal does not require a commitment to a derivational approach involving syntactic movement, and can be understood within any framework that distinguishes between filler–gap and filler–resumptive dependencies. The locus of change also need not be literally in the features of the complementizer, as long as it is understood as a change that affects the entire clause.

Supposing that grammatical resumption is derived from intrusive resumption, there should be room for intermediate stages of historical change. Let us now consider our ambiguous cases in this light. For Cantonese, Francis et al. (2015) observed in their production data that rate of resumption in coverb relatives varied by verb, apparently depending on the acceptability of the gapped variant with a particular verb.[20] To explain this systematic variation among verbs, they suggested that each coverb was at a different stage of grammaticalization along the path from ordinary transitive verb to serial verb to preposition. For example, for the coverb *tung4* 'with', the gapped option was very low in acceptability, and the resumptive pronoun option was always used in production. The authors suggest that this particular coverb may be farther along the grammaticalization path than the other coverbs. Correspondingly, the purported coverb stranding constraint could be understood as a soft constraint on its way to becoming a categorical constraint. Returning to Alexopoulou's (2010) proposal, the existence of a fully acceptable resumptive option in coverb relatives would appear to indicate that the complementizer already bears the syntactic features which allow for an anaphoric dependency. However, resumption is not manifested obligatorily due to the intermediate status of the coverb stranding constraint. Interestingly, Francis et al. (2015) found a similar pattern of acceptability and production in possessive relative clauses, suggesting that the syntactic constraint that prevents extraction of a possessor, commonly known as the Left Branch Constraint (Ross 1967), might also have an intermediate status in this language.

In Hebrew, as in Cantonese, resumptive pronouns are judged as highly acceptable in prepositional object relatives (Shlonsky 1992) (although this has not been formally tested), and in simple direct object relatives (Farby et al. 2010). Following Alexopoulou's (2010) proposal, this would suggest that the complementizer in Hebrew relative clauses bears the appropriate syntactic features to license an anaphoric dependency. In contrast, resumptive pronouns in English are judged as very low in

---

[20] It is notable that Morgan and Wagers (2018) found a similar correlation between rate of production and acceptability of the gapped variant in their study of English relative clauses. However their English data showed a low level of acceptability for resumptive pronouns even in contexts where they were commonly produced, unlike what Francis et al. (2015) found for Cantonese.

acceptability in direct object and prepositional object relatives (Han et al. 2012; Hitz and Francis 2016), suggesting that the complementizer does not license a resumptive dependency in English. Alternatively, it is possible that a resumptive dependency *can* be grammatically licensed in English relative clauses, but subject to semantic and register-based restrictions, as Radford (2019) proposed on the basis of corpus examples from spontaneous speech. As I noted above, Radford's proposals have not been tested experimentally, and it is unclear to what extent acceptability can be improved (if at all) by using more naturalistic sentence materials. However, McKee and McDaniel (2001) present experimental evidence suggesting that resumption might be grammatically licensed in some structural contexts, even for sentences which apparently violate the semantic and register-based restrictions that Radford observed. McKee and McDaniel (2001) examined restrictive relative clauses in adult and child English using a task in which the experimenter set up a context scenario and then spoke the target sentence. The participant then gave a binary (yes–no) acceptability judgment. Among the sentence types they examined were possessive relative clauses as in (20a–b).

(20)   a. *This is the pirate whose Minnie Mouse buried __ treasure.
       b. ?This is the pirate that Minnie Mouse buried **his** treasure.
       c. This is the pirate whose treasure Minnie Mouse buried.

(21)   a. This is the girl who **her** dog cries all night when it storms.
       b. This is the boy who I think **his** father recently won the lottery.

McKee and McDaniel (2001) found that adult participants never accepted a gap functioning as the possessor of the direct object, as in (20a), presumably due to a violation of the Left Branch Constraint. However, participants accepted a resumptive pronoun in this position, as in (20b), about 65% of the time (McKee and McDaniel 2001: 137). Possessive relative clauses with fronting of the entire object NP, as in (20c), were not tested, but would likely have been rated as acceptable more than 65% of the time. Even so, the strong contrast in acceptability between (20a) and (20b) is unexpected if resumptive pronouns are ungrammatical in the possessor function, just like gaps. This acceptability contrast has not been tested experimentally in any of the more recent studies of resumption in English. However, Chaves and Putnam (2021: 104–5) comment on the relative naturalness of constructed examples similar to (20b), as shown in (21a–b). Following Alexopoulou's (2010) proposal, it appears plausible (while admittedly speculative) that the complementizer licenses a conventional anaphoric dependency in the possessor function in English. If so, the anaphoric dependency type could potentially spread to other relative clause types in English at some later stage of grammaticalization. Given that grammatical resumption languages generally lack relative pronouns (Hawkins 1999; Keenan and Comrie 1977), such a change would most plausibly occur in the context of a general shift toward the use of *that*-relatives or relatives with zero marking of the complementizer.

What, then, do we make of the interesting parallels between English and Hebrew with regard to acceptability judgments of island-violating sentences? I believe the most straightforward answer is that the island constructions that were tested in these studies have a very marginal status and cannot be understood as 'grammatical' in the same sense as, for example, prepositional object relatives. In other words, resumption has not (yet) been established as a conventional option for forming relative clauses in *wh*-islands in English or in Complex NPs in Hebrew. It is intriguing that Radford (2019) found several corpus examples of *wh*-islands in resumptive relatives in English, while Keshev and Meltzer-Asscher (2017) found an amelioration effect of resumption as well as a filled-gap effect for Complex NP islands in Hebrew. However, a definitive explanation for these findings awaits future research.

In conclusion, the studies reviewed in this chapter are broadly consistent with the traditional distinction between intrusive and grammatical resumption. However, they suggest a more nuanced interpretation of this distinction whereby some grammatical constraints on extraction may be partially grammaticalized and realized synchronically in the form of soft constraints. This requires a more flexible notion of grammaticality than the one traditionally assumed in derivational and constraint-based approaches to grammar. For example, Francis et al. (2015) have argued that there exists a coverb stranding constraint in Cantonese which can be circumvented by the use of a resumptive pronoun. To account for the variable strength of this constraint as manifested by different coverbs at different stages of grammaticalization, they proposed that coverb stranding is best described synchronically as a soft constraint. This is only possible, however, within a theoretical approach that permits gradient grammaticality. Furthermore, the studies reviewed here generally support a key role for cognitive accessibility in motivating the use of resumption in both types of languages. This is evident especially in the elicited production data from Hebrew and English, as reported by Fadlon et al. (2019) and Morgan and Wagers (2018), which show clear facilitation effects of resumptive pronouns in less accessible contexts. Finally, the studies discussed in this chapter jointly illustrate the inherent difficulty of interpreting quantitative results from acceptability, reading time, corpus data, and production tasks in relation to theoretical proposals that were initially put forward on the basis of informal judgments. To make further progress in our understanding of these subtle phenomena, I believe we need a multimethodological approach in which corpus data from spontaneous language use begin to play a more central role. Radford's (2019) recent analysis of resumptive relatives in everyday spoken English is an excellent example of how corpus data can be applied to theoretical questions in syntax. Similar data on a larger scale and from a variety of languages and dialects will be of value both for quantitative corpus analyses and for designing more naturalistic stimuli in experimental tasks.

In the following and final chapter, I present additional arguments in favor of the idea of soft constraints in the grammar and consider the future of acceptability judgments as a tool for understanding grammar within an increasingly interdisciplinary and multimethodological research landscape.

8

Gradient acceptability, methodological diversity, and theoretical interpretation

In this book, I have reviewed evidence from recent experimental studies showing that various factors may affect acceptability judgments. These factors include syntactic, semantic, prosodic, and discourse-based constraints, as well as performance-based factors. Following the approach set out by Schütze (1996) in his foundational book *The Empirical Base of Linguistics*, I have argued that linguists interested in making theoretical claims about syntax should control for these factors as much as possible when designing a judgment task, and that they should follow standard experimental procedures to ensure statistically meaningful results. Also following Schütze's (1996) approach, I have emphasized that acceptability judgments are a type of performance data and therefore an indirect source of evidence about grammatical competence, and I have argued that considering other data sources in addition to judgments can be useful for deciding among alternative syntactic analyses. While drawing a lot of inspiration from Schütze (1996), the current book is rather different in its aims and emphasis. I have not evaluated the methodological implications of the many participant and task-related factors that can affect judgments, nor have I proposed any psychological model of the judgment process. Instead, I have focused on the implications of gradient judgment data for theoretical interpretation. I have examined the different assumptions about form–meaning isomorphism and gradient grammaticality in different theoretical frameworks and how these assumptions can potentially affect linguists' interpretation of acceptability judgment data (Chapter 2). I have discussed and evaluated several types of evidence that have been used to distinguish formal syntactic constraints from other factors, in the context of ongoing debates over the syntactic status of island constraints, auxiliary selection constraints, word order constraints, and Superiority effects (Chapters 3–4). I have also reviewed recent research on the complex relationship between corpus frequency and acceptability, including some studies involving machine learning (Chapter 5). Using case studies on relative clause extraposition in English and German (Chapter 6) and resumption in Cantonese, Hebrew, and English relative clauses (Chapter 7), I have further illustrated how different theoretical assumptions affect the interpretation of judgment data, and how different types of evidence can be used to support or refute a particular syntactic analysis. With respect to both case studies, I have argued that soft constraints within the grammar are helpful for capturing some gradient patterns of judgments.

Gradient Acceptability and Linguistic Theory. Elaine J. Francis, Oxford University Press.
© Elaine J. Francis (2022). DOI: 10.1093/oso/9780192898944.003.0008

In this final chapter, I revisit the issues of form–meaning isomorphism (Section 8.1) and soft constraints (Section 8.2), providing additional examples and arguments to support the positions I have taken in earlier chapters. I then discuss some additional types of psycholinguistic experiments that have been used to address theoretical questions in syntax, with reference to three studies of split intransitivity in Spanish and English (Section 8.3). Specifically, these studies employ visual probe recognition tasks, cross-modal lexical priming tasks, and structural priming tasks to test a widely accepted theoretical proposal which says that two classes of intransitive verbs differ syntactically with respect to the presence/absence of object-to-subject movement (Burzio 1986). I argue that while the results of these studies are open to different theoretical interpretations, the information gleaned from these and other alternative task types is potentially valuable for addressing syntactic questions. Finally, I offer some brief remarks on big data, neurolinguistics, and the future of syntactic theory within an increasingly diverse methodological landscape (Section 8.4) and conclude the book (Section 8.5).

8.1 Form–meaning isomorphism and the syntactic status of semantic contrasts

In Chapter 2, I argued that one of the main theoretical issues potentially affecting our interpretation of acceptability judgment data is the degree of form–meaning isomorphism assumed within a given theoretical framework. I then returned to this theme in the discussion of split intransitivity in German in Chapter 3, and in the discussion of RCE (relative clause extraposition) in English in Chapter 6. One of the cases I discussed in Chapter 6 was reported in Overfelt (2015), who examined the licensing of the polarity item *any* in English relative clauses in adjacent and extraposed positions. Evidence from an acceptability judgment task showed that this polarity item was equally acceptable in both contexts, suggesting that *any* is within the semantic scope of the quantifier *every* even when it is contained within an extraposed relative clause. From this, Overfelt deduced that the quantifier must syntactically c-command *any* at some underlying level of syntactic structure. This type of argumentation is typical of derivational theorists, in assuming that similarities (or differences) in semantic interpretation can be taken to reveal similarities (or differences) in syntactic structure. Although she did not cite Overfelt's (2015) judgment data, Walker (2017) provides an alternative analysis which does not require strict form–meaning isomorphism. According to Walker, RCE involves a special noncanonical mapping of syntactic constituent structure to semantic scope relations. Thus, the similarity of interpretation between canonical and extraposed relative clauses is dealt with at the level of semantics and is not taken to imply similar syntactic c-command relations. In my earlier discussion in Chapter 6, I concluded that both theoretical accounts appear to be equally compatible with the judgment data from Overfelt (2015). In the current section, I discuss a similar case in which the interpretation of a set of judgment data depends on one's theoretical assumptions about form–meaning isomorphism. However, in this case, the assumption of form–meaning isomorphism (or lack thereof) intersects in interesting ways with the other main theoretical idea introduced in Chapter 2—the notion of soft constraint.

With a series of acceptability judgment experiments, Jeffrey et al. (2015: 100) set out to distinguish among competing theoretical accounts of transitive subject control (henceforth, TSC) in English.

(1) a. Jane promised Sarah to do the dishes.
    b. Jane asked Sarah to do the dishes.
    c. Jane pledged to Sarah to do the dishes.
    d. Jane promised Sarah she would do the dishes.
    e. Jane pledged to Sarah that she would do the dishes

In (1a), which involves TSC, the matrix clause subject *Jane* is interpreted as the controller of the covert subject within the infinitive clause *to do the dishes.* By comparison, (1b) involves object control, in which the matrix clause object *Sarah* is interpreted as controlling the interpretation of the infinitive clause subject. According to one theoretical account, a syntactic locality condition prevents *Jane* from being interpreted as the controller of the implied subject of the infinitive clause in (1b). According to Larson's (1991) formulation, the Minimal Distance Principle (MDP) requires the infinitive clause subject to be controlled by the closest c-commanding antecedent: in this case, the matrix object, *Sarah.* This locality condition apparently fails to apply in (1a), in which *Jane* controls the interpretation of the infinitive clause subject. Why does it fail to apply? As Jeffrey et al. (2015) point out, a number of solutions to this problem have been proposed (Hornstein 1999; Landau 2003; Larson 1991). For the sake of concreteness, I will focus here on just two proposals, one of which involves strict form–meaning isomorphism, and the other of which involves a purely semantic account of control.

Hornstein and Polinsky (2010) present a syntactic analysis of TSC sentences like (1a) which assumes a version of the Minimal Distance Principle and which preserves form–meaning isomorphism. This is accomplished by positing distinct syntactic structures for TSC sentences like (1a) and object control sentences like (1b). In (1b), the direct object, *Sarah*, is the closest c-commanding antecedent, making it the controller of the infinitive subject. In (1a), however, *Sarah* is instead analyzed as embedded within a preposition phrase headed by a null preposition.[1] Therefore, the matrix subject *Jane* becomes the closest c-commanding antecedent and the controller of the infinitive subject. For the same reason, sentences like (1c) which contain the overt preposition phrase *to Sarah* are interpreted as having the matrix subject *Jane* as the controller of the infinitive subject. Hornstein and Polinsky (2010) further note based on their own and others' informal observations that TSC sentences like (1a) are only marginally acceptable, at least for some speakers. They attribute this to the difficulty of perceiving

---

[1] To accommodate Uniform Theta Assignment (Baker 1997), this difference is said to correspond to a subtle difference in semantic roles in which the oblique object of a null preposition is less directly affected by the action than the direct object of a transitive verb (Hornstein and Polinsky 2010: 21).

and learning the null preposition. In contrast, they assume that TSC sentences with an overt preposition like (1c) are fully acceptable. Jeffrey et al. (2015) then take Hornstein and Polinsky's (2010) analysis to predict that TSC sentences with a null preposition, as in (1a), should be judged as less acceptable than their finite paraphrase (1d). However, TSC sentences with an overt preposition, as in (1c) should be just as acceptable as their finite paraphrase (1e).

Jackendoff and Culicover (2003) present an alternative syntactic analysis which says that TSC sentences like (1a) share the same syntactic constituent structure as object control sentences like (1b). According to this approach, no syntactic locality condition applies, and the interpretation of control relations depends solely on the semantic properties of the verbs in relation to their arguments. Since the syntactic structure of the two control constructions is the same but the semantic interpretation is different, this analysis does not maintain strict form–meaning isomorphism. In addition, Jackendoff and Culicover (2003: 523) assume that TSC sentences like (1a) are fully grammatical. Grouping together several semantic accounts of TSC which similarly assume that TSC is grammatical, Jeffrey et al. (2015) take this type of account to predict no differences among the sentence types in (1a), (1c), (1d), and (1e). I would add, however, that Jackendoff and Culicover (2003: 530) briefly address the claim that TSC sentences like (1a) are less acceptable for some speakers. They argue that English speakers are strongly biased to interpret the constituent ordering in (1a–b) as object control, making TSC interpretations more difficult to get. This would seem to predict that TSC sentences as in (1a) should be judged as less acceptable on average than their finite paraphrases as in (1d). It is unclear from their discussion whether the same bias would apply to TSC sentences with an overt preposition as in (1c).

In a series of three acceptability judgment experiments, two of which I will discuss here, Jeffrey et al. (2015) set out to test these predictions regarding the acceptability of TSC. Experiment 1a examined the acceptability of TSC sentences with the matrix verb *promise* as compared to their finite paraphrases. This experiment also included the corresponding intransitive versions of these two sentence types as a control. The four test conditions were as in (2a–d). Grammatical and ungrammatical filler sentences with different verbs used in similar structures were also included. (2e) shows one of the ungrammatical filler types.

(2) a. Jane promised Sarah to do the dishes.   (TSC)
    b. Jane promised Sarah she would do the dishes.   (finite paraphrase of TSC)
    c. Jane promised to do the dishes.   (ISC)
    d. Jane promised she would do the dishes.   (finite paraphrase of ISC)
    e. *Jane declined Sarah to do the dishes.   (ungrammatical filler)

Results from 20 native English-speaking participants showed that TSC sentences as in (2a) were rated less acceptable than the other three sentence types, resulting in a significant interaction between finiteness and transitivity (Figure 8.1). The authors

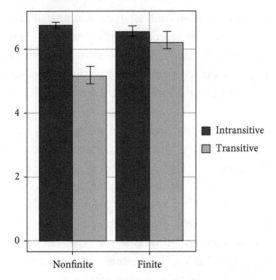

Fig. 8.1 Acceptability of transitive and intransitive control sentences with *promise* and their finite paraphrases

Source: Reprinted from Jeffrey et al. (2015: 108) with permission from Elsevier.

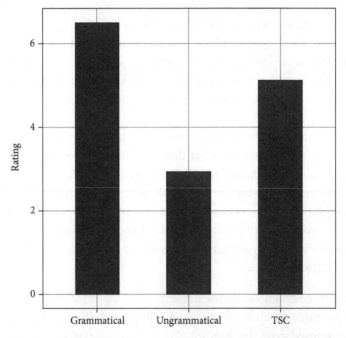

Fig. 8.2 Acceptability of grammatical and ungrammatical filler sentences and TSC sentences with *promise*

Source: Reprinted from Jeffrey et al. (2015: 108) with permission from Elsevier.

observe that the TSC sentences were still rated much higher than the ungrammatical filler sentences (Figure 8.2).

Experiment 1b tested a different group of participants on sentences similar to the ones in Experiment 1a. Instead of the verb *promise*, the test sentences in Experiment 1b used the verbs *vow*, *pledge*, *commit*, and *guarantee*. These verbs are similar to *promise* in inducing a subject control interpretation, but take preposition phrase complements rather than direct object noun phrases. The four test conditions are shown in (3a–d). The same filler sentences as in Experiment 1a were also included.

(3)   a. Jane vowed to Sarah to do the dishes.
      b. Jane vowed to Sarah that she would do the dishes.
      c. Jane vowed to do the dishes.
      d. Jane vowed that she would do the dishes.

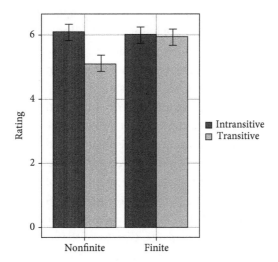

Fig. 8.3 Acceptability of transitive and intransitive control sentences with *vow*, *pledge*, *commit*, and *guarantee*, and their finite paraphrases

Source: Reprinted from Jeffrey et al. (2015: 110) with permission from Elsevier.

Results from 20 participants in Experiment 1b showed the same pattern for verbs like *vow* as were shown for the verb *promise* in Experiment 1a. Sentences like (3a) which involve TSC with an overt preposition were rated lower than the other three sentence types (Figure 8.3), but higher than the ungrammatical filler sentences. Jeffrey et al. (2015) interpret these results (along with the results of a third experiment that examined the related phenomenon of control shift) with respect to the two theoretical positions outlined briefly above. They claim that semantic approaches to TSC predict no differences in acceptability between TSC sentences with and without an overt preposition, or between TSC sentences and their finite paraphrases. They contrast the semantic approach with the approach of Hornstein and Polinsky (2010), who predict that TSC sentences with *promise*, as in (2a) should be less acceptable than their finite paraphrases, as in (2b). The latter prediction was confirmed (Figure 8.1). Since the reason given for the lower acceptability of (2a) is the presence of a null preposition, Hornstein and Polinsky (2010) also predict that TSC sentences with an overt preposition, as in (3a), should not be degraded in acceptability. This prediction was not confirmed. Rather, the results showed that TSC sentences with an overt preposition, like (3a), were less acceptable in comparison to their finite paraphrase (Figure 8.3) in the same way that TSC sentences with *promise* were (Figure 8.1). As also noted above, both types of TSC sentences (with and without an overt preposition) were only slightly degraded in acceptability and were rated higher than the ungrammatical fillers such as (2e) (results for *promise* type TSC sentences in Experiment 1a shown in Figure 8.2).

In interpreting these results, Jeffrey et al. (2015) propose that a syntactic locality condition is in fact responsible for the lower acceptability of TSC, but that it applies equally to TSC sentences with and without an overt preposition. They further argue that because the TSC sentences were only slightly degraded in acceptability, the relevant locality condition should not be subsumed under a more general syntactic principle, as has been proposed (Hornstein 1999). Instead, they interpret the relevant locality condition as a preference condition or soft constraint in the sense of Sorace and Keller (2005). Their soft constraint analysis is supported with data from the Corpus of Contemporary American English showing that speakers actually use TSC in spontaneous speech, even though they do not use it very often (about 1% of clauses with the verb *promise*) (Jeffrey 2014). Also in keeping with Sorace and Keller's (2005) idea of soft constraint, Jeffrey et al. (2015) present evidence of variation in acceptability ratings within and across participants. Graphs of the individual ratings for TSC items show that some participants gave consistently high ratings, some gave consistently low ratings, and others gave intermediate or variable ratings for different items (Jeffrey et al. 2015: 117). They surmise that some participants may be more sensitive to the purported syntactic locality violation than others. Where does this leave the semantic account of control? Jeffrey et al. (2015: 117) suggest that those speakers who provide consistently high ratings for TSC sentences appear to be adopting a semantic strategy for interpreting them, while those speakers who provide intermediate, low, or variable ratings may have access to syntactic and semantic strategies at the same time. At least with respect to speakers who fail to give consistently high ratings for TSC sentences, then, Jeffrey et al. (2015) suggest that a purely semantic account fails. An alternative explanation that is consistent with the semantic account is possible, however. As I mentioned above, Jackendoff and Culicover (2003: 530) discuss this issue in a footnote: "It is true, as Takagi (2001) observes, that there is a strong bias toward interpreting NP V NP to VP as object control, and this may be a default constructional meaning that makes it hard for some speakers…to get subject control readings."

According to this account, the interpretation of a sentence with the surface order [NP V NP to VP] as either TSC or object control is determined by the semantic properties of the verb and its arguments. However, the canonical syntax–semantics mapping involved in object control is more frequently used and more salient to speakers, creating some difficulty for interpreting the noncanonical mapping involved in TSC. Note that this account would need to be extended slightly to apply to [NP V PP to VP] surface order, as in Experiment 1b. This default interpretation analysis is, in essence, a soft constraint analysis similar to the one I proposed for capturing the Name Constraint on RCE in English in Chapter 6. It differs in a subtle way from the soft constraint analysis proposed by Jeffrey et al. (2015). Whereas the former analysis applies at the level of the construction (i.e. the preferred syntax–semantics mapping), the soft constraint proposed by Jeffrey et al. (2015) applies purely at the level of the syntactic representation.

In conclusion, the patterns of acceptability judgments shown in Experiments 1a and 1b appear to support an analysis in which the TSC construction (with or without a preposition) violates a soft constraint rather than a strict grammatical constraint. This analysis is further supported with corpus data showing that TSC is used (albeit infrequently) in spontaneous discourse (Jeffrey 2014: 27). I have argued that the relevant soft constraint may plausibly be interpreted in at least two ways, depending on whether one adopts a syntactic or a semantic account of control. A syntactic account assumes strict form–meaning isomorphism, distinct syntactic structures for TSC and object control, and an analysis of the relevant soft constraint as a syntactic locality condition. Jeffrey et al. (2015) propose such an account of their own data and reject a purely semantic account. An alternative semantic account assumes that TSC and object control constructions share the same syntactic structure but involve different syntax–semantics mappings. In this analysis, the relevant soft constraint takes the form of a preferred syntax–semantics mapping. Because the TSC construction violates the preferred mapping, it tends to be perceived as less acceptable. Possibly, this effect could be ameliorated with the addition of a supporting context that would allow readers/listeners to anticipate a TSC interpretation. Individual differences in patterns of judgments suggest that whatever the nature of the soft constraint (syntax only or syntax–semantics mapping), its expression is variable across speakers. Finally, it is important to note that a soft constraint analysis would not be possible within a theoretical framework that assumes a strict categorical notion of grammaticality. An alternative analysis, most likely involving performance-related factors, would need to be proposed instead. In the following section, I consider this contrast between categorical and gradient notions of grammaticality in more depth.

8.2 The case for gradient grammars

In the previous section, I followed Jeffrey et al. (2015) in arguing that the lower acceptability of TSC sentences compared to their finite paraphrases is plausibly due to a soft constraint within the grammar. I then showed two possibilities for how such a constraint might be formulated, depending on whether one assumes the same or different syntactic structures for TSC and object control. Indeed, throughout the book, I have presented similar arguments in favor of a soft constraint analysis of Superiority effects in German *wh*-questions (Featherston 2005a), subclausal locality in German RCE (Strunk and Snider 2013), definiteness and predicate type in English RCE (Francis and Michaelis 2014), and coverb stranding in Cantonese relative clauses (Francis et al. 2015). Recognizing that the idea of gradience within the grammar is controversial among generative linguists, I would like to reconsider the motivation for this type of analysis. What exactly do soft constraints buy us that we can't get from hard constraints in combination with non-syntactic factors? To address this question, I will first review how the idea of soft constraints developed, and some of the arguments I have given in favor of the notion so far. I will then discuss some additional arguments presented by Häussler and Juzek (2020) in their recent chapter on gradience in acceptability judgments. Finally, I will consider proposals by Schütze (1996), Kempen and Harbusch (2008), and Villata et al. (2019) to account for gradient constraint strength using a similarity-based metric.

In Chapter 2, I discussed how practitioners of derivational and constraint-based approaches to grammar have traditionally understood syntactic representations to be either well-formed (grammatical) or ill-formed (ungrammatical) in a categorical sense. Within these traditions, the pervasive phenomenon of gradience in acceptability has been understood as resulting from a combination of categorical syntactic constraints and various additional factors (Schütze 1996; 2011). To show that a categorical syntactic constraint has been violated, it has been sufficient in most cases to present informally obtained judgments showing that a syntactically ill-formed sentence is less acceptable than a well-formed control sentence which differs minimally in some aspect of its structure. In experimental work in syntax, this idea has been adapted to factorial designs in which one or more linguistic features is manipulated and statistical analysis is applied. Cowart's (1997) judgment experiment that tested *that*-trace effects in English is typical of this line of argumentation. Cowart (1997) manipulated two factors (gap location and presence/absence of *that*) to create four experimental conditions, as illustrated in (4a–d) (Cowart 1997: 19).

(4) a. I wonder **who** you think ___ likes John.   (subject gap, no *that*)
     b. I wonder **who** you think John likes ___.   (object gap, no *that*)
     c. I wonder **who** you think that ___ likes John.   (subject gap, with *that*)
     d. I wonder **who** you think that John likes ___.   (object gap, with *that*)

Results of an acceptability rating task showed a significant interaction between the two factors. Subject and object gaps without *that* (4a–b) were rated similarly to each other and higher than subject and object gaps with *that* (4c–d). More importantly, the difference between the conditions with and without *that* was greater for subject gaps than for object gaps. Cowart argues that this pattern of interaction supports an analysis in which the sentence type in (4c) violates a *that*-trace constraint and is ungrammatical, while the other three sentence types are grammatical. He attributes the minor effect of *that* on the acceptability of grammatical sentences like (4d) to a general bias (Cowart 1997: 19). More generally, when the results of an acceptability judgment experiment show a pattern of interaction similar to what Cowart (1997) reported, they are taken as a confirmation of the hypothesized constraint. As long as the sentence materials are well-controlled and the predicted interaction is found, any gradience in the observed ratings is attributed to additional factors that are irrelevant to the syntactic analysis.

In Chapter 2, I noted that a contrast in acceptability or a pattern of interaction similar to what Cowart (1997) found for *that*-trace effects in English has not always been taken as sufficient for supporting a categorical notion of grammar. Instead, some authors have proposed a notion of gradience *within* the grammar to account for the degraded acceptability of a construction that is attested in language use, or to account for differences in acceptability among different types of ungrammatical sentences. For example, I discussed how Chomsky (1986a) and other derivational theorists proposed different levels of constraint strength to account for the judgments obtained for different types of syntactic islands (Chomsky 1986a; Cinque 1990; Rizzi 1990; Szabolcsi 2006). I further noted that linguists working within several frameworks descended from Optimality Theory have developed the idea of gradient constraint strength more fully. These approaches, which include Stochastic OT (Bresnan, Dingare, and Manning 2001; Manning 2003), Linear OT (Sorace and Keller 2005), and the Decathlon Model (Featherston 2008), have operationalized the idea in quantitative terms to account for quantitative data from acceptability judgment tasks, preference tasks, and corpus frequencies. For example, in Chapter 2, I discussed Heidinger's (2015) Stochastic OT analysis of postverbal constituent ordering in Spanish. To account for gradient patterns of responses on a forced-choice preference task and an elicited production task, Heidinger (2015) proposed a set of soft constraints that interact with each other to determine which constituent ordering is preferred for a given input.[2] I pointed out that many of these soft constraints incorporate discourse or processing-related elements (e.g. discourse focus, phrase length), and asked whether the observed patterns of responses might alternatively be understood directly in terms of these non-syntactic factors. Indeed, a lurking question behind proposals of gradient grammar and gradient grammaticality has been whether there could be an alternative explanation of this nature. Do we really need to abandon the idea of categorical grammaticality to account for gradient patterns of judgments?

In Chapters 6–7, I argued that some patterns of judgments are indeed most compatible with a soft constraint analysis rather than either a hard constraint analysis or a purely performance-based account, especially when considered in the context of

---

[2] Based on the frequency values obtained in the two experiments, Heidinger (2015) calculated a ranking value for each constraint and also the range of its application above and below that value. The ranking value determines how the constraints are ranked relative to each other, while the range of application determines whether the rankings can be reversed on a probabilistic basis. If two constraints overlap in their range of application, their rankings can be reversed in the stochastic evaluation, resulting in different output forms on different occasions (i.e. optionality). The likelihood of such a reversal happening depends on how far apart the ranking values are. If the ranking values are nearly equal, for example, the reversal should happen about 50% of the time.

other types of data. For example, in my discussion of RCE in English in Chapter 6, I argued that the patterns of judgments associated with definiteness (Name Constraint) and predicate type (Predicate Constraint), as identified by Walker (2013), are good candidates for a soft constraint analysis. I first argued against a hard constraint analysis by showing attested examples from the International Corpus of English Great Britain in which the constraints are apparently violated (Francis and Michaelis 2014). I then argued against a purely performance-based account by referring to data from an elicited production experiment which suggest that the definiteness effect (Name Constraint) is construction specific, and not a more general effect of information flow in discourse (Francis and Michaelis 2017). I tentatively proposed a constructionist analysis in which the relevant soft constraints are understood with reference to a preferred subtype (form–meaning mapping) for the RCE construction. In accordance with MacDonald's idea of Plan Reuse (2013), instances of RCE which conform to the preferred subtype are more easily retrieved from memory, easier to produce and comprehend, and judged as more acceptable than those that do not. While acknowledging that these constraints can also be implemented in a theory of constraint interaction such as Linear OT or Stochastic OT, I presented this constructionist analysis as possible alternative, and showed how such an analysis might be extended using Goldberg's (2019) usage-based theory of the partial productivity of constructions.

Going beyond the analysis of individual constructions, Häussler and Juzek (2020) examine gradient patterns of judgments for many different types of grammatical and ungrammatical sentences and ask whether these patterns might be attributed to a combination of strict grammatical constraints and performance factors. If so, there would be no compelling need for a notion of gradient constraint strength. Their approach to this problem is somewhat different than the one I have taken in this book. I have started with a pair of sentence types that differ in acceptability and explored the possible reasons for this difference. By casting doubt on both a strict grammatical constraint (e.g. by showing that speakers sometimes use the constraint-violating sentence type) and a fully performance-based account (e.g. by showing that the constraint appears to be construction-specific), I have argued in favor of conventionalized preferences within the grammar. In contrast, Häussler and Juzek (2020) start with a corpus of English sentences that have been predetermined by linguists to be strictly grammatical or ungrammatical and then explore how consistent these predetermined categories are with speakers' gradient judgments. Of particular importance will be their finding that speakers rated many of the purportedly ungrammatical sentences as relatively acceptable.

Häussler and Juzek (2020) collected a set of test items selected from a large corpus of example sentences from syntactic studies of English published in the journal *Linguistic Inquiry* (2001–10). They first narrowed down their item list by excluding those items for which the ratings would be potentially influenced by non-syntactic factors. These factors included low plausibility, unintended alternative readings, garden path effects, complex or hard-to-process structures (e.g. with multiple antecedents), emotionally evocative vocabulary, and colloquial or socially stigmatized usage. From the 2,539 items that remained after this initial screening, they took measures to reduce the possible effects of scale bias imposed by the original authors. First, they narrowed their database to exclude the items from papers that used a binary scale ('*' or unmarked) to indicate grammaticality, leaving only the items from papers that used at least three types of marking (i.e. papers that at least included '?' to indicate lower acceptability or uncertainty about grammaticality). From that set, they included only the items that were either marked as '*' (ungrammatical) or unmarked (implying full grammaticality). Finally, from this smaller set, they randomly sampled 50 items marked with '*' and 50 unmarked items, which they then used as stimuli in three acceptability judgment experiments.

In Experiment 1, the test sentences were presented to 65 nonexpert raters (L1 speakers of American English) through the Mechanical Turk online platform. Participants read each item and rated it on a 7-point scale.[3] The authors then ran two more experiments (Experiments 2 and 3) using the same stimuli with new participants (L1 speakers of British English) recruited through the Prolific online platform. Experiment 2 replicated Experiment 1, but with 25 new participants recruited from Prolific. (This was necessary to set up Experiment 3 because the Mechanical Turk platform was temporarily unavailable.) Experiment 3 tested another set of 26 participants (also recruited from Prolific) on a subset of the stimulus items from Experiment 2, specifically to test for possible scale effects, as I explain below.

Results from Experiment 1 showed that the items marked with '*' in the original paper were generally rated lower than the unmarked items. However, there was a great deal of overlap among the two sets (Figure 8.4). In addition, 43 of the 100 items fell within the mid bin, receiving intermediate ratings between 3 and 5. Of these, 77% were marked with '*' indicating that the author considered them to be ungrammatical, while the remaining 23% were unmarked. Thus, the results show a wide range of variation in the ratings of sentences that were assumed by the original authors to be ungrammatical. The results of Experiment 2, which was a replication of Experiment 1 with different participants (British rather than American English speakers), were very similar: 45 of 100 items fell within the mid bin, and most had been originally marked as ungrammatical.

In interpreting these results, Häussler and Juzek (2020) first consider the possible effects of two task-related factors: aggregation of the ratings across individuals and scale effects. It is possible in a rating task that averaging over multiple participants could obscure the fact that some participants consistently gave high ratings for a particular item, while others consistently gave low ratings for the same item. However, their analyses of individual participants' responses revealed that there was no such bimodal distribution for the items with intermediate mean ratings. Rather, they found that many participants gave intermediate ratings for these items. They conclude that the

---

[3] Although each item was predetermined to be grammatical or ungrammatical based on the original author's marking, the stimulus sentences were presented to participants in the standard way, without any marking.

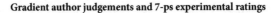

Gradient author judgements and 7-ps experimental ratings

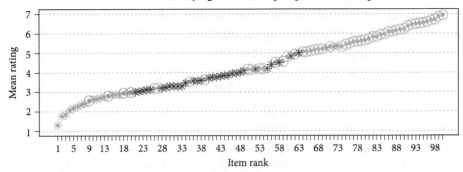

Fig. 8.4 Mean acceptability ratings of items marked grammatical and ungrammatical in the original *Linguistic Inquiry* publication. Items in the middle range of 3–5 are highlighted

Source: From Häussler and Juzek (2020: 247).

intermediate ratings cannot be due to an aggregation effect. The second task-related factor they looked at was a scale effect. A scale effect is the tendency for participants to use the entire rating scale when such a scale is provided, rather than providing responses mostly at either end of the scale. To examine this, they tested a new set of participants on the same items, but excluded the 45 items for which the ratings fell in the intermediate 3–5 range in Experiment 2. If the gradience observed in Experiments 1–2 were entirely due to a scale effect, we would expect approximately the same percentage of items to fall within the intermediate range in both experiments. However, this percentage was much lower in Experiment 3. The ratings for 45% of items in Experiment 2 fell into intermediate 3–5 range, as compared with 25% in Experiment 3. In addition, only 7% of the items in Experiment 3 fell into the narrower 3.5–4.5 range, compared with 24% in Experiment 2. The authors conclude that a scale effect can explain some but not all of the gradience observed in Experiments 1 and 2.

To explain the remaining gradience in judgments that was not due to a scale effect, Häussler and Juzek (2020) once more consider performance factors. Although they had prescreened the items to control for the potential effects of low plausibility, ambiguity, structural complexity, and colloquial usage, they acknowledge that these and other similar factors might still have exerted some influence on the ratings. Possibly, uncontrolled performance factors could help explain why a number of the unmarked (grammatical) items received intermediate or low ratings. However, as noted above, 77% of the items in Experiment 1 that received intermediate ratings in the 3–5 range were marked with '*', meaning that the original authors believed these items in fact violated a syntactic constraint. Häussler and Juzek (2020) acknowledge that grammatical illusions—special cases in which ungrammatical sentences are perceived as relatively acceptable—are a potential performance factor which was not considered in the prescreening process.[4] However, they observe that their stimulus items originally marked with '*' do not instantiate any known grammatical illusions. They give the following examples of ungrammatical items that received intermediate ratings. Mean ratings from Experiment 1 are given in parentheses following each item.

(5)   a. *John was hoped to win the game. (4.20)
      b. *If you want good cheese, you only ought go to the North End. (4.40)
      c. *John beseeched for Harriet to leave. (4.51)
      d. *John said to take care of himself. (4.83)
      e. *October 1st, he came back. (5.00)
      f. *John pounded the yam yesterday to a very fine and juicy pulp. (5.26)
      g. *Sue estimated Bill. (5.31)
      h. *I read something yesterday John had recommended. (5.33)

Having determined that the ungrammatical items with relatively high ratings do not involve any known grammatical illusions, Häussler and Juzek (2020) surmise that the original authors were unlikely to be completely wrong about the syntactic deviance of these items. They tentatively conclude that the most plausible explanation for the observed gradience comes from within the grammar itself.

Now that I have reviewed some of the evidence in favor of a gradient grammar approach, I will conclude this section by considering the alternative proposals of Schtüze (1996), Kempen and Harbusch (2008), and Villata et al. (2019). In chapter 6 of his trailblazing book, Schütze (1996) proposed a cognitive model of the acceptability judgment process. In this chapter, Schütze anticipates the problem of ungrammatical sentences showing a range of variation in acceptability (as strikingly exemplified much later in Häussler and Juzek's (2020) experiments) and offers a tentative solution. He suggests that assigning a scalar rating to an ungrammatical sentence might involve generating a grammatical version of the sentence: "In rating a marginal sentence, for example, one might first extract the intended meaning, then generate a grammatical sentence that is the expression of that meaning, then compare the two to decide how far off the original sentence was" (Schütze 1996: 174). Essentially, Schütze is proposing that the participant applies a similarity-based metric to determine the degree of difference between an ungrammatical stimulus sentence and its closest grammatical counterpart expressing the intended meaning, at least so far as this intended meaning can be recovered. As I discussed in Chapter 5, Kempen and Harbusch (2008) apply this idea to explain variation in the acceptability ratings of six word order variants in German. A corpus analysis showed that four of the six word orders were never used, and yet they differed from each other in acceptability. Following Schütze (1996), they proposed that all four of the unattested variants were ungrammatical. However, because

---

[4] For example, in Chapter 4, I discussed data showing that ungrammatical missing VP sentences in English and German are judged as relatively acceptable when they occur in a context with multiple center embeddings (Bader et al. 2003; Gibson and Thomas 1999). This hard-to-process context causes readers to overlook the missing VP and perceive the sentence as relatively acceptable.

the ungrammatical variants showed different degrees of deviance from the "ideal de-livery" version of the sentence, they received different acceptability ratings. In this way, both Schütze (1996) and Kempen and Harbusch (2008) maintain a categorical notion of grammaticality, while still accounting for variation in the ratings of ungrammatical sentences. They do so by attributing this variation to performance factors specific to the judgment process.

In more recent work based on a similar idea, Villata et al. (2019) present a compu-tational model that derives gradient acceptability ratings of island-violating English sentences using a simulated structure-building mechanism. They begin with a few key observations from previous acceptability judgment studies conducted by Sprouse and Messick (2015): (1) *whether*-islands (a type of weak island) are rated as more acceptable when the filler phrase is D-linked (e.g. *which car*), as in (6c), than when the filler phrase is a bare pronoun (e.g. *what*), as in (6b); (2) *whether*-islands with an uninterpretable dependency (intransitive verb), as in (6d), are less acceptable than *whether*-islands with an interpretable dependency (transitive verb), as in (6b–c); (3) D-linked *whether*-islands are still less acceptable than their non-island counterparts; and (4) subject islands (a type of strong island) are equally unacceptable regardless of filler type (7b–c).[5]

(6) a. **What** do you think that John bought __?   (non-island)
     b. *__**What** do you wonder whether John bought __?   (bare)
     c. ?**Which car** do you wonder whether John bought __?   (D-linked)
     d. *__**Which car** do you wonder whether John laughed __?   (intransitive)

(7) a. **What** does the leader think __ interrupted the TV show?   (non-island)
     b. *__**Who** does the leader think the speech by __ interrupted the TV show?
                                                                      (subj island)
     c. *__**Which politician** does the leader think the speech by __ interrupted the TV show?

Villata et al. (2019) then describe a computational model which simulates word-by-word parses for English sentences and derives a predicted acceptability judgment based on the harmony value of the final parse. In simple terms, the self-organized sentence processing (SOSP) model uses a simple constraint-based grammar consist-ing of a lexicon in which each entry encodes a partial phrase structure tree bearing the syntactic and semantic features of the word and its expected dependents. During word-by-word parsing, the model builds up a structure in a dynamic manner by forming bonds between the partial trees that are projected from each word and then adjusting the bonds as each new word is added. As each new word is added, there is a com-petition among all possible ways to form bonds among the partial trees. The parse

---

[5] The ameliorating effect of transitivity was greater when the filler phrase was D-linked, suggesting that D-linked *whether*-islands are easier to interpret than bare *whether*-islands. Examples in (6a–d) and (7a–c) are from Villata et al. (2019: 1179).

with the optimal matching of features generally wins the competition, resulting in a well-formed structure with a harmony value of 1. In the case of an ungrammatical sentence, the model still builds up a structure in the same way. If there is no possible way of forming bonds among the partial trees such that the features fully match, the model settles on a structure with a partial match. When the final word is added, the result is a fully formed structure, but with a harmony value of less than 1.

Recall that the goal of the model was to simulate the differences in acceptability that were shown in judgments experiments for *whether*-islands and subject islands. This was accomplished by assigning different penalties to the harmony value depending on how similar the ungrammatical structure is to a corresponding well-formed structure. In the case of a *whether*-island with D-linking, as in (5c), the structure of the non-island variant in (5a) is close enough to allow (5c) to be interpreted in the same way. Because the D-linked filler phrase *which car* has a strong requirement for a resolution to the filler–gap dependency, the model tends to look for a structure which allows this, and to settle on one which substitutes the features of *wonder whether* with the features of *think that*. This allows the filler–gap dependency to be resolved, and is consistent with previous findings showing that participants were good at interpreting dependencies within D-linked *whether*-islands. However, because of the required substitution, the harmony value for the sentence is slightly lower than that of a well-formed sentence such as (5a). This is again consistent with previous results showing that D-linked *whether*-islands are slightly less acceptable than the corresponding non-islands.

In the case of a *whether*-island with the bare filler phrase *what*, as in (5b), the features encoding the requirement for a filler–gap dependency are weaker, meaning that the model tends not to consider a *think that* substitution and instead builds an alternative structure with an unresolved gap. The harmony value is lower in this case because the unresolved gap causes a strong penalty. This is consistent with the finding that *whether*-islands with bare filler phrases are less acceptable than *whether*-islands with D-linked filler phrases. Finally, in the case of subject islands, as in (6b–c), the model settles on a parse in which the gap following the preposition *by* is not linked to any filler phrase. As in the case of a *whether*-island with a bare filler, the dependency cannot be interpreted, and the resulting harmony value is low. In addition, because there is no closely analogous structure allowing for a lexical substitution, D-linking of the filler phrase does not prompt the model to find an alternative structure that would allow the dependency to be formed. These simulations are therefore consistent with findings from judgment experiments showing that D-linking of the filler phrase did not improve the acceptability of subject islands.[6]

---

[6] Interestingly, in an unrelated set of experiments, Chaves and Dery (2014) found that the acceptability of subject islands in English improved with D-linking, and was also subject to repeated exposure effects. Their stimuli were slightly different than those of Sprouse and Messick (2015) in that the interrogative phrase was extracted from the main clause subject instead of an embedded subject. It is unclear whether the model of Villata et al. (2019) would predict a greater harmony value for subject islands of the type that Chaves and Dery (2014) studied.

In proposing a computational model that predicts the acceptability of different types of island-violating sentences, Villata et al. (2019) do not refer to the previous proposals by Schütze (1996) or Kempen and Harbusch (2008). However, the intuition behind their model is very similar to these proposals in that the acceptability rating of an ungrammatical sentence depends on the degree to which its structure deviates from that of an analogous well-formed sentence. For Schütze (1996) and Kempen and Harbusch (2008), the acceptability ratings of different types of ungrammatical sentences derive from a process of analogical reasoning which occurs during the judgment process and which is external to the grammar. In this way, a categorical notion of grammaticality can be maintained. Villata et al. (2019) do not see their model in the same way, however. In their view, the reasoning that allows ungrammatical sentences to be fully or partially interpreted is built into the grammar, where grammar is understood not as a static representation but as a process of structure building. They emphasize that the gradient judgments that the model derives do not depend on any grammar-external factors such as plausibility or working memory capacity but rather depend on features that are internal to the grammatical system. Their approach is therefore similar in spirit to that of other gradient grammar approaches such as Stochastic OT (Bresnan, Dingare, and Manning 2001) and Linear OT (Sorace and Keller 2005), while the implementation in terms of incremental structure building and harmony evaluation is more closely related to the Gradient Symbolic Computation parsing model (Cho, Goldrick, and Smolensky 2017).[7]

To sum up, I have presented two kinds of arguments in favor of gradience within the grammar. The first kind of argument, which I presented in Chapters 6–7, starts with a contrast in acceptability between an ostensibly ungrammatical sentence and a set of control sentences and proposes a grammatical constraint to account for this contrast. If corpus data suggest that the constraint-violating construction is well attested, this argues against its status as a hard constraint. Similarly, if construction-specific factors contribute to the lower acceptability of the constraint-violating construction, this argues against a purely performance-based account and instead suggests a conventionalized preference or soft constraint. The second kind of argument, which Häussler and Juzek (2020) present in their chapter, starts with a pattern of divergence among the acceptability ratings of grammatical and ungrammatical sentences of many different types. By minimizing the effects of performance factors related to the sentence materials, and showing that task-related effects cannot fully account for the variance in ratings, it is argued that a notion of gradient constraint strength can plausibly account for the remaining variance. Villata et al. (2019) further support this type of argument by showing that their computational model can predict variation in judgments of different types of island-violating sentences in English based solely on information

---

[7] Gradient Symbolic Computation (Cho, Goldrick, and Smolensky 2017) is a computational model of incremental parsing which posits a dynamic structure-building mechanism. I refer the reader also to Smolensky et al. (2014) for a detailed overview of the Gradient Symbol Systems theory. Like most of the other gradient grammar approaches discussed in this book, the Gradient Symbol Systems theory offers a way of understanding the competence grammar in the light of gradient patterns in language use, and is closely related to Optimality Theory (Prince and Smolensky 2004).

supplied by the grammar itself, and without reference to any grammar-external performance factors. I recognize that these arguments in favor of gradient grammar are suggestive and not definitive. However, I would argue that the burden of proof falls on those who favor a categorical notion of grammar to offer an alternative explanation for these findings in terms of performance and/or task-related factors.

8.3 The place of acceptability judgments in an expanding syntactic toolkit

In addition to emphasizing the importance of key theoretical assumptions about form–meaning isomorphism and gradient grammaticality, I have argued in favor of a multimethodological approach to interpreting contrasts in acceptability. To illustrate this multimethodological approach, I have primarily used examples from corpus analyses, elicitation tasks, and self-paced reading tasks. I will briefly review the utility of these methods in Section 8.3.1. Then in Section 8.3.2, I will discuss several additional experimental methods that have begun to gain ground for addressing syntactic questions. A review of these methods is beyond the scope of the current work. However, to provide some perspective on the role of acceptability judgments within an expanding syntactic toolkit, I will discuss how a particular phenomenon at the syntax–semantics interface—split intransitivity—has been studied in Spanish and English using three of these methods. With respect to both languages, I will show how different methods and sentence materials have led to different results. While some experiments have shown a statistically significant distinction between sentences with unaccusative and unergative verbs, others have not. Furthermore, I will argue that for both types of outcomes, alternative theoretical interpretations are possible. In this way, the methods used in these studies are similar to the more familiar methods I have emphasized throughout the book.

8.3.1 How corpus data, production tasks, and self-paced reading tasks can inform our syntactic analyses

Here, I briefly review some of the ways in which corpus data, production tasks, and self-paced reading tasks can inform our interpretation of acceptability judgment data. First, I have claimed that corpus data from natural discourse are especially useful for demonstrating the range of syntactic structures that people use as well as the contexts that permit their use. For example, in Chapter 6, I discussed an acceptability judgment experiment by Strunk and Snider (2013) which showed that extraposed relative clauses in German were rated as less acceptable when the antecedent was an embedded noun than when it was a head noun. One possible interpretation of this finding is that such sentences violate a syntactic constraint on subclausal locality. However, Strunk and Snider (2013) also presented corpus data showing that German speakers naturally produced constraint-violating relative clauses. Furthermore, they showed that speakers produced fewer such clauses as depth of embedding of the antecedent increased from two to three to four levels, suggesting a possible role for processing factors. Based on these corpus data, Strunk and Snider (2013) argue that a strict syntactic constraint on subclausal locality is not a very plausible interpretation of the judgment data.

In arguing for a multimethodological approach, I have also referred to evidence from spoken and written elicitation tasks. I have claimed that elicitation tasks are useful for discovering the conditions under which language users will choose a less favored or purportedly ungrammatical structure even when a more favored or clearly grammatical alternative is available. For example, in Chapter 7, I discussed a study of Cantonese relative clauses that included data from acceptability judgments and elicited production. With an acceptability judgment task, Francis et al. (2015) found that sentences containing a relative clause in which the object of a coverb (preposition-like serial verb) was extracted were significantly less acceptable than comparable sentences with a resumptive pronoun. These results appeared to support earlier proposals for a coverb stranding constraint. However, results from a spoken elicitation task showed that speakers produced constraint-violating sentences about 25% of the time, even though the resumptive pronoun option was both preferred and readily available. Francis et al. (2015) argue that these findings cast doubt on proposals for a strict grammatical constraint on coverb stranding. Elicited production data can sometimes be used to argue in favor of a grammatical constraint, however. For example, Fadlon et al. (2019) reported on a written elicitation task showing that English speakers never used a resumptive pronoun in an object relative clause. Although failure to produce a certain structure does not prove that it is ungrammatical, Fadlon et al. (2019) take these findings to be consistent with previous claims about the ungrammaticality of this structure. That is, ungrammaticality is taken to be a likely reason why this structure would not be readily accessible to the production system.

Besides corpus analysis and elicited production, a third method that I have discussed in a few instances is self-paced reading. An advantage of this method is that it provides information about the relative ease or difficulty of processing over time, at different locations within a sentence. I have shown that this method can also be used in conjunction with acceptability judgments to support or contest a particular syntactic analysis. For example, in Chapter 7, I discussed Hammerly's (2021) study of English showing that relative clauses with resumptive pronouns were read faster than relative clauses with gaps when the pronoun/gap was contained within a *wh*-island, while the opposite was true when the pronoun/gap was contained within an embedded declarative clause. In the light of evidence from several previous studies showing that *wh*-island configurations in English are just as unacceptable with or without a resumptive pronoun (Han et al. 2012; Heestand, Xiang, and Polinsky 2011; Polinsky et al. 2013), Hammerly claims that resumptive pronouns fail to repair the grammaticality of these configurations. Instead, he argues that the pronoun partially compensates for the difficulty that readers encounter when they attempt to interpret a gap in an unexpected context, by providing an overt cue to the identity of the filler phrase. While Hammerly (2021) is cautious in his conclusions, it is possible to argue further based on these results that processing ease might help explain why resumptive pronouns have developed a saving function in languages with grammatical resumption, in particular for grammatical structures where gaps are not permitted. According to Alexopoulou and Keller (2007) and Alexopoulou (2010), for example, a change in the feature structure of the complementizer allows for languages with only a movement-based strategy to develop a resumption strategy. Once the resumption strategy is conventionally available in the language, it can be invoked at an earlier stage of processing a sentence, allowing readers to more readily interpret the dependency when the pronoun is encountered. According to these authors, then, the facilitation effect of resumption is present for similar reasons in both language types (i.e. because it helps readers or listeners resolve the dependency), but should be stronger and therefore easier to detect in languages with grammatical resumption than in languages with intrusive resumption.

8.3.2 Split intransitivity in Spanish and English: evidence from acceptability judgments, visual probe recognition, structural priming, and cross-modal lexical priming

In Chapter 3, I discussed the phenomenon of split intransitivity in relation to Keller and Sorace's (2003) study of auxiliary selection and impersonal passives in German. To review, split intransitivity refers to a cross-linguistic pattern whereby two major classes of intransitive verbs, commonly known as unergative and unaccusative, tend to show distinct distributions (Burzio 1986; Perlmutter 1978). In terms of semantics, unergative verbs (e.g. *dance, fly, smile*) select an agent-like argument and tend to express atelic events, while unaccusative verbs (e.g. *float, fall, arrive*) select a patient-like argument and tend to express telic events. In terms of syntax, the subject of an unergative verb shows typical subject properties, while the subject of an unaccusative verb may in some ways resemble a transitive object. Although different constructions are diagnostic of the distinction in different languages, the standard syntactic analysis within derivational frameworks is uniform across languages. This analysis says that in a basic intransitive clause, the argument functioning as the subject is licensed in a different underlying position for unergative and unaccusative predicates (Burzio 1986). The sole argument of a unergative predicate originates in the subject position, just like the subject argument of a transitive clause. In contrast, the sole argument of an unaccusative predicate originates in an object position within the VP and undergoes movement to the subject position, leaving behind a trace in the original position. This analysis succinctly captures the general pattern whereby the subject of an unaccusative predicate tends to show some object-like properties. However, as discussed in Chapter 3, this analysis has been controversial. Some linguists working in constraint-based frameworks have offered an alternative account of split intransitivity, according to which the syntactic representation of intransitive clauses is uniform, involving a simple structure with no syntactic movements, and the observed distributional differences are predictable from semantics (Sadock 2012; Van Valin 1990). This approach has been supported with evidence for cross-linguistic and cross-constructional variation that is not easily captured in terms of a binary syntactic classification but seems to be predictable from the fine-grained semantic properties of the predicate (Bentley and Eythórsson 2004; Keller and Sorace 2003; Sorace 2000; Van Valin 1990).

Split intransitivity is an informative case for exploring the relationship between experimental data and theoretical interpretation from a multimethodological perspective because it has been studied using several psycholinguistic methods. These methods include acceptability judgments (Keller and Sorace 2003; Montrul 2005; 2006), visual probe recognition (Bever and Sanz 1997; Montrul 2004; 2006), structural priming (Flett 2006), cross-modal lexical priming (Friedmann et al. 2008), extended picture–word interference (Momma, Slevc, and Phillips 2018), and visual world paradigm (Huang and Snedeker 2020; Koring, Mak, and Reuland 2012). In psycholinguistic studies of split intransitivity, the basic logic is as follows. If there is a categorical syntactic distinction between unaccusative and unergative predicates, this distinction should be detectable in online comprehension and production tasks which are presumed to tap into syntactic representations. On the other hand, if unaccusative and unergative predicates share the same syntactic structure, they should evoke similar responses in such tasks. Below, I discuss three representative studies of split intransitivity in Spanish and English: Montrul (2006), Flett (2006), and Friedmann et al. (2008). Montrul (2006) used acceptability judgment tasks and visual probe recognition tasks in Spanish and English, Flett (2006) used structural priming tasks in Spanish, and Friedmann et al. (2008) used cross-modal lexical priming tasks in English. The authors of these studies not only used different methods but also found different patterns of results and came to different conclusions. As I discuss each study, I will elaborate on the specific predictions for each task type and how they were implemented in the research design. In exploring the theoretical implications of these studies, it will be important to consider the (undisputed) semantic differences among the different classes of verbs, and how these differences might have affected the results. I will argue that the results of all three studies are compatible with multiple theoretical interpretations.

In a series of four experiments, Montrul (2006) examined the unaccusative–unergative distinction in Spanish and English by administering an acceptability judgment task and a visual probe recognition task to speakers of each language. (I will elaborate on the nature of the visual probe recognition task below.) A group of monolingual Spanish speakers completed the two Spanish tasks, a group of monolingual English speakers completed the two English tasks, and a group of bilingual speakers of Spanish and English completed all four experiments. The study's main goal was to test whether bilingual speakers of Spanish and English living in the USA whose perceived weaker language is Spanish would differ from monolingual speakers of Spanish (in the Spanish tasks) or from monolingual speakers of English (in the English tasks) in their sensitivity to differences in verb type. Following up on Sorace's (2000) proposal for a semantic hierarchy of unaccusative and unergative verbs, Montrul (2006) was also interested in whether participants would respond differently to different seman-tic subclasses of verbs. Montrul hypothesized that 'core' subclasses of unaccusative and unergative verbs as identified by Sorace (2000) should show a clear contrast in both ex-perimental tasks, while the other subclasses might fail to show the expected contrasts, or might show more variability in the responses, especially for the bilingual partici-pants. Overall, results showed that the bilingual speakers responded very similarly to the monolingual Spanish speakers on the two Spanish tasks, and very similarly to the monolingual English speakers on the two English tasks. One point of interest is that the bilingual group showed some evidence of transfer from Spanish in their responses to the English visual probe recognition task, even though they perceived English to be their stronger language. For the remainder of this discussion, however, I will focus on the within-group variables (verb type and semantic subclass), and how the effects due to these variables might be interpreted with respect to the major theoretical ap-proaches to split intransitivity. While such theoretical implications were not the main focus for Montrul (2006), the results of that study provide an especially instructive example for the current discussion.

Adopting a derivational framework, Montrul (2006) follows Bever and Sanz (1997) and Sanz (2000) in assuming that unergative and unaccusative predicates are syntac-tically distinct in Spanish, but not in English. Specifically, unaccusative predicates in Spanish are understood to bear a movement trace in the object position, while unac-cusative predicates in English are understood to share the same structure as unergative predicates. Montrul (2006) acknowledges that the two verb types have distinct dis-tributions in both languages, but attributes such differences directly to semantics in the case of English. This theoretical analysis makes an interesting prediction for the two task types. Montrul (2006) predicted that with respect to the relevant construc-tions in Spanish and English, differences between unaccusative and unergative verbs should be easily detected in an acceptability judgment task, regardless of whether they are grounded in both syntax and semantics (Spanish) or only in semantics (English). Following Sorace (2000), Montrul (2006) further predicted that the strength of the contrasts might vary, depending on the construction tested and the semantic subclass of the predicate. To test these predictions, Montrul (2006) conducted acceptability judgment tasks testing three diagnostic constructions of split intransitivity and two control structures in each language. As predicted, speakers of both languages rated sentences instantiating the diagnostic constructions differently depending on verb type. For example, Spanish speakers rated sentences with a bare plural postverbal subject higher when the verb was unaccusative, as in (8a) (Montrul 2006: 48). Sim-ilarly, English speakers rated sentences with a cognate object higher when the verb was unergative, as in (9b) (Montrul 2006: 53).

(8) a. Llegaron   turistas   a la ciudad.
       arrived   tourists   at the city
    b. *Hablaron turistas   en el autobús.
       spoke   tourists   in the bus

(9) a. *This time, the plane arrived a timely arrival.

b. I dreamed a scary dream last night.

Also, as expected, the results showed some variation across constructions, semantic subclasses, and participant groups. For example, in the Spanish task, one semantic sub-class of unaccusative verbs (verbs of existence) received low ratings in the absolutive construction, just like the unergative verbs (Montrul 2006: 51). Most importantly for the current discussion, the results of the acceptability judgment experiments showed that both monolingual and bilingual participants were highly sensitive to verb type when rating the acceptability of sentences in Spanish and English.

For the visual probe recognition task, Montrul (2006) makes a different predic-tion. She hypothesizes that Spanish speakers will show evidence of encountering a movement trace when responding to simple intransitive sentences with an un-accusative verb, but not when responding to simple intransitive sentences with an unergative verb. She further predicts that this evidence should be clear for the "core" semantic subclasses of unaccusative and unergative verbs, but might fail to show up for the other subclasses. In such a case, there would be no main effect for verb type, but an interaction between verb type and semantic subclass. In con-trast, she hypothesizes that English speakers will show no evidence of encountering a movement trace, regardless of verb type or semantic subclass. To understand why Montrul (2006) makes different predictions for the acceptability judgment task and the visual probe recognition task, it is necessary to consider the nature of the vi-sual probe recognition task and why it is thought to tap into the detailed syntactic representation.

Montrul's (2006) visual probe recognition task for Spanish was modeled on a pre-vious study by Bever and Sanz (1997) and used some of the same sentence materials from that study. To test a new hypotheses related to Sorace's (2000) unaccusativity hi-erarchy, Montrul (2006) modified the stimuli to include verbs from three semantic subclasses of unaccusative verbs (directed motion, appearance, existence) and three semantic subclasses of unergative verbs (controlled process, motional process, un-controlled process). Following Sorace (2000), each subclass was categorized as 'core', 'less core', or 'peripheral' with respect to its verb type. For example, directed motion verbs were core unaccusatives, while controlled process verbs were core unergatives. In the task, participants were presented with an intransitive sentence divided into three segments. The subject noun was always modified by an adjective and a relative clause, and the main verb was selected to vary according to verb type (unaccusative, unergative) and semantic subclass (core, less core, peripheral). After the sentence was displayed for a short time, it disappeared, and a probe word appeared. Participants then had to decide whether the probe word had appeared earlier in the sentence and respond with a button press indicating 'yes' or 'no'. For the test trials, the probe word was always the subject-modifying adjective, and the correct answer was always 'yes'. (For the filler trials, probe words and correct answers varied.) Finally, following the probe question, participants were prompted to answer a comprehension question based on the content of the relative clause. An example trial for Spanish is shown in (10) (but note that the actual stimulus items did not contain English glosses) (Montrul 2006: 57).

(10) El apuesto referí   /   que oficiaba el partido   /   llegó en un auto
      The handsome umpire   who officiated the game   arrived in a car
      APUESTO
      Estaba el referí de vacaciones?
      Was the umpire on vacation?

Following Bever and Sanz (1997), Montrul (2006) predicted that Spanish speakers would be faster to indicate a 'yes' response to the probe word in unaccusative trials as compared with unergative trials. The idea is that the subject argument of an unaccusative verb should be reactivated at the position of the movement trace, causing participants to respond more quickly to the probe word.[8] Montrul (2006) further predicted that the 'core' subclasses of unaccusative and unergative verbs (i.e. directed motion and controlled process) should show the predicted contrast, while the other subclasses might or might not do so. Response times for the monolingual Spanish group showed no overall advantage for unaccusative verbs. However, consistent with Montrul's second prediction, there was a significant interaction between semantic subclass and verb type. The 'core' and 'peripheral' subclasses showed the expected advantage for unaccusative verbs, while the 'less core' subclasses showed a contrast in the opposite direction (Figure 8.5). Results for the bilingual group (not shown) followed the same pattern, except that response times were slower overall than for the monolingual group. In sum, the response times for the Spanish visual probe recognition task failed to show any overall effect of verb type, but showed the expected advantage for unaccusative verbs in two of the three subclasses.

For the English visual probe recognition task, which used sentence materials very similar to those used in the Spanish task, Montrul (2006) predicted that there would be no difference in response times due to verb type, regardless of semantic subclass, since unaccusative and unergative verbs in English were understood to share the same syntactic structure. Consistent with this prediction, response times for the monolingual English group showed no main effect of verb type and no interaction between verb type and semantic subclass (Figure 8.6).[9]

---

[8] Bever and Sanz (1997: 80) confirmed this prediction, but only for the subset of participants (16 out of 32) who spontaneously scanned the stimulus sentences in a 'sequence-sensitive' manner. These sequence-sensitive participants were identified independently of their responses on the test items through a positive correlation between sentence length and response time on the filler items. In a study of split intransitivity in L2 Spanish that used the same visual probe recognition task, Montrul (2004: 248) criticized Bever and Sanz (1997) for invoking sequence sensitivity, claiming that it was a poorly motivated post hoc method for explaining the results, and that it failed to explain why sequence-insensitive individuals showed shorter response times for unergative verbs. Although Montrul (2004) was able to replicate the effect of sequence sensitivity, she did away with this measure in her analysis of verb type and semantic subclass. Montrul (2006) only examined verb type and semantic subclass and did not include sequence sensitivity in the analysis.

[9] The bilingual group showed an interesting pattern of interaction in the English task. Bilingual participants responded faster to unergatives, but only in the 'less core' subclasses. Since this was similar to the pattern shown

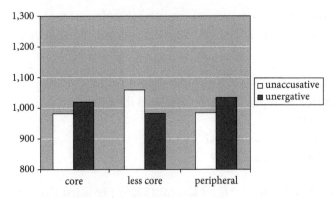

Fig. 8.5 Mean response times by verb type and semantic subclass for monolingual Spanish speakers in the Spanish visual probe recognition task

Source: Reproduced from Montrul (2006: 60) with permission from Sage Publishing.

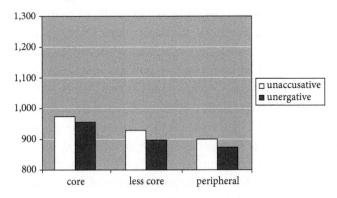

Fig. 8.6 Mean response times by verb type and semantic subclass for monolingual English speakers in the English visual probe recognition task

Source: Reproduced from Montrul (2006: 62) with permission from Sage Publishing.

Overall, the results of four experiments largely confirmed Montrul's (2006) predictions based on proposals from earlier work (Bever and Sanz 1997; Sanz 2000; Sorace 2000). The results for the acceptability judgment tasks were similar for Spanish and English, indicating that both monolingual and bilingual participants were sensitive to the syntactic and semantic requirements of the diagnostic constructions that were tested in each language. The judgment tasks were not meant to distinguish between syntactic and semantic manifestations of split intransitivity but rather to explore possible differences between the monolingual and bilingual participant groups. Also as

by the same bilingual participants on the Spanish task, Montrul (2006: 64) explained this interaction as due to transfer from Spanish. Such a transfer effect was somewhat unexpected, since the participants perceived Spanish to be their less dominant language.

expected, the results of the visual probe recognition tasks appear to support Montrul's (2006) hypothesis that there is a syntactic distinction between unergative and unaccusative predicates in Spanish which is not present in English. Finally, the results for the Spanish visual probe recognition task showed a different pattern of responses for the different subclasses of verbs. Specifically, there was a response time advantage for unergative verbs in the 'less core' (change of state and motional process) subclasses, in contrast to the other subclasses, which showed a response time advantage for unaccusative verbs.

What does this variation among subclasses mean for the syntactic analysis of Spanish? Montrul (2006) takes it as evidence in favor of Sorace's (2000) unaccusativity hierarchy, but she does not discuss the syntactic implications further. Here, I will briefly consider three possible interpretations. One is that change of state verbs do not share the same syntactic properties as other unaccusative verbs in Spanish. In that case, it would be puzzling why they patterned like other unaccusative verbs in the judgment tasks. A second possibility is that the semantic properties of change of state verbs prompted readers to process these sentences differently, such that any facilitation effect due to the presence of a movement trace was neutralized or overridden. A third, related option is that the task itself was not sensitive to movement traces, either because movement traces do not exist (as hypothesized in constraint-based frameworks) or because the probe word was presented only after the entire sentence was read. In either of these scenarios, the observed differences in response times would presumably be due to semantic or lexical factors. On both the second and third accounts, then, it is puzzling why the monolingual English group did not show any differences among the semantic subclasses in the English task. In sum, it is difficult to determine the theoretical implications because it is not entirely clear what factor or factors are driving the response times in this task. In the remainder of this section, I will discuss two additional studies of split intransitivity: Flett (2006) and Friedmann et al. (2008). As in the case of Montrul (2006), the results of these studies are consistent with the authors' theoretical predictions. However, these authors' predictions are different than those of Montrul (2006), as are the methods used. For each set of results, I will again argue that alternative theoretical interpretations are possible.

As part of a larger dissertation study comparing sentence production in first and second language speakers of Spanish and English, Flett (2006) conducted three experiments investigating split intransitivity in first and second language (henceforth L1 and L2) Spanish. The first experiment in this series was a preference task that directly compared subject–verb and verb–subject word order for the same intransitive sentence. In each trial, the participant was asked to provide a rating from 1 to 10, where 1 indicated a strong preference for the verb–subject order, and 10 indicated a strong preference for the subject–verb order. Each intransitive sentence contained either an unaccusative or an unergative verb. Based on previous descriptions of Spanish, Flett (2006) predicted that in a neutral discourse context, participants would prefer the subject–verb word order with unergative verbs, as in (11a), but would prefer verb–subject word order with unaccusative verbs, as in (12b).

(11) a. El médico gritó.
       the doctor shouted
    b. Gritó el médico.
       shouted the doctor

(12) a. El médico llegó.
       the doctor arrived
    b. Llegó el médico.
       arrived the doctor

The results of the preference task were largely compatible with these predictions. L1 Spanish speakers demonstrated a preference for subject–verb order with unergative verbs, but showed no preference for either order with unaccusative verbs. L2 Spanish speakers showed a general preference for subject–verb order, but no difference between unaccusative and unergative verbs.

Similar to Montrul's (2006) acceptability judgment tasks, Flett's (2006) preference task was designed to establish whether L1 and L2 speakers of Spanish were sensitive to the effects of predicate type on word order preference. Flett (2006) did not attempt to distinguish between syntactic and semantic accounts of split intransitivity using this task. However, the second and third experiments were designed to tap into the syntactic representation more specifically using structural priming. To review, structural priming is a facilitation effect caused by recent exposure to a particular grammatical structure. A common manifestation of structural priming both in spontaneous speech and in experimental tasks is the tendency for speakers to repeat structures that have been recently heard or read (Pickering and Ferreira 2008). In a traditional structural priming task, participants first read a prime sentence and then verbally describe a picture depicting a different scenario. Pictures are constructed to depict scenes that can be readily described using two (or sometimes more) alternative structures for the same message, for example active or passive. The priming effect is measured in terms of how often speakers use a particular structure under different priming conditions. For example, if speakers use a passive sentence significantly more often following a passive prime than following an active prime, this indicates a structural priming effect.

Crucially, many experimental studies have shown that structural priming occurs even when no lexical content words are repeated between the prime and the target. This has been taken as evidence that grammatical structure is represented independently of lexical content (Bock 1986; Pickering and Ferreira 2008: 429–31). It is also generally assumed that a structural priming effect depends on the prime and target sentences having the same or very similar structures. This is in fact a key assumption underlying Flett's (2006) experiments on split intransitivity in Spanish. Using the same word order alternation as in the preference task (intransitive sentences with subject–verb or verb–subject order), Flett (2006) conducted two structural priming tasks to investigate whether L1 and L2 Spanish speakers would show similar priming effects for unergative and unaccusative primes. Following Bock and Levelt (1994: 962), she hypothesized that object-to-subject movement of the type commonly believed to occur in Spanish unaccusatives has no psychological validity for production. Therefore, at least for the purposes of production planning, unaccusative and unergative sentences should serve equally well as primes. Flett's experiments also test an alternative hypothesis. If sentences with unaccusative and unergative verbs differ in syntactic structure according to the standard derivational analysis (i.e. only unaccusatives involve object-to-subject movement), and if this difference is in fact relevant for production planning, then verb–subject order should be primed more effectively when prime and target are of the same predicate type. For example, speakers should use verb–subject order in an unaccusative target sentence more often following an unaccusative prime with verb–subject order than following an unergative prime with verb–subject order. For the sake of brevity, I will describe the second structural priming experiment only.

In the experimental task, participants first read an intransitive prime sentence with either verb–subject or subject–verb order. As a comprehension check, they were shown a picture and asked to indicate whether it matched the sentence they read. They were then shown a picture depicting a different scenario and asked to describe it verbally. Below each picture was a written cue instructing participants to use a particular intransitive verb. The priming effect was determined by how often speakers used verb–subject order following four different types of primes that varied according to verb type (unergative, unaccusative) and word order (subject–verb, verb–subject). Target sentences were always unaccusative. In line with Flett's (2006) main hypothesis, the results showed that participants' responses did not differ according to predicate type. Although there was a significant increase in verb–subject order following verb–subject primes compared to subject–verb primes, the priming effect was the same for unergative and unaccusative primes. In addition, L1 and L2 participants showed the same pattern of responses and differed only in that the L2 participants used the verb–subject order more often than the L1 participants in all four conditions.

Flett (2006: 241) is relatively cautious in her conclusions and claims only that any syntactic differences are not relevant for L1 and L2 production. In a major position paper on the value of structural priming as evidence for linguistic representations, Branigan and Pickering (2017: 9) go further and argue that Flett's (2006) findings support a syntactic analysis in which unaccusative and unergative predicates share the same syntactic constituent structure. As I noted above and in Chapter 3, such an analysis has also been proposed by some authors working in constraint-based theories (Sadock 2012; Van Valin 1990). Some of the replies to Branigan and Pickering's position paper dispute this interpretation, arguing that while the priming effects indicate structural similarity *at some level*, structural priming tasks are not sensitive to the detailed syntactic representation (Adger 2017; Koring and Reuland 2017). They also point out that other types of experimental tasks such as acceptability judgments, cross-modal lexical priming, and visual world paradigm have in fact shown differences between the two verb types (Friedmann et al. 2008; Koring, Mak, and Reuland 2012). In their response to the replies, Branigan and Pickering (2017: 50) counter this objection by observing that priming effects are reduced between constructions that have the same order of constituents but a different number of arguments, suggesting that structural priming is sensitive to some non-overt elements (Griffin and Weinstein-Tull 2003). They further argue that structural priming provides more definitive evidence about syntactic representation compared with other methods: "Many experimental methods such as studies using reactivation or visual world paradigms provide results relating to interpretation; there may be an underlying syntactic cause of the effects or there may not, but we typically cannot tell. In contrast, priming is informative about syntactic representation" (Branigan and Pickering 2017: 50–1).

In essence, they are claiming that structural priming is unlike these other tasks because it allows us to detect structural similarities despite semantic differences. I agree with them that this is an advantage of structural priming as a method.[10] However, I would also concur with Adger (2017) and Koring and Reuland (2017) that structural identity may not be required for priming to occur. While we know that some types of structural differences preclude or mitigate priming effects, this does not prove that every type of structural difference should do so. Thus, Flett's (2006) findings appear to be compatible with both constraint-based accounts in which unaccusative and unergative predicates share the same constituent structure, and derivational accounts in which unaccusative predicates involve object-to-subject movement while unergative predicates do not.

While recognizing that split intransitivity is a big topic with a growing experimental literature, I will wrap up the current section by discussing one additional representative study. Friedmann et al. (2008) hypothesized that English has distinct syntactic representations for unaccusative and unergative predicates. To test this hypothesis, they conducted a cross-modal lexical priming experiment in which participants must make a lexical decision (word or nonword) about a sequence of letters on the screen while listening to a spoken English sentence. This task resembles the visual probe recognition task from Bever and Sanz (1997) and Montrul (2006) in purporting to detect a reactivation of the subject at a position following the hypothesized movement trace. However, unlike the visual probe recognition task, which only allows for one response time measurement following the presentation of the entire sentence, the cross-modal lexical decision task provides information about the activation of the subject at different points in time. This is possible because the task combines auditory presentation of the stimulus sentence with visual presentation of the probe word, meaning that the timing of the probe word relative to the stimulus sentence can be manipulated across different trials. The results of the cross-modal lexical priming experiment in fact showed a difference in strength of priming due to verb type, which Friedmann et al. (2008) take as evidence in support of a syntactic distinction between

---

[10] In my own reply to Branigan and Pickering's (2017) position paper, I argue along similar lines that structural priming is a promising method for identifying structural similarities and differences among historically related constructions which have diverged semantically due to grammaticalization (Francis 2017).

unergative and unaccusative predicates in English. Interestingly, these results differ from those of Montrul (2006), who found no effect of verb type in the English visual probe recognition task and concluded that this syntactic distinction is not present in English. While the difference in the results of the two studies might be attributed to a greater sensitivity of the cross-modal lexical priming task to detect movement traces, I will argue that the results are in fact open to different theoretical interpretations. Let us now examine the study by Friedmann et al. (2008) more closely.

For the spoken stimuli, Friedmann et al. (2008) compared three types of verbs: unergative, non-alternating unaccusative, and alternating unaccusative. Sample stimulus items are shown in (13a–c) (Friedmann et al. 2008: 362). The term 'alternating unaccusative' refers to an unaccusative verb which alternates with a transitive variant of the same verb (e.g. *the table dried/they dried the table*). These alternating verbs were included because their syntactic status (as involving a movement trace or not) has been controversial. Although the syntactic status of regular (non-alternating) unaccusative verbs has also been controversial, the authors do not present it as such and assume that sentences containing these verbs should show evidence of a movement trace following the verb.

(13) a. The tailor$_1$ from East Orange, New Jersey, mysteriously **disappeared**$_2$ when it was$_3$ time to adjust the tuxedos and dresses for the participants in the wedding party. (non-alternating unaccusative)
   b. The table$_1$ in the basement of the old house finally **dried**$_2$ after the leading$_3$ window was sealed a month ago. (alternating unaccusative)
   c. The surgeon$_1$ with a brown felt fedora hat and matching coat eagerly **smiled**$_2$ when the beautiful$_3$ actress walked down the corridor to exam room three. (unergative)

In each trial, the participant saw a visual probe word while listening to a stimulus sentence. The probe word was timed to occur at one of three locations within the sentence, as indicated by the numbered subscripts in examples (13a–c). The participant's task was to make a lexical decision about the probe word. For the test items, each probe word was a real word which was either semantically related or unrelated to the subject of the sentence. (Nonword probes were included for many of the filler items.) Participants were expected to respond faster to semantically related probes as compared with unrelated probes. Accordingly, the priming effect was defined as the difference in response time for related and unrelated probes. Although response times were measured at all three locations, the authors predicted an effect of verb type only at the third location. That is, they expected a stronger priming effect for unaccusative verbs than for unergative verbs at the third location (a position three words following the verb) due to a reactivation of the subject following the movement trace. Their expectation for a slightly delayed effect was based on the findings from a previous study that used the same method to test reactivation of the subject following the verb in English passive sentences, which are assumed to involve the same type of movement as in unaccusative sentences (Osterhout and Swinney 1993).

The results appear to support the authors' theoretical predictions. Comparing across the different probe locations, there was, as expected, a strong priming effect at the first position directly following the subject noun, and a weaker priming effect at the second position directly following the verb. Priming effects for the first two probe positions did not differ according to verb type. At the third probe location, however, there was a significant difference due to verb type. For the unergative and alternating unaccusative verbs, there was a further decay of activation of the subject, as shown by a weaker priming effect compared with the second probe position. For the non-alternating unaccusative verbs, however, the priming effect was significantly stronger than at the second position, indicating a reactivation of the subject. The authors argue that these findings support a syntactic analysis in which sentences with non-alternating unaccusative verbs involve a movement trace following the verb, while sentences with unergative verbs do not.[11]

As noted above, Friedmann et al. (2008) expected to find evidence of a syntactic distinction between unaccusative and unergative verbs in English, and in fact found a difference in response times that appears to support their predictions. In contrast, Montrul (2006) did not expect to find such a syntactic distinction in English, although she did expect to find one in Spanish. Montrul's results for the English visual probe recognition task showed no differences due to verb type, apparently confirming her alternative hypothesis for English. How can these different findings be reconciled? As noted above, the cross-modal lexical priming task differs from the visual probe recognition task in allowing for response time measurements at different points in the sentence. Arguably, the ability to measure activation at different points in time makes the former task more sensitive to the presence of movement traces. Friedmann et al. (2008) do not discuss the findings from Montrul's (2006) study of English, but they do discuss the visual probe recognition task from the original study of Spanish by Bever and Sanz (1997). They argue that because this task only measures response time after the entire sentence has been read, it cannot be used to distinguish between constant activation of the subject throughout the sentence and reactivation of the sub-ject following the verb. In contrast, they argue that "the cross-modal methodology allows us to examine sensitivity to grammatical structure before any conscious reflec-tion occurs" and at different locations within the sentence (2008: 359). Possibly, this difference between the two methods could help explain why Friedmann et al. (2008) found a facilitation effect for unaccusative verbs in English while Montrul (2006) did not. I would argue, however, that while these two methods measure reactivation of the subject in a different way, it is not clear in either case whether such reactivation indicates the presence of a movement trace. As I mentioned above in relation to the

---

[11] The status of the alternating unaccusative verbs was not clear. A verb-by-verb analysis showed variable be-havior, with six of the 15 verbs in this category showing the same pattern of reactivation as the non-alternating unaccusative verbs. Friedmann et al. suggest that this variable behavior might be due to a temporary ambiguity, since alternating unaccusatives share the same morphological form as their transitive counterparts, and transitive verbs should not exhibit any reactivation of the subject following the verb. Thus, they do not view this variable be-havior as evidence in favor of a shared structure for non-alternating unaccusative and unergative verbs. However, they acknowledge that additional experiments would be needed to better interpret the results.

findings of Flett (2006) for Spanish, Branigan and Pickering (2017: 50–1) argue that a reactivation of the subject as shown in tasks such as cross-modal lexical priming might be due to properties of the semantic relationship between the verb and the subject. Huang and Snedeker (2020) make a similar argument in their discussion of Friedmann et al. (2008), noting that the verbs used in their cross-modal priming task were not controlled for imageability. To test whether this might have made a difference to the results, Huang and Snedeker (2020) conducted a judgment task in which participants were asked to rate the imageability of the verbs used in Friedmann et al. (2008) and in another study. The results showed that the unergative verbs were rated significantly higher in imageability than the unaccusative verbs. Huang and Snedeker (2020) argue that this difference could have affected the timing of reactivation, leading to a different pattern of responses for unaccusative and unergative verbs.[12] Thus, they argue that additional experiments using cross-modal lexical priming would be needed to rule out possible effects of imageability. More generally, Huang and Snedeker (2020) argue that the mixed results from different psycholinguistic studies of split intransitivity across different task types and different languages are compatible with an approach such as that of Van Valin (1990), in which the language-specific constructions used as tests for unaccusativity do not depend on any two-way structural distinction, but rather on a set of semantic features that make each construction more or less compatible with the lexical semantic properties of different verbs. Huang and Snedeker state: "On such an account, we would have no reason to expect systematic differences in the processing of so-called unaccusative and unergative verbs, since each of these categories would contain a mix of verbs with different semantic structures" (2020: 18). At the same time, they acknowledge that the lack of consistent support from psycholinguistic studies does not rule out the possibility of a two-way syntactic distinction. I agree with Huang and Snedeker on both points and conclude that the results from Friedmann et al. (2008), much like the results from Flett (2006) and Montrul (2006), are compatible with both derivational and constraint-based theories of split intransitivity.

In summary, the studies of split intransitivity discussed in this section illustrate two main points. First, because grammar cannot be observed directly, different tools in the methodological toolkit may give what seem to be different answers to the same theoretical question, in this case the question of whether there exists any syntactic distinction between unergative and unaccusative predicates. For example, acceptability judgment tasks and visual probe recognition tasks showed a distinction between unergative and unaccusative predicates in Spanish (Montrul 2006), while structural

---

[12] Huang and Snedeker's main study similarly tested English sentences with unergative and unaccusative verbs, but using a visual world paradigm. They controlled for imageability of the verb and a few other factors that were not controlled for in the study by Friedmann et al. (2008) and found no differences attributable to verb type. The visual world paradigm similarly measures activation of the subject argument while listening to a sentence, except that instead of measuring responses to a semantically related visual probe word, it measures eye movements to a semantically related picture across different points in time. Huang and Snedeker's (2020) results were in contrast to those of Koring et al. (2012), who used the same visual world paradigm with Dutch stimuli and found a significant effect of verb type.

priming tasks showed no such distinction (Flett 2006). Second, attempting to reconcile such apparent conflicts can help elucidate the role that grammatical representations play in different types of tasks. As we have seen, one possible way of understanding the apparent conflict between structural priming and visual probe recognition is to assume that structural priming taps into a purely syntactic level of representation while visual probe recognition is more sensitive to the semantic relationship between the verb and its argument (Branigan and Pickering 2017). Another possible interpretation of this apparent conflict would be to say that structural priming is sensitive to superficial similarities in constituent order, while visual probe recognition is sensitive to the detailed syntactic representation (Adger 2017; Koring and Reuland 2017). While the former explanation is most compatible with a constraint-based framework which assumes a semantic difference between the two predicate types but no syntactic difference, the latter explanation is most compatible with a derivational framework which assumes a syntactic distinction at an abstract level. In this way, one's theoretical framework is a crucial guide for interpreting these types of apparent conflicts. Regardless of which theoretical framework is assumed, however, I would submit that employing a variety of different tools is essential for identifying cases of apparent misalignment in the first place and reconciling them within a coherent theoretical approach to grammar and processing.

How can we progress beyond identifying cases of apparent conflict and resolving them based on a particular set of assumptions about linguistic representation? As Lewis and Phillips (2015) argue in a review of the relationship between theories of language processing and theories of grammar, a better understanding of how abstract grammatical representations affect participants' performance on different tasks will require a closer alignment between theories of grammar, which have traditionally relied on untimed acceptability judgments, and theories of language processing, which have relied more on the results of time-sensitive measures. Although the specific studies they cite are different than the ones I have reviewed in this section, their conclusions are equally applicable here:

> Psycholinguists cannot ignore insights from offline data since, as we have reviewed above, existing evidence shows that grammatical distinctions typically have immediate impact on online processes. There have also been occasional waves of enthusiasm among theoretical linguists about the prospect of using evidence from real-time phenomena to decide among alternative grammatical theories. …In each case, the debate has been limited by the lack of clear timing predictions from linguistic theories.
>
> (Lewis and Phillips 2015: 41)

I agree with their assessment of the current situation, but also share their optimism that substantial progress can be made by examining "cases of apparent misalignment between online ('fast') and offline ('slow') responses" with a view toward developing "an explicit process model that explains how the offline judgments arise" (Lewis and Phillips 2015: 42).

One major class of misalignments that Lewis and Phillips (2015: 39) identify is that of complete but inaccurate computations, or what Phillips (2013a) calls overgeneration. As I discussed in Chapter 4 with reference to agreement attraction and missing VP illusions, overgeneration involves structures which are produced or accepted under limited circumstances, but which are typically judged as unacceptable in untimed judgment tasks. Phillips (2013a) argues that such cases can be best understood as ungrammatical structures which are produced or temporarily accepted due to noisy memory retrieval mechanisms. As I discussed in Chapter 7, resumptive pronouns in English relative clauses are widely understood to be an example of overgeneration because of the misalignment between acceptability judgments (which are generally low) and elicited production (in which resumptive pronouns readily occur within less accessible contexts such as island-violating structures). However, a few linguists have argued that these pronouns are in fact grammatical in English, but limited to informal registers and specific semantic or pragmatic contexts (Cann et al. 2005; Radford 2019). As I argued in Chapter 7, a better understanding of such misalignments will require not only experimental evidence from timed and untimed tasks, but also evidence from spontaneous language use indicating the conditions under which speakers typically use these purportedly ungrammatical structures. Such evidence is necessary to determine whether the use of these structures might be influenced by other factors besides noisy memory retrieval mechanisms (such as semantic or pragmatic constraints), and to develop experimental tasks that further investigate the factors that are identified in this way.

8.4 Expanding the toolkit further: some thoughts on big data, neurolinguistics, and the future of syntactic theory

Across generative and functionalist approaches, contemporary linguists share a basic understanding of language as both a social and a cognitive phenomenon. Language is inherently social because language users must adopt the language or languages that are common to the communities in which they live, and they must learn how to communicate with others and to convey socially relevant meanings through language. Language is inherently cognitive because language users must store and process linguistic information, whether of spoken, signed, or written modality, using their brains and senses. Through a strong focus on the study of competence as distinct from performance, generative linguists have developed a tradition of studying syntax in a way that abstracts away from various aspects of these social and cognitive dimensions. On the social side, understanding the structural similarities and differences among diverse languages and dialects has been a priority. However, understanding the socially meaningful syntactic choices of language users (for example, my choice to say *I done left* instead of *I already left* as an index of my Appalachian American identity) has mostly been relegated to the field of sociolinguistics. Similarly, on the cognitive side, understanding syntax as a rule-governed system of knowledge that interfaces with other rule-governed systems (phonology, semantics, pragmatics) has been crucial for building theories that can predict whether a particular combination of words will be judged as well-formed. However, understanding the cognitive mechanisms underlying sentence production and comprehension has mostly been relegated to the fields of psycholinguistics and neurolinguistics. While the examples in this book have focused only on the cognitive side, I believe that they help make the more general case for a tighter integration among subfields that traditionally study competence and those that traditionally study performance. I maintain that attention to relevant research on language use and language processing is necessary even for those linguists who espouse a narrow view of competence (i.e. one that does not include detailed information about previously experienced language use) for the simple reason that acceptability judgments and all other sources of linguistic data result from some manner of language use, and as such they are subject to influences from both linguistic knowledge and performance factors. This point has been illustrated extensively in my discussion of relative clause extraposition and PP extraposition in English and German in Chapter 6, and in my discussion of resumptive pronouns in Cantonese, Hebrew, and English relative clauses in Chapter 7. On that note, I will offer here some brief remarks on big data, neurolinguistics, and the future of syntactic theory.

In the current context, I understand 'big data' to consist of large corpora of texts or transcribed speech which have been used as the training input to computational language learning models. Based on probabilistic patterns learned from the input, the models perform a language-related task, such as word prediction, classification, or translation. In Chapter 5, I discussed how recurrent neural network (RNN) models trained on large unannotated corpora of English texts have been used to predict English speakers' acceptability judgments of a variety of different types of grammatical and ungrammatical sentences (Lau et al. 2017; Sprouse et al. 2018). Based on significant correlations between the predictions of their models and English speakers' acceptability judgments, Lau et al. (2017) suggest that human grammatical knowledge may be probabilistic in nature, in a manner analogous to the surface probabilities that RNN models learn from corpus input. Sprouse et al. (2018) ran a similar study and found similar correlations between the predictions of the RNN models and human judgments. However, they also observed that the models were poor predictors of acceptability judgments for certain complex sentence types, suggesting that the patterns learned by the models may be qualitatively different than the grammatical knowledge underlying participants' judgments. Given the more accurate predictions of linguists' grammaticality assignments for the same sentences, they argue that such findings pose a serious challenge for the hypothesis that human grammatical knowledge may be derivable from surface probabilities. However, they acknowledge that traditional syntactic theories also face a serious challenge. Unlike the RNN models, syntactic theories that assume a categorical notion of grammaticality have no way to capture gradience in judgments and must instead attribute such gradience to extra-syntactic factors.

They leave open the question of what a comprehensive theory of gradient judgments should look like. As I have argued in Section 8.2 and in previous chapters, however, there are good reasons to believe that such a theory should in some way incorporate gradience within the grammar.

Because Sprouse et al. (2018) included many types of ungrammatical sentences in their test sets, their analysis of the error patterns (i.e. the items for which the models' predictions deviated from the participants' actual judgments) provided only a few clues about the nature of the models' grammatical generalizations. Machine learning studies that focus on only one type of syntactic pattern have been more informative, however. For example, in a study of long-distance subject–verb agreement in English, Linzen and Leonard (2018) compared the performance of RNN models with that of human participants on analogous verb number prediction tasks. Both the RNN models and the human participants successfully posited agreement with the subject noun in most cases, and with a nonsubject attractor noun in a small percentage of cases. In other words, the responses of both the RNNs and the English speakers deviated slightly from the predictions of syntactic theories. For the human participants, the findings were in line with previous psycholinguistic studies of agreement attraction. One interesting finding was that the RNN model showed a significantly higher error rate (where an error is defined as agreement with a nonsubject attractor noun) when the attractor noun was within a relative clause as compared to a PP. By contrast, human participants made slightly fewer errors for relative clauses than for PPs. Further investigations showed that the model was unable to reliably detect the end of the relative clause (which is not overtly marked in English) and had instead relied on a gradient heuristic that favored short relative clauses. It is important to note that Linzen and Leonard (2018) based their conclusions on the performance of the models and did not attempt to probe the internal representations, which consist of numerical vectors which are opaque to interpretation. However, as Linzen and Baroni (2021) point out, a few different techniques have been developed for interpreting the vectors and linking them to the model's behavior, allowing researchers to begin to access more detailed information about what a model has learned.

The implications of deep learning models for theories of human grammatical knowledge remain controversial. To the extent that such models can predict human performance on judgment tasks, verb prediction tasks, and other types of tasks, they show that grammatical generalizations can be learned from surface probabilities. Lau et al. (2017) and others have taken such findings as tentative support for a usage-based approach to grammatical knowledge. To the extent that the predictions of the models diverge from human performance, they show that the models have learned different generalizations. Such divergences can be taken to imply that human grammatical knowledge must include something like the symbolic representations of generative syntax. (Such a view is also supported to some degree when computational models which incorporate explicit symbolic representations in the input perform in a more human-like manner than those that do not.) Alternatively, such divergences can be taken to imply simply that the usage-based patterns learned by the models are not yet as sophisticated as the usage-based patterns learned by humans (Linzen and Baroni 2021: 14). Either way, the study of computational learning from big data provides a fruitful area for developing hypotheses about human grammatical knowledge as well as language acquisition and processing.

Machine learning models show how linguistic generalizations can be abstracted from probabilistic patterns in corpora. While they offer a rich source of data for developing and testing hypotheses about human languages, they show no direct evidence for how people learn, use, and represent linguistic information. In contrast, neurolinguistics is concerned with identifying the cortical networks in the brain that people actually use during language processing, as well as the timing of neural activation. The field of neurolinguistics first developed from studies of aphasia—language impairment caused by an acquired brain injury. With the advent of noninvasive techniques for detecting neural activation, neurolinguistics now includes a broad range of studies of language processing in individuals with and without cortical injuries. Specific cortical regions involved in language processing are identified using neuroimaging techniques such as fMRI (functional magnetic resonance imaging), which measures changes in blood flow related to neural activation. Timing of neural activation is measured using electrophysiological techniques such as EEG (electroencephalography), which records activation from electrodes placed on the scalp. In general, the hypotheses on which neurolinguistic studies have been based depend crucially on linguistic theories that specify the various linguistic units and the well-formedness conditions on their combination, and on psycholinguistic theories that postulate the cognitive processes involved in language acquisition and processing. In turn, findings from neurolinguistic studies have been used to inform theories of language acquisition and processing and, to a lesser extent, theories of grammatical knowledge. Since the current book examines the implications of gradient responses to acceptability judgment tasks and other experimental tasks for theoretical interpretation, I will focus this brief discussion on three related studies illustrating the implications of fMRI evidence for a particular theoretical construct: syntactic movement.[13]

Much like the behavioral measures I have discussed so far (acceptability judgments, reading times, priming effects), measures of neural activation require somewhat different interpretations within different theoretical approaches, but they are typically compatible with the assumptions of different theories of grammatical knowledge (Sprouse and Lau 2013). In those cases where researchers have argued in favor of a particular theoretical construct on the basis of neurolinguistic evidence, the arguments have generally been subtle, complex, and controversial. As reviewed in Grodzinsky

---

[13] Staying within this very limited scope, I set aside the vast and important literature on aphasia and consider only studies with cognitively healthy participants. I also omit any treatment of the important literature on how ERPs (event-related potentials) as calculated from an EEG signal inform theories of linguistic knowledge and sentence processing with evidence from precise timing of neural activation. I refer readers to Kemmerer (2021) for an overview of the state of the art in the cognitive neuroscience of language, including two chapters covering the various types of aphasia, and comprehensive chapters on the neural bases of sentence comprehension and sentence production.

and Santi (2008), Kemmerer (2021), and Sprouse and Lau (2013: 995–1000), several fMRI studies have found increased activation in Broca's area (Brodmann areas 44 and 45 of the left inferior frontal gyrus) when participants are listening to sentences with a noncanonical word order such as relative clauses, *wh*-questions, topicalization, and scrambling, relative to various control conditions. Based on such findings as well as findings from studies of aphasia, Grodzinsky and colleagues have proposed that the function of Broca's area in sentence comprehension is to support the processing of syntactic movement as postulated in derivational theories. They point out that sentences with a noncanonical word order not only involve syntactic movement (according to derivational theories) but also involve structural complexity and working memory demands (Grodzinsky and Santi 2008: 478). To isolate the effects of syntactic movement from these other factors, the researchers compare movement constructions against comparable non-movement constructions. In one study, Ben-Shachar et al. (2004) conducted two fMRI experiments in which participants listened to different types of grammatical sentences in Hebrew and answered comprehension questions on some of the trials. The first experiment compared two types of argument displacement (topicalization and dative shift), while the second experiment compared two types of embedded questions (*wh*-questions and yes–no questions). Results showed a consistent pattern of increased activation in Broca's area and two other regions across both experiments, but only for the two constructions involving syntactic movement (topicalization and *wh*-questions).[14,15]

While the data are consistent with a movement account, other plausible analyses are available. First, it is not clear whether the movement and non-movement constructions were sufficiently similar in terms of working memory demands to rule out the possible influence of this factor. By all accounts, yes–no questions involve no filler–gap dependency and should be less taxing on working memory resources for this reason. Similarly, dative shift involves a short displacement within the verb phrase (where displacement means fronting from the canonical position), while topicalization involves a longer displacement to a position before the subject. Second, the movement and non-movement constructions that are being compared differ in their semantic and discourse functions. For example, topicalized objects and *wh*-phrases in Hebrew serve prominent discourse functions (topic and focus, respectively), in contrast to the interrogative complementizer '*im* 'if' in yes–no questions and non-topicalized objects in dative sentences. Finally, filler–gap dependencies are given a similar syntactic analysis across different constructions (topicalization, *wh*-questions, relative clauses) in

---

[14] The anatomical boundaries of Broca's area are controversial (Tremblay and Dick 2016), but the term most commonly refers to the left inferior frontal gyrus (Brodmann areas 44 and 45), as is the case for Ben-Shachar et al. (2004). The other two regions Ben-Shachar et al. (2004) identified as being associated with syntactic movement were left ventral precentral sulcus (Brodmann areas 6 and 9) and bilateral posterior superior temporal sulcus (Brodmann areas 39, 22, and 37).

[15] Ben-Shachar et al. (2004) distinguish between A-bar movement of the type found in filler–gap constructions (e.g. relative clauses, *wh*-questions, topicalization), and A-movement of the type found in verb-argument constructions (e.g. passive, raising). They claim that these findings apply specifically to A-bar movement, since according to some syntactic analyses, dative shift involves A-movement.

constraint-based theories that do not invoke syntactic movement (Culicover and Jack-endoff 2005; Pollard and Sag 1994), meaning that a similar syntax-specific explanation could be given without reference to movement.

Extending this line of research, Santi and Grodzinsky (2007) manipulated both syntactic structure (movement vs. non-movement) and dependency distance (short, medium, long) in an fMRI study of reflexive binding and object relative clauses in English. In the task, participants listened to English sentences and then judged them in a binary acceptability judgment task. Although the stimuli included ungrammatical sentences, only the responses to the grammatical sentences were analyzed. Example stimulus sentences for the longest dependency distance are given in (14a–b) (Santi and Grodzinsky 2007: 10).

(14) a. Anne assumes that the **mailman** who loves the sister of Kim pinched **himself**.
　　　b. Kate loves the **woman** who the mailman and the mother of Kim pinched __.

Reflexive pronouns such as *himself* in (14a) are bound to an antecedent via an anaphoric dependency, while relative clauses as in (14b) involve a filler–gap dependency. In derivational theories, filler–gap dependencies require syntactic movement while anaphoric dependencies do not. By manipulating the dependency distance in the same way for both sentence types, the authors were able to test for independent effects of syntactic movement and working memory demands. Results showed that for object relative clauses, activation in Broca's area increased with increased linear distance, whereas there was no such distance effect for reflexive binding. However, there was increased activation for reflexive binding in a different brain region (right middle frontal gyrus, Brodmann area 10). The authors interpret this finding to mean that working memory demands affect activation in Broca's area, but only for structures involving syntactic movement. At the end of the paper, however, they hint at a different factor that might have affected their results. In a filler–gap dependency, participants actively search for a gap after encountering the filler phrase, whereas in a reflexive binding dependency, the reflexive pronoun cannot be predicted in advance (Santi and Grodzinsky 2007: 16).

Following up on the idea that the role of Broca's area in sentence comprehension might be related to predictive processing, Matchin et al. (2014) conducted a similar fMRI study that compared *wh*-questions and backward anaphora sentences in English, each with short and long dependency distances. Examples of the long dependency conditions are given in (15a–b).

(15) a. **Which song** did the band that won the contest play __ at the concert?
　　　b. Because **he** extinguished the flames that burned all night, **the fireman** saved the resident.

This study again contrasts a filler–gap (movement-based) dependency with an anaphoric dependency, but differs from Santi and Grodzinsky's (2007) study in that backwards anaphora (unlike reflexive binding) involves predictive processing. That is, in the absence of any antecedent preceding the pronoun, an antecedent is predicted to occur following the pronoun. Results of a listening task in fact showed increased activation in Broca's area with increased dependency distance for both sentence types, suggesting that predictive processing rather than syntactic movement is the most relevant factor. Following the alternative theoretical approach of Novick et al. (2005), they interpret these results as possibly supporting a general role for Broca's area in cognitive control: "demands on cognitive control may increase while holding the filler or anaphor in memory and processing additional syntactic/semantic content from the ongoing sentence during the longer conditions" (Matchin, Sprouse, and Hickok 2014: 10).

As Matchin and Hickok (2020) discuss in their recent review, the role of Broca's area in sentence comprehension remains a highly controversial topic with a large literature involving several competing theoretical approaches. My modest aim here has been to provide a brief illustrative example of how evidence from fMRI can be given different theoretical interpretations with respect to the role of syntactic representation. While the measurements involved with fMRI and other brain mapping techniques are considerably more complex than simple Likert-scale ratings or response times, the problems for theoretical interpretation turn out to be quite familiar.

For many linguists, machine learning techniques and brain mapping techniques are unfamiliar and apparently of limited relevance to theories of grammatical knowledge. However, I believe both types of techniques will play an important role in the future of syntactic theory as we move toward a more integrated approach to cognitive science. Machine learning studies help us understand what people *might* be learning when they learn a language. Importantly, they allow researchers to manipulate the input in specific ways to test how input characteristics (e.g. different frequency distributions, presence/absence of explicit grammatical coding, or overall amount of input) affect the grammatical generalizations that are learned. Thus, they are a powerful tool for hypothesis testing, especially when used to predict the results of psycholinguistic studies, including acceptability judgment tasks. Neurolinguistic studies help us understand the cognitive mechanisms underlying sentence comprehension and production. Along with traditional behavioral techniques, neuroimaging and electrophysiological techniques allow us to better define the role of grammatical representations and their well-formedness conditions in online processing. More pertinent to the current discussion, they also provide an important source of information about the nature of those representations.

Insofar as psycholinguistic, neurolinguistic, and computational methods will play a role in the future of syntactic theory, their utility will be limited if the languages and cultures studied are also limited. Polinsky (to appear) observes that a number of experimental studies of syntax and syntactic processing have been published examining constituent order (Koizumi et al. 2014; Yasunaga et al. 2015) and relative clauses (Clemens et al. 2015) in Mayan languages as well as questions, relative clauses, and agreement phenomena in the Austronesian language Chamorro (Wagers et al. 2015; 2018), and that additional experimental studies of these languages are ongoing.

I would also point to exemplary experimental studies of constituent order in Malay-alam (Namboodiripad 2017) and relative clause processing in Ojibwe (Hammerly 2020), both of which represent the foundational work for ongoing research programs on these languages.[16] However, to date, the vast majority of studies in experimental syntax and syntactic processing have been conducted on well-described languages. Polinsky (to appear) attributes this state of affairs to the fact that experimental stud-ies tend to rely on existing linguistic descriptions and theoretical analyses. Indeed, the illustrative examples I have chosen for this book are primarily from experimental studies of English and a few other well-studied languages. This choice reflects my main goals of comparing different theoretical interpretations of acceptability judgments with respect to the same syntactic phenomenon and showing how different methods can be used to arrive at a theoretical interpretation of a particular phenomenon. How-ever, in the interest of increasing the empirical coverage of syntactic theory with an expanded methodological toolkit and from an interdisciplinary perspective, it will be important to apply experimental and computational techniques to a broader set of diverse languages, expanding upon the foundational work that is already being done.

As Norcliffe et al. (2015) observe in their introduction to a special journal issue de-voted to cross-linguistic psycholinguistics, experimental research on adult language processing has expanded to a wider range of languages, including indigenous lan-guages and sign languages, since the 1980s, but still lacks the diversity that would be most desirable for advancing the field.[17] Kemmerer (2019) further notes that neurolinguistic studies have been far less linguistically diverse than linguistic and psycholinguistic studies. These authors make the case that data from a broader set of languages is crucial for progress in their respective fields, psycholinguistics and cognitive neuroscience. For example, Norcliffe et al. (2015) point to psycholinguistic studies of Basque (Carreiras et al. 2010), Avar (Polinsky et al. 2012), and Q'anjob'al and Ch'ol (Clemens et al. 2015) showing that languages with ergative–absolutive alignment systems provide distinct morphological and syntactic cues for parsing and have impor-tant implications for theories of relative clause processing.[18] Likewise, I would argue that a comprehensive theory to accommodate gradient acceptability judgments will depend on data from typologically diverse languages. Namboodiripad (2017) takes a significant step in this direction by developing acceptability judgment tasks which are amenable to many fieldwork contexts and which measure gradient differences in word order flexibility in active transitive clauses within and across languages, using

---

[16] Chamorro is an Austronesian language spoken in Guam and in the US Commonwealth of the North-ern Mariana Islands. Malayalam is a Dravidian language spoken in the state of Kerala in India. Ojibwe is an Algonquian language spoken in parts of what is now Minnesota and Ontario.

[17] Anand et al. (2011) analyzed 4,000 psycholinguistics abstracts from leading conferences and journals, find-ing that 85% covered 10 languages, while 57 languages were studied in total. Similarly, out of 550 corpora from the Linguistics Data Consortium, they found that 22 languages were represented, with 85% of the corpora representing English, Chinese, Arabic, Spanish, and Japanese.

[18] Basque is a language isolate spoken in the Basque Country of Northern Spain and Southwestern France. Avar is a Northeastern Caucasian language spoken in Dagestan, Azerbaijan, Kazakhstan, and Turkey (Polinsky et al. 2012). Q'anjob'al and Ch'ol are Mayan languages. Q'anjob'al is spoken in Huehuetenango, Guatemala, while Ch'ol in spoken in Chiapas, Mexico (Clemens et al. 2015).

English and Malayalam as test cases. This work is important in showing that differences in acceptability between canonical and noncanonical word orders are a matter of degree, and not fully predictable from the hypothesized status of the noncanonical orders as either grammatical or ungrammatical. For example, although all possible permutations of subject, verb, and object are grammatical in Malayalam (in contrast to English), older Malayalam speakers showed greater flexibility (i.e. a smaller penalty in acceptability for noncanonical orders) as compared with younger speakers, suggesting a possible grammatical change in progress related to greater contact with English among the younger speakers. Such findings arguably support a role for soft constraints in the grammatical systems of the younger speakers.

Polinsky (to appear) and Anand et al. (2011) lay out some important ethical considerations and practical challenges for this endeavor, to ensure that researchers work with language communities in a collaborative manner, including community members on the research team when possible. They also point to the importance of determining whether experimental techniques are appropriate in a given context, and if so, ensuring that such techniques are adapted to each community in a culturally relevant way. As one notable example, Sedarous and Namboodiripad (2020) provide practical advice for adapting experimental tasks to a much wider range of languages and cultures through the use of audio stimuli. Norcliffe et al. (2015) observe that significant time, money, preparation, and multidisciplinary training that includes the languages and cultures of interest will be required to diversify experimental research. These challenges are very substantial. However, I am optimistic that as more linguists are trained in some combination of fieldwork, theoretical linguistics, corpus and computational methods, and experimental methods, and as more linguists (even those with minimal training in experimental methods) join collaborative interdisciplinary teams that draw on the complementary expertise of different members, a tighter integration between theories of language acquisition and processing and theories of grammatical knowledge based on data from a more diverse set of languages will become possible.

8.5 Conclusions

In this book, I have shown that the design and interpretation of acceptability judgment tasks requires close attention to the various syntactic, semantic, pragmatic, prosodic, and processing-based factors that can affect them, and I have reviewed the major strategies that have been proposed in experimental syntax research for teasing these factors apart. In addition, I have shown that theoretical assumptions about form–meaning isomorphism and gradient grammaticality are important for the theoretical interpretation of quantitative data from acceptability judgments and other experimental tasks. Thus, it is crucial to be aware of these assumptions as we design our experiments and interpret the results. I have argued that regardless of one's theoretical framework, a multimethodological approach that includes a combination of corpus data, judgment tasks, and other types of behavioral experiments can help narrow down the range of plausible explanations. Finally, I have shown that compelling evidence is available in support of gradience within the grammar, and I have argued that such evidence should somehow be accounted for within any linguistic theory. In the service of developing linguistic theories that can more fully account for gradience in acceptability judgments, and which can be better integrated with theories of language acquisition and processing, I believe that drawing on a broad range of data from different methods and languages, keeping informed of developments outside one's own specialization, and maintaining an openness to collaboration with colleagues in neighboring fields or subfields is the best way forward.

Glossary

A-bar movement Leftward syntactic movement targeting a position higher than the clausal subject position, such as Spec CP.

Acceptability judgments Judgments by language users as to the perceived naturalness of a linguistic expression, often given in the form of numerical ratings in the context of an experiment or a structured interview.

Accessibility Relative ease with which specific linguistic information can be accessed during online language production or comprehension.

Additive effect Cumulative effect of two independent variables on a response variable such that each variable shows an independent main effect and no statistical interaction is observed.

Agentivity Degree to which the referent of a nominal argument is perceived as intentionally causing an action.

Aggregation effect Effect of averaging over multiple participants which can potentially obscure the systematic effects of individual differences among participants.

Agreement attraction Phenomenon in which speakers produce or accept sentences with subject–verb agreement errors due to the presence of a distracting nonsubject noun, as in: *The key to the cabinets are on the table.*

Amelioration effect Improvement in acceptability ratings resulting from some experimental manipulation, such as changing the lexical items used or the context in which the target sentence occurs.

A-movement Leftward syntactic movement targeting a subject or complement position, such as Spec TP.

Anaphoric dependency Relationship between a pronoun and its antecedent within the same sentence.

Aphasia Language deficits resulting from an acquired brain injury.

Atelic Event depicted as having no definite endpoint (e.g. *They are listening to music*).

Backgroundedness Degree to which a proposition is presupposed to be true.

Barrier Phrasal category occurring within a filler–gap dependency which renders syntactic movement ungrammatical.

Binary judgment task Acceptability judgment task in which participants rate sentences on a scale with only two options, such as 'acceptable' or 'unacceptable'.

Binding Relationship between two constituents within a sentence such that one determines the reference of the other. For example, *Kim* binds *herself* in the sentence *Kim helped herself*.

Broca's area Brain region in the left hemisphere associated with aspects of speech and language processing (left inferior frontal gyrus, Brodmann areas 44 and 45).

C-command Relationship between two nodes in a syntactic tree. A c-commands B when either B is a sister to A (i.e. B and A are directly dominated by the same node) or B is dominated by the node that is the sister to A.

Ceiling effect Pattern of responses in an experimental task which are consistently at the high end of the response scale.

Ceiling mismatch Equally high acceptability ratings given to two syntactic structures which differ in frequency of occurrence.

Complex NP Constraint Restriction on long-distance dependencies (a type of island constraint) which prevents movement out of the clausal complement of a noun, as in *Who did she make the claim that she knows __?

Comp-trace violation Restriction on long-distance dependences which prevents the occurrence of an embedded subject gap following an overt complementizer, as in: *What did you think that __ would happen?

Conservatism via entrenchment Phenomenon in which speakers are less accepting of the novel use of a verb in a particular construction to the extent that the verb is frequently encountered in other constructions.

Constraint 1. Restriction of some kind (syntactic, semantic, processing-based, prosodic, etc.) that limits how language is used or what constitutes a well-formed linguistic expression; 2. In constraint-based grammars, a prefabricated piece of grammatical structure which licenses utterances which instantiate that structure.

Constraint-based grammar Family of grammatical theories which claim that grammatical sentences are positively licensed by a set of pre-specified pieces of structure (constraints) specific to each language. Such structures are learned in the way that words are learned.

Construction Learned pairing of form and meaning such as a word, phrasal idiom (e.g. *spill the beans*), or abstract grammatical pattern (e.g. active transitive clause).

Coordinate Structure Constraint Restriction on long-distance dependencies (a type of island constraint) which prevents movement out of only one conjunct of a coordinate structure, as in: *Which movie did you read a book and watch __?

Correlation Common expression to refer to the Pearson correlation coefficient (r), which measures the strength and direction of the linear relationship between two variables.

Coverb Grammaticalized verb which co-occurs with one or more other verbs within a serial verb construction.

Cross-modal lexical priming task Experimental task in which participants make a lexical decision (word or nonword) about a sequence of letters on the screen while listening to a spoken sentence. Priming effects (faster decisions) may occur when the letter sequence expresses a real word that is related to a word in the spoken sentence.

Deep learning models Computational models that mimic human learning using an artificial neural network. Such models consist of multiple layers of nodes (neurons) whose connections (weights) are gradually adjusted through error-based learning from examples observed in a set of training data (e.g. a text corpus).

Dependence Constraint on Input–Output Correspondence (DEP-IO) In Optimality Theory, a constraint which states that elements in the output should correspond in a one-to-one manner with elements in the input.

Dependency Locality Theory Theory of resource allocation in sentence processing which predicts that the cost of integrating a word with a syntactically related constituent earlier in sentence is modulated by the number of intervening discourse referents.

Derivation Step-by-step sequential process for combining syntactic constituents together to form a sentence.

Derivational grammar Family of grammatical theories which posit a step-by-step derivation as the process by which sentences are formed.

Discourse-given information Information which has been mentioned in the preceding context or is otherwise already known.

Distributed neural network model Computational learning model consisting of nodes (neurons) whose connections (weights) are gradually adjusted through error-based learning from examples observed in a set of training data (e.g. a text corpus).

D-linking Weakening or neutralization of certain restrictions on syntactic movement in interrogative sentences resulting from the use of a D-linked question phrase—a question phrase such as *which car* that presupposes the existence of a set of entities in the discourse.

Electroencephalography (EEG) Electrophysiological technique which records neural activation from electrodes placed on the scalp.

Empty Category Principle (ECP) In Government and Binding Theory, the requirement that a movement trace must be properly governed by a lexical head (for an object trace) or by a coindexed antecedent (for a subject or adjunct trace).

EVAL In Optimality Theory, the process of evaluating a set of candidate forms according to a set of ranked or weighted constraints.

Event-related potentials (ERP) Electrical activity in the brain as measured from an EEG signal at a particular point in time in relation to the presentation of a stimulus. ERPs relevant for sentence processing include the N400, P600, and ELAN (early left anterior negativity).

Exemplar cluster Grouping of stored instances of a category perceived to instantiate the same linguistic expression.

Experiment trial Within a psychological experiment, a single stimulus presentation and the associated response.

Extended picture–word interference task Language production task in which participants must describe a picture after viewing a distractor verb that is either semantically related or unrelated to the target verb for describing the picture. Related distractors are expected to interfere with production planning, resulting in longer response latencies or longer duration in producing the first part of the sentence.

Extended Projection Principle (EPP) Requirement for an overt subject in a finite clause.

Extraposition from NP Rightward displacement of the modifier or complement of a noun to a position outside the NP.

Eye-tracking Experimental technique which measures eye movements during the presentation of visual stimuli.

Factorial design Experimental design which includes a condition for each combination of factors and levels. For example, a 3×3 factorial design has two factors (e.g. verb and structure) with three levels each (e.g. three verbs and three structures), for a total of nine conditions.

Filled-gap paradigm Self-paced reading task with sentence materials designed to induce a kind of syntactic reanalysis. At a position where a gap might be expected, the reader encounters a pronoun or NP instead and must then assign a different interpretation to the sentence.

Filler–gap dependency Structural relationship between a fronted element (e.g. interrogative word, relative pronoun, or topicalized object) and a coindexed gap (missing element) occurring later in the sentence.

Filler phrase Word or phrase (e.g. interrogative word, relative pronoun, or topicalized object) that signals the beginning of a long-distance dependency and on which the interpretation of the following gap depends (e.g. *who* in *Who did you see __?*).

Filler sentences Stimulus sentences that are used in a psycholinguistic experiment primarily to distract participants from the experimental manipulation.

Floor effect Pattern of responses in an experimental task which are consistently at the low end of the response scale.

Floor mismatch Differences in acceptability ratings between two syntactic structures, both of which fail to occur or very rarely occur in a corpus.

Form–meaning isomorphism Requirement for a consistent mapping between syntactic structures (e.g. structural positions) and meaningful elements (e.g. semantic roles).

Free relative clause Type of relative clause which includes a filler and a gap, but no overt head noun. For example, *whatever he told you* in the sentence: *Whatever he told you was wrong.*

Frozen Structure Constraint Restriction on syntactic movement out of a rightward extraposed PP or relative clause.

F-structure In Lexical-Functional Grammar, the level of structure at which grammatical relations such as subject, direct object, and oblique object, and morphosyntactic categories such as nominative case and past tense are specified.

Functional magnetic resonance imaging (fMRI) Neuroimaging technique which measures changes in blood flow related to neural activation.

Gap (site) Tail end of a long-distance dependency where the filler phrase is interpreted (e.g. position following the verb *say* in the question: *What did you say __ ?*).

GEN In Optimality Theory Syntax, a generative process which takes as its input an abstract representation of the meaning and lexical content of an expression and generates a set of candidate forms for its syntactic realization.

Grammatical illusion Type of ungrammatical sentence which is often perceived to be acceptable due to inaccurate or incomplete comprehension.

Grammaticalization Gradual process of language change whereby lexical items (e.g. nouns, verbs, adjectives) become grammatical function words (e.g. classifiers, auxiliaries, prepositions) or grammatical morphemes.

High/low attachment Interpretation of a word or phrase as modifying a preceding head word that occurs either higher or lower in the structure.

Island constraints Restrictions on syntactic movement out of certain structural configurations known as 'islands' following Ross (1967).

Left Branch Constraint Restriction on long-distance dependencies (a type of island constraint) which prevents movement out of the left branch of a noun phrase, as in: *How many did you read __ books?*

Long-distance dependency Type of syntactic dependency that can extend across one or more clausal boundaries; typically in reference to a filler–gap dependency.

Magnitude estimation task As applied to acceptability judgment tasks, a task in which participants assign an acceptability score to each sentence in relation to a fixed reference sentence with a preassigned score. In psychophysics, a perceptual task in which participants assign a score to the perceived magnitude of a stimulus (e.g. perceived loudness of a sound) in relation to a fixed reference stimulus.

Merge In Minimalist syntax, a structure-building procedure which combines two constituents together to form a larger phrase, applying in a step-by-step manner until the entire sentence is formed.

Minimal Distance Principle (MDP) Requirement that the non-overt subject of an infinitive clause must be interpreted as co-referential with the closest c-commanding antecedent.

Missing VP illusion Grammatical illusion in which participants often fail to detect the missing verb phrase in an ungrammatical sentence with multiple embeddings.

Mixed-effects regression model Statistical regression model that includes random effects in addition to fixed effects. In experimental language research, random effects are useful for capturing systematic variation due to properties of individual participants and stimulus items.

Move In Minimalist syntax, a displacement operation which copies a constituent that occurs lower in the structure and merges it into a position higher in the structure, leaving behind an unpronounced copy or trace in the original position.

N-back task Task for measuring individual working memory capacity in which participants are presented with a sequence of stimuli (e.g. letters) and must indicate whether the current stimulus matches the one that was presented n trials earlier in the sequence. The difficulty of the task increases as the value of n is increased.

Negative Polarity Item (NPI) Word or phrase which occurs most readily in negative, interrogative, or conditional contexts, or in the presence of certain quantifiers (e.g. *anything* and *at all* in the sentence: *They don't want anything at all*).

N-gram model Simple computational language model which calculates the probability of a word based on the previous (n − 1) words in the sentence, based on the observed frequency of the word sequence in a training corpus.

NP Accessibility Hierarchy Implicational hierarchy describing which grammatical roles can be relativized across languages. If a language can relativize a role that occurs lower on the hierarchy (e.g. oblique object), it can also relativize the roles that occur higher on the hierarchy (e.g. subject, direct object, indirect object).

Optimality Theory (OT) Theoretical approach to phonology, morphology, and syntax which centers the idea of competition among ranked or weighted constraints which apply to a set of candidate forms to select an optimal output form.

Outbound anaphora Phenomenon in which an independent pronoun takes a word-internal element as its antecedent (e.g. the pronoun *its* takes part of a compound word as its antecedent in the sentence: *Coffee drinkers tend to enjoy its taste*).

Overgeneration Cases in which apparently ungrammatical representations are produced or accepted under limited circumstances. A typical example is agreement attraction, in which speakers may produce or accept verb forms that agree with a nonsubject.

Preposition Phrase Extraposition (PPE) Rightward displacement of the PP modifier or complement of a noun to a position outside the NP (e.g. *Three reasons were given for the decision*).

Preposition stranding constraint Syntactic restriction which prevents leftward movement of the object of a preposition by itself, leaving the preposition behind (stranded).

Projection Principle In Government and Binding Theory, the requirement that representations at all levels of structure (D-Structure, S-Structure, and Logical Form) adhere to the subcategorization properties of lexical items.

Reading span task Task for measuring individual working memory capacity in which participants must read a list of unrelated sentences and then recall the last word of each sentence in the correct order. Difficulty is increased by increasing the number of sentences.

Recurrent Neural Network (RNN) model Deep learning model commonly used for simulating language learning because of its ability to keep track of previously observed word sequences, allowing it to detect linguistic dependencies across a distance.

Relative Clause Extraposition (RCE) Rightward displacement of the relative clause modifier of a noun to a position outside the NP (e.g. *Three experiments were conducted which confirmed our predictions*).

Relative clause island Restriction on long-distance dependencies (a type of island constraint) which prevents movement out of the relative clause modifier of a noun, as in: *What did you see the guy who found __?*

Relativized Minimality Syntactic locality condition which prevents syntactic dependencies from occurring across an intervening element which shares the same structural type as the first element of the dependency. This condition is commonly used to explain the degraded acceptability of *wh*-islands.

Repeated exposure effect Effect of repetition of the same or similar stimuli during an experiment session, resulting in faster response times, higher acceptability ratings, or some other type of facilitation.

Resumptive pronoun Pronoun occurring at the tail of a long-distance dependency in the position where a gap would otherwise go (e.g. the pronoun *his* in: *the guy that I can never remember his name*).

Satiation In an acceptability judgment task, an increase in acceptability ratings resulting from presentations of multiple sentences with the same structure but distinct lexical content. Satiation is a specific type of repeated exposure effect.

Scalable line-drawing task Acceptability judgment task in which participants draw a line to indicate how much better or worse a sentence is perceived to be in relation to a reference sentence with a fixed line length. This task is a variant of the magnitude estimation task which uses lines instead of numerical scores.

Scalar judgment task Acceptability judgment task in which the dependent measure is a rating on an ordinal scale.

Scale effect Tendency for participants to use the entire rating scale when such a scale is provided, rather than providing responses mostly at either end of the scale.

Self-organized sentence processing model (SOSP) Dynamic computational model for syntactic parsing which builds syntactic structures in an incremental manner by forming bonds between partial trees that are projected from each word and adjusting the bonds as each new word is added.

Self-paced reading task Sentence comprehension task in which participants read sentences one word (or multi-word chunk) at a time at their own pace by pressing a button to view each new word. Slower times between button presses are assumed to indicate processing difficulty in that region.

Sentential Subject Constraint Restriction on long-distance dependencies (a type of island constraint) which prevents movement out of a clausal subject, as in: *Who is that she has met __ likely?*

Serial recall task Memory task in which participants are presented with a sequence of stimulus items (e.g. words) and must then recall all of the items in the same order.

Soft constraint Conventionalized preference for a particular structural configuration or form–meaning mapping which is manifested as a statistical tendency rather than a strict grammatical requirement (e.g. the tendency for transitive verbs to occur in a position directly adjacent to their direct objects in English).

Split intransitivity Cross-linguistic tendency for two general classes of intransitive predicates, commonly known as unaccusative and unergative predicates, to show distinct syntactic distributions.

Statistical preemption Degraded acceptability of a lexical item used in a new construction due to the fact that it has been frequently observed in a different (preempting) construction to express the same meaning and function.

Structural priming task Language production task in which participants first read a prime sentence and then verbally describe a picture depicting a different scenario. Pictures are constructed to depict scenes that can be readily described using two alternative structures for the same message, for example active or passive. Priming effects are observed to the extent that the prime sentence prompts participants to use a particular structure.

Subjacency condition Syntactic locality constraint on long movement across more than one bounding node, resulting in the requirement for shorter cyclic movements. This condition is used as a general explanation for various types of island effects.

Subject island Restriction on long-distance dependencies (a type of island constraint) which prevents movement out of the subject, as in: *Who does the brother of __ look like Tom?*

Superadditive effect Type of statistical interaction in which the cumulative effect of two independent variables on a response variable is greater than would be expected based on the effect of each factor in isolation.

Superiority constraint Restriction on syntactic movement in interrogative clauses with more than one *wh*-phrase which says that only the phrase in the highest (most superior) position in the structure can move. This constraint rules out sentences such as: *What did who say __ ?*

Telic Event depicted as having a definite endpoint (e.g. *They ate all the cookies*).

Transitive subject control (TSC) Co-reference relation in which the subject of a transitive clause (rather than the direct object) controls the interpretation of the non-overt subject of an infinitive complement clause. For example, Jake is understood as the dish washer in *Jake promised Sarah to do the dishes.*

T-to-C movement In Minimalist syntax, an analysis of subject–auxiliary inversion involving head-to-head movement of the finite verb or auxiliary from T (Tense or INFL) to C (complementizer) positions.

Unaccusative Class of intransitive predicates which tend to express telic events and which select a patient-like argument (e.g. *arrive, fall, appear*).

Unergative Class of intransitive predicates which tend to express atelic events and which select an agent-like argument (e.g. *talk, dance, laugh*).

Unification In constraint-based theories, a structure building procedure which combines pieces of prefabricated structure together in a non-procedural (simultaneous) fashion and checks those pieces for compatibility.

Usage-based theories Approaches to linguistic analysis which view grammar as a dynamic system of knowledge which includes detailed information about previous language use.

Visual probe recognition task Experimental task in which participants must decide whether a probe word had appeared in a sentence they just read which is no longer visible. Faster response times are expected to the extent that the probe word is accessible, in trials where the probe word matches a word in the sentence.

Visual world paradigm Experimental paradigm in which participants speak or listen to spoken language while looking at pictures or objects. Eye movements to the pictures or objects are measured with an eye-tracker while the participant performs the linguistic task, providing information about the time course of comprehension or production planning.

Wh-island Restriction on long-distance dependencies (a type of island constraint) which prevents movement out of an embedded question, as in: *What did she wonder whether they said __ ?

Working memory capacity Limit on the amount of information that can be temporarily held in memory for use in performing a cognitive task. This limit differs across individuals and can be measured using various memory tasks such as the n-back and reading span tasks.

References

Aarts, Bas. 2007. *Syntactic Gradience: The Nature of Grammatical Indeterminacy*. Oxford: Oxford University Press.

Abrusán, Márta. 2011. "Presuppositional and Negative Islands: A Semantic Account." *Natural Language Semantics* 19 (3): 257–321.

Ackerman, Lauren, Michael Frazier, and Masaya Yoshida. 2018. "Resumptive Pronouns Can Ameliorate Illicit Island Extractions." *Linguistic Inquiry* 49 (4): 847–59.

Adger, David. 2003. *Core Syntax: A Minimalist Approach*. Oxford: Oxford University Press.

Adger, David. 2017. "The Limitations of Structural Priming Are Not the Limits of Linguistic Theory." *Behavioral and Brain Sciences* 40: 18–19.

Aissen, Judith. 2003. "Differential Object Marking: Iconicity vs. Economy." *Natural Language & Linguistic Theory* 21: 435–83.

Akmajian, Adrian. 1975. "More Evidence for an NP Cycle." *Linguistic Inquiry* 6 (1): 115–29.

Alexopoulou, Theodora. 2010. "Truly Intrusive: Resumptive Pronominals in Questions and Relative Clauses." *Lingua* 120 (3): 485–505.

Alexopoulou, Theodora, and Frank Keller. 2007. "Locality, Cyclicity, and Resumption: At the Interface between the Grammar and the Human Sentence Processor." *Language* 83 (1): 110–60.

Ambridge, Ben. 2013. "How Do Children Restrict Their Linguistic Generalizations? An (Un-) Grammaticality Judgment Study." *Cognitive Science* 37 (3): 508–43.

Ambridge, Ben, and Adele E. Goldberg. 2008. "The Island Status of Clausal Complements: Evidence in Favor of an Information Structure Explanation." *Cognitive Linguistics* 19 (3): 357–89.

Anand, Pranav, Sandra Chung, and Matthew Wagers. 2011. "Widening the Net: Challenges for Gathering Linguistic Data in the Digital Age." Response to NSF SBE 2020: Future Research in the Social, Behavioral & Economic Sciences. https://people.ucsc.edu/~schung/anandchungwagers.pdf.

Aoun, Joseph, Lina Choueiri, and Norbert Hornstein. 2001. "Resumption, Movement, and Derivational Economy." *Linguistic Inquiry* 32 (3): 371–403.

Ariel, Mira. 1999. "Cognitive Universals and Linguistic Conventions: The Case of Resumptive Pronouns." *Studies in Language* 23 (2): 217–69.

Arnold, Doug, and Evita Lindardaki. 2007. "HPSG-DOP: Towards Exemplar-Based HPSG." In *Proceedings of the 12th ESSLLI Workshop on Exemplar-Based Models of Language Acquisition and Use*. Dublin: The Association for Logic, Language, and Information.

Arnold, Jennifer E., Anthony Losongco, Thomas Wasow, and Ryan Ginstrom. 2000. "Heaviness vs. Newness: The Effects of Structural Complexity and Discourse Status on Constituent Ordering." *Language* 76 (1): 28–55.

Arnon, Inbal, Neal Snider, Philip Hofmeister, T. Florian Jaeger, and Ivan A. Sag. 2006. "Cross-Linguistic Variation in a Processing Account: The Case of Multiple Wh-Questions." In *Annual Meeting of the Berkeley Linguistics Society*, 32: 23–35. Berkeley: Berkeley Linguistics Society.

Asudeh, Ash. 2011. "Local Grammaticality in Syntactic Production." In *Language from a Cognitive Perspective: grammar, Usage and Processing*, edited by Emily M. Bender and Jennifer E. Arnold, 51–79. Stanford, CA: CSLI Publications.

Asudeh, Ash. 2012. *The Logic of Pronominal Resumption*. Oxford: Oxford University Press.

Bader, Markus. 2016. "Complex Center Embedding in German—The Effect of Sentence Position." In *Quantitative Approaches to Grammar and Grammatical Change*, edited by Sam Featherston and Yannick Versley, 9–32. Berlin: de Gruyter.

Bader, Markus, Josef Bayer, and Jana Häussler. 2003. "Explorations of Center Embedding and Missing VPs." Poster presented at the 16th CUNY Conference on Sentence Processing, Cambridge, MA.

Bader, Markus, and Jana Häussler. 2010. "Toward a Model of Grammaticality Judgments." *Journal of Linguistics* 46 (2): 273–330.

Baker, Mark. 1997. "Thematic Roles and Syntactic Structure." In *Elements of Grammar: handbook in Generative Syntax*, edited by Liliane Haegeman, 73–137. Dordrecht: Springer.

Baltin, Mark R. 1981. "Strict Bounding." In *The Logical Problem of Language Acquisition*, edited by C. L. Baker and John J. McCarthy, 257–95. Cambridge, MA: MIT Press.

Baltin, Mark R. 1982. "A Landing Site Theory of Movement Rules." *Linguistic Inquiry* 13 (1): 1–38.

Baltin, Mark R. 2006. "Extraposition." In *The Blackwell Companion to Syntax Volume I*, edited by Martin Everaert and Henk van Riemsdijk, 237–71. Malden, MA: Blackwell.

Barak, Libby, and Adele E. Goldberg. 2017. "Modeling the Partial Productivity of Constructions." In *Proceedings of the American Association of Artificial Intelligence (AAAI) Symposium on Computational Construction Grammar and Natural Language Understanding*, 131–8. Stanford, CA: AI Access Foundation.

Bates, Elizabeth, and Brian MacWhinney. 1989. "Functionalism and the Competition Model." In *The Crosslinguistic Study of Sentence Processing*, edited by Brian MacWhinney and Elizabeth Bates, 3–76. Cambridge, UK: Cambridge University Press.

Beltrama, Andrea, and Ming Xiang. 2016. "Unacceptable but Comprehensible: The Facilitation Effect of Resumptive Pronouns." *Glossa: A Journal of General Linguistics* 1 (1): 1–24.

Ben-Shachar, Michal, Dafna Palti, and Yosef Grodzinsky. 2004. "Neural Correlates of Syntactic Movement: Converging Evidence from Two FMRI Experiments." *NeuroImage* 21 (4): 1320–36.

Bentley, Delia, and Thórhallur Eythórsson. 2004. "Auxiliary Selection and the Semantics of Unaccusativity." *Lingua* 114 (4): 447–71.

Bever, Thomas G, and Montserrat Sanz. 1997. "Empty Categories Access Their Antecedents during Comprehension: Unaccusatives in Spanish." *Linguistic Inquiry* 28 (1): 69–91.

Birner, Betty J., and Gregory L. Ward. 1998. *Information Status and Noncanonical Word Order in English*. Amsterdam: John Benjamins.

Bloomfield, Leonard. 1933. *Language*. New York: Holt, Rinehart and Winston.

Boas, Hans Christian. 2003. *A Constructional Approach to Resultatives*. Stanford, CA: CSLI Publications.

Bock, Kathryn. 1986. "Syntactic Persistence in Language Production." *Cognitive Psychology* 18 (3): 355–87.

Bock, Kathryn, and J. Cooper Cutting. 1992. "Regulating Mental Energy: Performance Units in Language Production." *Journal of Memory and Language* 31 (1): 99–127.

Bock, Kathryn, and Willem Levelt. 1994. "Language Production: Grammatical Encoding." In *Handbook of Psycholinguistics*, edited by Morton Ann Gernsbacher, 945–84. San Diego: Academic Press.

Bod, Rens. 2000. "An Empirical Evaluation of LFG-DOP." In *COLING 2000 Volume 1: The 19th International Conference on Computational Linguistics*, 62–8. Saarbrüken, Germany.

Boeckx, Cedric. 2012. *Syntactic Islands*. Cambridge, UK: Cambridge University Press.

Boersma, Paul, and Bruce Hayes. 2001. "Empirical Tests of the Gradual Learning Algorithm." *Linguistic Inquiry* 32 (1): 45–86.

Boguslavsky, Igor, Ivan Chardin, Svetlana Grigorieva, Nikolai Grigoriev, Leonid Iomdin, and Nadezhda Frid. 2002. "Development of a Dependency Treebank for Russian and Its Possible Applications in NLP." In *Proceedings of the 3rd International Conference on Language Resources and Evaluation*, 852–6. Las Palmas, Gran Canaria.

Borer, Hagit. 1984. "Restrictive Relatives in Modern Hebrew." *Natural Language & Linguistic Theory* 2 (2): 219–60.

Borer, Hagit. 1994. "The Projection of Arguments." In *Functional Projections*, 17: 19–48. Occasional Papers in Linguistics. University of Massachusetts.

Branigan, Holly P., and Martin J. Pickering. 2017. "An Experimental Approach to Linguistic Representation." *Behavioral and Brain Sciences* 40: 1–18.

Bresnan, Joan. 2000. *Lexical-Functional Syntax*. Malden, MA: Blackwell.

Bresnan, Joan. 2007. "Is Syntactic Knowledge Probabilistic? Experiments with the English Dative Alternation." In *Roots: Linguistics in Search of Its Evidential Base*, edited by Sam Featherston and Wolfgang Sternefeld, 22. Berlin: de Gruyter.

Bresnan, Joan, Anna Cueni, Tatiana Nikitina, and R. Harald Baayen. 2007. "Predicting the Dative Alternation." In *Cognitive Foundations of Interpretation*, edited by G. Boume, I. Kraemer, and J. Zwarts, 69–94. Amsterdam: Royal Netherlands Academy of Science.

Bresnan, Joan, and Judith Aissen. 2002. "Optimality and Functionality: Objections and Refutations." *Natural Language & Linguistic Theory* 20: 81–95.

Bresnan, Joan, Shipra Dingare, and Christopher D. Manning. 2001. "Soft Constraints Mirror Hard Constraints: Voice and Person in English and Lummi." In *Proceedings of the LFG 01 Conference*, edited by Miriam Butt and Tracy Holloway King, 177–84. Stanford, CA: CSLI Publications.

Bresnan, Joan, and Tatiana Nikitina. 2010. "The Gradience of the Dative Alternation," In *Reality Exploration and Discovery: Pattern Interaction in Language and Life*, edited by Linda Uyechi and Lian Hee Wee, 161–84. Stanford, CA: CSLI Publications.

Burzio, Luigi. 1986. *Italian Syntax: A Government-Binding Approach*. Dordrecht: Foris.

Bybee, Joan L. 2006. "From Usage to Grammar: The Mind's Response to Repetition." *Language* 82 (4): 711–33.

Bybee, Joan L. 2010. *Language, Usage and Cognition*. Cambridge, UK: Cambridge University Press.

Bybee, Joan L., and David Eddington. 2006. "A Usage-Based Approach to Spanish Verbs of 'Becoming.'" *Language* 82 (2): 323–55.

Bybee, Joan L., and Paul J. Hopper. 2001. *Frequency and the Emergence of Linguistic Structure*. Amsterdam: John Benjamins.

Bybee, Joan L., and James L. McClelland. 2005. "Alternatives to the Combinatorial Paradigm of Linguistic Theory Based on Domain General Principles of Human Cognition." *Linguistic Review* 22 (2–4): 381–410.

Cann, Ronnie, Tami Kaplan, and Ruth Kempson. 2005. "Data at the Grammar–Pragmatics Interface: The Case of Resumptive Pronouns in English." *Lingua* 115 (11): 1551–77.

Carreiras, Manuel, Jon Andoni Duñabeitia, Marta Vergara, Irene de la Cruz-Pavía, and Itziar Laka. 2010. "Subject Relative Clauses Are Not Universally Easier to Process: Evidence from Basque." *Cognition* 115 (1): 79–92.

Chacón, Dustin A. 2019. "Minding the Gap? Mechanisms Underlying Resumption in English." *Glossa: A Journal of General Linguistics* 4 (1): 68.

Chafe, Wallace. 1994. *Discourse, Consciousness, and Time: The Flow and Displacement of Conscious Experience in Speaking and Writing*. Chicago: University of Chicago Press.

Chaves, Rui P. 2012. "On the Grammar of Extraction and Coordination." *Natural Language & Linguistic Theory* 30 (2): 465–512.

Chaves, Rui P. 2013. "An Expectation-Based Account of Subject Islands and Parasitism." *Journal of Linguistics* 49 (2): 285–327.

Chaves, Rui P., and Jeruen E. Dery. 2014. "Which Subject Islands Will the Acceptability of Improve with Repeated Exposure?," In *Proceedings of the 31st West Coast Conference on Formal Linguistics*, edited by Robert Santana-LaBarge, 96–106. Somerville, MA: Cascadilla Proceedings Project.

Chaves, Rui P., and Jeruen E. Dery. 2018. "Frequency Effects in Subject Islands." *Journal of Linguistics* 55 (3): 475–521.

Chaves, Rui P., and Michael T. Putnam. 2021. *Unbounded Dependency Constructions: Theoretical and Experimental Perspectives*. Oxford Surveys in Syntax & Morphology. Oxford, New York: Oxford University Press.

Chen, Yunchuan, and Shin Fukuda. 2018. "The Acceptability of the Resumptive Pronoun in the Subject and Object Positions of Chinese Relative Clauses." In *Proceedings of the 30th North American Conference on Chinese Linguistics (NACCL-30)*, 18. Columbus, OH: NACCL Proceedings Online.

Cho, Pyeong Whan, Matthew Goldrick, and Paul Smolensky. 2017. "Incremental Parsing in a Continuous Dynamical System: Sentence Processing in Gradient Symbolic Computation." *Linguistics Vanguard* 3 (1).

Chomsky, Noam. 1956. *"The Logical Structure of Linguistic Theory."* Cambridge, MA: MIT Library.

Chomsky, Noam. 1957. *Syntactic Structures*. The Hague: Mouton.

Chomsky, Noam. 1964. "Degrees of Grammaticalness." In *The Structure of Language: Readings in the Philosophy of Language*, edited by Jerry Fodor and Jerrold Katz, 384–9. Englewood Cliffs, NJ: Prentice-Hall.

Chomsky, Noam. 1965. *Aspects of the Theory of Syntax*. Cambridge, MA: MIT Press.

Chomsky, Noam. 1973. "Conditions on Transformations." In *A Festschrift for Morris Halle*, edited by Stephen Anderson and Paul Kiparsky, 232–86. New York: Holt, Rinehart & Winston.

Chomsky, Noam. 1981. *Lectures on Government and Binding*. Dordrecht: Foris.

Chomsky, Noam. 1982. *Some Concepts and Consequences of the Theory of Government and Binding*. Linguistic Inquiry Monographs. Cambridge, MA: MIT Press.

Chomsky, Noam. 1986a. *Barriers*. Cambridge, MA: MIT Press.

Chomsky, Noam. 1986b. *Knowledge of Language: Its Nature, Origin, and Use*. Westport, CT: Greenwood.

Chomsky, Noam. 1995. *The Minimalist Program*. Cambridge, MA: MIT Press.

Chomsky, Noam. 2000. *The Architecture of Language*. Oxford: Oxford University Press.

Chomsky, Noam. 2004. "Beyond Explanatory Adequacy." In *Structures and Beyond: The Cartography of Syntactic Structures*, edited by Adriana Belletti, 104–31. Oxford University Press.

Chomsky, Noam, and Howard Lasnik. 1977. "Filters and Control." *Linguistic Inquiry* 8 (3): 425–504.

Chomsky, Noam, and Howard Lasnik. 1993. "The Theory of Principles and Parameters." In *Syntax: An International Handbook of Contemporary Research*, edited by Arnim von Stechow, Joachim Jacobs, W. Sternefeld, and T. Vennemann, 506–69. Berlin: de Gruyter.

Christiansen, Morten H., and Nick Chater. 2016. "The Now-or-Never Bottleneck: A Fundamental Constraint on Language." *Behavioral and Brain Sciences* 39: 1–19.

Christiansen, Morten H., and Maryellen C. MacDonald. 2009. "A Usage-Based Approach to Recursion in Sentence Processing." *Language Learning* 59: 126–61.

Cinque, Guglielmo. 1990. *Types of A' Dependencies*. Cambridge, MA: MIT Press.

Clark, Brady. 2005. "On Stochastic Grammar." *Language* 81 (1): 207–17.

Clemens, Lauren Eby, Jessica Coon, Pedro Mateo Pedro, Adam Milton Morgan, Maria Polinsky, Gabrielle Tandet, and Matthew Wagers. 2015. "Ergativity and the Complexity of Extraction: A View from Mayan." *Natural Language & Linguistic Theory* 33 (2): 417–67.

Clifton, Charles, Gisbert Fanselow, and Lyn Frazier. 2006. "Amnestying Superiority Violations: Processing Multiple Questions." *Linguistic Inquiry* 37 (1): 51–68.

Cowart, Wayne. 1994. "Anchoring and Grammar Effects in Judgments of Sentence Acceptability." *Perceptual and Motor Skills* 79 (3): 1171–82.

Cowart, Wayne. 1997. *Experimental Syntax: Applying Objective Methods to Sentence Judgements*. Thousand Oaks, CA: Sage.

Crawford, Jean. 2012. "Using Syntactic Satiation to Investigate Subject Islands." In *Proceedings of the 29th West Coast Conference on Formal Linguistics*, edited by Jaehoon Choi, 38–45. Somerville, MA: Cascadilla Proceedings Project.

Croft, William. 1991. *Syntactic Categories and Grammatical Relations: The Cognitive Organization of Information*. Chicago: University of Chicago Press.

Croft, William. 2001. *Radical Construction Grammar: Syntactic Theory in Typological Perspective*. Oxford: Oxford University Press.

Culicover, Peter W. 1993. "Evidence against ECP Accounts of the That-t Effect." *Linguistic Inquiry* 24 (3): 557–61.

Culicover, Peter W. 2013. *Grammar and Complexity: Language at the Interface of Competence and Performance*. Oxford: Oxford University Press.

Culicover, Peter W., and Ray S. Jackendoff. 2005. *Simpler Syntax*. Oxford: Oxford University Press.

Culicover, Peter W., and Susanne Winkler. 2018. "Freezing: Between Grammar and Processing." In *Freezing: Theoretical Approaches and Empirical Domains*, edited by Jutta Hartmann, Marion Jäger, Andreas Kehl, Andreas Konietzko, and Susanne Winkler, 353–86. Boston, MA: de Gruyter.

Dąbrowska, Ewa. 2008. "Questions with Long-Distance Dependencies: A Usage-Based Perspective." *Cognitive Linguistics* 19 (3): 391–425.

Deane, Paul. 1991. "Limits to Attention: A Cognitive Theory of Island Phenomena." *Cognitive Linguistics* 2 (1): 1–63.

Diessel, Holger, and Martin Hilpert. 2016. "Frequency Effects in Grammar." In *Oxford Research Encyclopedia of Linguistics*, edited by Mark Aronoff, 1–30. Oxford: Oxford University Press.

Dillon, Brian. 2017. "Incremental Syntactic Processing and the Right Roof Constraint." In *A Schrift to Fest Kyle Johnson*, edited by Nicholas LaCara, Keir Moulton, and Anne-Michelle Tessier, 119–30. Amherst, MA: ScholarWorks.

Dillon, Brian, and Norbert Hornstein. 2013. "On the Structural Nature of Island Constraints." In *Experimental Syntax and Island Effects*, edited by Jon Sprouse and Norbert Hornstein, 208–22. Cambridge, UK: Cambridge University Press.

Divjak, Dagmar. 2017. "The Role of Lexical Frequency in the Acceptability of Syntactic Variants: Evidence From *That*-Clauses in Polish." *Cognitive Science* 41 (2): 354–82.

Eberhard, Kathleen M., J. Cooper Cutting, and Kathryn Bock. 2005. "Making Syntax of Sense: Number Agreement in Sentence Production." *Psychological Review* 112 (3): 531–59.

Edelman, Shimon, and Morten H. Christiansen. 2003. "How Seriously Should We Take Minimalist Syntax?" *Trends in Cognitive Sciences* 7 (2): 60–1.

Elman, Jeffrey L. 1990. "Finding Structure in Time." *Cognitive Science* 14 (2): 179–211.

Elman, Jeffrey L., Elizabeth A. Bates, Mark H. Johnson, Annette K. Smith, Domenico Parisi, and Kim Plunkett. 1996. *Rethinking Innateness: A Connectionist Perspective on Development*. Cambridge, MA: MIT Press.

Embick, David. 2004. "On the Structure of Resultative Participles in English." *Linguistic Inquiry* 35 (3): 355–92.

Erteschik-Shir, Nomi. 2006. "What's What?" In *Gradience in Grammar: Generative Perspectives*, edited by Gisbert Fanselow, Caroline Fery, Matthias Schlesewsky, and Ralf Vogel, 317–35. Oxford: Oxford University Press.

Erteschik-Shir, Nomi, and Shalom Lappin. 1979. "Dominance and the Functional Explanation of Island Phenomena." *Theoretical Linguistics* 6 (1–3): 41–86.

Fadlon, Julie, Adam M. Morgan, Aya Meltzer-Asscher, and Victor S. Ferreira. 2019. "It Depends: Optionality in the Production of Filler–Gap Dependencies." *Journal of Memory and Language* 106 (June): 40–76.

Fanselow, Gisbert. 2001. "Features, θ-Roles, and Free Constituent Order." *Linguistic Inquiry* 32 (3): 405–37.

Farby, Shira, Gabi Danon, Joel Walters, and Michal Ben-Shachar. 2010. "The Acceptability of Resumptive Pronouns in Hebrew." In *Proceedings of Israeli Association for Theoretical Linguistics (IATL)*, edited by Yehuda N. Falk. Vol. 26, 1–16. Jerusalem: Israel Association for Theoretical Linguistics. http://www.iatl.org.il/?page_id=46.

Featherston, Sam. 2005a. "Universals and Grammaticality: Wh-Constraints in German and English." *Linguistics* 43 (4): 667–711.

Featherston, Sam. 2005b. "That-Trace in German." *Lingua* 115 (9): 1277–302.

Featherston, Sam. 2005c. "Magnitude Estimation and What It Can Do for Your Syntax: Some Wh-Constraints in German." *Lingua* 115 (11): 1525–50.

Featherston, Sam. 2007. "Data in Generative Grammar: The Stick and the Carrot." *Theoretical Linguistics* 33 (3): 269–318.

Featherston, Sam. 2008. "The Decathlon Model of Empirical Syntax." In *Linguistic Evidence: Empirical, Theoretical and Computational Perspectives*, edited by Stephan Kepser and Marga Reis, 187–208. Berlin: de Gruyter.

Featherston, Sam. 2011. "Three Types of Exceptions—and All of Them Rule-Based." In *Expecting the Unexpected: Exceptions in Grammar*, edited by Horst J. Simon and Heike Wiese, 291–324. Berlin: de Gruyter.

Featherston, Sam. 2019. "The Decathlon Model." In *Current Approaches to Syntax*, edited by András Kertész, Edith Moravcsik, and Csilla Rákosi, 155–86. Berlin: de Gruyter.

Fedorenko, Evelina, and Edward Gibson. 2008. "Syntactic Parallelism as an Account of Superiority Effects: Empirical Investigations in English and Russian." Unpublished manuscript. MIT.

Ferreira, Fernanda. 2003. "The Misinterpretation of Noncanonical Sentences." *Cognitive Psychology* 47 (2): 164–203.

Ferreira, Fernanda, and Benjamin Swets. 2005. "The Production and Comprehension of Resumptive Pronouns in Relative Clause 'Island' Contexts." In *Twenty-First Century Psycholinguistics: Four Cornerstones*, edited by Anne Cutler, 263–78. Mahwah, NJ: Lawrence Erlbaum Associates.

Fillmore, Charles J., and Paul Kay. 1993. "Construction Grammar Coursebook." University of California, Berkeley.

Fillmore, Charles J., Paul Kay, and Mary Catherine O'Connor. 1988. "Regularity and Idiomaticity in Grammatical Constructions: The Case of Let Alone." *Language* 64 (3): 501–38.

Flett, Susanna. 2006. "A Comparison of Syntactic Representation and Processing in First and Second Language Production." University of Edinburgh.

Fox, Danny, and Martin Hackl. 2006. "The Universal Density of Measurement." *Linguistics and Philosophy* 29 (5): 537–86.

Fox, Danny, and Jon Nissenbaum. 1999. "Extraposition and Scope: A Case for Overt QR." In *Proceedings of the 18th West Coast Conference on Formal Linguistics*, edited by Sonya Bird, Andrew Carnie, Jason D. Haugen, and Peter Norquest, 132–44. Somerville, MA: Cascadilla Press.

Francis, Elaine J. 2010. "Grammatical Weight and Relative Clause Extraposition in English." *Cognitive Linguistics* 21 (1): 35–74.

Francis, Elaine J. 2011. "Constraining Mismatch in Grammar and in Sentence Comprehension: The Role of Default Correspondences." In *Pragmatics and Autolexical Grammar: In Honor of Jerry Sadock*, edited by Etsuyo Yuasa, Tista Bagchi, and Katharine Beals, 279–98. Amsterdam: John Benjamins.

Francis, Elaine J. 2017. "Structural Priming Can Inform Syntactic Analyses of Partially Grammaticalized Constructions." *Behavioral and Brain Sciences* 40: 22–3.

Francis, Elaine J., Charles Lam, Carol Chun Zheng, John Hitz, and Stephen Matthews. 2015. "Resumptive Pronouns, Structural Complexity, and the Elusive Distinction between Grammar and Performance: Evidence from Cantonese." *Lingua* 162 (July): 56–81.

Francis, Elaine J., and Stephen Matthews. 2006. "Categoriality and Object Extraction in Cantonese Serial Verb Constructions." *Natural Language & Linguistic Theory* 24 (3): 751–801.

Francis, Elaine J., and Laura A. Michaelis, eds. 2003. *Mismatch: Form–Function Incongruity and the Architecture of Grammar*. Stanford, CA: CSLI Publications.

Francis, Elaine J., and Laura A. Michaelis. 2014. "Why Move? How Weight and Discourse Factors Combine to Predict Relative Clause Extraposition in English." In *Competing Motivations in Grammar and Usage*, edited by Brian MacWhinney, Andrej Malchukov, and Edith Moravcsik, 70–87. Oxford: Oxford University Press.

Francis, Elaine J., and Laura A. Michaelis. 2017. "When Relative Clause Extraposition Is the Right Choice, It's Easier." *Language and Cognition* 9 (2): 332–70.

Franck, Julie, Gabriella Vigliocco, and Janet Nicol. 2002. "Subject–Verb Agreement Errors in French and English: The Role of Syntactic Hierarchy." *Language and Cognitive Processes* 17 (4): 371–404.

Francom, Jerid. 2009. "Experimental Syntax: Exploring the Effect of Repeated Exposure to Anomalous Syntactic Structure—Evidence from Rating and Reading Tasks." PhD diss., University of Arizona. http://search.proquest.com/docview/304844660/?pq-origsite=primo.

Frazier, Lyn, and Charles Clifton Jr. 1989. "Successive Cyclicity in the Grammar and the Parser." *Language and Cognitive Processes* 4 (2): 93–126.

Fried, Mirjam, and Jan-Ola Östman, eds. 2004. *Construction Grammar in a Cross-Language Perspective*. Amsterdam: John Benjamins.

Friedmann, Naama, Gina Taranto, Lewis P. Shapiro, and David Swinney. 2008. "The Leaf Fell (the Leaf): The Online Processing of Unaccusatives." *Linguistic Inquiry* 39 (3): 355–77.

Gazdar, Gerald, Ewan H. Klein, Geoffrey K. Pullum, and Ivan A. Sag. 1985. *Generalized Phrase Structure Grammar*. Cambridge, MA: Harvard University Press.

Gennari, Silvia P., Jelena Mirković, and Maryellen C. MacDonald. 2012. "Animacy and Competition in Relative Clause Production: A Cross-Linguistic Investigation." *Cognitive Psychology* 65 (2): 141–76.

Gibson, Edward. 1998. "Linguistic Complexity: Locality of Syntactic Dependencies." *Cognition* 68 (1): 1–76.

Gibson, Edward, and Evelina Fedorenko. 2013. "The Need for Quantitative Methods in Syntax and Semantics Research." *Language and Cognitive Processes* 28 (1–2):88–124.

Gibson, Edward, and James Thomas. 1999. "Memory Limitations and Structural Forgetting: The Perception of Complex Ungrammatical Sentences as Grammatical." *Language and Cognitive Processes* 14 (3): 225–48.

Ginzburg, Jonathan, and Ivan Sag. 2000. *Interrogative Investigations: The Form, Meaning, and Use of English Interrogatives.* Stanford, CA: CSLI Publications.

Givón, Talmy. 1984. *Syntax: A Functional-Typological Approach.* Amsterdam: John Benjamins.

Givón, Talmy. 1993. *English Grammar Volume II: A Function-Based Introduction.* Amsterdam: John Benjamins.

Goldberg, Adele E. 1995. *Constructions: A Construction Grammar Approach to Argument Structure.* Chicago: University of Chicago Press.

Goldberg, Adele E. 2006. *Constructions at Work: The Nature of Generalization in Language.* Oxford: Oxford University Press.

Goldberg, Adele E. 2013. "Backgrounded Constituents Cannot Be 'Extracted.'" In *Experimental Syntax and Island Effects,* edited by Jon Sprouse and Norbert Hornstein, 221–38. Cambridge, UK: Cambridge University Press.

Goldberg, Adele E. 2016. "Partial Productivity of Linguistic Constructions: Dynamic Categorization and Statistical Preemption." *Language and Cognition* 8 (3): 369–90.

Goldberg, Adele E. 2019. *Explain Me This: Creativity, Competition, and the Partial Productivity of Constructions.* Princeton, NJ: Princeton University Press.

Goodall, Grant. 2010. "Experimenting with Wh-Movement in Spanish." In *Current Issues in Linguistic Theory,* edited by Karlos Arregi, Zsuzsanna Fagyal, Silvina A. Montrul, and Annie Tremblay, 313: 233–48. Amsterdam: John Benjamins.

Goodall, Grant. 2011. "Syntactic Satiation and the Inversion Effect in English and Spanish Wh-Questions: Syntactic Satiation and Inversion in English and Spanish." *Syntax* 14 (1): 29–47.

Goodall, Grant. 2015. "The D-Linking Effect on Extraction from Islands and Non-Islands." *Frontiers in Psychology* 5: 1–11.

Greenbaum, Sidney. 1976. "Contextual Influence on Acceptability Judgments." *Linguistics* 15 (187): 5–12.

Griffin, Z., and Justin Weinstein-Tull. 2003. "Conceptual Structure Modulates Structural Priming in the Production of Complex Sentences." *Journal of Memory and Language* 49 (4): 537–55.

Grimshaw, Jane. 1997. "Projection, Heads, and Optimality." *Linguistic Inquiry* 28 (3): 373–422.

Grimshaw, Jane, and Vieri Samek-Lodovici. 1998. "Optimal Subjects and Subject Universals." In *Is the Best Good Enough?,* edited by Pilar Barbosa, Danny Fox, Paul Hagstrom, Martha McGinnis, and David Pesetsky, 193–219. Cambridge, MA: MIT Press.

Grodzinsky, Yosef, and Andrea Santi. 2008. "The Battle for Broca's Region." *Trends in Cognitive Sciences* 12 (12): 474–80.

Guéron, Jacqueline. 1980. "On the Syntax and Semantics of PP Extraposition." *Linguistic Inquiry* 11 (4): 637–78.

Guéron, Jacqueline, and Robert May. 1984. "Extraposition and Logical Form." *Linguistic Inquiry* 15 (1): 1–31.

Gundel, Jeanette K. 1988. "Universals of Topic–Comment Structure." In *Studies in Syntactic Typology,* edited by Michael Hammond, Edith A. Moravcsik, and J. R. Wirth, 209–39. Amsterdam: John Benjamins.

Haider, Hubert. 1993. *Deutsche syntax, generativ: vorstudien zur Theorie einer projektiven Grammatik.* Tübingen: Gunter Narr Verlag.

Hale, Kenneth, and Samuel Jay Keyser. 1993. "On Argument Structure and the Lexical Expression of Syntactic Relations." In *The View from Building 20: Essays in Linguistics in Honor of Sylvain Bromberger,* edited by Kenneth Hale and Samuel Jay Keyser, 53–109. Cambridge, MA: MIT Press.

Hammerly, Christopher. 2020. "Person-Based Prominence in Ojibwe." PhD diss., University of Massachusetts Amherst.

Hammerly, Christopher. 2021. "The Pronoun Which Comprehenders Who Process It in Islands Derive a Benefit." *Linguistic Inquiry* Advance publication.

Han, Chung-hye, Noureddine Elouazizi, Christina Galeano, Emrah Görgülü, Nancy Hedberg, Jennifer Hinnell, Meghan Jeffrey, Kyeong-min Kim, and Susannah Kirby. 2012. "Processing Strategies and Resumptive Pronouns in English." In *Proceedings of the 30th West Coast Conference on Formal Linguistics*, edited by Nathan Arnett and Ryan Bennett, 153–61. Somerville, MA: Cascadilla Proceedings Project.

Häussler, Jana, and Markus Bader. 2015. "An Interference Account of the Missing-VP Effect." *Frontiers in Psychology* 6: 1–16.

Häussler, Jana, Gisbert Fanselow, Thórhallur Eythórsson, Radek Šimik, and Luis Vicente. 2018. "Crossing Movement Paths: Multiple Wh-Questions in Seven Languages." Unpublished manuscript. University of Leipzig.

Häussler, Jana, Margaret Grant, Gisbert Fanselow, and Lyn Frazier. 2015. "Superiority in English and German: Cross-Language Grammatical Differences?" *Syntax* 18 (3): 235–65.

Häussler, Jana, and Tom Juzek. 2020. "Linguistic Intuitions and the Puzzle of Gradience." In *Linguistic Intuitions: Evidence and Method*, edited by Samuel Schindler, Anna Drożdżowicz, and Karen Brøcker, 233–54. Oxford: Oxford University Press.

Hawkins, John A. 1999. "Processing Complexity and Filler–Gap Dependencies across Grammars." *Language* 75 (2): 244.

Hawkins, John A. 2004. *Efficiency and Complexity in Grammars*. Oxford: Oxford University Press.

Hawkins, John A. 2014. *Cross-Linguistic Variation and Efficiency*. Oxford: Oxford University Press.

Heestand, Dustin, Ming Xiang, and Maria Polinsky. 2011. "Resumption Still Does Not Rescue Islands." *Linguistic Inquiry* 42 (1): 138–52.

Heidinger, Steffen. 2015. "Optionality and Preferences in Spanish Postverbal Constituent Order: An OT Account without Basic Constituent Order." *Lingua* 162: 102–27.

Hitz, John, and Elaine J. Francis. 2016. "On the Usefulness of Formal Judgment Tasks in Syntax and in Second-Language Research: The Case of Resumptive Pronouns in English, Turkish, and Mandarin Chinese." *Linguistics* 54 (6).

Hoeksema, Jack. 1986. "Monotonicity Phenomena in Natural Language." *Linguistic Analysis* 16: 25–40.

Hofmeister, Philip. 2007. "Representational Complexity and Memory Retrieval in Language Comprehension." PhD diss., Stanford University.

Hofmeister, Philip, Laura Staum Casasanto, and Ivan A. Sag. 2012. "How Do Individual Cognitive Differences Relate to Acceptability Judgments? A Reply to Sprouse, Wagers, and Phillips." *Language* 88 (2): 390–400.

Hofmeister, Philip, Laura Staum Casasanto, and Ivan A. Sag. 2013. "Islands in the Grammar? Standards of Evidence." In *Experimental Syntax and Island Effects*, edited by Jon Sprouse and Norbert Hornstein, 42–63. Cambridge, UK: Cambridge University Press.

Hofmeister, Philip, Peter W. Culicover, and Susanne Winkler. 2015. "Effects of Processing on the Acceptability of 'Frozen' Extraposed Constituents." *Syntax* 18 (4): 464–83.

Hofmeister, Philip, T. Florian Jaeger, Inbal Arnon, Ivan A. Sag, and Neal Snider. 2013. "The Source Ambiguity Problem: Distinguishing the Effects of Grammar and Processing on Acceptability Judgments." *Language and Cognitive Processes* 28 (1–2): 48–87.

Hofmeister, Philip, and Elisabeth Norcliffe. 2013. "Does Resumption Facilitate Sentence Comprehension?" In *The Core and the Periphery: Data-Driven Perspectives on Syntax Inspired by Ivan A. Sag*, edited by P. Hofmeister and E. Norcliffe, 225–46. Stanford, CA: CSLI Publications.

Hofmeister, Philip, and Ivan A. Sag. 2010. "Cognitive Constraints and Island Effects." *Language* 86 (2): 366–415.

Hornstein, Norbert. 1999. "Movement and Control." *Linguistic Inquiry* 30 (1): 69–96.

Hornstein, Norbert, and Maria Polinsky. 2010. "Control as Movement: Across Languages and Constructions." In *Movement Theory of Control*, edited by Norbert Hornstein and Maria Polinsky, 1–41. Amsterdam: John Benjamins.

Hornstein, Norbert, and Amy Weinberg. 1995. "The Empty Category Principle." In *Government and Binding Theory and the Minimalist Program: Principles and Parameters in Syntactic Theory*, edited by Gert Webelhuth, 241–96. Oxford: Wiley-Blackwell.

Huang, Yujing, and Jesse Snedeker. 2020. "Evidence from the Visual World Paradigm Raises Questions about Unaccusativity and Growth Curve Analyses." *Cognition* 200 (July): 104251.

Huck, Geoffrey J., and Younghee Na. 1992. "Information and Contrast." *Studies in Language* 16 (2): 325–34.

Jackendoff, Ray. 1992. "Mme. Tussaud Meets the Binding Theory." *Language and Linguistic Theory* 10 (1): 1–31.

Jackendoff, Ray. 2007. "Linguistics in Cognitive Science: The State of the Art." *Linguistic Review* 24 (4): 347–401.

Jackendoff, Ray. 2011. "Alternative Minimalist Visions of Language." In *Non-Transformational Syntax*, edited by Robert D. Borsley and Kersti Börjars, 268–96. Oxford: Wiley-Blackwell.

Jackendoff, Ray, and Peter W. Culicover. 2003. "The Semantic Basis of Control in English." *Language* 79: 517–56.

Jeffrey, Meghan. 2014. "Control Over Objects: An Experimental Investigation of Transitive Subject Control." PhD diss., Vancouver: Simon Fraser University.

Jeffrey, Meghan, Chung-hye Han, and Panayiotis Pappas. 2015. "Experimental Evidence of Variation and Gradience in the Syntax and Semantics of Transitive Subject Control." *Lingua* 164 (September): 100–31.

Joshi, Aravind K., and Yves Schabes. 1997. "Tree-Adjoining Grammars." In *Handbook of Formal Languages: Volume 3 Beyond Words*, edited by Grzegorz Rozenberg and Arto Salomaa, 69–123. Berlin: Springer.

Kandybowicz, Jason. 2006. "Comp-Trace Effects Explained Away." In *Proceedings of the 25th West Coast Conference on Formal Linguistics*, edited by Donald Baumer, David Montero, and Michael Scanlon, 220–8. Somerville, MA: Cascadilla Proceedings Project.

Kaplan, Ronald M., and Joan Bresnan. 1982. "Lexical-Functional Grammar: A Formal System for Grammatical Representation." In *Formal Issues in Lexical-Functional Grammar*, edited by Mary Dalrymple, Ronald M. Kaplan, John T. Maxwell, and Annie Zaenen, 29–130. Stanford, CA: CSLI Publications.

Kay, Paul, and Charles J. Fillmore. 1999. "Grammatical Constructions and Linguistic Generalizations: The What's X Doing Y? Construction." *Language* 75 (1): 1–33.

Kay, Paul, and Ivan A. Sag. 2012. "Cleaning up the Big Mess: Discontinuous Dependencies and Complex Determiners." In *Sign-Based Construction Grammar*, edited by Hans Boas and Ivan A. Sag, 229–56. Stanford, CA: CSLI Publications.

Keenan, Edward L., and Bernard Comrie. 1977. "Noun Phrase Accessibility and Universal Grammar." *Linguistic Inquiry* 8 (1): 63–99.

Keffala, Bethany. 2011. "Resumption and Gaps in English Relative Clauses: Relative Acceptability Creates an Illusion of 'Saving.'" Edited by Chundra Cathcart, I-Hsuan Chen, Greg Finley, Shinae Kang, Clare S. Sandy, and Elise Stickles. *Annual Meeting of the Berkeley Linguistics Society* 37 (1): 140–54.

Keller, Frank. 2000. "Gradience in Grammar: Experimental and Computational Aspects of Degrees of Grammaticality." PhD diss., University of Edinburgh. https://rucore.libraries.rutgers.edu/rutgers-lib/38303/.

Keller, Frank. 2006. "Linear Optimality Theory as a Model of Gradience in Grammar." In *Gradience in Grammar: Generative Perspectives*, edited by Gisbert Fanselow, Caroline Féry, Matthias Schlesewsky, and Ralf Vogel, 270–87. Oxford: Oxford University Press.

Keller, Frank, and Antonella Sorace. 2003. "Gradient Auxiliary Selection and Impersonal Passivization in German: An Experimental Investigation." *Journal of Linguistics* 39 (1): 57–108.

Kemmerer, David. 2019. *Concepts in the Brain: The View From Cross-Linguistic Diversity*. New York: Oxford University Press.

Kemmerer, David. 2021. *Cognitive Neuroscience of Language*. 2nd ed. New York: Psychology Press.

Kempe, Vera, and Brian MacWhinney. 1999. "Processing of Morphological and Semantic Cues in Russian and German." *Language and Cognitive Processes* 14 (2): 129–71.

Kempen, Gerard, and Karin Harbusch. 2005. "The Relationship between Grammaticality Ratings and Corpus Frequencies: A Case Study into Word Order Variability in the Midfield of German Clauses." In *Linguistic Evidence*, edited by Stephan Kepser and Marga Reis, 329–50. New York: Mouton de Gruyter.

Kempen, Gerard, and Karin Harbusch. 2008. "Comparing Linguistic Judgments and Corpus Frequencies as Windows on Grammatical Competence: A Study of Argument Linearization in German Clauses." In *The Discourse Potential of Underspecified Structures*, edited by Anita Steube, 179–92. Berlin: de Gruyter.

Kertész, András, and Csilla Rákosi. 2012. *Data and Evidence in Linguistics: A Plausible Argumentation Model*. Cambridge, UK: Cambridge University Press.

Kertész, András, and Csilla Rákosi. 2014. "The P-Model of Data and Evidence in Linguistics." In *Studies in Language Companion Series*, edited by András Kertész and Csilla Rákosi, 153: 15–48. Amsterdam: John Benjamins.

Keshev, Maayan, and Aya Meltzer-Asscher. 2017. "Active Dependency Formation in Islands: how Grammatical Resumption Affects Sentence Processing." *Language* 93 (3): 549–68.

Kimball, John, and Judith Aissen. 1971. "I Think, You Think, He Think." *Linguistic Inquiry* 2 (2): 241–46.

Kiparsky, Paul, and Carol Kiparsky. 1970. "Fact." In *Progress in Linguistics*, edited by Manfred Bierwisch and Karl Erich Heidolph, 143–73. The Hague: Mouton.

Kiss, Katalin. 1993. "Wh-Movement and Specificity." *Natural Language and Linguistic Theory* 11: 85–120.

Kitagawa, Yoshihisa, and Janet Dean Fodor. 2006. "Prosodic Influence on Syntactic Judgements." In *Gradience in Grammar: Generative Perspectives*, edited by Gisbert Fanselow, Caroline Fery, Matthias Schlesewsky, and Ralf Vogel, 336–58. Oxford: Oxford University Press.

Kluender, Robert. 1998. "On the Distinction between Strong and Weak Islands: A Processing Perspective." *Syntax and Semantics*, 241–80.

Kluender, Robert, and Marta Kutas. 1993. "Subjacency as a Processing Phenomenon." *Language and Cognitive Processes* 8 (4): 573–633.

Koizumi, Masatoshi, Yoshiho Yasugi, Katsuo Tamaoka, Sachiko Kiyama, Jungho Kim, Juan Esteban Ajsivinac Sian, and Lolmay Pedro Oscar García Mátzar. 2014. "On the (Non)Universality of the Preference for Subject–Object Word Order in Sentence Comprehension: A Sentence-Processing Study in Kaqchikel Maya." *Language* 90 (3): 722–36.

Konieczny, Lars. 2000. "Locality and Parsing Complexity." *Journal of Psycholinguistic Research* 29 (6): 627–45.

Konietzko, Andreas, Susanne Winkler, and Peter W. Culicover. 2018. "Heavy NP Shift Does Not Cause Freezing." *Canadian Journal of Linguistics/Revue Canadienne de Linguistique*, March, 1–11.

Koring, Loes, Pim Mak, and Eric Reuland. 2012. "The Time Course of Argument Reactivation Revealed: Using the Visual World Paradigm." *Cognition* 123 (3): 361–79.

Koring, Loes, and Eric Reuland. 2017. "What Structural Priming Can and Cannot Reveal." *Behavioral and Brain Sciences* 40: 31–2.

Kothari, Anubha. 2008. "Frequency-Based Expectations and Context Influence Bridge Quality." Unpublished manuscript. Stanford University.

Kroch, Anthony. 1981. "On the Role of Resumptive Pronouns in Amnestying Island Constraint Violations." In *Proceedings of the Sixteenth Annual Meeting of the Chicago Linguistic Society*, 125–35. Chicago: Chicago Linguistic Society.

Kroch, Anthony. 1989. "Amount Quantification, Referentiality, and Long Wh-Movement." Unpublished manuscript. University of Pennsylvania. http://157.138.8.12/jspui/bitstream/11707/682/3/Kroch.pdf.

Kučerová, Ivona. 2012. "Grammatical Marking of Givenness." *Natural Language Semantics* 20 (1): 1–30.

Kuhn, Jonas. 2000. "Faithfulness Violations and Bidirectional Optimization." In *Proceedings of the LFG 2000 Conference*, edited by Miriam Butt and Tracy Holloway King, 161–81. Berkeley: CSLI Proceedings Online.

Kuhn, Jonas. 2003. *Optimality-Theoretic Syntax: A Declarative Approach*. Stanford, CA: CSLI Publications.

Kuno, Susumu. 1987. *Functional Syntax: Anaphora, Discourse and Empathy*. Chicago: University of Chicago Press.

Kuno, Susumu, and Jane J. Robinson. 1972. "Multiple Wh Questions." *Linguistic Inquiry* 3 (4): 463–87.

Labov, William. 1972. "Some Principles of Linguistic Methodology." *Language in Society* 1 (1): 97–120.

Ladusaw, William A. 1979. "Polarity Sensitivity as Inherent Scope Relations." PhD diss., University of Texas at Austin.

Lakoff, George. 1987. *Women, Fire, and Dangerous Things: What Categories Reveal about the Mind*. Chicago: University of Chicago Press.

Landau, Idan. 2003. "Movement Out of Control." *Linguistic Inquiry* 34 (3): 471–98.

Langacker, Ronald W. 1987. *Foundations of Cognitive Grammar: Theoretical Prerequisites*. Stanford, CA: Stanford University Press.

Lappin, Shalom, and Jey Han Lau. 2018. "Gradient Probabilistic Models vs Categorical Grammars: A Reply to Sprouse et al. (2018)." *Science of Language* (blog). 2018. http://thescienceoflanguage. com/2018/07/22/gradient-probabilistic-models-vs-categorical-grammars-a-reply-to-sprouse-et-al-2018/.

Larson, Richard. 1991. "Promise and the Theory of Control." *Linguistic Inquiry* 22(1): 103–39.

Lau, Jey Han, Alexander Clark, and Shalom Lappin. 2017. "Grammaticality, Acceptability, and Probability: A Probabilistic View of Linguistic Knowledge." *Cognitive Science* 41 (5): 1202–41.

Lee, Seung Han. 2017. "Factors at Play in Extraposing English Relative Clauses." PhD diss., Chonnam National University.

Legendre, Géraldine. 2001. "An Introduction to Optimality Theory in Syntax." In *Optimality-Theoretic Syntax*, edited by Géraldine Legendre, Jane Barbara Grimshaw, and Sten Vikner, 1–27. Cambridge, MA: MIT Press.

Legendre, Géraldine, Jane Barbara Grimshaw, and Sten Vikner. 2001. *Optimality-Theoretic Syntax*. Cambridge, MA: MIT Press.

Legendre, Géraldine, Paul Smolensky, and Colin Wilson. 1998. "When Is Less More? Faithfulness and Minimal Links in Wh-Chains." In *Is the Best Good Enough? Optimality and Competition in Syntax*, edited by Pilar Barbosa, Danny Fox, Paul Hagstrom, Martha McGinnis, and David Pesetsky, 249–89. Cambridge, MA: MIT Press.

Levelt, Willem J.M. 1972. "Some Psychological Aspects of Linguistic Data." *Linguistische Berichte* 17: 18–30.

Levin, Beth. 1993. *English Verb Classes and Alternations*. Cambridge, MA: MIT Press.

Levinson, Stephen C. 1987. "Pragmatics and the Grammar of Anaphora: A Partial Pragmatic Reduction of Binding and Control Phenomena." *Journal of Linguistics* 23 (2): 379–434.

Levinson, Stephen C. 1991. "Pragmatic Reduction of the Binding Conditions Revisited." *Journal of Linguistics* 27 (1): 107–61.

Levy, Roger, Evelina Fedorenko, Mara Breen, and Edward Gibson. 2012. "The Processing of Extraposed Structures in English." *Cognition* 122 (1): 12–36.

Lewis, Shevaun, and Colin Phillips. 2015. "Aligning Grammatical Theories and Language Processing Models." *Journal of Psycholinguistic Research* 44 (1): 27–46.

Linzen, Tal, and Marco Baroni. 2021. "Syntactic Structure from Deep Learning." *Annual Review of Linguistics* 7 (1).

Linzen, Tal, Emmanuel Dupoux, and Yoav Goldberg. 2016. "Assessing the Ability of LSTMs to Learn Syntax-Sensitive Dependencies." *Transactions of the Association for Computational Linguistics* 4 (December): 521–35.

Linzen, Tal, and Brian Leonard. 2018. "Distinct Patterns of Syntactic Agreement Errors in Recurrent Networks and Humans." In *Proceedings of the 40th Annual Conference of the Cognitive Science Society*, 692–97. Austin, TX: Cognitive Science Society. http://arxiv.org/abs/1807.06882.

Liu, Yingtong, Rachel Ryskin, Richard Futrell, and Edward Gibson. 2019. "Verb Frequency Explains the Unacceptability of Factive and Manner-of-Speaking Islands in English." In *Proceedings of the 41st Annual Conference of the Cognitive Science Society*, 685–91. Austin, TX: Cognitive Science Society.

Lohse, Barbara, John A. Hawkins, and Thomas Wasow. 2004. "Domain Minimization in English Verb–Particle Constructions." *Language* 80 (2): 238–61.

Luka, Barbara J., and Lawrence W. Barsalou. 2005. "Structural Facilitation: Mere Exposure Effects for Grammatical Acceptability as Evidence for Syntactic Priming in Comprehension." *Journal of Memory and Language* 52 (3): 436–59.

Lutz, Uli. 1996. "Some Notes on Extraction Theory." In *On Extraction and Extraposition in German*, edited by Uli Lutz and J. Pafel, 1–44. Vol. 11. Linguistik Aktuell. Amsterdam: Benjamins.

Manning, Christopher D. 2003. "Probabilistic Syntax." In *Probabilistic Linguistics*, edited by Rens Bod, Jennifer Hay, and Stefanie Jannedy, 289–342. Cambridge, MA: MIT Press.

Marantz, Alec. 2013. "Verbal Argument Structure: Events and Participants." *Lingua* 130: 152–68.

Matchin, William, and Gregory Hickok. 2020. "The Cortical Organization of Syntax." *Cerebral Cortex* 30 (3): 1481–98.

Matchin, William, Jon Sprouse, and Gregory Hickok. 2014. "A Structural Distance Effect for Backward Anaphora in Broca's Area: An FMRI Study." *Brain and Language* 138 (November): 1–11.

Matthews, Stephen, and Virginia Yip. 2011. *Cantonese: A Comprehensive Grammar*. London: Routledge.

McCarthy, John J., and Alan Prince. 1995. "Faithfulness and Reduplicative Identity." *Linguistics Department Faculty Publication Series*.

McCawley, James D. 1968. "The Role of Semantics in a Grammar." In *Universals in Linguistic Theory*, edited by Emmon Bach and Robert Harms, 125–70. New York: Holt, Rinehart, and Winston.

McCawley, James D. 1998. *The Syntactic Phenomena of English*. Chicago: University of Chicago Press.

McClelland, James L. 2015. "Capturing Gradience, Continuous Change, and Quasi-Regularity in Sound, Word, Phrase, and Meaning." In *The Handbook of Language Emergence*, edited by Brian MacWhinney and William O'Grady, 53–80. Hoboken, NJ: Wiley.

McClelland, James L., and Joan L. Bybee. 2007. "Gradience of Gradience: A Reply to Jackendoff." *Linguistic Review* 24 (4): 437–55.

McCloskey, James. 2003. "Working on Irish." *Glot* 7: 3–63.

McCloskey, James. 2006. "Resumption." In *The Blackwell Companion to Syntax*, edited by Martin Everaert and Henk van Riemsdijk, 94–117. Malden, MA: Blackwell.

McCloskey, James. 2011. "Resumptive Pronouns, Ā-Binding, and Levels of Representations in Irish." In *Resumptive Pronouns at the Interfaces*, edited by Alain Rouveret, 65–119. Amsterdam: John Benjamins.

McClure, William. 1995. *Syntactic Projections of the Semantics of Aspect*. Tokyo: Hitsujishobo.

McDaniel, Dana, and Wayne Cowart. 1999. "Experimental Evidence for a Minimalist Account of English Resumptive Pronouns." *Cognition* 70 (2): B15–24.

MacDonald, Maryellen C. 2013. "How Language Production Shapes Language Form and Comprehension." *Frontiers in Psychology* 4: 1–16.

McKee, Cecile, and Dana McDaniel. 2001. "Resumptive Pronouns in English Relative Clauses." *Language Acquisition* 9 (2): 113–56.

McKoon, Gail, Gregory Ward, Roger Ratcliff, and Richard Sproat. 1990. "Morphosyntactic and Pragmatic Manipulations of Salience in the Interpretation of Anaphora." Unpublished manuscript. Northwestern University and AT&T Bell Laboratories.

Meltzer-Asscher, Aya. 2021. "Resumptive Pronouns in Language Comprehension and Production." *Annual Review of Linguistics* 7 (1): 177–94.

Meltzer-Asscher, Aya, Julie Fadlon, Kayla Goldstein, and Ariel Holan. 2015. "Direct Object Resumption in Hebrew: How Modality of Presentation and Relative Clause Position Affect Acceptability." *Lingua* 166 (October): 65–79.

Meyer, Roland. 2004. "Superiority Effects in Russian, Polish, and Czech: Judgments and Grammar." *Cahiers Linguistiques d'Ottawa* 32: 44–65.

Michaelis, Laura A. 1994. "A Case of Constructional Polysemy in Latin." *Studies in Language* 18 (1): 45–70.

Michaelis, Laura A. 2004. "Type Shifting in Construction Grammar: An Integrated Approach to Aspectual Coercion." *Cognitive Linguistics* 15 (1): 1–67.

Michaelis, Laura A. 2009. "Sign-Based Construction Grammar." In *The Oxford Handbook of Linguistic Analysis*, edited by Bernd Heine and Hengeveld Narrog, 155–76. Oxford: Oxford University Press.

Michaelis, Laura A. 2012. "Making the Case for Construction Grammar." In *Sign-Based Construction Grammar*, edited by Hans Boas and Ivan A. Sag, 31–69. Stanford, CA: CSLI Publications.

Michaelis, Laura A., and Knud Lambrecht. 1996. "Toward a Construction-Based Theory of Language Function: The Case of Nominal Extraposition." *Language* 72 (2): 215.

Miller, George A., and Noam Chomsky. 1963. "Finitary Models of Language Users." In *Handbook of Mathematical Psychology*, edited by Duncan Luce, Robert R. Bush, and Eugene Galanter, II: 419–91. New York: Wiley.

Momma, Shota, L. Robert Slevc, and Colin Phillips. 2018. "Unaccusativity in Sentence Production." *Linguistic Inquiry* 49 (1): 181–94.

Montrul, Silvina. 2004. "Psycholinguistic Evidence for Split Intransitivity in Spanish Second Language Acquisition." *Applied Psycholinguistics* 25 (2): 239–67.

Montrul, Silvina. 2005. "On Knowledge and Development of Unaccusativity in Spanish L2 Acquisition." *Linguistics* 43 (6).

Montrul, Silvina. 2006. "On the Bilingual Competence of Spanish Heritage Speakers: Syntax, Lexical-Semantics and Processing." *International Journal of Bilingualism* 10 (1): 37–69.

Morgan, Adam Milton, and Matthew W. Wagers. 2018. "English Resumptive Pronouns Are More Common Where Gaps Are Less Acceptable." *Linguistic Inquiry* 49 (4): 861–76.

Myers, James. 2009. "Syntactic Judgment Experiments." *Language and Linguistics Compass* 3 (1): 406–23.

Nagata, Hiroshi. 1988. "The Relativity of Linguistic Intuition: The Effect of Repetition on Grammaticality Judgments." *Journal of Psycholinguistic Research* 17 (1): 1–17.

Namboodiripad, Savithry. 2017. "An Experimental Approach to Variation and Variability in Constituent Order." PhD diss., University of California San Diego.

Newmeyer, Frederick J. 1996. *Generative Linguistics: A Historical Perspective*. New York: Routledge.

Newmeyer, Frederick J. 2003. "Grammar Is Grammar and Usage Is Usage." *Language* 79 (4): 682–707.

Newmeyer, Frederick J. 2016. "Nonsyntactic Explanations of Island Constraints." *Annual Review of Linguistics* 2 (1): 187–210.

Norcliffe, Elisabeth, Alice C. Harris, and T. Florian Jaeger. 2015. "Cross-Linguistic Psycholinguistics and Its Critical Role in Theory Development: Early Beginnings and Recent Advances." *Language, Cognition and Neuroscience* 30 (9): 1009–32.

Novick, Jared M., John C. Trueswell, and Sharon L. Thompson-Schill. 2005. "Cognitive Control and Parsing: Reexamining the Role of Broca's Area in Sentence Comprehension." *Cognitive, Affective, & Behavioral Neuroscience* 5 (3): 263–81.

Oshima, David Y. 2006. "On Factive Islands: Pragmatic Anomaly vs. Pragmatic Infelicity." In *New Frontiers in Artificial Intelligence: Joint JSAI 2006 Workshop Post-Proceedings*, edited by Takashi Washio, Ken Satoh, Hideaki Terada, and Akihiro Inokuchi, 147–61. Dordrecht: Springer.

Osterhout, Lee, and David Swinney. 1993. "On the Temporal Course of Gap-Filling during Comprehension of Verbal Passives." *Journal of Psycholinguistic Research* 22 (2): 273–386.

Overfelt, Jason. 2015. "Extraposition of NPIs from NP." *Lingua* 164 (September): 25–44.

Palangi, Hamid, Paul Smolensky, Xiaodong He, and Li Deng. 2017. "Deep Learning of Grammatically-Interpretable Representations Through Question-Answering." ArXiv:1705.08432 [Cs.CL], 1–22. https://arxiv.org/abs/1705.08432v1.

Pater, Joe. 2019. "Generative Linguistics and Neural Networks at 60: Foundation, Friction, and Fusion." *Language* 95 (1): e41–74.

Perek, Florent. 2014. "Rethinking Constructional Polysemy: The Case of the English Conative Construction." In *Human Cognitive Processing*, edited by Dylan Glynn and Justyna A. Robinson, 43: 61–85. Amsterdam: John Benjamins.

Perlmutter, David. 1978. "Impersonal Passives and the Unaccusative Hypothesis." In *Proceedings of the Fourth Annual Meeting of the Berkeley Linguistics Society*, edited by Anthony Woodbury, Farrell Ackerman, John Kingston, Eve Sweetser, Henry Thompson, and Kenneth Whistler, 157–89. Berkeley: University of California.

Pesetsky, David. 1982. "Complementizer-Trace Phenomena and the Nominative Island Condition." *Linguistic Review* 1 (3): 297–344.

Pesetsky, David. 1987. "Wh-in Situ: Movement and Unselective Binding." In *The Representation of (in) Definiteness*, edited by Eric Reuland and Alice Ter Meulen, 98–129. Cambridge, MA: MIT Press.

Phillips, Colin. 2013a. "Some Arguments and Nonarguments for Reductionist Accounts of Syntactic Phenomena." *Language and Cognitive Processes* 28 (1–2): 156–87.

Phillips, Colin. 2013b. "On the Nature of Island Constraints I: Language Processing and Reductionist Accounts." In *Experimental Syntax and Island Effects*, edited by Jon Sprouse and Norbert Hornstein, 64–108. Cambridge, UK: Cambridge University Press.

Pickering, Martin J., Stephen Barton, and Richard Shillcock. 1994. "Unbounded Dependencies, Island Constraints, and Processing Complexity." In *Perspectives on Sentence Processing*, edited by Charles Clifton, Lyn Frazier, and Keith Rayner, 199–224. London: Lawrence Erlbaum Associates.

Pickering, Martin J., and Victor S. Ferreira. 2008. "Structural Priming: A Critical Review." *Psychological Bulletin* 134 (3): 427–59.

Pickering, Martin J., and Matthew J. Traxler. 2001. "Strategies for Processing Unbounded Dependencies: Lexical Information and Verb-Argument Assignment." *Journal of Experimental Psychology: Learning, Memory, and Cognition* 27: 1401–10.

Polinsky, Maria. to appear. "Experimental Syntax and Linguistic Fieldwork." In *Oxford Handbook of Experimental Syntax*. Oxford University Press.

Polinsky, Maria, Lauren Eby Clemens, Adam Milton Morgan, Ming Xiang, and Dustin Heestand. 2013. "Resumption in English." In *Experimental Syntax and Island Effects: Toward a Comprehensive Theory of Islands*, edited by Jon Sprouse and Norbert Hornstein, 341–59. Cambridge, UK: Cambridge University Press.

Polinsky, Maria, Carlos Gómez Gallo, Peter Graff, and Ekaterina Kravtchenko. 2012. "Subject Preference and Ergativity." *Lingua* 122 (3): 267–77.

Pollard, Carl, and Ivan A. Sag. 1994. *Head-Driven Phrase Structure Grammar*. Chicago: University of Chicago Press.

Post, Emil L. 1943. "Formal Reductions of the General Combinatorial Decision Problem." *American Journal of Mathematics* 65 (2): 197–215.

Postal, Paul M. 1969. "Anaphoric Islands." In *Proceedings from the Fifth Annual Meeting of the Chicago Linguistic Society*, 205–39. Chicago: Chicago Linguistic Society.

Postal, Paul M. 1974. *On Raising: One Rule of English Grammar and Its Theoretical Implications*. Cambridge, MA: MIT Press.

Postal, Paul M. 1998. *Three Investigations of Extraction*. Cambridge, MA: MIT Press.

Prince, Alan, and Paul Smolensky. 2004. *Optimality Theory: Constraint Interaction in Generative Grammar*. Malden, MA: Blackwell.

Prince, Ellen F. 1990. "Syntax and Discourse: A Look at Resumptive Pronouns." In *Annual Meeting of the Berkeley Linguistics Society* 16: 482–97.

Pritchett, Bradley L. 1991. "Subjacency in a Principle-Based Parser." In *Principle-Based Parsing: Computation and Psycholinguistics*, edited by Robert C. Berwick, Steven P. Abney, and Carol Tenny, 301–45. Studies in Linguistics and Philosophy. Dordrecht: Springer.

Pullum, Geoffrey K. 2010. "Creation Myths of Generative Grammar, and the Mathematics of Syntactic Structures." In *The Mathematics of Language. MOL 2009, MOL 2007*, edited by Christian Ebert, Gerhard Jäger, and Jens Michaelis, 6149: 238–54. Lecture Notes in Artificial Intelligence. Dordrecht: Springer.

Radford, Andrew. 2009. *Analysing English Sentences: A Minimalist Approach*. Cambridge, UK: Cambridge University Press.

Radford, Andrew. 2019. *Relative Clauses: Structure and Variation in Everyday English*. Cambridge, UK: Cambridge University Press.

Ramchand, Gillian. 2013. "Argument Structure and Argument Structure Alternations." In *Cambridge Handbook of Generative Syntax*, edited by M. Den Dikken, 275–331. Cambridge, UK: Cambridge University Press.

Richter, Stephanie N., and Rui P. Chaves. 2020. "Investigating the Role of Verb Frequency in Factive and Manner-of-Speaking Islands." In *Proceedings of the 42nd Annual Conference of the Cognitive Science Society*, 1771–7. Austin, TX: Cognitive Science Society.

Rizzi, Luigi. 1990. *Relativized Minimality*. Cambridge, MA: MIT Press.

Rizzi, Luigi. 2004. "Locality and Left Periphery." In *Structures and beyond: The Cartography of Syntactic Structures*, edited by Adriana Belletti, 3: 223–51. Oxford: Oxford University Press.

Robenalt, Clarice, and Adele E. Goldberg. 2015. "Judgment Evidence for Statistical Pre-emption: It Is Relatively Better to Vanish than to Disappear a Rabbit, But a Life-guard Can Equally Well Backstroke or Swim Children to Shore." *Cognitive Linguistics* 26 (3).

Rochemont, Michael S., and Peter W. Culicover. 1990. *English Focus Constructions and the Theory of Grammar*. Cambridge, UK: Cambridge University Press.

Rosenbach, Anette. 2005. "Animacy versus Weight as Determinants of Grammatical Variation in English." *Language* 81 (3): 613–44.

Rosenbaum, Peter. 1967. *The Grammar of English Predicate Complement Constructions*. Cambridge, MA: MIT Press.

Rosenbloom, Paul. 1950. *The Elements of Mathematical Logic*. New York: Dover.

Ross, John Robert. 1967. "Constraints on Variables in Syntax." PhD diss., Massachusetts Institute of Technology.

Ross, John Robert. 1973a. "A Fake NP Squish." In *New Ways of Analyzing Variation in English*, edited by Charles-James Bailey and Roger Shuy, 96–140. Washington, DC: Georgetown University Press.

Ross, John Robert. 1973b. "Nouniness." In *Three Dimensions of Linguistic Theory*, edited by Osamu Fujimura, 137–257. Tokyo: TEC Company.

Ross, John Robert. 1987. "Islands and Syntactic Prototypes." In *Papers from the Twenty-Third Regional Meeting of the Chicago Linguistic Society*, 309–20. Chicago: Chicago Linguistic Society.

Rudin, Catherine. 1988. "On Multiple Questions and Multiple WH Fronting." *Natural Language & Linguistic Theory* 6 (4): 445–501.

Rudin, Catherine. 1996. "Multiple Wh-Questions South, West and East: A Government-Binding Approach to the Typology of Wh-Movement in Slavic Languages." *International Journal of Slavic Linguistics and Poetics* 39/40: 103–22.

Sadock, Jerrold M. 1991. *Autolexical Syntax: A Theory of Parallel Grammatical Representations*. Chicago: University of Chicago Press.

Sadock, Jerrold M. 2012. *The Modular Architecture of Grammar*. Cambridge, UK: Cambridge University Press.

Sag, Ivan A. 2012. "Sign-Based Construction Grammar: An Informal Synopsis." In *Sign-Based Construction Grammar*, edited by Hans C. Boas and Ivan A. Sag, 69–202. Stanford, CA: CSLI Publications.

Sag, Ivan A., Thomas Wasow, and Emily M. Bender. 2003. *Syntactic Theory*. Stanford, CA: CSLI Publications.

Santi, Andrea, and Yosef Grodzinsky. 2007. "Working Memory and Syntax Interact in Broca's Area." *NeuroImage* 37 (1): 8–17.

Sanz, Montserrat. 2000. *Events and Predication: A New Approach to Syntactic Processing in English and Spanish*. Amsterdam: John Benjamins.

Saussure, Ferdinand de. 1916. *Cours de Linguistique Générale*. Paris: Payot.

Saussure, Ferdinand de. 1983. *Course in General Linguistics*. Edited by Charles Bally, Albert Sechehaye, and Albert Riedlinger. Translated by Roy Harris. La Salle, IL: Open Court.

Schütze, Carson T. 1996. *The Empirical Base of Linguistics: Grammaticality Judgments and Linguistic Methodology*. Chicago: University of Chicago Press.

Schütze, Carson T. 2011. "Linguistic Evidence and Grammatical Theory." *Wiley Interdisciplinary Reviews: Cognitive Science* 2 (2): 206–21.

Sedarous, Yourdanis, and Savithry Namboodiripad. 2020. "Using Audio Stimuli in Acceptability Judgment Experiments." *Language and Linguistics Compass* 14 (8).

Sells, Peter. 1984. "Syntax and Semantics of Resumptive Pronouns." PhD diss., University of Massachusetts.

Shlonsky, Ur. 1992. "Resumptive Pronouns as a Last Resort." *Linguistic Inquiry* 23 (3): 443–68.

Šimík, Radek, and Marta Wierzba. 2015. "The Role of Givenness, Presupposition, and Prosody in Czech Word Order: An Experimental Study." *Semantics and Pragmatics* 8: 1–103.

Smolensky, Paul, Matthew Goldrick, and Donald Mathis. 2014. "Optimization and Quantization in Gradient Symbol Systems: A Framework for Integrating the Continuous and the Discrete in Cognition." *Cognitive Science* 38 (6): 1102–38.

Snow, Catherine, and Guus Meijer. 1977. "On the Secondary Nature of Syntactic Intuitions." In *Acceptability in Language*, edited by Sidney Greenbaum, 163–77. The Hague: Mouton.

Snyder, William. 1994. "A Psycholinguistic Investigation of Weak Crossover, Scope, and Syntactic Satiation Effects: Implications for Distinguishing Competence from Performance." Poster presented at the CUNY Conference on Human Sentence Processing, New York.

Snyder, William. 2000. "An Experimental Investigation of Syntactic Satiation Effects." *Linguistic Inquiry* 31 (3): 575–82.

Snyder, William. 2018. "On the Nature of Syntactic Satiation." Unpublished manuscript. University of Connecticut.

Snyder, William. 2021. "Satiation." In *The Cambridge Handbook of Experimental Syntax*, edited by Grant Goodall. Cambridge, UK: Cambridge University Press.

Sobin, Nicholas. 2002. "The Comp-Trace Effect, the Adverb Effect and Minimal CP." *Journal of Linguistics* 38 (3): 527–60.

Sorace, Antonella. 2000. "Gradients in Auxiliary Selection with Intransitive Verbs." *Language* 76 (4): 859.

Sorace, Antonella, and Frank Keller. 2005. "Gradience in Linguistic Data." *Lingua* 115 (11): 1497–524.

Spencer, Nancy Jane. 1973. "Differences between Linguists and Nonlinguists in Intuitions of Grammaticality-Acceptability." *Journal of Psycholinguistic Research* 2 (2): 83–98.

Sprouse, Jon. 2007a. "A Program for Experimental Syntax: Finding the Relationship between Acceptability and Grammatical Knowledge." PhD diss., University of Maryland.

Sprouse, Jon. 2007b. "Continuous Acceptability, Categorical Grammaticality, and Experimental Syntax." *Biolinguistics* 1: 123–34.

Sprouse, Jon. 2008. "The Differential Sensitivity of Acceptability Judgments to Processing Effects." *Linguistic Inquiry* 39 (4): 686–94.

Sprouse, Jon, and Norbert Hornstein, eds. 2013. *Experimental Syntax and Island Effects*. Cambridge, UK: Cambridge University Press.

Sprouse, Jon, and Ellen F. Lau. 2013. "Syntax and the Brain." In *Cambridge Handbook of Generative Syntax, The*, edited by Marcel den Dikken, 971–1005. Cambridge, UK: Cambridge University Press.

Sprouse, Jon, and Troy Messick. 2015. "How Gradient Are Island Effects?" Poster presented at the North East Linguistic Society 46, Concordia University, Montreal.

Sprouse, Jon, Carson Schütze, and Diogo Almeida. 2013. "Assessing the Reliability of Journal Data in Syntax: Linguistic Inquiry 2001–2010." *Lingua* 134: 219–48.

Sprouse, Jon, Matt Wagers, and Colin Phillips. 2012. "A Test of the Relation between Working-Memory Capacity and Syntactic Island Effects." *Language* 88 (1): 82–123.

Sprouse, Jon, Beracah Yankama, Sagar Indurkhya, Sandiway Fong, and Robert C. Berwick. 2018. "Colorless Green Ideas Do Sleep Furiously: Gradient Acceptability and the Nature of the Grammar." *Linguistic Review* 35 (3): 575–99.

Stallings, Lynne M., Maryellen C. MacDonald, and Padraig G. O'Seaghdha. 1998. "Phrasal Order-ing Constraints in Sentence Production: Phrase Length and Verb Disposition in Heavy-NP Shift." *Journal of Memory and Language* 39 (3): 392–417.

Staub, Adrian. 2009. "On the Interpretation of the Number Attraction Effect: Response Time Evidence." *Journal of Memory and Language* 60 (2): 308–27.

Staum Casasanto, Laura, Philip Hofmeister, and Ivan Sag. 2010. "Understanding Acceptabil-ity Judgments: Additivity and Working Memory Effects." In *Proceedings of the 32nd Annual Conference of the Cognitive Science Society*, 224–9. Austin, TX: Cognitive Science Society. http://toc.proceedings.com/09137webtoc.pdf.

Steedman, Mark. 2000. *The Syntactic Process*. Cambridge, MA: MIT Press.

Steels, Luc. 2011. "Introducing Fluid Construction Grammar." In *Constructional Approaches to Language*, edited by Luc Steels, 11: 3–30. Amsterdam: John Benjamins.

Steels, Luc. 2013. "Fluid Construction Grammar." In *The Oxford Handbook of Construction Grammar*, edited by Thomas Hoffman and Graeme Trousdale, 153–67. Oxford: Oxford University Press.

Stepanov, Arthur. 2007. "The End of CED? Minimalism and Extraction Domains." *Syntax* 10 (1): 80–126.

Stowe, Laurie A. 1986. "Parsing WH-Constructions: Evidence for on-Line Gap Location." *Language and Cognitive Processes* 1 (3): 227–45.

Stowell, Timothy Angus. 1981. "Origins of Phrase Structure." PhD diss., Massachusetts Institute of Technology.

Strunk, Jan. 2014. "A Statistical Model of Competing Motivations Affecting Relative Clause Ex-traposition in German." In *Competing Motivations in Grammar and Usage*, edited by Brian MacWhinney, Andrej Malchukov, and Edith Moravcsik, 88–106. Oxford: Oxford University Press.

Strunk, Jan, and Neal Snider. 2013. "Subclausal Locality Constraints on Relative Clause Extraposi-tion." In *Rightward Movement in a Comparative Perspective*, edited by Gert Webelhuth, Manfred Sailer, and Heike Walker, 99–144. Amsterdam: John Benjamins.

Szabolcsi, Anna. 2006. "Strong versus Weak Islands." In *The Blackwell Companion to Syntax*, edited by Martin Everaert and Henk van Riemsdijk, 479–531. Malden, MA: Blackwell.

Szabolcsi, Anna, and Frans Zwarts. 1997. "Weak Islands and an Algebraic Semantics for Scope Taking." In *Ways of Scope Taking*, edited by Anna Szabolcsi, 217–62. Dordrecht: Springer.

Takami, Ken-ichi. 1992. "On Definiteness Effect in Extraposition from NP." *Linguistic Analysis* 22: 100–16.

Takami, Ken-ichi. 1999. "A Functional Constraint on Extraposition from NP." In *Function and Struc-ture: In Honor of Susumu Kuno*, edited by Akio Kamio and Ken-ichi Takami, 23–56. Amsterdam: John Benjamins.

Talmy, Leonard. 1985. "Lexicalization Patterns: Semantic Structure in Lexical Forms." In *Language Typology and Syntactic Description Vol. 3: Grammatical Categories and the Lexicon*, edited by Timothy Shopen, 36–149. Cambridge, UK: Cambridge University Press.

Tang, Sze-Wing, Fan Kwok, Thomas Hun-Tak Lee, Caesar Lun, Kang Kwong Luke, Peter Tung, and Kwan Hin Cheung. 2002. *Guide to LSHK Cantonese Romanization of Chinese Characters*. Hong Kong: Linguistic Society of Hong Kong.

Tanner, Darren, Janet Nicol, and Laurel Brehm. 2014. "The Time-Course of Feature Interference in Agreement Comprehension: Multiple Mechanisms and Asymmetrical Attraction." *Journal of Memory and Language* 76: 195–215.

Taylor, John R. 2003. *Linguistic Categorization*. Oxford: Oxford University Press.

Telljohann, Heike, Erhard W. Hinrichs, Sandra Kübler, Heike Zinsmeister, and Kathrin Beck. 2006. "Stylebook for the Tübingen Treebank of Written German (TüBa-D/Z)." Universität Tübingen. http://www.sfs.uni-tuebingen.de/resources/tuebadz-stylebook-0607.pdf.

Thornton, Robert, and Maryellen C. MacDonald. 2003. "Plausibility and Grammatical Agreement." *Journal of Memory and Language* 48 (4): 740–59.

Tomasello, Michael. 2003. *Constructing a Language*. Cambridge, MA: Harvard University Press.

Tremblay, Pascale, and Anthony Steven Dick. 2016. "Broca and Wernicke Are Dead, or Moving Past the Classic Model of Language Neurobiology." *Brain and Language* 162 (November): 60–71.

Uszkoreit, Hans, Thorsten Brants, Denys Duchier, Brigitte Krenn, Lars Konieczny, Stephan Oepen, and Wojciech Skut. 1998. "Studien zur performanzorientierten Linguistik." *Kognitionswissenschaft* 7 (3): 129–33.

Van Valin, Robert D. Jr. 1990. "Semantic Parameters of Split Intransitivity." *Language* 66 (2): 221.

Van Valin, Robert D. Jr. 1993. "A Synopsis of Role and Reference Grammar." In *Advances in Role and Reference Grammar*, edited by Van Valin, Robert D. Jr, 1–158. Amsterdam: John Benjamins.

Van Valin, Robert D. Jr. 2005. *Exploring the Syntax–Semantics Interface*. Cambridge, UK: Cambridge University Press.

Van Valin, Robert D. Jr, and Randy J. LaPolla. 1997. *Syntax: Structure, Meaning, and Function*. Cambridge, UK: Cambridge University Press.

Vasishth, Shravan, and Richard L. Lewis. 2006. "Argument-Head Distance and Processing Complexity: Explaining Both Locality and Antilocality Effects." *Language* 82 (4): 767–94.

Vetter, Harold J., Jerry Volovecky, and Richard W. Howell. 1979. "Judgments of Grammaticalness: A Partial Replication and Extension." *Journal of Psycholinguistic Research* 8 (6): 567–83.

Villata, Sandra, Jon Sprouse, and Whitney Tabor. 2019. "Modeling Ungrammaticality: A Self-Organizing Model of Islands." Edited by A. K. Goel, C. M. Seifert, and C. Freksa. In *Proceedings of the 41st Annual Conference of the Cognitive Science Society*, 1178-1184. Austin, TX: Cognitive Science Society.

Wagers, Matthew, Manuel F. Borja, and Sandra Chung. 2015. "The Real-Time Comprehension of WH-Dependencies in a WH-Agreement Language." *Language* 91 (1): 109–44.

Wagers, Matthew, Manuel F. Borja, and Sandra Chung. 2018. "Grammatical Licensing and Relative Clause Parsing in a Flexible Word-Order Language." *Cognition* 178 (September): 207–21.

Wagers, Matthew, Ellen F. Lau, and Colin Phillips. 2009. "Agreement Attraction in Comprehension: Representations and Processes." *Journal of Memory and Language* 61 (2): 206–37.

Walker, Heike. 2013. "Constraints on Relative Clause Extraposition in English: An Experimental Investigation." In *Rightward Movement in a Comparative Perspective*, edited by Gert Webelhuth, Manfred Sailer, and Heike Walker, 145–72. Amsterdam: John Benjamins.

Walker, Heike. 2017. "The Syntax and Semantics of Relative Clause Attachment." PhD diss., Goethe-Universität Frankfurt am Main.

Ward, Gregory, Richard Sproat, and Gail McKoon. 1991. "A Pragmatic Analysis of So-Called Anaphoric Islands." *Language* 67 (3): 439–74.

Wasow, Thomas. 2002. *Postverbal Behavior*. Stanford, CA: CSLI Publications.

Wasow, Thomas. 2009. "Gradient Data and Gradient Grammars." In *Proceedings from the Forty-Third Annual Meeting of the Chicago Linguistic Society*, 255–71. Chicago: Chicago Linguistic Society.

Wasow, Thomas, and Jennifer Arnold. 2005. "Intuitions in Linguistic Argumentation." *Lingua* 115 (11): 1481–96.

Wasow, Thomas, T. Florian Jaeger, and David Orr. 2011. "Lexical Variation in Relativizer Frequency." In *Expecting the Unexpected: Exceptions in Grammar*, edited by Horst J. Simon and Heike Wiese, 175–96. Berlin: de Gruyter.

Wunderlich, Dieter. 2001. "How Gaps and Substitutions Can Become Optimal: The Pronominal Affix Paradigms of Yimas." *Transactions of the Philological Society* 99 (2): 315–66.

Yasunaga, Daichi, Masataka Yano, Yoshiho Yasugi, and Masatoshi Koizumi. 2015. "Is the Subject-before-Object Preference Universal? An Event-Related Potential Study in the Kaqchikel Mayan Language." *Language, Cognition and Neuroscience* 30 (9): 1209–29.

Yuasa, Etsuyo. 2005. *Modularity in Language: Constructional and Categorial Mismatch in Syntax and Semantics*. Berlin: de Gruyter.

Name Index

Aarts, B. 44
Abrusán, M. 24
Ackerman, L. 185, 187
Adger, D. 119–21, 222
Aissen, J. 40, 88
Akmajian, A. 136–7, 142
Alexopoulou, T. 74–5, 79, 183, 190–2, 213
Ambridge, B. 59–63, 71–2, 115
Anand, P. 234–5
Aoun, J. 159, 178
Ariel, M. 161–3, 166–8, 170, 172, 175, 177, 180, 190
Arnold, D. 51
Arnold, J. 6, 39, 41, 150
Arnon, I. 93, 95–6, 101
Asudeh, A. 170, 178

Bader, M. 90, 112–14, 117, 162
Baker, M. 196n
Baltin, M.R. 60, 127–8, 130, 136
Barak, L. 51, 154
Baroni, M. 123, 229
Bates, E. 47
Beltrama, A. 178n
Ben–Shachar, M. 231
Bentley, D. 70, 214
Bever, T. 215–17, 222, 224
Birner, B. 152
Bloomfield, L. 3
Boas, H.C. 48
Bock, K. 221
Bod, R. 51
Boeckx, C. 24–5
Boersma, P. 19, 39, 56, 154n
Boguslavsky, I. 96
Borer, H. 160, 179
Branigan, H.P. 221–2, 225
Bresnan, J. 40, 106, 108–10, 115
Burzio, L. 67, 195, 213
Bybee, J.L. 20, 47–50, 53, 106, 112

Cann, R. 170
Carreiras, M. 234
Chafe, W. 152
Chaves, R.P. 56, 62–3, 72, 82–4, 192, 209
Chen, Y. 163
Cho, P.W. 51, 210

Chomsky, N. 2–8, 10–12, 18, 20–1, 42–6, 74–5, 89, 136, 203
Christiansen, M.H. 90
Cinque, G. 45–6
Clark, B. 41–2
Clemens, L.E. 234
Clifton, C. 74
Comrie, B. 157–8, 161
Cowart, W. 6, 46, 104, 183–5, 188, 202–3
Crawford, J. 83
Croft, W. 19, 26
Culicover, P.W. 18, 22, 134, 146, 148, 197, 200

Dąbrowska, E. 107–8, 110
Deane, P. 34
Dery, J.E. 82–4, 209
Diessel, H. 47, 106
Dillon, B. 135
Divjak, D. 113–15, 117, 122

Eberhard, K.M. 88
Eddington, D. 49–50, 106
Elman, J.L. 123
Embick, D. 23, 28
Erteschik-Shir, N. 8, 56, 100
Eythórsson, T. 70, 214

Fadlon, J. 165–70, 193, 212
Farby, S. 161–5, 168, 179–82, 190
Featherston, S. 56, 92, 96–101
Fedorenko, E. 93–6, 98, 100, 102
Ferreira, F. 91, 170
Flett, S. 214, 219–22, 225
Fodor, J.D. 64
Fox, D. 24, 130
Francis, E.J. 15–16, 51, 147–54, 156, 173–7, 187, 190–1, 193, 212
Franck, J. 88
Francom, J. 82–3
Frazier, L. 74
Fried, M. 30
Friedmann, N. 214, 219, 222–5
Fukuda, S. 163

Gazdar, G. 19
Gennari, S.P. 166n, 167
Gibson, E. 89–90, 93–6, 98, 100, 102, 138

Ginzburg, J. 8
Goldberg, A.E. 18, 26, 31, 51, 59–63, 71,
    115–17, 154, 156, 204
Goodall, G. 77–80, 82–4
Greenbaum, S. 5
Griffin, Z. 222
Grimshaw, J. 19, 35–6
Grodzinsky, Y. 230–2
Guéron, J. 130, 144–51, 153, 155
Gundel, J.K. 152

Haider, H. 97
Hale, K. 23
Hammerly, C. 186–7, 212–13
Han, C. 164
Harbusch, K. 111, 113–14, 124, 202, 207–8, 210
Häussler, J. 90, 92–3, 98–101, 112–14, 117, 135,
    162, 164, 202, 204–7, 210
Hawkins, J.A. 38, 158, 175, 190
Hayes, B. 19, 39, 56, 154n
Heestand, D. 159, 178, 188–9, 212
Heidinger, S. 40–1, 203
Hickok, G. 233
Hilpert, M. 47, 106
Hitz, J. 189, 191
Hoeksema, J. 128
Hofmeister, P. 25, 34–5, 56, 76–82, 86–7, 102,
    127, 132–6, 143, 164–5, 182
Hornstein, N. 35, 80, 196–7, 200
Huang, Y. 225
Huck, G. 144

Jackendoff, R. 18, 22, 48, 197, 200
Jeffrey, M. 196–201
Juzek, T. 202, 204–7, 210

Kandybowicz, J. 10
Kaplan, R.M. 19, 26
Kay, P. 19, 26, 30n, 47
Keenan, E.L. 157–8, 161
Keffala, B. 164
Keller, F. 46, 66–7, 69, 71–2, 74–5, 79, 82, 111,
    146, 183, 200, 213
Kemmerer, D. 230–1, 234
Kempe, V. 96
Kempen, G. 111, 113–14, 124, 202, 207–8, 210
Kertész, A. 53
Keshev, M. 180–3, 188, 190, 193
Keyser, S.J. 23
Kimball, J. 88
Kiss, K. 45
Kitagawa, Y. 64
Kluender, R. 13–14, 16, 24–5, 34, 46, 56, 74–5,
    78–9

Koizumi, M. 233
Konieczny, L. 138
Konietzko, A. 134
Koring, L. 222, 225
Kothari, A. 63
Kroch, A. 24, 171
Kučerová, I. 63–6
Kuhn, J. 36–7
Kuno, S. 56, 93
Kutas, M. 13–14, 16, 24–5, 34, 56, 74–5, 78–9

Labov, W. 5–6
Ladusaw, W.A. 128
Landau, I. 196
Langacker, R.W. 20, 47–8
Lappin, S. 120–2
Larson, R. 196
Lasnik, H. 10
Lau, E.F. 230–1
Lau, J.H. 117–24, 228–9, 231
Lee, S.H. 147–8, 150, 152
Legendre, G. 35, 37
Leonard, B. 122, 229
Levelt, W.J.M. 5–6, 221
Levin, B. 106
Levinson, S.C. 8
Levy, R. 134
Lewis, S. 226–7
Linzen, T. 121–3, 229
Liu, Y. 61–3, 72
Lohse, B. 150

McCarthy, J.J. 35
McCawley, J.D. 2, 7–8
McClelland, J.L. 48, 50
McCloskey, J. 157–8, 178, 190
McClure, W. 67, 70
McDaniel, D. 46, 183–5, 188, 192
MacDonald M.C. 90, 88, 152, 204
McKee, C. 192
McKoon, G. 58
MacWhinney, B. 47, 96
Manning, C.D. 39, 104–5
Marantz, A. 23
Matchin, W. 232–3
Matthews, S. 173–5
Meijer, G. 5
Meltzer-Asscher, A. 157, 160–1, 163–4, 168,
    180–3, 188, 190, 193
Messick, T. 208–9
Meyer, R. 94
Michaelis, L.A. 30–1, 51, 147–54, 156
Miller, G.A. 89
Momma, S. 214

Montrul, S. 214–20, 222–5
Morgan, A.M. 169, 171–2, 185–6, 188, 191, 193
Myers, J. 6

Na, Y. 144
Namboodiripad, S. 234–5
Newmeyer, F.J. 3, 103–6, 110, 124
Nikitina, T. 106
Nissenbaum, J. 130
Norcliffe, E. 164–5, 234–5
Novick, J.M. 233

Oshima, D.Y. 8
Osterhout, L. 223
Östman, J. 30
Overfelt, J. 128–32, 139, 195

Palangi, H. 123
Pater, J. 121, 123
Perek, F. 151
Perlmutter, D. 67, 213
Pesetsky, D. 9, 77
Phillips, C. 8, 15–16, 76–7, 79–80, 87–92, 95, 101–2, 226–7
Pickering, M.J. 182, 221–2, 225
Polinsky, M. 172, 196–7, 200, 233–5
Pollard, C. 11–12
Post, E.L. 4
Postal, P.M. 12, 45
Prince, A. 35, 210n
Prince, E.F. 158, 171
Pritchett, B. 56
Pullum, G.K. 4
Putnam, M.T. 56, 192

Radford, A. 21, 171–2, 178, 185, 188–9, 192–3
Rákosi, C. 53
Ramchand, G. 67
Reuland, E. 222
Richter, S.N. 62–3, 72
Rizzi, L. 24, 45–6
Robenalt, C. 51, 116–17, 154
Rochemont, M.S. 146, 148
Rosenbach, A. 150
Rosenbaum, P. 11
Rosenbloom, P. 4n
Ross, J.R. 43–4, 46, 55, 132
Rudin, C. 94n

Sadock, J.M. 27–9, 71–2
Sag, I.A. 11–12, 33–5, 56, 76–80
Samek-Lodovici, V. 36
Santi, A. 231–2
Sanz, M. 215–17, 222, 224
Saussure, F. 3

Schütze, C.T. 4–6, 105–7, 111, 194, 202, 207–8, 210
Sedarous, Y. 235
Sells, P. 159, 178
Shlonsky, U. 157, 160
Šimík, R. 63–4, 66, 72
Smolensky, P. 35, 51, 210
Snedeker, J. 225
Snider, N. 127, 136, 140, 142–4, 149, 156, 211–12
Snow, C. 5
Snyder, W. 80–1, 83
Sobin, N. 9–10
Sorace, A. 46, 66–7, 69–72, 82, 146, 200, 213–16, 219
Spencer, N.J. 5
Sprouse, J. 25, 35, 80–1, 83, 85–7, 118–22, 124, 208–9, 228–9, 231
Stallings, L.M. 150
Staub, A. 88
Staum Casasanto, L. 133
Steedman, M. 18n
Steels, L. 19, 26, 47, 51
Stepanov, A. 92
Stowe, L.A. 181
Stowell, T.A. 9
Strunk, J. 127, 136, 140, 142–4, 149, 156, 211–12
Swets, B. 170
Swinney, D. 223
Szabolcsi, A. 24, 45, 77, 80, 203

Takagi, H. 200
Takami, K. 144
Talmy, L. 19
Tang, S.W. 173n
Tanner, D. 88
Thomas, J. 89–90
Thornton, R. 88
Tomasello, M. 19, 47
Traxler, M.J. 182
Tremblay, P. 231n

Uszkoreit, H. 142–3

Van Valin, R.D., Jr. 19, 26, 31, 56, 214, 225
Vasishth, S. 76
Vetter, H.J. 5
Villata, S. 202, 207–10

Wagers, M. 88, 169, 171–2, 185–6, 188, 191, 193
Walker, H. 128, 130–1, 145–9, 151–3, 155, 195, 204

Ward, G. 12–13, 57–9, 63, 71
Wasow, T. 19, 38–40, 105, 135n, 150
Weinstein-Tull, J. 222
Wierzba, M. 63–6, 72
Winkler, S. 134
Wunderlich, D. 35

Xiang, M. 178n, 212

Yasunaga, D. 233
Yip, V. 173–5
Yuasa, E. 19, 26, 31

Subject Index

accessibility 58, 95, 154, 161–7, 170–1, 175, 181, 190, 193; *see also* NP Accessibility Hierarchy

agentivity 22–3, 27–8, 67–70

aggregation effect 205–6

agreement attraction 88–9, 229; *see also* grammatical illusions; missing VP illusions

amelioration 9, 14, 24, 56–7, 59, 71, 75–80, 83, 89–90, 181, 185, 188

anaphora, *see* backwards anaphora; outbound anaphora; reflexive binding

animacy 7, 68–70, 99–100, 167

Automodular Grammar 19, 26–9; *see also* level-mapping theories

auxiliary selection 67–71; *see also* impersonal passive; split intransitivity

Avar 234

backwards anaphora 232–3

Basque 234

Berkeley Construction Grammar 19, 26, 47; *see also* sign-based theories

Broca's area 231–3

Cantonese 172–7, 179–83, 189–91

case marking 96–7

c-command 129–31, 195–6

Chamorro 234

Ch'ol 234

cleft sentences 91

Cognitive Construction Grammar 19, 26, 47, 51, 154–5; *see also* sign-based theories

Cognitive Grammar 20, 47–8

competence and performance 3–5, 38–41, 53, 103–7, 175–7, 194, 204–7, 210–11, 227–8

complement selection 14, 113–15; *see also* verb-argument constructions

Complex Noun Phrase Constraint, *see* Complex NP islands

Complex NP islands 13, 44–5, 55, 60, 74–81, 85, 94, 99, 108, 179–83; *see also* island constraints

comprehension, *see* processing ease

comp-trace, *see that*-trace

constituent order 38–42, 63–6, 111–13, 203, 235; *see also* weight effects; Heavy-Last

constraint-based theories, *see* level-mapping theories; sign-based theories

Coordinate Structure Constraint 180–3; *see also* island constraints

corpus frequency 40, 103–24, 141–2, 148–52, 161, 171, 200, 211–12, 228–9

coverb stranding constraint 173, 175, 177, 190–1, 193; *see also* preposition stranding constraint

cross-modal lexical priming task 222–5

Czech 63–6, 100

Decathlon Model 19, 39, 53, 56, 92, 97–8, 153, 177; *see also* Optimality Theory (OT)

definiteness 64–6, 144–55, 171–2, 177, 201, 204; *see also* Name Constraint

dependency distance 74–5, 85–7, 136–44, 161–2, 164–5, 169; *see also* Dependency Locality Theory; subclausal locality condition

Dependency Locality Theory 138; *see also* dependency distance

depth of embedding, *see* dependency distance

derivational theories 21–6, 52; *see also* Government and Binding; Minimalist Program

discourse function 12–13, 30, 40, 57–66, 134, 144–55, 231

  backgroundedness 59–63

  focus 41, 59–63, 134, 144–55

  topic 12–13, 40, 57–9, 105, 144–55, 231

  see also D-linking

ditransitive clauses 106, 109–10

D-linking 77–9, 93, 96–7, 209; *see also* discourse function

elicited production task 41, 152–3, 165–70, 174–7, 193, 203, 212; *see also* structural priming task

Empty Category Principle (ECP) 9–10, 45–6, 183–5; *see also* island constraints

English 2, 7–16, 22–6, 28–9, 31–6, 38–46, 55, 57–63, 74–89, 97–100, 104–6, 108–10, 116–17, 128–35, 144–55, 158, 164–6, 169–72, 183–7, 192, 195–202, 204–11, 213–18, 222–5, 232–3

  colloquial 171–2

entrenchment 20, 48, 116, 154–5
event-related potentials (ERP) 46, 230
event structure 23, 28, 51, 67–71, 116–17,
    154–5, 213–26; *see also* split intransitivity;
    verb-argument constructions
exceptional case marking 11–12
exemplar-based learning 48–52, 154–5
expletive subject 11, 29, 36–7
Extended Projection Principle (EPP) 21–2
extraposition from NP, *see* relative clause
    extraposition (RCE); preposition phrase
    extraposition (PPE)

factive islands 59–63, 71–2; *see also* island
    constraints; manner-of-speaking islands
Fake NP Squish, *see* squishy categories
filled-gap paradigm 181–3, 187
finiteness 15, 21, 36, 45, 61–2, 113, 137,
    197–200
Fluid Construction Grammar 19, 26, 47, 51; *see*
    also sign-based theories
form-meaning isomorphism 17, 22–3, 28–9,
    32, 37, 52, 70–2, 130–1, 146–7, 151, 153,
    195–201
freezing effects 132–6; *see also* island
    constraints
Frozen Structure Constraint, *see* freezing
    effects
functional magnetic resonance imaging
    (fMRI) 230–3

German 66–71, 90–1, 96–100, 111–13, 134,
    137–44
Government and Binding 9, 18, 35; *see also*
    derivational theories; Minimalist Program
GoVP$_{bare}$ construction 31–2
gradient grammaticality, *see* soft constraints
grammatical illusions 87–92, 206–7; *see also*
    agreement attraction; missing VP illusions;
    overgeneration
grammaticalization 177, 190–3

Head-Driven Phrase Structure Grammar 19,
    26, 33, 51, 130–1; *see also* sign-based
    theories
Heavy-Last 40–1; *see also* constituent order;
    weight effects
Hebrew 157, 160–4, 166–8, 189–91
high/low attachment 137–44

impersonal passive 67–71; *see also* auxiliary
    selection; passive clauses; split intransitivity
information structure, *see* discourse function

interrogative clauses 13–15, 24–5, 34, 44–6,
    55, 59–63, 74–5, 80–4, 93–101, 132–6,
    158–9, 170, 183–7, 212; *see also* Superiority
    constraint; *wh*-islands
Irish 178, 190
island constraints 33–5, 44–5, 55–6, 76–81,
    83–7, 92–101, 178–89; *see also* Complex NP
    islands; Coordinate Structure Constraint;
    coverb stranding constraint; Empty
    Category Principle (ECP); factive islands;
    freezing effects; Left Branch Constraint;
    manner-of-speaking islands; preposition
    stranding constraint; Relativized Minimal-
    ity; Sentential Subject Constraint; strong
    and weak islands; Subjacency condition;
    Subject islands; Superiority constraint;
    that-trace; *wh*-islands
Italian 36

Lebanese Arabic 178
Left Branch Constraint 191–2; *see also* island
    constraints
length effects, *see* weight effects
level-mapping theories 27–9; *see also* Auto-
    modular Grammar; Lexical-Functional
    Grammar; Role and Reference Grammar;
    Simpler Syntax
Lexical-Functional Grammar 19, 26, 35, 37, 51;
    see also level-mapping theories
Linear OT 19, 39, 56, 82–3, 153; *see also*
    Optimality Theory (OT)

machine learning 117–23, 228–30, 233; *see also*
    N-gram models; recurrent neural network
    (RNN) models
magnitude estimation task 68, 97, 112
Malayalam 234–5
Mandarin 163n, 173
manner-of-speaking islands 59–63, 71–2; *see*
    also factive islands; island constraints
Merge 21, 48, 130
Minimal Distance Principle (MDP) 196
Minimalist Program 21–6, 29, 56, 130, 183–5;
    see also derivational theories; Government
    and Binding
missing VP illusions 89–91, 227; *see also*
    agreement attraction; grammatical illusions
multiple *wh*-questions, *see* Superiority
    constraint

Name Constraint 144–55, 177, 201, 204; *see*
    also definiteness
n-back task 86; *see also* reading span task; serial
    recall task; working memory

negation 60–3, 130n
negative polarity item (NPI) 128–31
neurolinguistics 230–3
N-gram models 118; *see also* machine learning;
    recurrent neural network (RNN) models
NP Accessibility Hierarchy 157–8, 161; *see also*
    accessibility

Ojibwe 234
Optimality Theory (OT) 35–42, 53; *see also*
    Decathlon Model; Linear OT; Stochastic
    OT
outbound anaphora 12–13, 57–9
overgeneration 87–92, 159, 188–9, 227; *see
    also* agreement attraction; grammatical
    illusions; missing VP illusions

passive clauses 22, 27–31, 40, 105, 148, 166–9;
    see also impersonal passive
Polish 113–15
Predicate Constraint 144–55, 204
preposition phrase extraposition (PPE) 128–
    31; *see also* relative clause extraposition
    (RCE)
preposition stranding constraint 157, 173; *see
    also* coverb stranding constraint
processing ease 13–16, 24–6, 33–5, 38–42,
    74–102, 131–6, 138–44, 150–1, 158, 162–3,
    165–7, 169–70, 185–7, 208–10, 212–26,
    230–3
production, *see* elicited production task
prosody 10, 63–6

Q'anjob'al 234
quantifier scope 128–31

Radical Construction Grammar 19, 26; *see also*
    sign-based theories
reading span task 86–7; *see also* n-back task;
    serial recall task; working memory
reading time, *see* self-paced reading task
recurrent neural network (RNN) models 118–
    22, 228–9; *see also* machine learning;
    N-gram models
reflexive binding 232
relative clause extraposition (RCE) 131–53; *see
    also* preposition phrase extraposition (PPE)
relative clause islands, *see* Complex NP islands
relative clauses 9–11, 13, 15–16, 45, 86–8,
    131–53, 157–93, 229, 232–4
    extraposed 131–53
    free 15–16
    nonrestrictive 161, 166–8, 171
    prenominal 173–4

resumptive 157–93, 212–13, 227
Relativized Minimality 45; *see also* island
    constraints
repeated exposure effects 80–4, 209, 220–2; *see
    also* satiation; structural priming task
resumptive pronouns 157–93, 212–13, 227
    grammatical 160–4, 166–9, 173–7, 189–93
    intrusive 164–6, 170–2, 183–7, 189–93
    see also relative clauses
Role and Reference Grammar 19, 26; *see also*
    level-mapping theories
Russian 93–7

satiation 80–4; *see also* repeated exposure
    effects; structural priming task
scale effect 205–6
selectional restrictions 7–8, 42–3
self-organized sentence processing (SOSP)
    model 208–11
self-paced reading task 34, 58–9, 63, 76–8, 84,
    89–90, 181–3, 186–7, 212–13
semantic roles 11–12, 21–3, 27–31, 91, 196
Sentential Subject Constraint 55, 92; *see also*
    island constraints; Subject islands
serial recall task 86; *see also* n-back task;
    reading span task; working memory
Sign-Based Construction Grammar 19, 26, 33;
    see also sign-based theories
sign-based theories 30–3; *see also* Berkeley
    Construction Grammar; Cognitive Con-
    struction Grammar; Fluid Construction
    Grammar; Head-Driven Phrase Structure
    Grammar; Radical Construction Grammar;
    Sign-Based Construction Grammar
Simpler Syntax 19, 26, 47; *see also*
    level-mapping theories
soft constraints 38–47, 51–2, 56, 75, 80, 82–3,
    140, 143–6, 151–6, 175–7, 191, 193, 200–11,
    235; *see also* strong and weak islands
Spanish 41, 49, 82–3, 213–22
split intransitivity 66–71, 213–26; *see also* event
    structure
squishy categories 43–4
statistical preemption 115–17
stative predicate 23, 28, 32
Stochastic OT 19–20, 38–42, 49, 104–5, 153,
    203–4; *see also* Optimality Theory (OT)
strong and weak islands 24, 44–7, 75, 77, 80, 93;
    see also island constraints; soft constraints
structural priming task 220–2; *see also* elicited
    production task; satiation; repeated
    exposure effects
subclausal locality condition 136–44; *see also*
    dependency distance

Subjacency condition 13–14, 24–5, 44–5, 60,
75–6, 136, 183–5; *see also* island constraints
subject-auxiliary inversion 82–3
Subject islands 83–4, 208–9; *see also* island
constraints; Sentential Subject Constraint
superadditivity 25, 78, 85, 133, 143
Superiority constraint 92–101, 164; *see also*
island constraints
syntactic satiation, *see* satiation

telicity 67–70, 213
that-trace 9–10, 104, 202–3; *see also* island
constraints
thematic roles, *see* semantic roles
theta roles, *see* semantic roles
transitive subject control (TSC) 196–201

unaccusative verbs, *see* split intransitivity
unergative verbs, *see* split intransitivity
unification 19, 26, 31–2, 48

usage-based approaches 47–53, 106–10,
115–23, 154–5, 228–9
Usage-based Theory (of Bybee) 47–50, 53

verb-argument constructions 51, 116–17,
154–5; *see also* complement selection; event
structure
visual probe recognition task 214–19, 222–6

weight effects 38–42, 150–1; *see also* constituent
order; Heavy-Last
wh-islands 34, 44–6, 74–5, 80–1, 158–9, 170,
183–7, 212; *see also* interrogative clauses;
island constraints
wh-questions, *see* interrogative clauses
word order, *see* constituent order
working memory 25, 78, 84–7, 163, 231–2; *see
also* n-back task; reading span task; serial
recall task

OXFORD SURVEYS IN SYNTAX AND MORPHOLOGY

General Editor
Robert D Van Valin, Jr.
Heinrich-Heine University and the University at Buffalo,
State University of New York

Advisory Editors
Guglielmo Cinque, University of Venice; Daniel Everett, Illinois State University;
Adele Goldberg, Princeton University; Kees Hengeveld, University of Amsterdam;
Caroline Heycock, University of Edinburgh; David Pesetsky, Massachusetts Institute of
Technology; Ian Roberts, University of Cambridge; Masayoshi Shibatani, Rice University;
Andrew Spencer, University of Essex; Tom Wasow, Stanford University

PUBLISHED
1. **Grammatical Relations**
Patrick Farrell

2. **Morphosyntactic Change**
Olga Fischer

3. **Information Structure**
The Syntax-Discourse Interface
Nomi Erteschik-Shir

4. **Computational Approaches to Syntax and Morphology**
Brian Roark and Richard Sproat

5. **Constituent Structure**
(Second edition)
Andrew Carnie

6. **Processing Syntax and Morphology**
A Neurocognitive Perspective
Ina Bornkessel-Schlesewsky and Matthias Schlesewsky

7. **Syntactic Categories**
Gisa Rauh

8. **The Interplay of Morphology and Phonology**
Sharon Inkelas

9. **Word Meaning and Syntax**
Approaches to the Interface
Stephen Wechsler

10. **Unbounded Dependency Constructions**
Theoretical and Experimental Perspectives
Rui P. Chaves and Michael T. Putnam

11. **Gradient Acceptability and Linguistic Theory**
Elaine J. Francis

IN PREPARATION
The Syntax-Discourse Interface
Extraction from Coordinate Structures
Daniel Altshuler and Robert Truswell

Complex Sentences
Toshio Ohori

Periphrasis
Gergana Popova and Andrew Spencer